LEPROSY, RACISM,
AND PUBLIC HEALTH

LEPROSY, RACISM, AND PUBLIC HEALTH

Social Policy in Chronic Disease Control

Zachary Gussow

Westview Press
Boulder, San Francisco, & London

Copyright © 1989 by Westview Press, Inc.

Published in 1989 in the United States of America by Westview Press, Inc., 5500 Central Avenue, Boulder, Colorado 80301, and in the United Kingdom by Westview Press, Inc., 13 Brunswick Centre, London WC1N 1AF, England

Library of Congress Cataloging-in-Publication Data
Gussow, Zachary, 1923–
    Leprosy, racism, and public health: social policy in chronic
disease control / Zachary Gussow.
    p. cm.
  Includes index.
  ISBN 0-8133-0674-4
  1. Leprosy—Social aspects—United States—History. 2. Leprosy—
Government policy—United States—History. 3. Racism—United
States—History. I. Title.
  [DNLM: 1. Leprosy—history. 2. Leprosy—prevention & control.
3. Prejudice. 4. Public Health—history. 5. Public Policy. WC
335 G982L]
RA644.L3G878 1989
362.1'96998'0097—dc19
DNLM/DLC
for Library of Congress   88-5567
                                                                                  CIP

Printed and bound in the United States of America

The paper used in this publication meets the requirements of the American National Standard for Permanence of Paper for Printed Library Materials Z39.48-1984.

10   9   8   7   6   5   4   3   2   1

⟡—— Contents

Tables and Figures

◇——— *Preface*

I had given no thought whatsoever to leprosy prior to my moving to New Orleans in 1961. Leprosy was not a disease that affected those I knew or with whom I had grown up. My people developed cancer and had strokes and heart attacks; earlier they would have contracted an acute infectious disease. At the time I journeyed south, mental illness attracted research attention, and when I joined the faculty in the Department of Psychiatry, Louisiana State University School of Medicine, I fully expected to be preoccupied with diseases of the mind. Instead, to phrase it in medieval terms, I became involved with a "disease of the soul."

The ideas presented in this book and, above all, its perspective that the modern Western stigmatization of leprosy is of recent origin and not, as is generally believed, the result of tradition that dates from ancient biblical times, emerged out of ongoing fieldwork conducted at the United States Public Health Service Hospital, Carville, Louisiana—the only leprosarium in the continental United States.

Fieldwork at Carville, along with side excursions among outpatients attending clinics in New Orleans and San Francisco, continued throughout most of the 1960s. In 1973, my work was extended to East Africa, particularly Tanzania; it also included brief surveys in Kenya and Ethiopia.

An invitation extended to me by Dr. Oliver W. Hasselblad, then president of the American Leprosy Missions, to present a paper at the Ninth International Leprosy Congress, London, 1968, had provided me an opportunity to review the current thinking about leprosy stigma. A new approach, based on mid-nineteenth- and early twentieth-century Western social history, was presented. A paper based on it was subsequently published in 1970 in the *Bulletin of the History of Medicine* and later, in 1971, in more analytic form, in the *American Anthropologist*.

Ideas I first outlined in 1968, to which I later added my observations of leprosy control programs in hyperendemic Third World nations, provide the central historical assumptions and background on which the present work builds. The work encompassed in this book thus spans a period of more than two decades of investigation, thought, and writing.

Generally, social scientists seek out institutions for study. Less well appreciated are those situations wherein administrators seek to have their own institutions examined by social scientists. Late in the 1950s, Carville

was experiencing profound changes in leprosy policy, and the new administration strongly felt the need for studies of hospital sociology. Discussions
about research were initiated by Dr. Edgar B. Johnwick, medical officer in
charge, early in 1957 with members of the Department of Psychiatry,
Louisiana State University School of Medicine. Dr. George Devereux, a
psychoanalytically trained anthropologist and visiting consultant to the
department, later joined the discussion. Three years later, Dr. Devereux,
with whom I had earlier worked, called to ask if I would consider a position
"in the South." Leprosy was never mentioned, nor was it mentioned when
I was interviewed for the job in New Orleans.

Leprosy, as disease or as stigma, had not previously been studied by
social scientists in the United States or abroad, and locally, in Louisiana,
there had been only a few minor psychological and epidemiological studies.
There was a growing literature in the early 1960s on hospitals and other
places of inmate confinement, but the situation at Carville was atypical,
and I was soon intrigued.

Although my own involvement with leprosy may be termed an accident
of a personal nature, the involvement of Carville with social science at this
time was not accidental. It came during a period when hospital personnel
favored social science inquiry and at a time in the history of leprosy when
events were rapidly changing. It was only later, after I had thought that
the idea of studying the leprosarium had been my own, that I learned that
the groundwork had already been laid. I no longer wonder that my reception
at Carville was so cordial.

*   *   *

Numerous people and institutions have been involved in the study that
has led to this book. My deepest obligation is to the Department of Psychiatry.
Psychiatry was an exciting subject during the 1960s, when psychiatrists,
psychoanalysts, and anthropologists freely interfered with each other's dis-
ciplines. Dr. Charles Watkins, who was then chairman of the department
and assistant to the chancellor, viewed psychiatry in broad and humanistic
terms. His personal encouragement led me to become more deeply involved
in the study than I might otherwise have been. Two other members of the
department, Drs. Edward H. Knight, Jr., and Marvin F. Miller, were involved
when the idea of the research originated in the late 1950s, and later they
collaborated in the early years of data collection. Dr. Miller was psychiatric
consultant to Carville and for two years held monthly patient group meetings,
data from which have been used in this book. Dr. Knight, a psychoanalyst,
saw two patients with leprosy in therapy, one for a period of a year.
Although his material remains unpublished, discussions about leprosy with
Dr. Knight have always been provocative.

My study of leprosy eventually turned from fieldwork at Carville to
history. Here I wish to thank John P. Isché, former head of the Medical
School Library at LSU, and his staff for the many courtesies they extended

to me during the years that I had need of archival sources. Without the rare book collection that John Ische so insisted on maintaining, my research into the early history of leprosy and public health in Louisiana would have been infinitely more difficult. I am also grateful for the open stacks at the Tulane University School of Medicine Library and to the Rudolph Matas Collection housed there. I also made extensive use of the Tulane University Library and the Louisiana Collection at the New Orleans Public Library.

Fieldwork during the first years of the study went slowly. Carville is about 85 miles from New Orleans, and during the 1960s the trip by car took about two hours each way. Often I stayed overnight as "guest" in the administration building. Because of hospital work hours and patient and staff residential patterns, fieldwork after 4:30 p.m. and on weekends and holidays yielded diminished returns. At first, I simply made the round trip two and even three times a week.

During this phase of the study I informally interviewed patients and staff as I roamed around the leprosarium sampling staff meetings and conferences and hanging around the patient canteen. Carville is not a typical hospital; it is more of a residential-treatment community, and the patients live private lives in private living quarters in the colony portion of the leprosarium. I soon realized that there was far more here to study than I had previously imagined and that getting to know the "universe" of Carville and that of leprosy could not be accomplished by a single fieldworker spending hours traveling. Besides, I had classes to teach. Thus, I approached the Department of Sociology at nearby Louisiana State University in Baton Rouge seeking to interest colleagues in joining the study. Here I found two, George S. Tracy and S. Lee Spray. Along with their graduate students, they collected and analyzed a large body of observational and interview data.

George Tracy became my closest collaborator and coauthor of a number of papers. His training brought to the study a rigor and a logic that anthropologists may lack. Fieldwork is an exhausting business. It is also lonely, and especially so when the research has to do with studying people. The fun and excitement of research that fuel the staying power required by extended work come from the intellectual growth and emotional support that bind collaborators together. Later, our earlier mutual interest changed direction: I pursued leprosy abroad and in the library, while George followed the abstract lure of experimental statistics.

Three graduate students—James D. Ebner, Dorothy S. Nichols, and Carolyn M. Rutledge—whose work was supervised by George Tracy and S. Lee Spray, produced theses about Carville and about community attitudes toward the disease; their data have contributed to this book. Sue Drysdale conducted a number of patient interviews.

The administration at Carville left me remarkably free to pursue the study in my own way. This was enormously important in view of the fact that in the decade that project members were interviewing everybody in sight and observing everything that was going on, there were three different chief medical officers at Carville. Dr. Johnwick died in 1965; he was replaced temporarily by Dr. Merlin L. Brubaker, and then later, and more permanently, by Dr. John R. Trautman. I am indebted to Drs. Brubaker and Trautman for allowing the work to continue without interruption, and especially to Dr. Trautman, who has never refused a request. Although Dr. Johnwick endured me for a shorter period, I feel an enormous obligation to him. His vision had initiated the study, and he loved to talk about his work at Carville and was an enthusiastic correspondent. The acceptance by the administration of our presence at Carville spilled over to the staff, and although many may have had little idea of what we were up to, invariably we were well received.

We were also well received by the patients. Appointments for formal, often lengthy interviews were almost always honored. Interviews were tape-recorded, and some patients were apprehensive that their identities might be disclosed. All interviews, those of both patients and staff, have remained confidential. Among the patients, I am especially indebted to Stanley Stein, who for many years was editor of the patient publication, *The Star. The Star* was an extraordinary publication in its day, and Stein was an extraordinary person. During one of my early visits to *The Star*'s office, Stein made me a present of all back issues of that publication dating to its rebirth in 1941. Whatever impelled Stein to make this offer, I trust that this book will acknowledge my debt to him, for without these issues my knowledge of Carville history would be woefully incomplete.

A number of people in the wider world of leprosy have assisted me over the years. I wish to express my gratitude to Dr. Paul Fasal, former chief, Leprosy Service, U.S. Public Health Service Hospital, San Francisco, who graciously allowed me to observe the operation of his clinic during the summer of 1963 and who introduced me to patients in the Bay Area; to Dr. Oliver W. Hasselblad, who has supported my efforts in numerous ways; and to Gene Phillips Clemes, friend and former public relations officer, American Leprosy Missions, for many kindnesses. I wish to remember Dr. Stanley G. Browne, O.B.E., former secretary-treasurer, International Leprosy Association, who chided me years ago, saying that if I wanted to understand leprosy I would have to venture beyond Carville. Dr. John H. Hanks, teacher, friend, and former director, Leonard Wood Memorial Laboratory, Johns Hopkins School of Hygiene & Public Health, initiated me into the biopathology of leprosy via lectures and an inoculation of lepromin.

Funding for my research has been made possible from a number of sources. A generous grant from the Edward G. Schlieder Educational Foundation, New Orleans, arranged by LSU Medical School, covered most of the costs of fieldwork at Carville. The trustees of the foundation were gentlemen, their only stipulation being that my reports to them not be written in jargon. A small grant from the National Institute of Mental Health helped to defray some final expenses. In 1970, a special award from the National Institutes of Health and sabbatical leave from LSU allowed me to spend a year of study at the Johns Hopkins School of Hygiene & Public Health. In 1973, the World Health Organization awarded me a travel fellowship to study the delivery of leprosy services in East Africa; this grant was supplemented by a small award from the American Philosophical Society. The year I spent at Johns Hopkins and the people I met there, plus the experience in East Africa, profoundly affected my perspective on leprosy. I cannot mention all the leprosy and health workers I met in East Africa, and at the All Africa Leprosy Research and Training Centre (ALERT), in Ethiopia, who made the trip both worthwhile and enjoyable, but I especially want to express my gratitude to the officials and personnel of the World Health Organization—who assisted my travel plans and, in Tanzania, gave me the use of a Land-Rover—and the Ministry of Health, Tanzania, who welcomed me to their country and provided me with the multifarious services of an experienced driver.

This has not been an easy matter to digest or to write. I am deeply indebted to the late Marion Pearsall, anthropologist and editor, who read most of the manuscript while undergoing intensive chemotherapy. Her critical reading has helped sharpen the conceptualization. Charles F. Chapman, LSU Editorial Office, has provided counsel, nurturance, and, with help from Susan L. Rogers, word-processor wizardry.

My most important debt, however, is to my wife, Ann Raney Gussow, who is both an anthropologist and an editor. She "land-rovered" with me throughout Tanzania and shared in the tasks of interviewing, observing, and note taking. On the book, I used every minute of her time that she would give, which was enormous, and extracted every bit of critical advice that she could give; we are still married and still friends.

Zachary Gussow

However repulsive the disease itself in some of its phases may be, there is nothing whatever of that nature about its study. It is a sort of aristocrat amongst diseases.

Jonathan Hutchinson,
On Leprosy and Fish-Eating. London, 1906.

PART 1

Introduction

1

Symbol and Disease

Disease, Susan Sontag has noted,[1] has often been used as a metaphor for dread and mystifying things considered to be socially or morally wrong. Some diseases are more heavily burdened by metaphoric trappings than are others. Those diseases that appear to act in capricious and unruly ways, that are not understood, and that have no known cause and cure tend to mystify the most. During the Middle Ages, people drew a strong connection between disease and immorality and equated particular diseases with the cardinal sins. The people of later centuries attached exaggerated fantasies to epidemic calamities. More recently, insanity, syphilis, tuberculosis, cancer, and now AIDS have similarly captured the public imagination. Another disease to inspire vivid fantasies has been leprosy.

That leprosy is the ultimate disease and that the leper is the ultimate pariah are pervasive ideas in Western society. To a mind attuned to the Old Testament, leprosy is abomination, a matter of ritual uncleanliness. For those who believe in the New Testament, the stories of Christ miraculously curing the lepers become metaphors for divine salvation. From very early times, leprosy was seen as a divine punishment for sinfulness and was viewed "as no other sickness known to man has ever been."[2]

The particular way in which disease becomes metaphor and turns into myth depends on the context and the expectations of the times. Many of the major illnesses of the past have since lost their former expressive power; they have been demythicized. The diseases of the Middle Ages no longer convey notions of sin; and insanity, tuberculosis, and syphilis have ceased to be effective metaphors. The fantasies about cancer keep changing. Only leprosy continues to be encumbered with something like its original connotations.

Within the Western world leprosy has been written about extensively in relation to church dogma, medieval leprosaria, the work and activities of missionaries, the fiction of Ben Hur, and the parables of Christ. Such sources gave rise to a massive literature that asserts the relationship of modern leprosy with the "leprosies" of the past. In this *Ur*-version the relationship is continuous and the imagery of leprosy endures. As a "dreadful manifestation of . . . a disease of the soul," the leprosy cited in the Scriptures was intensely tainted. So deeply rooted is this stigma that the taint of the disease has withstood the test of time, infusing "all aspects of culture, whether religious, medical, legal, literary, or popular." As the historian Saul Nathaniel Brody put it: "The stigma of leprosy is thus the product of a long tradition."[3]

Such beliefs about the persistence of leprosy's taint are endorsed by those of the medical world most involved with the disease, by religious groups and in Bible schools, and also by academic historians. Although puzzled by the long history of the taint, the latter nevertheless accept it as fact. These ideas are presumed to constitute the general public's view.

The historical disgrace of leprosy is held responsible for setting the disease apart, for arousing horror in the public mind, and for turning the afflicted into moral and civil outcasts. Humanity's dread is termed a natural response; some argue that the response has appeared nearly everywhere the disease has appeared, back to time immemorial. So prominently has the disgrace been proclaimed, so closely associated are leprosy and stigma, that it was maintained scarcely a generation ago that there could be no medical hope until the stigma was first removed.[4]

Negative disease metaphors persist as powerful images as long as a disease remains salient. But the mere presence of a disease, even if common and mysterious, does not automatically confer on it a sense of social importance. Salience has social and political overtones. The condition must threaten a class of citizens, a way of life; it must arouse public concern; above all, it must give rise to action. It must become a social problem. Many diseases, prevalent and harmful though they may be, never attain this status. They remain personal tragedies. Epidemic yellow fever in nineteenth-century Louisiana was ignored until it brought sickness and death to the landed and wealthy classes. Pellagra, thought by some earlier in this century to be communicable from person to person, and once common in the American rural South and among European peasants, aroused little public concern.[5] Many conditions of today—mental illness, alcoholism, and drug abuse—common as they are to broad segments of society, have only achieved special status after years of bitter struggle. The competitive struggle among diseases for social recognition is fierce. Many push for this recognition, but only a few succeed.[6] The politics of funding cancer research is well documented.[7] Other conditions, long known but neglected, are currently making a bid for public attention and support, for example, sickle cell anemia, thalassemia, and lead poisoning. Methods involving political activism are apparent.[8]

Leprosy is acknowledged to have been a moral issue in biblical and medieval times but has been of little significance on the continent of Europe since at least the sixteenth century and has never been of any importance in the Americas north of Mexico. Nevertheless, the Western world continues to view its taint as real. An intense aversion to leprosy has been displayed in modern times. Unprecedented laws have been enacted and special places of confinement have been created to contain lepers. A group of special caretakers has evolved. These caretakers and patients alike testify to overwhelming public stigmatization. Gross stereotypes about the disease persist—fierce contagion and mutilating deformity—along with a Western imagery that supports fantasies of biblical and medieval taint. Yet in retaining its status as a social problem, leprosy seems to have managed to bypass the social and political processes that other diseases have had to contend with in order to sustain public recognition. As reflected in myth and belief, the special status of leprosy has been maintained through the power of literary imagery and tradition alone.

The power of tradition has been used to account for the survival of numerous social patterns from the past. One explanation of how tradition functions asserts that phenomena are produced by a set of constant causes. The set of causes that reproduces phenomena occurring now is the same set of causes that produced them in the first place. Another explanation is that some social patterns *not* reproduced by a set of constant causes may reproduce themselves nonetheless. Where constant causes fail to explain the reproduction of patterns, historical forces must be examined.

Popular beliefs about the persistence of leprosy stigma fall into the first category of explanation. Here, constant causes are invoked to explain the continuity of the stigma. This mode of explanation is not confined to popular beliefs, however. It is also the central explanatory premise found in recent institutional and scholarly examinations of the phenomenon. The failure of such explanations to conceptualize beyond constant causes both reinforces the belief in constant causes and adds to the paradox of the persistence of leprosy stigma.

When we consider such questions as the enduring survival of beliefs and attitudes, the problem of explanation, as Arthur L. Stinchcombe has noted, can be divided into two sets of causal components. The initial set comprises the complex circumstances that cause an attitude to arise. Such explanations may or may not be sociological. The second, and more important, set comprises the general processes by which attitudes are maintained. Such explanations definitely are sociological.[9] In the case of the taint of leprosy, my problem does not center about origination. I accept that leprosy was tainted in the medieval and biblical past, even that it was especially tainted. The difficulty lies with how this taint is said to have been maintained. The premises that have been advanced simply do not seem equal to the task.

MEDICAL CHARACTERISTICS AND UNCERTAINTIES

The stigma of leprosy and stereotypes about the disease have played a crucial role in its social history. Stigma and stereotypes have influenced the formulation of social policies for the management and control of leprosy, rationales for keeping leprosy separate from the rest of medicine, and the creation of special institutions—leprosaria. The stereotypes have played an unusually important role in raising funds for patient care and a decidedly negative role in matters of patient rehabilitation, social acceptance, and medical research.

Views that attribute stigma to constant causes have had a considerable impact on leprosy policies. Such views themselves are a part of the history of the taint. I will consider these views and present an alternative explanation, based *not* on the continuity of stigma but instead on the retainting of leprosy in modern times. But it is first necessary to review the medical characteristics of the disease, for these characteristics figure in the development of views about stigma.

The medical characteristics presented here describe the disease as it is explained today. It is not known to what extent the disease may have altered its form with time; the disease is so protean in its manifestations that regional variations in description have been the subject of much confusion and controversy. Indeed, when the World Health Organization first entered into international leprosy work, it argued the need for standardization.[10]

Variations in the descriptions of leprosy and the many differing explanations about the disease—for example, in the degree of contagion and in the emphasis placed on deformity—are reflected in the picture of the disease that is presented to public audiences. Historically, the view most widely disseminated about leprosy has tended to be an extreme view, which further reflects the way that scientific description is shaped by social expectations. Uncertainties about leprosy continue to vex scientists, and different assessments about the nature of the disease frequently appear. The major uncertainties and medical characteristics are as follows.

- Leprosy is a chronic infectious disease that chiefly involves the skin and peripheral nerves. But it may also affect certain other tissues, notably the eye, the mucosa of the upper respiratory tract, muscle, bone, and testes. Leprosy has been called the great imitator because it mimics and therefore can be confused with a profusion of other conditions.

- *Mycobacterium leprae* is regarded as the causative agent. The bacillus was first described by Gerhard Armauer Hansen of Norway in 1873–1874 and was the first bacterium associated with a disease affecting humans. In leprosy, Koch's postulates have not been definitively fulfilled. However, the mycobacteria are consistently present in the lepromatous form of the disease and decline in number or disappear as the disease is controlled by treatment or undergoes spontaneous remission. Morphologically, *M. leprae* is similar to *M. tuberculosis* and, like the latter, is acid-fast.

- *M. leprae* has not been cultivated in vitro. The disease resists experimental transmission in humans, despite scores of attempts by leprosy workers to inoculate themselves, patients, friends, and students. However, a few instances of accidental inoculation have been reported. For years efforts to induce leprosy in animals were unproductive. More recently, experiments with hamsters, mice, armadillos, and certain species of monkeys are yielding results.

- The mode of transmission is still uncertain. Prolonged and intimate contact with an active case has for some time been believed to be necessary for infection to take place. However, some persons apparently acquire the disease after a relatively brief exposure. Entry is commonly thought to be through the skin or, secondarily, via the respiratory tract. The role of insect vectors, however, has not been totally ruled out. A human carrier is suspected to be necessary by some.

- Genetic factors are believed to be crucial in determining the degree of susceptibility. Those whose tissue defense mechanisms are least able to cope with the bacillus develop lepromatous leprosy; others develop more benign forms. Thus, in areas of the world where there is little leprosy and a high degree of immunity, the disease is held to be only mildly contagious or even noncontagious. In hyperendemic areas among populations with a low degree of immunity, or in virgin populations with minimal resistance, the disease is considerably more infectious. Finally, the incubation period is often prolonged and nonspecific; it varies from a few months to many years.

- Until recently, there were no diagnostic tests to detect the presence of early infection. Now a specific serodiagnostic test has been devised but, at this writing, has not been subjected to the full array of routine field trails.

- Treatment of leprosy is also uncertain and problematic. Sulfone therapy, introduced in the early 1940s, is more effective than earlier medications but is only bacteriostatic. The development of primary and secondary drug resistance is an increasing problem. Newer drugs, some of which are bacteriocidal, become available slowly. Drug manufacturers have little interest in leprosy. The newer drugs are expensive, need to be taken in combination, and when used intermittently may produce serious side effects. These circumstances place an ever-increasing burden on leprosy-care systems in the developing countries. The question of how to treat leprosy has involved leprologists in innumerable controversies.

- Epidemiologically, the characteristics of leprosy vary depending on whether it is in an epidemic or endemic state. In epidemic states the disease spreads rapidly, no particular foci can be identified, and all ages of the population are at risk; the tuberculoid form, which represents a high degree of resistance, tends to predominate. In endemic states, the disease spreads slowly, cases are often clustered in villages or in families, and children and young adults are commonly affected; the lepromatous form of the disease predominates, and contact greatly increases the risk of infection and affects the pattern of spread. Generally, leprosy is twice as common among males as among females.

- The number of cases of leprosy in the world today is conservatively estimated at 10 million to 15 million. The bulk of the cases are in impoverished Third World countries, mainly in Asia and Africa. Although the disease today tends to concentrate in tropical rural areas, it has also appeared in temperate and not so temperate climates.[11]

MODERN THEORIES OF LEPROSY STIGMA

Social scientists are not the only group interested in stigma, nor are they the only ones to develop theories. Those who themselves are stigmatized and those who mediate between the stigmatized groups and society have long had a practical interest in the matter. They emphasize ways to ameliorate the stigma and to counter the disqualifying ideology.[12] Not all leprosy theorists have destigmatization as their primary concern. But some theorists, puzzled or fascinated by the attitudes and emotionalism involving the stigma and its persistence, seek to elucidate its base.

I will now present three modern theories of leprosy stigma. The first view, advanced by Olaf Kristen Skinsnes, M.D., Ph.D., a missionary leprologist, although highly sophisticated, is based on the beliefs of an earlier generation that saw stigma as a natural response to the disease. A second view is from historical scholarship. The third view was developed by institutionalized leprosy patients in the United States.

Skinsnes's Theory

Skinsnes was born of missionary parents in Sinyang, China. He became a professor of pathology, John A. Burns School of Medicine, Honolulu, Hawaii, and director of the American Leprosy Missions' Leprosy Atelier. Skinsnes is eminent in both the scientific and missionary worlds, a prolific contributor to technical journals, and dedicated to solving the mysteries of *Mycobacterium leprae*. His interests extend far beyond the laboratory, into the history, art, literature, and sociology of the disease.

In an early publication Skinsnes provided details on an exquisite hypothetical disease that would express the ultimate in physical deterioration and disability and would elicit the most negative possible societal response. This hypothetical disease would:

1. Be externally manifest. Prominent and disfiguring skin swelling and ulceration would appear over the much of the body.

2. Be progressively crippling and deforming with increasing loss of function. Such physical deterioration, when prolonged, would place an economic strain on a society with limited resources and a shortage of facilities for the care of the disabled. The social strain would be greatest where the disease progressively involved nerves of the face and of the extremities. Although such impairment would not totally jeopardize individual survival, it would impair adaptation. The deformity would present a "visual horror." As the central nervous system would not be involved, victims of the disease would remain aware of their condition, which would further add to their predicament.

3. Be nonfatal and chronic, subjecting sufferers to secondary disease complications. Epidemic diseases, by contrast, result in recovery or death in a relatively short time. They may cause "fear and horror,

but the epidemic passes and community immunity builds up. Such epidemics are more likely to be regarded by the community as a special visitation from the gods, directed at the whole group. The society may then feel united in affliction, and perhaps in wrongdoing, for which the visitation is believed to be the punishment, rather than being revolted by certain 'punished' individuals."

4. Have an insidious onset, "bedeviling and confusing the scholars."

5. Have a fairly high endemicity, only limitedly epidemic. A disease with such a pattern "might well be dismissed by society as an oddity, or perhaps a strange personal affliction," whereas "a common disease would demand action and explanation."

6. Have an incidence rate associated with low standards of living, thereby providing a

> favorable milieu for the development of superstitions and misconceptions. . . . This association occurs when disease is transmitted primarily by person to person contact and has such a low degree of infectivity that prolonged contact under crowded and perhaps unhygienic conditions are necessary for usual transmission. Alternatively, the same effect could be accomplished by coupling low infectivity with high, but not complete, native immunity. . . . Another mechanism of achieving this effect would be for transmission to be accomplished by insect vectors.

7. Appear to be incurable, owing to the lack of knowledge, or apparently incurable, owing to residual deformity.

8. "As a master-stroke," the disease would have a long incubation period. A long lapse of time between "infection and manifestation . . . reduces . . . the likelihood of determining the specific source of the infection, especially when the infecting agent is invisible to the unaided eye. In a society where superstition and magical explanations . . . are in vogue, a long incubation period might well add the mysterious touch that would cause the disease to appear as if striking from the unknown . . . as if it were a special punishment from heaven or 'the gods.'"[13]

Clearly, the disease complex postulated is leprosy, as Skinsnes intended it to be. Although "each of the characteristics," he wrote, "can be found in a variety of diseases and are not unique, [the] complex provided by the association of all these characteristics in one disease is . . . unique." This premise allows Skinsnes to formulate the following theorem about leprosy stigma: Leprosy possesses a unique medical pathology; this unique pathology produces a unique social response.[14] A set of constant causes thus produces stigma wherever the disease appears.

Skinsnes did more than formulate a position. He also documented it: among Occidental nations, notably Europe; in centuries long past through the writings of Dante and Chaucer; in the post-Medieval period by the

Romantic writers; as a nonmedical and opprobrious literary term in the publications found on contemporary newsstands; as accretions to biblical definitions; and in works from Oriental antiquity in China, Japan, and India as well as those from pre-Christian Western history.[15]

Skinsnes is critical of the view that attributes lepraphobia solely to biblical teaching. He noted that the stigma observed in the ancient Orient can hardly be derived from such a tradition. As far as the West is concerned, "Europe lived with leprosy for several centuries [during the Dark and Middle Ages], reacting with both leprophobia and leprophilia." Thus, "it is not unlikely that much of the reaction to leprosy derived from direct experience, observation and reaction, and was not merely a parroting of ancient beliefs."[16]

The proposition that a unique medical pathology is the cause of a unique social reaction is reminiscent of a bacteriological model. For Skinsnes, social reaction to leprosy is "virtually specific," so specific in fact that the existence of the particular social reaction may be considered as evidence of the existence of the disease itself, "even though the records of the age may be naive, inconclusive, or inclusive of" other diseases mislabeled leprosy. When such a pattern of intensely negative "social reaction and belief exists in a society it is evidence of the presence of leprosy even if the medical witness is deficient."[17]

Leprosy is the core odium, Skinsnes wrote. Noting that the word has been used in a wide sense, not always directly related to the disease itself, he wrote: "It seems, however, to be a fact that leprosy has always been a part of the moiety that has been designated 'leprosy'. . . . As increasing medical and social understanding have peeled away the other entities that were complexed with leprosy, leprosy has emerged and been left as the sole assignee of the odium for which its core characteristics were originally and predominantly responsible."[18]

"Disease is not a metaphor," Susan Sontag wrote in *Illness as Metaphor*. But "any important disease whose causality is murky, and for which treatment is ineffectual, tends to be awash in significance. First, the subjects of deepest dread (corruption, decay, pollution, anomie, weakness) are identified with the disease. The disease itself becomes a metaphor. Then, in the name of the disease (that is, using it as a metaphor), that horror is imposed on other things. The disease becomes adjectival."[19] Other master illnesses, such as tuberculosis and cancer, have also been heavily encumbered by the trappings of metaphor. But, as Sontag noted, these metaphors change with context and expectation. Even when the disease remains "mysterious," as does cancer, the images and fantasies change with the times. Not so with leprosy. Skinsnes's metaphor is immutable.

Historians' Views of Leprosy Stigma

Philip A. Kalisch is the only professional historian to write about leprosy stigma within the context of modern events. His work therefore merits special attention. In his major paper "Lepers, Anachronisms, and the Progressives: A Study of Stigma, 1889–1920," Kalisch focused on the national leprosarium movement that flourished in the United States between the last decade of the nineteenth century and the period that coincided with U.S. entry into World War I.[20]

Leprosy was a social and political issue around the turn of the century. In 1898, the United States Public Health Service was authorized to investigate the prevalence of leprosy in the United States. Although the study documented only 278 cases in the country, the commission recommended that one or two leprosaria be established. A bill to confine lepers was introduced in 1905, and the issue was debated in the House of Representatives. The bill failed, but it was later reintroduced a number of times. Finally, in the 1916–1917 session of Congress, the bill passed. World War I delayed its implementation until 1921, when the national leprosarium was located on the site of the Louisiana Home for Lepers, Carville, Louisiana.

It is in this context of national events that Kalisch sought to evaluate the federal government's policy, which compelled the incarceration of lepers and maintained a strong antileprosy sentiment, "a tendency . . . that was entirely out of keeping with early twentieth century America."[21] The reforms that the "Progressive Era" produced in the United States, Kalisch wrote, "resulted in the enlightened amelioration of stigma surrounding such illnesses as insanity, tuberculosis, and syphilis, but failed to break through the barrier of stigma surrounding leprosy."[22]

Leprosy was the first disease to elicit a socialized response at the federal level. The move to establish a national leprosarium was unprecedented. Leprosy was considered to be contagious and disfiguring and was thought to be spreading. But other contagious diseases were also spreading in the United States and to a far greater extent. The federal response to leprosy was a response to the "conservative sector of public opinion." "The moral powers of Congress," Kalisch wrote, "seem to have been unduly dulled by fear of contagion and by an unwillingness to compromise the almost instinctive primitive reaction to the disease." But, according to Kalisch, the stigma of leprosy "was no simple delusion of a bigoted and ignorant few, rather it comprised a set of beliefs whose structures were based in the deepest level of human lives with antecedents from the beginning of time."[23]

For Kalisch, the modern stigma of leprosy represents a reversion to the Middle Ages, when "lepraphobia was institutionalized and incorporated into a host of social and political practices, most of which became ritualistic." The centuries of leprosy stigma "from time immemorial with its unique dehumanization are no mere accident. If such an infantile 'fear' of leprosy can maintain such lasting intensity in the most 'normal' of adults, then there must be something at large in culture to sustain it." In accounting for the endurance of leprosy stigma, Kalisch invoked a constant cause: "the significance of skin blemishes appears all important as the aversion fantasies seem to emanate from a most primitive level of mental organization. This deepest, least rational social meaning . . . seems to have served certain deep-seated unconscious psychological needs."[24]

Leprous people are viewed as the personification of "dirt" and "uncleanliness." Dirt and uncleanliness "absorb aggression and help sustain the 'clean' elements by binding up the 'unclean.'" In the United States "it was only natural that the tension created by the leprous brought a reversion to ancient and medieval times when lepers had their place and authority was secure."

Thus, the public focus on leprosy, according to Kalisch, resolves a structural tension. It sublimates societal matters of order and disorder.

Saul Nathaniel Brody, a historian of medieval literature, is also intrigued with why it is that, although other diseases lost their medieval connotations long ago, leprosy has not. The stigma of leprosy, Brody noted in his book *The Disease of the Soul: Leprosy in Medieval Literature*, is far older than ecclesiastic tradition: "To locate the source of leprosy stigma in the Bible is tempting—but the Bible merely contains evidence of the stigma, not its origin. The connotation between leprosy and immorality was established before the Bible was written, and it has appeared nearly everywhere the disease has."[25] The importance of the Bible is that it "preserves, codifies, and elaborates tradition" and "even if it is not the source of the leper's reputation for sinfulness, no other document can claim to have helped so much in propagating that reputation."[26]

Brody, however, more than other theorists, acknowledges a gap in Western leprosy history. From the sixteenth century on, the disease ceased to be prevalent in Europe and was limited to a few isolated areas. But the association of leprosy with immorality continued, even though "audiences were not familiar with leprosy and had no direct experience with it."[27] The disease remained a powerful literary image nonetheless, "an emblem of sin," a symbol of "general ethical decay." The moral implications of the disease, Brody noted, "were so firmly established in Western culture during the medieval period that they have lasted into our own time. . . . That tradition has survived because it is the expression of a complex array of cultural forces."[28]

A Destigmatization Theory: The National Leprosarium, Carville, Louisiana

The national leprosarium (now known as the Gillis W. Long Hansen's Disease Center) is the only hospital for the treatment of the general civilian population for a specific disease that the U.S. Government has ever created. Founded in 1894 as the Louisiana Home for Lepers, the hospital came under federal jurisdiction in 1921. It is still in existence today. In the interest of improving their status in life, patients at the hospital have evolved their own theory of leprosy stigma.

Interest in destigmatizing leprosy understandably first came from within the world of leprosy itself. Two sets of circumstances contributed to this interest in destigmatization. One had to do with the state of medical treatment for leprosy earlier in the century. Chaulmoogra (hydnocarpus) oil had been an ancient remedy for the disease, and Western interest in its effectiveness was aroused in the years just before World War I. But by the 1930s this enthusiasm for the ancient substance had waned. With no truly effective medication in sight, a spirit of pessimism pervaded clinical circles. As the hope of caring for the diseased bodies of lepers diminished, attention was turned increasingly to their discredited status. Concerns about the damaging effect the stigma had on the lives of patients was for the first time now addressed in professional circles.

The other set of circumstances had to do with the emergence of a coherent patient community at the Carville leprosarium. Patient activists there began to address the issue of stigma at about the same time as the leprologists and for similar reasons. That intense patient involvement in the social issues affecting them occurred at Carville, rather than at any of the other leprosaria around the world, is not surprising. Carville is the only major leprosarium located in an industrial nation; hence, over the years, many, though not all, of its inmates have been citizens of the United States, relatively well educated, and often articulate.

From the early 1930s to the present day, patients at the leprosarium have been active in combatting the stigma of leprosy. One of their major achievements has been the formulation of a theory of stigma that explicates the basis of modern lepraphobia. It provides a basis for arguments that seek to alter public beliefs about the disease. The theory is re-educative and demythologizes leprosy. It is articulated in *The Star*, a bimonthly journal edited and published by the patients since it was founded in the 1930s.

The context of the Carville position is Christian-Judaic civilization; its boundaries are the whole of the Western world, including non-Christian areas influenced by biblical teachings. The Carville position is revolutionary. The Carville activists acknowledge that leprosy is publicly tainted by a set of beliefs that associates the modern disease with the "leprosies" of the past. However, they argue that the two conditions are *not* the same, that the public has erroneously equated them, and furthermore, that it is the continued belief that they *are* the same that accounts for the social prejudice that surrounds the disease today. Patients maintain that the use of such words as "leper" and "leprosy" perpetuates the myth of continuity and sustains a pejorative view of the disease that they claim is ubiquitous.

Early in their new career at Carville, patients learn that society's view of the disease is defective. The basic re-educative assumption of the theory is that societal rejection will diminish appreciably, and perhaps even disappear entirely, once social misconceptions about the disease are corrected. Serious proposals have been advanced to change the name of the illness to Hansen's disease in honor of the discoverer of *Mycobacterium leprae*, Armauer Hansen. This move was affirmed by the International Leprosy Congress, Havana, 1948, and again in Madrid, 1953.[29] The United States Public Health Service hospital at Carville actively disseminates the theory through public tours, seminars, and planned programs in which both staff and patients participate.

The Carville theorists have also attempted to deal with the issue of contagion. However, because a number of medical uncertainties exist related to communicability and transmission, the theory understandably encounters certain difficulties here. Much is made of leprosy as a "mildly communicable" disease. In the continental United States, outside of the endemic foci of Louisiana, Texas, Florida, and California, it is "so rarely communicated to contacts that from a public health standpoint it might be considered a non-communicable disease,"[30] a statement that reflects the regional limitations of the theory. It has been routinely related at Carville that in more than three-quarters of a century only one employee ever acquired the disease, and that man, it is pointed out, was a native of the endemic area of southern Louisiana. This record of near perfection is not shared by all leprosaria.[31]

The following case history, extracted from an extended interview, illustrates how patients reformulate their attitudes toward leprosy and deal with basic problems of revealing their illness to others.

> The patient has been a regular Carville resident since his first admission more than five years ago. He has a benign form of leprosy with few visible symptoms. The disease seems dormant at present. The patient is below middle age and his general health is good.
>
> The patient's view of the disease has been modified considerably since his diagnosis. At that time he believed leprosy to be highly contagious, painful, and fatal, and that he would soon lose various body parts—nose, ears, toes, etc. He continually tested for signs of atrophy and also experienced depression. He carefully concealed his disease from others, passing his symptoms off as due to a nonstigmatized condition. He was upset on arriving at Carville that the staff did not immediately confine him. Now he believes that leprosy is a minimal disease, especially when treatment is begun early. He ranks cancer, heart disease, tuberculosis, arthritis, and rheumatism as worse than leprosy. He views genetic susceptibility as a prime factor in acquiring the disease. Now he never denies having leprosy and pointedly informs others of his condition.
>
> He acknowledges the existence of public fear and believes that continuous efforts are necessary to correct erroneous public views. He links the maximal illness fantasy and the stigma held by the public to the teachings of the churches and to writers and film makers who continue to hold stereotypic views of leprosy.
>
> The patient cites his own experience and marked shift in viewpoint as an example of the "conversion" anticipated in the public once an understanding of the disease is achieved. He believes he has avoided developing a discredited self-identity through engaging in public education and the opportunity it has provided him for disclosing that he has leprosy. Concealers, he notes, deny themselves this opportunity; thus, they remain self-stigmatized.
>
> At present he lives at Carville, but works outside the institution. His employer and co-employees know he has leprosy. He would not have it otherwise, he says. Informally he reveals his disease in almost all appropriate situations with only minor reservations.

A selection from an interview with a patient who is more typical, less articulate, and less well educated, illustrates how patients incorporate elements of the Carville theory to account for public prejudice:

> This woman has been at Carville for 15 years and is now married to another patient at the leprosarium. She reports that the disease has never given her

trouble. Her bacteriological status is close to negative at the present time. She believes cancer and heart disease are worse than leprosy. Yet, to this day, "my family don't know about my having this disease. My brothers and sisters just know I'm sick and in a hospital, that's all."

Interviewer: "What do you think there is about leprosy that makes people afraid of it?"

Patient: "Actually, because they don't know anything about it. When you say 'leprosy' everybody gets so scared. It's so contagious they think, and it has always been in the Bible that it was so contagious that they naturally connect the two and think you had better get away from it."

Interviewer: "How realistically afraid of the disease do you think people should be?"

Patient: "Well, I don't think they should be afraid of it no more than you would be afraid of tuberculosis. You're not afraid to go out there among people with tuberculosis. The name itself makes people afraid because they don't know anything about it. But, I don't think people would be afraid if they knew more about it."

The Carville theory elaborates the view that society's negative image arises from, and has been perpetuated by, faulty biblical exegesis based, at best, on poorly substantiated linguistic evidence and historical reasoning. The theory dwells less on the medical and physiologic aspects of leprosy; it represents an attempt to inject a measure of certainty and hope into a markedly uncertain and, for some, less than hopeful experience. There is, however, some truth to the theory. Leprosy is not, except in rare instances, the ultimate disease it is fantasied to be; nor is it the same as the disease referred to in the Bible. Although the theory is incomplete as a social and historical explanation for the prejudices encountered, it nevertheless has value for patient adaptation.[32]

The Carville patient journal, *The Star*, was the first public voice to take a programmatic stand divorcing the modern disease from biblical leprosy. The position ran counter to popular belief and clerical teaching. It would be some time before leprologist historians and organizations that raise funds for leprosy work would address the issue raised by *The Star*.

CRITIQUE

The central thesis of modern theories of leprosy stigma is that the taint of leprosy is continuous from the distant past. The taint is also described as ubiquitous. Writers differ only to the extent that they assign different sets of constant causes to explain the perdurance of the stigma. Only the Carville position—that Western stigma endures because the public has erroneously equated the modern disease with biblical leprosy—does not depend on constant causes.

Although they have constructed a massive literature on lepraphobia, theorists have failed to address the question of whether ancient "leprosy" is the same as the disease known today. The assumption is that the diseases are the same, although diseases are known to alter their form. As Brody has shown, descriptions of medieval leprosy are remarkably simplistic when compared with the modern condition.[33] How it came about that ancient descriptions became equated with modern leprosy is an interesting example of how a disease may acquire an extended genealogy.

Modern theorists tend to ignore those situations in which the disease has been present, recognized, and even treated by physicians but in which strong aversion has been absent. Most remarkable is the failure of the theorists to acknowledge the history of leprosy in Norway during the nineteenth century, where leprosy was hyperendemic but regarded only as an unfortunate condition of life, much like poverty and illiteracy. Nowhere was it regarded in Norway as an ultimate disgrace. Nor was leprosy, until the very end of the nineteenth century, regarded negatively in southern Louisiana, where it was endemic. The absence of any special fear of leprosy is found in various parts of the world where the disease is found: for example, in the Upper Mississippi Valley, where Scandinavian immigrants to the United States were known to have the disease; in Hawaii, among native Polynesians; among the indigenous peoples of Australia, the Ryukyu Islands, and other parts of Oceania; in parts of South Russia; and throughout the Islamic world. Where apprehension is encountered, it is related to the diffusion of Western fears and the Western practice of isolating lepers from the community.[34]

The thesis that the taint of leprosy is ubiquitous is related to judgments about the alleged intensity of human aversion. As one sociologist has put it: "It is difficult to imagine a socially created status more damaging to self-esteem. Even the word 'leper' is frightening to almost all of us."[35] Nowhere in the vast documentation on lepraphobia is societal response to leprosy compared with societal responses to other known diseases, behaviors, or human predicaments. This near-total absence of comparative data is perhaps the weakest element in views about the intensity of lepraphobia; at the same time it represents one of the stronger arguments for regarding such views less as detached observation than as belief or ideology. Leprosy has been excluded from the test of comparison with other diseases and conditions. By piling extreme example of aversion atop extreme example and by citing tragic stories almost exclusively, writers have fashioned an image of the disease purportedly in agreement with popular Western views.

Lepraphobia may be likened to a "culture-bound syndrome response," present in some cultures, but not in all. The failure of theorists to locate lepraphobia in historical time and place, in context and expectation, gives lepraphobia the appearance of "received truth."

Yet the issue of leprosy stigma persists. By doubting the rationales behind the theories of leprosy stigma, I do not intend to dismiss or minimize the existence of the stigma itself. Leprosy is a real disease. It is highly prevalent in many parts of the world; it remains a disease with many uncertainties; and it has been and is now stigmatized. Two analytic problems present themselves: One is the need for an alternative explanation to account for the modern stigma of leprosy; the other is the need to place existing views in historical perspective.

THE RETAINTING OF LEPROSY

I first encountered the reality of the association of biblical and medieval sin with disease while conducting what I thought would be a modest study of leprosy patients at the United States Public Health Service Hospital, Carville, Louisiana—the only leprosarium in the continental United States. My initial plan was to investigate patterns of adaptation among patients with a chronic and disabling illness. What I did not know at the time and had not anticipated was the extent to which stigma and beliefs about stigma surrounded leprosy; nor was I aware of the sensitivity that leprosy patients and the staff have toward the views the public holds, or is presumed to hold, about those with the illness.

At Carville, beliefs about stigma have been especially strong. The official view held at the leprosarium is that the disease and its name evoke considerable public opprobrium. This view first came under research scrutiny when, during the course of interviewing patients and staff, I began to discover discrepancies about societal response. Interviews indicated that not all patient experiences had been negative. Many patients reported social encounters devoid of stigma and encounters that were neutral, if not positive; as such, those experiences were directly contrary to the position that the disease was categorically stigmatized. To be sure, negative encounters were reported more emotionally and lingered longer in the patients' minds, but within the accumulated data there were enough instances of neutral and positive experiences to offset the pervasive belief in societal rejection. Nonetheless, the Carville community, its culture, and especially the re-educative function of the patients' theory of stigma—namely, the defective view of leprosy believed to be held by the public—all seemed to reinforce a reporting of negative events. Patients attempted to explain this discrepancy by noting that the positive experiences might be the result of re-educational campaigns conducted over the years by patients at the hospital. "But the stigma of leprosy is real," they cautioned, "it is worse than the disease itself."

All views about the disease presumed the existence of intense opprobrium, yet these views had never been demonstrated in any survey. The literature on the subject of public views about leprosy in the United States was sparse and of little help. Reports on only three studies, all brief, could be found. One used the term "leprosy" as an item in a semantic differential investigation of mental illness, and the second was a reanalysis of the first. The third study was largely admonitory.[36] At this point, what the public actually thought about leprosy was unclear, and I felt the need for some objective data. I therefore carried out a community study. Conducted in a southern metropolitan area, the survey investigated knowledge and attitudes toward leprosy relative to a number of other diseases more in the public purview. The study produced the somewhat surprising finding that people do not particularly see leprosy as a threat. The general public surveyed viewed it as something that existed elsewhere (in the legendary past or "perhaps out there in the jungle somewhere"); therefore there was little or no concern and no categorical stigmatization. Although the survey was limited to one community and queried people only in relation to the word "leprosy," it nevertheless served to raise a number of further questions.[37]

The results of the survey framed a disjunction between actual public responses to leprosy and the convictions generally assumed to be held by the public. Earlier, I had found a historical incongruence between the view that leprosy stigma was continuous from the past and the Carville position questioning the relationship between the modern disease and the leprosy mentioned in the Bible. At this juncture the need to resort to the library became evident. Two items from the historical record stood out. One was the agreement among authorities that, with the exception of a few small endemic foci, leprosy had virtually disappeared from the continent of Europe since at least the sixteenth century and had never been of any importance in the Americas north of Mexico. The second item was the observation that the decline of leprosy in Europe corresponded to the decline in the power and prestige of the medieval church.

The disappearance of leprosy from Europe toward the end of the Middle Ages poses something of a dilemma. Although there is consensus among historians and leprologists alike that the prevalence of the disease declined dramatically, no one is sure why. Various explanations have been offered. The decline of leprosy in Europe has been attributed to the episodic nature of epidemics; to the depopulation produced by the Black Plague; to improvements in hygiene, diet, and standards of living; to changing concepts in the classification and nosology of disease; and even to the replacement of leprosy by the more urban tuberculosis bacillus. Michel Foucault has offered the intriguing suggestion that as a salient concept in European thought, the idea of "leprosy" was replaced in church theology at the end of the Middle Ages by the paradigm of "madness."[38] Medieval church theology and practice had required "the leper," and so lepers had appeared. Foucault's reasoning suggests to me that the saliency of "lepers" and "leprosy" as concepts may very well have loomed larger than the actual prevalence in Europe of leprosy as a disease; the "decline" in leprosy, then, was not necessarily an actual decline in the prevalence of the disease but rather a decline in the importance of the concepts as the structure and teachings of the church itself changed.

In considering questions of stigma, one can understand how such a set of beliefs was maintained during the Middle Ages. The disease was considered to be everywhere and was condemned by ecclesiastic authority as an extreme moral perversion. But it seems to me that, given the physical disappearance of the disease and the changes·in the medieval church, little in the way of direct experience, either with the disease or with its symbolism, could have kept alive an awareness of leprosy equal to the intensity that one finds expressed in modern views. If the taint of leprosy is still alive in modern times, and it seems that this is so, then it would have to be perpetuated by mechanisms other than the old church-carried stigma and maintained by something other than literary and pulpit references and metaphors.

The historical record provides a possible answer as to why the taint of leprosy is with us today. Whereas leprosy had disappeared from Europe and had declined as a salient theological concept by the end of the Middle Ages, by the nineteenth century it had reappeared and by the end of that century had caused Western nations to panic. During the period of nineteenth-century imperialism, the disease was discovered to be hyperendemic in those parts of the world that Western nations were annexing and colonizing. The discovery of leprosy in the colonial world, and the excitement in the 1860s generated by the announcement of an epidemic in Hawaii, revived Western concerns about a disease that otherwise remained but a memory. Leprosy became salient once again as Western nations, which had in the recent past experienced devastating epidemics of their own, became fearful that this disease might prove pandemic.

When they discovered that the disease was hyperendemic abroad, Europeans and Americans immediately—and logically within the intellectual climate of the day—labeled leprosy a disease of "inferior" peoples. In fearing that such a disease might contaminate the "civilized" world, Western nations became intensely lepraphobic by the turn of the century. Powerful social and political forces were activated to prevent leprous people from coming into contact with Westerners. Leprosy became an international social problem. In the United States, for example, amid late nineteenth- and early twentieth-century national apprehensions about immigration and about the biological and cultural status of those seeking entry into the country, appeals were made that the potential spread of the disease be addressed by the U.S. Congress.

Leprosy gained enormous importance as a social problem of Western nations during the final decades of the nineteenth century. That century was marked by grand imperialistic designs and by the movement of masses of people across oceans. It was a century of considerable intellectual and scientific ferment as controversies arose about the origin of man and other species and about evolution and social heredity. Spencerian ideas of social Darwinism dominated much of the thinking about cultural and biological progress.

The century also witnessed vast changes in the medical sciences. The germ theory of disease emerged as one of the most important scientific advances. This new theory ushered in a totally new era in clinical and experimental medicine. The germ theory was of the utmost importance in public health, but it also played an incisive role in race relations. Whole populations became labeled "contaminants" in ways never previously considered. The germ theory was instrumental in altering popular conceptions of disease and transformed conditions viewed as morally ambiguous, like tuberculosis or syphilis, into "crimes."[39] New immigration laws were written, particularly in the United States. The germ theory heightened fears that contact with "inferior" peoples would threaten the safety and future of the "superior" race. Race mixture, it was believed, would ultimately erode Anglo-Saxon effectiveness. Infection and contagion increased the sense of danger.

National anxieties were further aroused by the fact that germs were invisible and could contaminate even when precautions were taken.

Modern leprosy was not clinically described until the 1840s, with the work in Norway of Danielssen and Boeck. It was not until the early 1870s that Hansen would observe that *spedalskhed*, as the disease was known in Norway, contained mycobacteria. Hansen's observation added strength to the growing conviction late in the nineteenth century that leprosy was a germ disease and therefore contagious. But just how contagious leprosy is, which populations are susceptible, and how the disease is transmitted are not only questions that were unanswered during Hansen's time but also questions that are still being asked today. Notwithstanding these uncertainties, once Western nations learned that the disease was abundant in colonial areas, leprosy was almost immediately characterized as highly contagious; this characterization of the disease has still not been totally dispelled.

The late nineteenth-century Western opinion that leprosy was highly contagious, however, was not formed through extended observation and careful studies of the behavior of the disease. Rather, it was formed by the general attitudes held in Western nations about the character and the symbolic attributes supposedly possessed by the colonial populations in which the disease was presumed to be inherent. Western fears of a leprosy pandemic coincided with that period late in the nineteenth century when apprehensions about the Chinese and their "alien germs" were at their height and when, in the United States, the immigration of foreign populations deemed "undesirable" was being restricted. Racial connotations enhanced the stereotype of leprosy. Because of the awesomely negative image held in the West toward the Chinese—the "yellow peril"—Western peoples had exaggerated fears and elaborate fantasies about the diseases that might be introduced. The mantle of racism had condemned the colonial world as "inferior" and "undesirable." These adjectives and their imagery formed almost the total Western conception about non-Western, non-Anglo-Saxon humankind. This perspective came to be applied to all of the attributes of the peoples of the "backward" world; according to this perspective, their bodies were degenerate, their minds primitive, and their diseases loathsome. Leprosy gained in recognition because it was perceived to be a firm part of the other major issues of the day.

As leprosy was being stereotyped through descriptions that reflected European perceptions of "coolies" and "Hindoos," yet another set of images linked it with the biblical and medieval taint. The expansion of European imperialism late in the nineteenth century was accompanied by a religious revival in England and by an intensification of missionary activity. Starting in the 1870s, missionaries began going abroad in large numbers. The analogy that leprologist historians saw between their own Christian past and the leprosy from abroad was not lost on the growing overseas evangelical missionary movement. Systematic and focused attention on leprosy as an area of service formally began in 1874 with the formation in England of The Mission to Lepers.

Church-affiliated agencies have dominated the field of leprosy work worldwide to the present day. This involvement is unparalleled in the history of disease. Agencies raise and expend considerable sums of money and reach a large audience in efforts to promote community interest in the leper. Their appeal is emotional, Christian, and often scriptural. Even when they no longer directly equate contemporary leprosy with the leprosy of the Bible, the Christian appeal, message, and context within which funds are raised reinforce in the public mind an association of the modern disease with the ancient sacred writings of Western civilization.

In undertaking the worldwide care of lepers, missionary societies discovered more than just another group of people in need. They found a key word that for them linked the present with some of the most poignant teachings and practices of Christ. In sponsoring lepers, mission societies added a parabolized moral status to an already existing secular stigma.

The contribution of missionary activity in engendering modern lepraphobia has not gone unrecognized by those within that world. Dr. Stanley G. Browne, himself a medical missionary and leprologist, has noted: "While in some countries where leprosy is highly endemic, social prejudice against the disease is minimal, or nonexistent, it is generally true that leprosy is regarded with an inordinate fear and loathing accorded to no other disease. . . . Where such prejudice did not exist, it may even be engendered by Christian preachers who derive their ideas from Biblical references to 'leprosy' and 'lepers.'"[40]

Although scientific, rational alternate approaches for dealing with leprosy were proposed and sometimes tried in Europe and in the United States, the worldwide leprosarium movement that began in the late nineteenth century came to be the Western model-of-choice in the disposition of lepers. The move to establish leprosaria spoke of extraordinary motives. Special communities were created, along with a special group of caretakers. The segregation of lepers in these communities, and the presumed necessity for such segregation, engendered a labeling and fostered a fantasy of the disease that have been difficult to counteract.

The segregation of lepers in isolated asylums under missionary care tended to alleviate Western anxieties about the disease and to reduce the status of leprosy as an international problem. But attention to leprosy did not diminish. Unlike most tropical diseases, about which Westerners knew and heard little, leprosy held the public interest. The widespread distribution of leprosy throughout the colonial world and the special affinity of mission societies in caring for lepers resulted in the identification of leprosy with missionary care and Christianity. Soon the churches, through the work of missionaries and missionary hospitals, became the principal custodians and treatment providers for persons with the disease. This care and treatment evolved into a separatist tradition, with missionaries providing lepers with distinct and separate services. The institutionalized categorization of persons with leprosy as biblical "lepers" may be traced to this structured relationship. Because of this connection, leprosy has been enmeshed in a public religious aura—an aura that has preserved the professional insularity of the disease along with its special taint.

The role played by the United States in maintaining a separatist leprosy tradition has been significant. Abroad, two of the world's largest leper colonies were established under U.S. influence: Molokai, in Hawaii, and Culion, in the Philippines, were established in 1865 and 1901, respectively, soon after U.S. annexation of those islands. But U.S. involvement in the leprosarium movement has not been limited to hyperendemic areas. In 1917, the United States extended the concept of confining lepers to its own mainland, in a country where the prevalence in 1909 was only 0.018 per 1,000 population, a rate that has never been exceeded.[41] The conservatism of the United States with regard to leprosy policy did not stop there. Not only is the leprosarium at Carville, in this last quarter of the twentieth century, still a viable institution where patients are accorded a special status, but the United States failed to develop outpatient treatment centers for leprosy until the 1960s, long after such an approach was feasible.

The symbolic significance of leprosy has been an important part of the history of the fear of the disease. U.S. military excursions abroad, first in the Philippines at the end of the nineteenth century and later in World Wars I and II, once more raised the specter of pandemicity. This time the fear was not that foreigners would bring leprosy into the country, but that U.S. soldiers would bring the disease back home with them. It was no accident that the U.S. Congress, after years of defeating a bill to establish a federal leprosarium, finally passed such a measure in 1917 on the verge of U.S. entry into World War I. In calling for a leprosarium at that time, Congress was not seeking a solution to a medical problem; it was expressing the mood of the country: Lepers, along with all other things foreign, were considered "un-American."

CONCLUSION

The history of Western nations during the period of nineteenth- and twentieth-century imperialism and my own observations on the contemporary leprosy scene led me to theorize that leprosy stigma had reappeared through the influence of modern forces and events. In place of the continuity of stigma, one can look at the "retainting" of leprosy. The notion that present-day stigma represents *not* a continuity from a distant past but, instead, a retainting of the disease in modern dress derives, in part, from the historical record. I cannot, however, claim to be the only person conversant with that record. Others before me have read the same material and have written on the disease and its stigma. Nonetheless, they have tenaciously clung to the idea that the taint of leprosy has persisted from the past through tradition. The answer to this riddle does not lie in any special perspicacity on my part. Involvement in leprosy work is not primarily a secular matter. Modern-day leprosy has little relevance for most clinicians, historians of medicine, social scientists, and health planners in the everyday professional and academic Western world. Few secular theorists are concerned with the disease and its history. Leprosy work worldwide is carried out principally by members of church-affiliated agencies. The aggregate of leprosy workers comprises a coherent collectivity of mutual interests, similar beliefs, and considerable interaction. It is from this special group of sponsors, caretakers, and fundraisers that much of society's understanding and perception of the disease derives. In writing about leprosy and history, its members, perhaps understandably, have been concerned more with stigma than with historical process.

The estimated magnitude of leprosy in the world today undoubtedly is greater than it was during the period of alarm late in the nineteenth century. Modern surveys and improved case-finding methods have refined the means whereby cases of the disease are enumerated. The amount of public attention being paid to leprosy, however, is declining. It is tempting to attribute this lessening of attention to the belief that modern medicine has the disease under control, but such is not the case. Modern chemotherapy is bacteriostatic, at best. More important, most people with the disease live in countries with poorly developed health delivery systems. In Asia and in Africa many cases of the disease have not been detected and many patients receive treatment irregularly.[42] It is also tempting to speculate that Western perception about tropical populations has changed over the decades sufficiently so as to lessen the fear of foreign disease. However, in answering the question of why public interest in leprosy is declining, it is less important to examine how Western perceptions about foreign populations have changed than it is to look at how the public interest in leprosy that once was aroused was institutionalized.

Since the end of World War II, the old colonial empires have dissolved, newly independent Third World nations have emerged, and an international organization, the World Health Organization (WHO), has come into being. One function of WHO is to assist developing countries in national health planning. Early in the 1950s WHO declared leprosy to be a public health problem, not "a disease apart." Since its inception, WHO has been working toward the integration of leprosy care into general health systems. The developments that have taken place since the end of World War II have also changed the role of Western overseas mission societies. With the increasing secularization of leprosy and the changing role of mission societies has come a decline in religious fundraising for leprosy work and a lessening of public attention to leprosy as a dramatic disease.

In approaching the phenomenon of lepraphobia, I approach it as a Western phenomenon without implying that it has been exclusively a Western response. Western contributions to the stigmatization of leprosy, however, have been noteworthy.

I believe it is unnecessary to search the human psyche deeply or to reach far back into history to account for modern lepraphobia. A close look at the expanding Western world during the late nineteenth and early twentieth centuries suffices. Among the events and forces that have contributed to the retainting of leprosy are Western imperialism and colonialism, the germ theory of disease, missionary activity, the yellow peril, and racism. These are the issues that bear examining.

PART 2

The Western World in Transition: The Nineteenth Century

2

The Port City of New Orleans: A "Necropolis"

New Orleans has long been known as one of the more exotic cities of the United States—a "good-time town" known and remembered for its food and architecture, for jazz, and for Mardi Gras. Throughout the nineteenth century, New Orleans was the commercial center of the South, the entrepôt for the vast Mississippi-Missouri basin, an international seaport, and a city known for its distinctive mixture of cultures. Less well known and remembered, however, is that during much of the nineteenth century New Orleans was also one of the unhealthiest of U.S. cities and, in terms of the crude death rate, unhealthier than most major European cities as well.

Throughout most of the nineteenth century, the United States was hit repeatedly by a series of epidemics—cholera, smallpox, yellow fever—that declined in frequency and virulence only late in the century. These epidemics coincided with the expansion of population and the development of industries and cities throughout the nation. There had been epidemics in America during the colonial period, but they did not have the magnitude of the later epidemics. In terms of the crude death rate, colonial America was a far healthier place than America during the nineteenth century.[1]

New Orleans's reputation as a "pest-hole" and as a "necropolis" was based not only on its high mortality rate—which city officials, newspapers, and many physicians endeavored to deny or suppress—nor on its severe and periodic epidemics—news of which was also suppressed when possible. That reputation derived from the more tangible and more visible indifference the city leaders showed toward matters of urban sanitation and maritime quarantine. This indifference to sanitation and quarantine did not stem from apathy or from ignorance. It was reinforced by representatives of powerful commercial interests centered in New Orleans who regarded quarantine measures as costly to business and as unwarranted interference with the rights of free trade and free enterprise. It was further reinforced by influential and wealthy citizens who were indifferent to how the city's impoverished majority lived and who resented the idea of spending tax dollars on sanitation and public improvement.[2] "It was much simpler and—they thought—cheaper," historian John Duffy noted, "to ascribe the filthy and festering conditions of the slums to the immorality and irresponsibility of the slum tenants."[3]

New Orleans's population grew from about 8,000 in 1803, when Louisiana became part of the United States, to more than 17,000 seven years later. During this first period of expansion, French refugees from Saint-Domingue arrived in large numbers, many having fled first to Cuba. German immigrants also began arriving early in the century. Many, unable to pay their passage across the Atlantic, became indentured servants, whereby they worked for the person who paid the ship's captain for their crossing. A second population explosion occurred in the 1830s and 1840s, when the city more than doubled in size, mainly owing to the arrival of Irish and more German immigrants. The 1840 census showed New Orleans to have a population of 102,193, an increase of nearly 54,000 in ten years. By the eve of the Civil War, New Orleans had grown to have more than 168,000 inhabitants. Almost 41 percent of the 155,000 whites were foreign-born, with more than 24,000 Irish and almost 20,000 Germans. Italian immigration did not begin until after the Civil War.

The growth and prosperity of New Orleans through domestic and foreign commerce resulted from the city's geographical location, which combines the advantages of lying near the mouth of North America's most extensive river system—the Mississippi-Missouri river basin—and of commanding the Gulf coastline from the Florida Keys to the Yucatan with easy access to the sea-lanes and ports of the Caribbean and the Atlantic Ocean.

As the one great seaport of the Mississippi delta, New Orleans was the marketplace for the upriver antebellum plantation economy. The cotton, sugar, molasses, tobacco, grain, vegetables, spirits, and packaged freight that came downriver totaled receipts of nearly $3 billion in cargo from 1816 through 1861. Shipments upriver from New Orleans were also large, averaging about 57 percent of the value of those coming down the Mississippi.[4] Unlike the upriver plantation economy, New Orleans's commerce required a different labor base, and before the Civil War it was one of the few southern cities with a substantial working class and the only southern city with a large community of "freedmen of color."

The growth and expansion of New Orleans during the nineteenth century were accompanied by an enormous toll in human lives. From about 1820 until the turn of the century, the crude death rate in New Orleans was exceedingly high, averaging more than 40 per 1,000 population. For the thirty-year period from 1830 through 1859, the rate climbed to more than 60 per 1,000, outstripping the birth rate in the city for that period.[5] The period of ebullient commercial expansion and population growth coincided with the period of the great epidemics and pervasive endemic diseases. Population growth was achieved only through the constant immigration of the foreign-born and the influx of large numbers of "Americans" coming to New Orleans from all parts of the Upper Mississippi Valley and the Atlantic seaboard.

Money and people poured into New Orleans during its gilded age of growth and prosperity. From the North and from Europe came capital investment, and along with capital came people and families looking for opportunities, positions, and jobs. Both the skilled and the unskilled came in large numbers. From the northern states came brokers, businessmen, clerks, doctors, lawyers, boatmen, and farmers. From Germany came thousands of skilled artisans and laborers. Emigrant ships from Ireland unloaded Irish peasants to supply the construction gangs engaged in draining and filling the swamps of the well-below-sea-level city, building roads and railways, and erecting the many sumptuous and elaborate homes and buildings. During this period of growth and wealth, many prospered, many family names were transformed into "French" surnames—and many more people died of disease.

The great epidemics of the nineteenth century were regarded then, as now, as terrifying disasters. They appeared insidiously, striking suddenly and with dramatic force. In comparison with the acute and chronic endemic diseases, however, they were relatively less important in terms of morbidity and mortality. The main causes of death in the nineteenth century were the endemic diseases of everyday life—pulmonary tuberculosis, diarrheal diseases of infancy, bacillary dysentery, typhoid fever, and the infectious diseases of childhood, especially scarlet fever, diphtheria, and lobar pneumonia—diseases that by their very familiarity were often regarded with an almost casual and inevitable acceptance. Although a number of epidemics hit New Orleans during the nineteenth century, the disease most identified with the city was yellow fever, which was largely responsible for the port city's reputation as a "pest-hole." Yellow fever was not the sole disease affecting the city's reputation, however.

The common endemic diseases, especially malaria, smallpox, and the many forms of dysentery, seemed to take a particularly virulent form in the warm, humid, semitropical climate of New Orleans. Smallpox may actually have killed more people in Louisiana between 1865 and 1900 than yellow fever, but it never aroused the same degree of apprehension and alarm that the mosquito-borne disease produced.[6] Compared with yellow fever, which struck indiscriminately, smallpox was less of a threat to the middle- and upper-class citizens of New Orleans, who endeavored to protect themselves by vaccination or—as they did during yellow fever epidemics— by leaving the city. Smallpox was preponderantly a disease of the unvaccinated freedmen, of ex-slaves and immigrant groups and of other poor and disadvantaged groups. Hence, unlike the response to yellow fever, there was never any real sense of urgency about smallpox on the part of the press, among civic leaders, or among other socially prominent groups who determined community reactions to the threat from epidemic diseases. Occasionally the medical journals cited the need for a more extensive system of vaccination, and the press would carry articles about smallpox expressing worry about conditions in the smallpox hospitals more often than about preventing the disease.[7]

Unlike endemic disease, the great epidemics created acute alarm and compelled people to ponder their causes and effects. The power of the nineteenth century epidemics lay in the impetus they aroused for public health and social reform. But the social impetus that epidemics may produce is not due to their extent or even their severity. Epidemics, even calamitous ones, do not automatically raise the public consciousness. Like other phenomena, epidemics achieve the status of a recognized social problem only when their anticipated consequences or damaging effects become part of a political or ideological process. Only then is an epidemic socially defined as a public issue commanding community action.

The political history of yellow fever in New Orleans during the nineteenth century is an excellent example of how a series of devastating epidemics failed to gain the attention of public authorities until its damaging effects were felt by those in control of the city's socioeconomic structure. This history is important for yet another reason. The belated acknowledgment by the leaders of New Orleans of its past failure in public health helps to explain the actions of city and state officials when a far less familiar disease—namely, leprosy—came to public awareness in the city late in the century.

Yellow fever is first known to have struck unquestionably in New Orleans in 1796, when an estimated 3.5 percent of the population died.[8] Thereafter, and throughout the nineteenth century, the disease continued to strike the city almost yearly until the epidemics ceased early in the twentieth century, the last one occurring in 1905. The worst year was 1853, when 8,101 persons died of the disease, probably constituting the worst single epidemic ever to strike a major U.S. city. The death rate from yellow fever during the epidemic of 1853 was 52.55 per 1,000 population. Of the 15,787 persons who died in New Orleans in that year, 51 percent died of yellow fever.[9] In ten of the years between 1833 and 1878, the annual death toll from yellow fever exceeded 1,000.[10] For the epidemic years 1817 to 1854, yellow fever alone accounted for 25 percent of all deaths.

At midcentury New Orleans was the fourth largest city in the nation, ranking only behind the large northeastern cities of New York, Philadelphia, and Baltimore.[11] Compared with other southern cities, it was by far the largest. Charleston, South Carolina, was a poor second, having nearly 100,000 fewer persons than New Orleans.[12] The yellow fever epidemic of 1853, with its incredibly high mortality of 51 percent, drew increasing public attention not only to the disease but also, and more important, to the high overall mortality rate that had existed in New Orleans year in and year out. In 1854 Barton[13] calculated the average mortality rate in New Orleans from all causes, 1787 to 1853, to have been 59.63 per 1,000 population. For the six-year period from 1847 to 1852, the average mortality rate reached a high of 67.45 per 1,000.[14]

Compared with those of other cities and countries, New Orleans's cemeteries were distinctive for far more than their architecture. Throughout the same period, the average annual mortality rate for the entire United States was 22.47 per 1,000 population and, by comparison, England, France, Prussia, Austria, and Russia were health resorts. For the years 1838 to 1842 the average annual mortality rate for England, France, and Austria was 2.2,

2.4, and 2.9 percent, respectively. For Prussia, during 1838 to 1841, the rate was 2.7 percent, and for Russia in 1842, 3.6 percent.[15]

Although the epidemic of 1853 produced the largest number of cases and the highest mortality from yellow fever that ever affected the city, the case-fatality ratio was, according to Barton,[16] one of the lowest ever to occur in a great yellow fever epidemic. The ratio of 1 in 3.58 was lower than the ratio of 1 in 2.12 for the various yellow fever epidemics in Philadelphia between 1793 and 1819, 1 in 2 in New York, and 1 in 2.87 in Baltimore.

Some writers and historians, including Barton,[17] have suggested that this favorable ratio of fatalities to cases in New Orleans during the 1853 epidemic was due in large part to active work in providing nursing care to victims of yellow fever. Given the lack of medical knowledge about yellow fever at the time and the extraordinary diversity of treatments recommended, attentive nursing was probably the most effective of all nineteenth-century therapeutic aids. In this area, and this alone, New Orleans could claim some credit. Long before the Red Cross became a symbol of help and before Florence Nightingale showed the world what good nursing care could accomplish, a group of young clerks had organized in New Orleans in the early 1830s to care for victims of yellow fever. The group was later named the Howard Association in honor of the English philanthropist John Howard, who devoted his life to hospital research, quarantine, and prison reform. In the absence of city services and state agencies, other voluntary groups, such as the Society of the Good Samaritans, also sprang up at this time. Composed of middle-aged men from some of the older families in the city, the Samaritans limited their activities to friends and neighbors, whereas the Howard Association sought to provide aid to all residents of the city, especially to the poor and the immigrants. The activities of the Howard Association were thorough. It circulated lists of pharmacies where patients might obtain free medicine, paid for a panel of physicians, established temporary infirmaries and orphan asylums, and distributed emergency funds and food to the needy. Association members were assigned areas of the city where, aided by their wives, auxiliary members, and hired nurses, they visited the indigent sick. At each fever-ridden house they provided medicine, acquainted the family with methods of treatment, arranged for drugs and a doctor's care, occasionally left a nurse at the home, and, in severe cases, arranged for the sick to be removed to a hospital or public infirmary. In many cases they even took care of funeral arrangements.[18] During the 1853 epidemic, it is estimated that the Howard Association took care of more than 11,000 cases of yellow fever among the poor alone.[19]

Yellow fever was not confined to New Orleans, and in the 1870s the Howard Association expanded its activities to include other stricken towns and cities in Louisiana, Mississippi, and Alabama, as well as the city of Memphis, Tennessee, where a branch of the association was founded during the epidemic of 1878.[20] New Orleans was the contact city, so to speak; after invading the port city the disease would continue up the Mississippi River and along other waterways into the interior. This was the general epidemic pattern, and in 1878 the disease hit as far north as St. Louis. In that same year Memphis was also particularly hard hit, with 3,500 persons dying.[21]

In contrast to elected officials of the New Orleans government, and other groups that influenced public opinion and exercised municipal power, such as the press, the medical societies, and business corporations—all of whom showed their eagerness to suppress news of an epidemic—the Howard Association was alert to the first signs of disaster and immediately mobilized the community. Funds to support its work came generously from private donors from within the city and throughout the United States but less amply from the city government, which, in New Orleans, repeatedly censured the association for advertising the epidemic to the world. During the epidemic of 1853, the Howard Association received donations in excess of $225,000, of which only $10,000 was appropriated by the New Orleans City Council, which then immediately adjourned so that its members and their families could flee the diseased city.[22]

The activities of the Howard Association in the epidemic of 1853 were a high point in the association's work in aiding victims of yellow fever and a turning point in the role of voluntary agencies in coping with major and recurring health disasters. Thereafter, municipal and state actions increased greatly in scope and responsibility. After battling yellow fever for forty-five years, the Howard Association quietly disbanded after the epidemic of 1878.

The sheer magnitude of the 1853 epidemic—29,020 cases of yellow fever and 8,101 deaths out of a total population of 150,000—in the wake of the epidemic of the late 1840s that claimed nearly 4,000 deaths, spurred demand for a description of the city's health status. It was among the new arrivals and the city's poor that disease exacted its greatest toll. Travel weary and uprooted to a climate much different from what they had known, many immigrants in the early decades of the nineteenth century arrived in sickly condition and highly susceptible to the diseases prevalent in the semitropical port city of New Orleans. The overall mortality rate from 1830 to 1839, the decade of the second major population increase, was the highest ever recorded in the history of the city—63.5 per 1,000 population. For the year 1832 alone, it reached the incredible height of 147.02 per 1,000 population. Deaths from yellow fever were recorded in each year of the decade.[23]

In September 1853, the New Orleans Board of Health established a five-man sanitary commission to investigate all aspects of the devastating diseases that periodically swept through the city of New Orleans. The commission consisted of A. Foster Axson, Edward H. Barton, J. C. Simonds, John L. Riddell, and S. D. McNeil. All five men were outstanding physicians: Axson was also a crusading editor; Riddell was a professor of chemistry; McNeil was a well-known practitioner; and Barton and Simonds were emerging as leading figures in the Louisiana public health movement. The movement endeavored to awaken New Orleans to its incredibly high death rates and deplorable sanitary conditions—conditions that outsiders knew about and condemned. The preponderant local view, Barton[24] noted, was that "the city was one of the healthiest in the Union, although subject to occasional epidemics." This view was shared by most physicians, including Simonds, who, in a candid note published in 1851, told how he came to be dissuaded:

Two years ago, I attended a meeting of the American Medical Association, which was held in Boston. I there found that the subject of sanitary reform was exciting considerable attention, and that this was based, as it always must be, upon statistical investigations into the actual and comparative number of the births, marriages and deaths, in different localities. In my intercourse with various persons there and elsewhere, I found that New Orleans enjoyed a very undesirable reputation of being one of the most unhealthy localities in the United States. I knew that here we thought our city very healthy. My colleague on that occasion, who had long been a resident of this city, did not hesitate to avow his opinion of its general salubrity. In reply to an attempt to prove its unhealthiness by a reference to the very violent epidemic of 1847, he said that *only* about 3,000 died of yellow fever during that year; and I heard the remark afterwards quoted as a most astounding difference of opinion regarding the value of human life. I then proposed to myself to undertake the investigation of this question, with the determination to set it, if possible, finally at rest, and with the hope of being able to convince the world, by an array of unquestionable statistical details and impregnable arguments, that it had done injustice to New Orleans, and that our city was not the Golgotha which it was every where represented to be. The subject had not been pursued long, when I found that we were laboring under a delusion, and that we had long deceived ourselves regarding the salubrity of our city.[25]

The sanitary commission established by the Board of Health in September 1853 to investigate the yellow fever epidemic was "the only body then acting," Barton noted,[26] "that had the power—the City Council having adjourned for the summer." The commission published its report the following year. The report blamed yellow fever largely on the unsanitary conditions then prevailing in New Orleans and strongly advocated a comprehensive sanitary program, including improved sewerage and water systems, control of food supplies, and the strict regulation of buildings and houses. In 1849 Barton had for the first time shown that the city was the antithesis of a health resort;[27] his work, along with that of Lemuel Shattuck of Boston, materially assisted in the federal census of 1850—the first attempt to obtain the mortality statistics during one year in all of the states of the union.[28] Barton was chairman of the sanitary commission and wrote most of the 542 pages of its report.

In the report of 1854, Barton's condemnation of New Orleans's state of health was vitriolic. "New Orleans," he wrote,

is one of the dirtiest, and with other conjoint causes, is consequently the sickliest city in the Union, and scarcely anything has been done to remedy it. . . . No city can bear many inflictions of such a calamity as that of last year without serious deterioration. Concealment and boasting will not help us much. Public confidence is plainly on the wane; the disparaging truth that almost every official as well as unofficial means have been used to conceal, deny, explain away, has been resorted to, and now it stands forth in all its unabashed effrontery, in the very face of well attested and repeated proofs afforded by our Board of Health and our Medical Faculty, that the evil exists. . . .

The wealth of a city depends mainly upon the number of its inhabitants— labor is wealth—population and labor are its most productive elements;—a system of measures that is irrespective of the *poor*,—of the immigrant,—of that class that has raised this city from the *swamp and made it what it is:*—that has cleared the land and drained it,—made the streets—constructed the dwellings, and done so much to develop its destiny, is void of justice to the laborers who are worthy of their hire, and is a reflection upon the proprietors who profit by it. The value of real estate rises with competition when there is no overplus in market—the quantity of merchandise sold, depends upon the number of consumers and purchasers. If there is increased risk and jeopardy of life, an enhanced price is put upon every article sold. High food, (when we ought to have the cheapest market in America)—clothing—merchandise of every description,—high rents,—low real estate,—high wages for mechanical labor of all kinds—high price for professional talent;—these are the real reasons, as I am informed by intelligent merchants at *home and abroad*, why we have the dearest market in the United States; for comparatively few will risk their lives or trust their capital, *without additional compensation*, for the additional risk run![29]

It was the poor that Barton felt most strongly about, for they "are the greatest sufferers always, and especially in insalubrious places, and during epidemics. . . . [They] are the *hands*, the *machinery*, that make the wealth of a community, and give it its power; and hence, are the rightful claimants of its fostering care."[30]

Barton did more than assert a relationship between social position and health status. Combining a variety of sources, he assembled data estimating the mortality risk from yellow fever among the population of New Orleans and calculated what he called the "Life Cost of Acclimation; or Liabilities to Yellow Fever From Nativity, as Exhibited by the Epidemic of 1853, in New Orleans."[31] According to Barton's data (Table 2.1), only 35 percent of the population of New Orleans in 1853 consisted of persons born either in the city or elsewhere within the state of Louisiana. Over half of the population of the city were foreign-born. The Irish and German-Prussians constituted the largest groups, with 20 and 14 percent, respectively. The bulk of the European-born population also comprised relative newcomers to the city and to the climate, many having arrived only within the preceding decade or two.

A clinical characteristic of yellow fever is that nonfatal cases confer life-long immunity. Relapses do not occur, there are no sequelae, and complications are rare.[32] Barton's data show a distinct relationship between the nativity status of the population and mortality. The mortality rate among those born within the state was exceptionally low compared with the rate among other residents of the city—only 3.5 per 1,000, and, as Barton[33] noted, these deaths "have almost entirely been confined to those under ten," among children growing up during the comparatively mild yellow fever years between 1848 and 1853.

The immigrants from Europe suffered the most from yellow fever, both in terms of mortality and in absolute numbers affected. For Barton's eight European groups, the average mortality during the epidemic of 1853 was 138 per 1,000 population, with a high of 329 per 1,000 for those born in Holland and Belgium. In terms of absolute numbers, the Irish and the German-Prussians were the heaviest losers—3,569 Irish men, women, and children died, and 2,339 Germans.

The black population in New Orleans was the most acclimated. According to the federal census, 35,076 blacks lived in New Orleans in 1850. Of that population, 24,264 were classified as slaves and 10,812 as freedmen and women of color.[34] Although the mortality among blacks in New Orleans from yellow fever in 1853 was only 0.56 per 1,000,[35] Barton[36] nevertheless considered this to be a remarkably high rate.

Writing about a quarter of a century before Max von Pettenkofer delivered his two famous lectures on the value of health to a city (Munich), Simonds[37] calculated that, for the period from January 1846 to May 1850, the economic cost of disease and premature death to the city of New Orleans was $45,437,700, or "an average annual loss of $10,485,623 to the city, and of nearly $105 to every individual in it."[38] With the annual cost of preventable disease calculated to be $3,530,000 and an estimated loss of interest for the fifty-two-month period of $17,003,250, Simonds's argument was designed to draw attention to the relationship between sanitary conditions and economic prosperity. "Is it, then, surprising," he asked, "that New Orleans has not progressed more rapidly? What other city has had to encounter such losses, and what other city could stand them? New York, when her population was what ours is now, could not have stood it, if indeed, even now, she could. Is it wonderful that we are heavily taxed, when so large a portion of our wealth has been lost in the sick chamber, and swallowed up by the grave?"[39,40]

Immunity through previous exposure was not the only means useful to the native-born residents of the city for reducing the risk of yellow fever. The wealthy and affluent could afford the needed rest and the comfort of good nursing care, and many others simply fled the city. Yellow fever divided New Orleans into two seasons. May through November was the "unhealthy season," rainy and humid, when the air was full of myriad insects, mosquitoes, and miasma. The rest of the year was the so-called "healthy season," when temperatures cooled and spirits rose. For the middle and upper classes this was the social season, a time for lavish entertaining made possible by an abundant supply of household servants who lent an air of graciousness to the way that life was lived and enjoyed by the wealthy and landed families of the city.

Epidemic year or not, the oppressive summer heat of the city and the inexorable variety of its insect life added another dimension to the social lives of those who could afford it—a general exodus from the city at the beginning of summer to the resort areas of the North and along the Gulf Coast. Here they could escape the sultry humidity of the city, enjoy in

TABLE 2.1

Cost of Acclimation: Showing the Life Cost of Acclimation; or Liabilities to Yellow Fever from Nativity, as Exhibited by the Epidemic of 1853, in New Orleans

Nativities: State and Country	Pop. of New Orleans, 1850 (U.S. Census)	Est. Pop. of New Orleans 1853	Est. Mortality from Y.F., 1853	Mortality ratio per 1,000 Pop.	Percent Nativity/ Total Pop., N.O., 1853
1 New Orleans	} 38,337	} 46.004	140	} 3.58	} 34.92
2 State of Louisiana			25		
3 Southern States: Arkansas, Mississippi, Alabama, Georgia, South Carolina	2,655	3,176	42	13.22	2.41
4 Northern Slave States: North Carolina, Virginia, Maryland, Tennessee, Kentucky	4,160	4,984	153	30.69	3.78
5 Northern States: New York, Vermont, Massachusetts, Maine, Rhode Island, Connecticut, New Jersey, Pennsylvania, Delaware	8,898	10,751	353	32.83	8.16

6	N. Western States: Ohio, Indiana, Illinois, Missouri	1,693	2,030	92	44.23 (45.32)	1.54
7	British America (Canada)	318	381	20	50.24 (52.49)	0.29
8	West Indies, S. America, Mexico	1,693	1,790	11	6.14	1.36
9	Great Britain	3,832	4,598	240	52.19	3.49
10	Ireland	22,093	26,611	3,569	204.97 (134.11)	20.20
11	Northern Europe: Denmark, Sweden, Russia	491	588	96	163.26	0.45
12	Middle Europe: Prussia, Germany	14,765	17,718	2,339	132.01	13.45
13	Lowlands, W. Europe: Holland, Belgium	127	152	50	328.94	0.12
14	Mountainous Europe: Austria, Switzerland	663	797	176	220.08 (220.82)	0.60
15	France	8,306	9,967	480	48.13 (48.15)	7.56
16	Southern Europe: Spain, Italy	1,848	2,217	61	22.06 (27.52)	1.68
	TOTALS: Barton / Gussow	109,679 (109,879)	131,764	7,011 (7,847)	111.91 (86.08)	100.01

Source: Barton, Edward H. Report of the Sanitary Commission of New Orleans on the Epidemic Yellow Fever of 1853. Published by Authority of the City Council of New Orleans. (New Orleans: Office of the Daily Picayune, 1854): Table H, p. 248. Note: Figures in parentheses are my corrections of Barton's arithmetic; the final column has been added.

comfort the cooler salt air breezes of the Gulf of Mexico, and, as a bonus, afford themselves some added protection against the summer epidemics. Dowler[41] estimated that as many as 30,000 persons may have left the city during the summer of 1853. Barton[42] placed the figure precisely at 36,283, whereas Duffy[43] claimed that by time the epidemic had struck in full force the exodus may have reached as high as 75,000. The exodus for the summer of 1853 may have been higher than usual owing to the magnitude of the epidemic that year, but each summer large numbers of residents left the city for more salubrious climates, even as they still do to this day.

In leaving New Orleans during the "unhealthy season," whether as vacationer or refugee, many residents, nonetheless, were already infected and helped spread the disease beyond the boundaries of the city. With the city's failure to contain the spread of yellow fever, the apprehension was publicly raised in the newspapers as early as November 1853 that New Orleans might eventually find itself quarantined from the rest of the nation.[44] This prediction was to be realized a quarter of a century later, after the last major yellow fever epidemic in 1878.[45] In summing up his detailed study of the yellow fever epidemic of 1853, historian John Duffy wrote:

It is impossible to read the New Orleans newspapers and journals in the late fall of 1853 and not be astounded at the way in which the tragedy of the preceding summer was seemingly disregarded. . . . The loss of a tenth of its population scarcely seems to have affected the growth and prosperity of New Orleans. Within a few months the influx of newcomers had more than compensated for any losses, and the city continued to participate in the booming prosperity of the 1850's. . . . New Orleans, in December of 1853, was a thriving, bustling city with what seemed a short past and a great and glorious future. The yellow fever epidemic was over, the people were healthy, and the future would take care of itself.[46]

Many "insalubrities" existed in New Orleans in the 1850s. As Barton[47] listed them, they were "Bad air; Privies, Cemeteries, various manufactories, stables, slaughter houses, etc.; Bad water—stagnant water; Bad habits; Bad milk." These conditions, however, did not improve, nor were they effectively remedied in the decades to follow. Neither did yellow fever abate. It struck again with ferocity in 1854, 1855, 1858, 1867, and 1878, accounting for a total of 17,093 deaths in those five years alone.[48]

The epidemic of 1878 started in New Orleans and reached as far north as Gallipolis, Ohio. It affected some 120,000 persons throughout the Mississippi Valley and claimed between 13,000 and 20,000 lives. Economic loss to the Mississippi Valley was estimated by the Congressional Yellow Fever Commission to be about $30 million, but according to Ellis,[49] President Rutherford B. Hayes in his annual message on December 2, 1878, noted a "loss to the country . . . to be reckoned by the hundred millions of dollars." Estimates of the losses for the city of New Orleans ranged from $12 million to $100 million.

No case of yellow fever was officially reported for that year in the city of New Orleans until July 12, 1878, when Dr. Samuel M. Bemiss notified the Board of Health that he had attended a young child on Constance Street the previous day—although the first victim had already died on May 25. The health authorities did not announce the existence of an epidemic even as late as August, when thousands of citizens were already fleeing the city, about 40,000 of a population of 211,000.[50] New Orleans in 1878 reacted with uncustomary alarm. "In the many epidemics that New Orleans witnessed since 1796," Dr. John Dell Orto observed a year later, "there [was] not a single instance of such a panic" comparable to the public response in 1878. The panic in New Orleans was due largely to the fact that severe cases of the disease were appearing in the wealthier areas of the city. In July "rumors were going around . . . of some cases of yellow fever in the upper district, but the houses had been so well disinfected" that people were convinced "there could not be any danger of any epidemic . . . [and] when the President of the board of health announced that . . . he could control its spreading by the irrigation of the street with carbolic acid . . . [the] population had such confidence in the statement, that there was no uneasiness at the end of July." Many people believed that "children born in the city could not have yellow fever. . . . But when they saw their infants, their boys and young girls dying with symptoms similar to those of foreigners . . . they were seized by such a panic, as to cause an exodus unheard of in the history of the epidemics in New Orleans."[51] The New Orleans Board of Health published a complete list of everyone who had died of yellow fever in that year, including names, ages, nativity, location of residences, and dates of death. A total of 3,937 deaths was recorded, of which 1,642 (41.7 percent) were of persons born either in New Orleans or in the rest of Louisiana. Of that number 82.8 percent were among children ten years of age and younger.[52]

The epidemic of 1878 had a devastating effect on the entire urban South. In addition to the deaths and damage it caused in New Orleans, the disaster severely disrupted the Gulf Coast seaports, interior river towns, and smaller communities throughout the Mississippi Valley; it extended east as far as Atlanta, Georgia. The epidemic was virulent enough in the larger cities that "panic" in New Orleans and "madness" and "stampeding" in Memphis were new public reactions replacing the relative indifference that had characterized the response of the older social order to the epidemics of the past. Nearly 20,000 persons died of yellow fever in 1878, and the economic cost ran into hundreds of millions of dollars.

The catastrophe was so extensive in life and property that serious questions were raised about the adaptability of the older southern cities as viable centers of business growth. Southern commerce and industry had been badly shaken by the Civil War and its aftermath. Even before that, national trends in population movement, transport, and commerce had brought people and wealth to other parts of the country. New Orleans, which once ranked first in the nation in the value of its exports, had fallen to second by the outbreak of the war. From a population standing of third in the United States in 1840, New Orleans dropped to sixth place in 1860 and to tenth in 1880.

The acute disruption of trade and the huge business losses caused by the 1878 epidemic exacerbated the negative effects of the period of Reconstruction, which lasted in Louisiana from the end of the Civil War until 1877, when federal troops were withdrawn. Reconstruction had ushered in a pattern of lasting political corruption and had run up a staggering debt that affected the entire state. Debt and corruption hampered whatever will and ability the people of New Orleans had to deal with its many public problems.

In the 1880s, New Orleans entered a new and troubled political era. "Machine" politics, now in the hands of bosses of working-class origin, represented immigrant groups interested in patronage and not in taxation. These groups were at considerable odds with other segments within the community that argued for budgetary responsibility. Post-Reconstruction events and ideology gave the politics of New Orleans a turbulent character. Many voters, however, remained apathetic, and before the century was over, black citizens, who during Reconstruction had been politically active, were disenfranchised. Louisiana was also divided internally. Urban New Orleans and the rural interests that dominated the rest of the state were at odds, and in 1880 the state capital was moved upriver from New Orleans to Baton Rouge.[53]

Following the disaster of 1878, maritime quarantine became an important priority. The disasters of 1853 and 1854 had prompted the establishment of the first State Board of Health in 1855. But the board's efforts to administer an effective system of maritime quarantine and to enforce the inspection and fumigation of vessels arriving at New Orleans from yellow fever ports proved inadequate owing to the opposition of powerful commercial interests in the city and to laxity on the part of the state legislature. Physicians in New Orleans at the time were divided on the efficacy of maritime quarantine. Businessmen, especially those with railroad and shipping interests, considered such restrictions as unwarranted government interference in the rights of free enterprise. In 1876 the state legislature had passed an act allowing the board of health to permit any ship arriving from a tropical port to avoid quarantine if no disease could be shown to be on board and to submit only to fumigation with carbolic acid. Many later considered this lenient act to be responsible for the epidemic of 1878.[54]

Until 1878 the question of yellow fever in New Orleans had been addressed mainly by state and municipal voices, abetted by loud protests and threats of "shot-gun" quarantine from the leaders of neighboring cities along the Gulf Coast and up the Mississippi Valley, who demanded to be protected. The epidemic of 1878 raised the issue of maritime quarantine to the federal level, and in 1879 the U.S. Congress established a National Board of Health. The board's purpose was to aid state and municipal authorities in administering and enforcing local quarantine regulations. The National Board of Health added further fuel to the local quarantine controversy in Louisiana;

to many in the South the board represented federal interference in states' rights and reminded those in Louisiana that Union generals had occupied the state during the Civil War and that federal intervention had made life difficult for the South in the days of Reconstruction. Many commercial firms thought that the twenty-day quarantine on ships proposed by the board was an excessive regulation.

Maritime quarantine was too important an issue, however, not to be taken seriously. Locally it was linked to sanitary reform and New Orleans business prosperity. Outside the city it meant restoring confidence to the entire Mississippi Valley, for the failure of the Louisiana State Board of Health to provide protection was deeply resented by upriver states. Although the need for maritime quarantine went undisputed, the means by which a system of quarantine would be enforced and administered were intensely debated. The commercial cost of quarantine was the most divisive issue. Effective quarantine was desired only if it did not greatly obstruct the commerce of the city and did not prove to be too expensive in fees and taxes and in terms of goods not moving. The Louisiana State Board of Health was caught in the middle of the controversy, and in 1880 the board had to be reorganized.[55]

The reorganization proved effective. Although the board remained a state agency, control was now vested mainly in the hands of members from New Orleans and it was almost exclusively concerned with protecting the port. By stiffening quarantine regulations, perfecting methods of disinfection, and resisting the pressures of influential commercial groups who wanted quarantine regulations to be relaxed, the board averted a potential epidemic in 1880 and the city suffered only mild outbreaks of yellow fever in 1897 and 1898. A final epidemic in 1905—when the role of the *Stegomyia* mosquito in transmitting yellow fever was already known—might have been avoided if city ordinances attacking the breeding grounds of mosquitoes had been allowed to pass.[56]

New Orleans achieved a fair degree of success in dealing with maritime quarantine owing to the importance of the issue and to the combined efforts of municipal, state, and national resources. In dealing with its own sanitary problems, however, New Orleans was on its own, and here the city was far from successful. New Orleans continued to be plagued by unsanitary conditions, endemic disease, and high mortality, and it lacked adequate provision for taking care of the indigent sick and infirm. The social and governmental structures of the city were not equal to the task of adjusting to new national standards and trends. The number of local business failures was high; new municipal debts had been incurred; and taxation for public works was an unpopular idea.

After the epidemic of 1878, some segments of the community were able to find common cause, to set aside their intense southern sectionalism, and to distance themselves from cultural ties to the antebellum South. A new form of voluntarism emerged, this time not to assist victims of yellow fever, as the Howard Association had done earlier, but to enlist support for those public works that the city lacked. In 1879, the New Orleans Auxiliary Sanitary Association was formed, composed of 200 members representing diverse business interests and including a number of physicians, lawyers, and clergymen. The activities of this group of civic and business leaders, along with those of similar groups being formed in other southern cities, marked a turning point in the social and commercial history of the South. Henceforth, businessmen and members of the medical profession increasingly sought access to the political process.

Initially, the New Orleans Auxiliary Sanitary Association addressed a broad range of sanitary deficiencies affecting the overall health of the city, but with time the association limited its activities to fit business and commercial needs. Their maxim that "Public Health Is Public Wealth" reflected a circumscribed approach to the inadequacies of municipal services.[57]

An adequate and safe water supply had high priority in the city. The initial demand was for adequate water for flushing purposes and for fire protection. Later, clear, not muddy and polluted, water was sought by manufacturing firms. Water was pumped from the Mississippi River, near where the "nuisance" boats discharged their waste. The water company, privately owned, refused to undertake the expense of filtration. Frustrated by the intransigence of the water company and by increasing rates, many businessmen began to experiment with digging artesian wells on their property.

The majority of the citizens of New Orleans, however, relied on simple wells and cisterns for their daily water supply. In 1879, Dr. Thomas Layton observed that the contents of cisterns were "often so unclean as not to require microscopical examination for the detection of living organisms."[58] That opinion was shared a year later by Dr. Charles Smart, a U.S. Army water expert attached to the National Board of Health, who advised the New Orleans Auxiliary Sanitary Association that the wells he had examined had about the same proportion of raw sewage content as the city's drainage canals.[59]

In 1884, when the Cotton Centennial Exposition was held amidst expensively prepared gardens and new buildings especially erected for the purpose, New Orleans had no sewerage system and no municipal means for collecting garbage. The semitropical rainfall of the city made street flooding a hazard of daily life, especially in those sections of town without drainage facilities. Even during relatively dry months the deep gutters and drainage canals that primarily existed only in the wealthier neighborhoods "reeked with slimy, stagnant water" strewn with garbage. Muddy, unpaved streets, broken bridges across gutters and drainage ditches, uncollected refuse, stray livestock, filthy dairies, diseased cattle, and adulterated food and drugs complete a view of the city's landscape.[60]

Historians refer to the period in New Orleans between 1880 and 1896 as its "gilded age." Visitors like Mark Twain wrote about the glamour of the city and praised its progressive and sagacious leadership, its fashionable men's clubs, and its newly renovated pleasure resorts.[61] The period of Reconstruction was over, federal troops had been withdrawn from the state, and the epidemic of 1878 was a thing of the past. New Orleans had returned to its former pattern of arrogance and indifference. The voluntary business movement for public health reform had produced few city-wide results. Benefits accrued principally to the business sector and to the residential neighborhoods of the middle and upper classes.[62] The incidence of endemic diseases such as dysentery, malarial disease, pneumonia, and tuberculosis remained high, and in 1883, 1,226 deaths from smallpox were recorded. Conditions at the city isolation hospital were periodically investigated and periodically found wanting. The reduction in overall mortality between 1880 and 1900 was due in large measure to the absence of severe epidemics. The link between poverty and ill health remained unbroken and, in the case of black minorities, was strengthened by racial prejudice. The public institutions of the city saw little improvement. Money for the city's almshouses erratically came from fees on gambling, which were frequently diverted to other purposes. Public education received scant attention. A shortage of city funds, and more important, the lack of belief in the value of public education, contributed to a high rate of illiteracy. Public school teachers were often paid in city certificates rather than in cash.[63]

During its gilded age, the citizens of New Orleans did not know how to go forward. It was during this troubled period in its history, at a time when New Orleans was struggling for a sense of purpose and direction, that the existence of leprosy in the city came to the public's attention. The mode in which leprosy was perceived, and then managed, reflected the provincialism that characterized the public health history of the city and of the state.

3

Endemicity in the United States: Leprosy in Louisiana

The Spaniards who ruled over the Colony of Louisiana in the late eighteenth century had a long career of trafficking in African slaves. The slave trade attuned Spanish physicians and surgeons serving in the Spanish West Indies to what Captain Bernard Romans called "the chronic disease amongst the blacks . . . the leprosy, so-called." The disease was also known to the Spaniards of the time as "body yaws," "elephantiasis," and the "lame distemper."[1] Included were a wide assortment of visible and deforming neurological and dermatological conditions, among them afflictions variously recorded as the Barbadoes leg, scrotal tumor, syphilis vel lues aethiopica, sympathic hypertrophy or varix of the lymphatics, syphilis africana, pian, lepra tuberculosa, epian, and elephantiasis arabium. All of these conditions were seemingly bound together by a common unpleasantness of physical appearance.[2]

Spaniards objected strongly to these "chronic diseases" of blacks and former West Indian slaves, and these objections led Antonio de Ulloa, the first Spanish governor of Louisiana, to attempt in 1776 to banish diseased persons to an area distant from the center of the colony. This measure, Gayarré later wrote, "created great discontent."[3] The discontent came from the Creoles, the early French colonists, who were unhappy with the transfer of Louisiana from French to Spanish rule and who charged Ulloa with, among other things, "removing leprous children from the town to the inhospitable settlement at the mouth of the river."[4] The project was abandoned three years later, aided by a hurricane that devastated the region.

In 1785, when Don Estevan Miro became governor, the issue was again raised and a recommendation was made to the Cabildo, or City Council, that "a hospital . . . be erected for the reception of these unfortunate beings in the rear of the city."[5] According to the minutes of the Cabildo, Don Andres Almonester y Rojas announced that he had built a hospital for lepers. He informed the members of the Cabildo, in April 1785, that the hospital was built "so that the lepers may be kept together, of whom there are large numbers."[6] Known by the French name "La terre des Lepreux," or Leper's Land, the hospital was located in the rear of the city of New Orleans.

In 1799, Almonester's leper hospital was briefly described in the minutes of the Cabildo. The hospital at the time housed five lepers, "one white man, one Negro, one mulatto, and two Negresses."[7] Paul Alliot, a Frenchman, corroborated the existence of La terre des Lepreux when visiting New Orleans in 1802.[8]

Records of the City Council show that the hospital was still there in 1804.[9] The records also show that between 1800 and 1804 the City Council received a number of complaints concerning La terre des Lepreux. The first and repeated charge was that conditions at the hospital were deplorable. In 1800, Dr. Luis Giovellina addressed a letter to the Cabildo complaining about the lack of medical attention available to the inmates of the hospital.[10]

In the spring of 1804 a new and far more serious charge was leveled— that none of the patients at the hospital had leprosy. A committee of four physicians appointed to examine the patients reported to the Council that the five inmates did not have leprosy, though what they might have had was not mentioned. The inmates were subsequently discharged. In 1806, with no more lepers occupying the facility and with local Indians now demolishing the structure, the hospital was ordered to be surveyed with the intent of putting the property up for rent. A month later the City Council named the same four physicians to examine all suspected cases of leprosy in the city. But no further evidence was found, and public attention to leprosy vanished.[11]

It vanished, that is, until the 1870s. In 1872 Dr. W. G. Kibbe of Abbeville, Vermillion Parish, sent Felicien Ourblanc to New Orleans to be examined by Dr. Joseph Jones. On examining the patient, Jones concluded that "the case was one of leprosy," a diagnosis that does not seem to have been very disturbing to Jones, as he admitted to having "lost sight of the case" for the next five years. Then, on October 12, 1877, Jones received a letter from Kibbe in which Kibbe mentioned Felicien Ourblanc's visit five years earlier, informed Jones of several similar cases he and other physicians had seen, and formally requested Jones to give "us all the facts in your possession upon the history of this disease and related diseases in the Southern States."[12]

The selection of Jones as the physician to whom to address these inquiries was probably not fortuitous. Professor Jones was a formidable figure in Louisiana medicine. A prolific writer on scientific and medical subjects, Jones was foremost a crusader in matters of preventive medicine and public health. It was Jones who later, in 1880, was chosen to be president of the new State Board of Health when it was reorganized after the disastrous yellow fever epidemic of 1878.

Jones had had a long career in public health epidemiology. As a surgeon in the Confederate cavalry, he had earlier investigated health conditions among soldiers, prisoners of war, and civilians. He had conducted massive studies on hospital gangrene in the Confederate Army and diseases among Union prisoners at Camp Sumpter.[13] Though faced with the formidable task of running the State Board of Health, there was no let up in Jones's scientific output.

Between 1872, when Felicien Ourblanc was first sent to Jones, and 1877, when Kibbe wrote to Jones "for the facts upon the history of this disease," Kibbe had learned of seven cases of leprosy, in addition to several questionable ones, in and around Abbeville. Kibbe sent Jones a lengthy description of these cases along with his letter. The correspondence between Kibbe and Jones shows that although the physical signs of leprosy were recognized by some physicians in Louisiana at the time, little, if anything, was known about the disease itself.

When he became interested in a subject, Jones apparently lost little time in researching it. At a meeting of the New Orleans Medical and Surgical Association held on October 27, 1877, he delivered a paper on a case of yaws, with accompanying observations "upon the history of this disease in the West Indies and Southern States, together with certain facts establishing the existence of Leprosy in Louisiana, during the French and Spanish domination, and at the present time."[14]

That paper, which Jones presented only fifteen days after the dating of Kibbe's request for information, is an important one. It provides us with a clear exposition of the nosological confusion that existed at the time and of how these diseases were viewed by medical scholars in Louisiana. The paper is rich in historical detail, complete with a description from Gayarré on the Spanish leper hospital at La terre des Lepreux. Jones traced leprosy from Africa and the south of Europe to the West Indies and then to the southern states. In describing yaws, syphilis, and leprosy, and in furnishing a history and a source of entry into Louisiana, the southern states, and the New World, Jones made it clear that the diseases under discussion were characteristic of Africans and their descendants. Although whites, he noted, were not altogether exempt, the diseases were primarily peculiar to slaves and Negroes.

In placing this history into the medical record, Jones revealed for his audience that leprosy had had an earlier existence in Louisiana. His inquiry also established an important epidemiological fact: that cognizance about leprosy in Louisiana in the late 1870s extended no further than Kibbe's cases in Abbeville and the four cases that Jones now said had come under his observation during the preceding years.[15]

Jones's paper, published the following year in the *New Orleans Medical and Surgical Journal*, is important for another reason. The *NOM&SJ*, published since 1844, was a major source of information on developments in medicine and medical practice in the South. Jones's paper was only the second article about leprosy to appear in that journal, and the first one to discuss leprosy in relation to Louisiana. A general historical account of the disease, written by a former assistant surgeon in the U.S. Navy and based on a four-month visit to the Hawaiian Islands, had appeared in 1875.[16] This first article, however, made no reference to Louisiana.

If any thought was given to leprosy in Louisiana before Jones's paper appeared, it was confined to historians writing about an earlier period. The historical assumption was that leprosy had once existed in Louisiana, that

Spanish physicians and authorities had known of the disease, and that it had disappeared early in the nineteenth century through the death or migration of the lepers. Gayarré, one of Jones's historical sources, wrote: "It is remarkable that leprosy, which is now so rare a disease, was then not an uncommon affection in Louisiana. . . . In the course of a few years, the number of these patients gradually diminished, either by death or transportation, the disease disappeared almost entirely, the hospital [Leper's Land] went into decay.[17]

Jones's presentation to the New Orleans Medical and Surgical Association was about a disease known to have existed in other places and at other times and recently observed locally, one about which little was then known, but nevertheless a condition that Jones thought important enough to pursue further and, if necessary, to regulate.

Once the subject was opened up—and pronounced to be serious—it was perhaps inevitable that additional cases would soon be reported or remembered, as in the case of Dr. Thomas Layton. In delivering the annual address on the fifth anniversary of the New Orleans Medical and Surgical Association on December 7, 1878, Layton took note of the Spanish heritage of leprosy and recalled the case of a 54-year-old woman of Spanish extraction, a longtime resident of New Orleans, whom he had personally attended in the past.

> She was suffering from a skin disease of several years standing, totally unlike anything I had ever seen. My suspicions became aroused, and I determined to study the matter carefully. . . . In the meanwhile, the surroundings of my patient, of Spanish extraction themselves, began to suggest the possibility which had already occurred to my mind. . . . Whilst I was studying the case, the lady died. . . . Since that time, having continued my readings upon the topic, I have become almost certain that I had, in the person of my patient, met with the opportunity of seeing a veritable case of leprosy.[18]

In this same address Layton noted that the discussion of leprosy "was agitated" at a recent meeting of the Louisiana State Medical Association and that a committee was appointed to frame a report concerning the existence of leprosy in the state. The committee consisted of Dr. L. F. Salomon as its sole member, who, in his report published in 1879, commented that the investigation was ordered on "the information conveyed at the last meeting of this association, that the disease existed to an alarming extent."[19] Duffy offers the note that Jones had prodded the association into undertaking the study.[20]

The information on hand concerning the existence of leprosy in Louisiana consisted at that time of seven cases from Abbeville and the four that Jones recalled; these cases had attracted no attention until Jones tackled the subject. It is difficult to know what Jones had in mind in pronouncing that the disease existed to an "alarming extent." It is possible that he considered even a few cases to be alarming. Jones had read widely and, as evident from his extended research published in 1881, was not unaware of leprosy events current in other parts of the world. Jones may have envisioned the known cases as containing the seeds of a future threat. He was an activist and a catalyst, and his main concerns were quarantine and sanitary measures. Obstructive commercial interests and a slowly moving and oftentimes indifferent medical profession were his main targets. It is plausible that Jones was genuinely serious about leprosy as he sought to mobilize government and the private sector in all matters concerning the public's health.

Salomon attempted to communicate with every physician in the state and, "with the exception of four or five parishes," he succeeded. He addressed a letter to them all asking a series of questions about leprosy. The investigation drew a total blank. Salomon received "replies from about one-fourth of the physicians so addressed," and with the exception of Drs. Young and Kibbe of Vermillion Parish, whose cases were already known, all stated "that they were not cognizant of any cases of leprosy."[21]

Salomon, in his report to the Louisiana State Medical Association, questioned the need for such an investigation: "Either there has not been sufficient interest taken in the subject by physicians throughout the State, or many cases of Leprosy have not been recognized as such; else, the information conveyed at the last meeting of this association, that the disease existed to an alarming extent, was founded on error."[22]

Abbeville, where Kibbe reported the first seven cases, is about 160 miles west-southwest of New Orleans. Implicit in the investigation was the expectation that the disease would be encountered in rural Louisiana—that is, in parishes outside the city. Although he drew a blank in rural parishes, Salomon did somewhat better within New Orleans itself, where he identified seven cases, three of whom were then on the female surgical ward at Charity Hospital. Thus, the official report on the existence of leprosy in Louisiana in 1879 consisted of "fourteen cases in all, of which eleven remain in the State."[23]

When Jones became president of the State Board of Health in 1880, his new position provided him another avenue through which to communicate his ideas. Under his presidency, the annual reports of the board were changed in format and doubled in length. Whereas previously these reports had been statistical documents submitted by district sanitary inspectors, they now contained scholarly and polemical papers on the important health issues of the day.

Despite his activities as president of the board, Jones did not forget about leprosy. In the annual report of 1880, he published a section called "Leprosy in Louisiana."[24] In it he added to the material previously published in 1878. The section contained a miscellany of information, correspondence, excerpts from various official reports, and bits and pieces from the then current medical literature. There were subsections on the history of yaws and leprosy in the West Indies, Mexico, and New Brunswick, Canada; case reports of leprosy at Charity Hospital; and, finally, a report of Jones's own field investigation of leprosy in Lafourche Parish in south Louisiana. From the range of data presented, and especially from the fact that he personally went into the field himself, it is clear that Jones was not dissuaded by the lack of results reported earlier by Salomon.

Lafourche Parish is closer to the city of New Orleans than Abbeville is. Thibodaux,* the town on the Bayou Lafourche that Jones on October 2, 1880, selected as the starting point of his inquiry, is about 40 miles southwest of New Orleans. Disentangling the sequence of events that led Jones to Lafourche Parish is difficult. The southern parishes of "French" Louisiana were settled by politically displaced Acadians from Nova Scotia, who began arriving in Louisiana in 1764. By 1790 their numbers had increased to about 4,000, and at the end of the nineteenth century an estimated 40,000 to 50,000 Acadians were living in southern Louisiana. Leprosy is recorded to have first been noticed in New Brunswick, Canada, in 1815; by 1844 it was proposed that a lazaretto be established in Tracadie.[25] By the time Jones journeyed to Lafourche Parish he had already formed a connection in his mind between the early settlers of southern Louisiana and leprosy in Nova Scotia. In his "Leprosy in Louisiana" compilation, he included a section on leprosy in New Brunswick and referred to a relationship between the inhabitants of the lower Lafourche and the disease imported from the French settlements of Canada.[26]

Jones attributed the investigation in Lafourche Parish to a request from the Police Jury (the parish civic government). The request was forwarded to the State Board of Health on February 27, 1880. Samuel Choppin was president of the board at the time, but there is no evidence that Choppin acted on the matter. Jones succeeded Choppin a few months later, and on July 13, according to Jones, he received an "earnest communication" from the president of the Police Jury of the Parish of Lafourche, "urging an immediate investigation as to the nature of the disease called leprosy, which was reported to be prevalent more especially in the lower Lafourche."[27] Jones responded on July 26 that he would personally initiate an investigation. Whether Jones's fine hand was behind this request or whether the investigation was independently requested is not clear. What is clear, however, is that Jones almost single-handedly brought the issue of leprosy to medical attention.

Jones seems to have approached Lafourche with the expectation of finding the public in a state of panic: "It having been reported that the children of lepers, and some who were suffering with this disease, were attending the public schools and mingling with healthy children, an intense feeling of anxiety and distrust had been excited in the minds of some of the citizens of Lafourche."[28] Jones spent October 2 and 3 in Lafourche Parish, talking with the president of the Police Jury and with practitioners of surgery and medicine in Thibodaux. From these men he learned that "at this time no case of leprosy existed in this neighborhood, and only two had come within the knowledge of . . . physicians since the close of Civil War in 1865."[29] During this meeting "the belief was expressed that cases of leprosy would

---

*Variant spellings were common throughout the nineteenth century. One such spelling was "Thibodeaux," used by Jones.

be found in and around Lockport, some twenty-one miles below Thibodeaux."
But Dr. J. Gazzo, Sr., who lived closer to Lockport and had practiced in
the area for nearly half a century, informed Jones "that no lepers would
be found [until Jones] had passed beyond Lockport." Gazzo also stated
"that there were at present, fewer persons afflicted with this disease in
Lafourche than formerly."[30] When Jones reached Lockport and held discussions with physicians there, he was told "that nearly all the authenticated
cases of leprosy were situated below Harang's canal [several miles farther
down the bayou]."[31]

From this two-day survey, Jones estimated that there were no more than
twelve cases of leprosy in Lafourche Parish. Major S. J. Grisamore, president
of the Police Jury, put the entire number "at about fourteen cases." It is
uncertain how many cases Jones personally saw, for much of his information
came to him in a letter from someone identified only as "F. C." Jones
described F. C. as "a citizen of great . . . intelligence . . . although not a
graduate of a regular school of medicine," but a man with "extended
experience from Thibodeaux to the Gulf." According to F. C., "scrofula or
leprosy" was confined to six families in the parish. In describing these cases
to Jones, F. C. pointed out an important distinction: "The families affected
or tainted with that malady, ought to be divided into two distinct classes:
. . . those who, through inheritance, may only be tainted with *elephantiasis*;
and . . . those who are actually affected with the malady."[32]

On returning from Lafourche, Jones turned his attention to Charity Hospital
once again. Here he located records of nine cases of leprosy: five male and
four female patients with leprosy had been admitted to the hospital since
April 1874. All nine were adult and white. Five had been born in the United
States: four in Louisiana and one in Virginia. Four had been born in Europe.
All nine were diagnosed as having "Oriental leprosy." Jones provided
extensive case material and identified the patients by name, sex, age, place
of birth, and photograph:

Numa Kern: male, age 25, Bayou Lafourche, Louisiana
Donacien Ourblanc, male, age 36, Lafayette Parish, Louisiana
Madame Rosetta Francisco, female, age 63, Richmond, Virginia
Miss Wilhelmena Boyens, female, age 22, New Orleans, Louisiana
Miss Glendena Boyens, female, age 19, New Orleans, Louisiana
Father Charles Boglioli, Catholic priest, age 66, Italy
Antonio Gaspaire, male, age 58, France
Johann Domingo, male, no age given, Germany
William Ross, male, no age given, Russia.

Three of the four foreign-born patients had lived in or near New Orleans
for between ten and forty years. Johann Domingo, described as a "homeless"
man, had been in the city for only one day before his admission to the
hospital.[33]

It was noted earlier that the Spanish hospital for lepers was abandoned
at the beginning of the nineteenth century, after which the physicians of

New Orleans no longer found or sought to find further evidence of the disease. The demise of "La terre des Lepreux" and the disappearance of leprosy from the Colony of Louisiana coincided with the end of European dominion over New Orleans. From that time on, Louisiana was to be American territory. But historian John Duffy is less certain than earlier historians that leprosy had in fact disappeared from Louisiana. "More probably," he wrote, leprosy "was neither diagnosed nor reported for much of the nineteenth century."[34]

Neither view is consistent with the historical evidence. Leprosy had not disappeared. Cases were diagnosed in Louisiana as early as 1849,[35] and leprosy patients were freely admitted to Charity Hospital for as long as the annual reports of the hospital have been preserved—since 1857. In the mortality statistics of the Seventh Census of the United States, 1850, leprosy was listed as a cause of death, and eleven persons were reported to have died of the disease "in the twelve months preceding the first of June of that year." Of the eleven cases enumerated, four deaths were recorded for Louisiana, including two slaves from the northern section of the state and two white males from New Orleans and its environs.[36]

In 1897 Dr. Isadore Dyer of New Orleans presented a paper on endemic leprosy in Louisiana at the First International Leprosy Conference in Berlin.[37] Dyer tabulated all cases of leprosy recorded in the annual reports of Charity Hospital between 1857 and 1896 (Table 3.1). In 1915, at a symposium on leprosy sponsored by the Orleans Parish Medical Society, Dr. Rudolph Matas recalled that some twenty-five years earlier, when he was an intern at Charity Hospital in 1878–1880, as many as 112 leprous patients were housed in special wards in that institution during those years[38]—cases of the disease that had seemingly eluded Jones, who searched hospital records for leprosy in 1880.

What is so noteworthy about the cases of leprosy that are recorded for Louisiana before the 1880s is that the presence of the disease appears unaccompanied by any special concern or sense of alarm. The situation is analogous to that described in 1909 by Dr. L. Duncan Bulkley in characterizing the calm attitude held toward leprosy in New York Hospital in 1868 and in clinics all over Europe. Writing at the beginning of the twentieth century when leprosy was viewed with horror and alarm, Bulkley contrasted 1909 with how things were viewed and done forty years earlier.

In regard to the manner in which leprosy, as we now know it, is considered by those who come often in contact with it, it may be mentioned that in all the clinics in Europe, and in this country, as far as I know, patients thus afflicted mingle freely with others and are lectured upon and handled just as any other patients, and never has there been known any instance of harm therefrom. They are also constantly admitted to the beds of hospitals, without any thought of danger. In 1868, over forty years ago, before the days of antisepsis, when the writer was interne in the old New York Hospital, a most distressing case of tubercular anesthetic leprosy, with much ulceration and mutilation, was for a long time in the medical wards, and was then transferred

TABLE 3.1

A List of Cases Recorded in Such Annual Reports of the Charity Hospital,
New Orleans, as Have Been Preserved

Date of Report	Color	Remarks
1857	2 whites, 1 black	No reports preserved to 1857.
1858	1 white	
1859	2 whites	
1860	2 whites	
1861–1868	--	Reports missing.
1869	none	
1870–1873	--	Reports missing.
1874	1 white	
1875	4 whites	
1876	5 whites	
1877	5 whites[a]	
1878	--	Report missing.
1879	7 whites	
1880	7 whites	
1881	none	
1882	3 whites	
1883	3 whites, 2 blacks	
1884	6 whites, 2 blacks	
1885	5 whites, 1 black	
1886	1 black	
1887	5 whites, 1 black[b]	
1888	9 whites, 3 blacks	
1889	4 whites, 2 blacks	
1890	2 whites	
1891	2 whites	
1892	4 whites, 3 blacks[c]	
1893	2 whites, 3 blacks	
1894	1 white, 1 black	
1895	2 whites, 3 blacks	
1896	3 whites, 2 blacks	

[a]From 1877, or even 1876, these cases are more than likely already enumerated under Jones's cases, as he was connected with the Charity Hospital at that time. Salomon, also, in 1880, reported three of his cases from the Charity Hospital.

[b]These cases are most likely identical with those reported by Blanc, as he was dermatologist to the Hospital at the time.

[c]All of these cases are only useful in this report as correlative evidence of the existence of the disease, and, therefore, as argument for the endemic nature of the disease.

Source: Dyer, I. "Endemic Leprosy in Louisiana: With a Logical Argument for the Contagiousness of This Disease." The Philadelphia Medical Journal 2, no. 12, 1898, 571.

to the surgical service, where a portion of the foot was amputated without an anesthetic, there being no pain.[39]

It is possible that the leprosy so salient to the earlier Spanish rulers was not viewed with any special concern by the Americans when they acquired Louisiana in 1803; at least not until late in the century. The number of cases of leprosy that can be documented in Louisiana between 1849 and the late 1870s—vis-à-vis earlier Spanish suggestions of "scores" of cases and the sizable figure of forty-two cases that Dr. Henry W. Blanc documented for Charity Hospital alone between 1883 and 1888,[40] later amended to eighty-four cases in 1892[41]—may only reflect the fact that leprosy was not perceived with any special attention or considered to be noteworthy in the intervening period. However, once the disease came to international attention in the 1880s, more cases were discovered as physicians began actively to ferret them out, and in looking for leprosy in Louisiana they may have only found what possibly had been there all along.

SCIENTIFIC CONCERNS

Theories of disease causation and how specific diseases were acquired were undergoing profound changes late in the nineteenth century. The dominant scientific view held for a long time in Europe was that leprosy was a household, hereditary disease of multiple and disparate origins—the "hereditary dyscrasia sanguinis," as D. C. Danielssen had termed it. However, with the emergence of modern bacteriology and the discovery by Hansen early in the 1870s of *Mycobacterium leprae*, the proponents of a contagion theory now had a strong argument that leprosy was a germ disease.

Hansen's bacteriological research, along with recent reports from Hawaii of an epidemic in the 1860s, had heightened Western fears that the "loathsome" malady, known to be extensive overseas, might spread to the West through contact with leprous populations. The belief that leprosy might be a germ disease and therefore contagious left many scientists previously wedded to alternative hypotheses, such as heredity, miasmatic conditions, and fish-eating, uncertain and divided in their opinions. Many were in a quandary; Jones was no exception.

By the time Jones presented his paper to the New Orleans Medical and Surgical Association in 1877, he had read extensively about leprosy and its history and current status. Knowing that the disease historically had been reported among peoples who later came to populate the southern states of America, Jones sought to investigate the disease locally. When Jones went to Lafourche to see leprosy for himself, he found fewer cases than he had expected. Some were called "scrofula" or "elephantiasis." Jones added another name to the list, noting that "undoubted cases of Oriental leprosy were met with on both banks of the Bayou Lafourche." Jones speculated that while environmental factors may be important in the persistence of the disease in certain impoverished populations, "the disease on the Lower

Lafourche has been propagated by hereditary influences, and by personal contact, rather than engendered by climate, soil and food."[42]

Jones left Lafourche in the belief that, in the cases of leprosy he encountered there, two mechanisms were involved in the prolongation of the disease: heredity and contagion. Heredity was responsible for most of the cases. "The leprosy of the Lower Lafourche," Jones wrote, "in many of the cases if not all, can be shown to be inherited."[43] In discussing the incidence of the disease in the family tree of "Mr. G.," Jones speculated on the hereditary pattern: "Such facts would seem to indicate that the disease may apparently skip over one or more generations, and that an apparently healthy man, although descended from a leprous mother, may engender both healthy and leprous children, without contaminating his wife."[44] In a few instances, Jones noted, "cases of leprosy appear to have been contracted from contact or contagion. Instances were cited where the disease was said to have been propagated to men by contact with leprous women."[45]

Jones addressed the issue of contagion in more detail in discussing cases of the disease he found at Charity Hospital. The case of Father Charles Boglioli, Jones wrote, "presents special points of interest, and appears to sustain the generally received opinion as to the contagious nature of Oriental leprosy."[46] Father Boglioli was born in the Apennine mountains in the province of Lombardy, Italy. He arrived in New Orleans in 1840 at about the age of twenty-seven and spent the next twenty-six years at various posts in Missouri, Ohio, and Louisiana. He returned to New Orleans in 1866. According to Jones's history, the disease began to manifest itself in 1876 or 1877.

> During the past fourteen years, Father Boglioli has attended daily in the wards of the Charity Hospital, administering religious consolation and extreme unction to the sick and dying in both the male and female wards. . . . I have myself for eleven years been witness to his faithful labors in behalf of the Catholic Church. He says that about six years ago he attended two cases of leprosy in ward No. 7 and administered extreme unction to them, and rubbed their hands with oil during the administration of certain religious rites. [He] has in like manner attended the several cases of leprosy in his capacity of religious adviser and pastor in the male and female wards.

> This case has given rise to the belief that he has contracted his distressing disease, which has altered his aspect, causing a thickened and nodulated and bronzed, mottled appearance of the entire cuticle, by contact with those suffering with leprosy in the wards of the Charity Hospital.[47]

Thus, in 1880, after returning from his epidemiological investigation in Lafourche Parish and examining the history of cases of leprosy at Charity Hospital, Jones believed that the disease propagated itself in two ways. In the case of the Acadians of southern Louisiana, leprosy was usually acquired through heredity. But where the disease appeared in persons working at Charity Hospital, filled with poor immigrants, the mode of transmission was direct contact.

Jones's work in leprosy in the late 1870s and early 1880s took the form of public health epidemiology. He sought to determine the extent to which leprosy existed in the state. He also formulated a control policy, which contained a provision for the seclusion of patients in a leper house, ward, or hospital to be constructed in the districts where the disease existed. He warned of the danger of placing patients on the crowded wards of Charity Hospital, where he believed that Father Boglioli had acquired the disease. Jones's recommendations were consistent with his public health efforts at controlling other diseases in Louisiana, including the quarantine of men and ships in the case of yellow fever and malaria and the isolation of smallpox patients. Aware of the state's neglect with regard to helping sufferers of other diseases, Jones wrote "it is manifestly the duty of the State to provide for the maintenance of the victims of leprosy." The policy that Jones envisioned provided for medical care. It was also humane, in that it recommended that patients not be removed from the districts in which they lived but that they be placed under the care of local practitioners.[48]

Jones published on leprosy only once more, in 1887, nine years before his death. In volume 2 of a three-part series entitled *Medical and Surgical Memoirs*, a collection of Jones's writings, he included a long section on "Leprosy in America." Here he reprinted all of his earlier papers and added some new material and further reflections on the disease.[49]

In his 1887 writings, Jones again reviewed the history of leprosy in Louisiana, noting the several sources of the disease: (1) the early settlers to the shores of the Gulf of Mexico who came from countries in Europe (France, Spain, Italy) where the disease was not yet extinct, (2) slaves imported from Africa, with "their peculiar diseases, the yaws and the Grecian and Arabian leprosy," and (3) the Acadian refugees driven from Canada, who arrived in southern Louisiana in the eighteenth century. Jones does not comment on whether the leprosy of the first two groups had lingered on in Louisiana or, if it had, how the disease had been passed along. He does comment on the Acadian leprosy, however. Jones considered the leprosy in southern Louisiana among descendants of Acadians to be inherited in most instances. The original Acadian leprosy was explained by Jones as an example of how an unhealthy environment could prolong the disease through several generations:

> Those cases of leprosy which have arisen amongst the descendants of the Acadians without doubt derived their origin from the French settlers of barren and rocky coasts of Nova Scotia, where the winter lasts seven months and is of dreadful severity, where the summer comes suddenly, and where perpetual fogs render the country equally unwholesome and unpleasant.[50]

Contagion was an entirely different matter. "The contagious nature of leprosy," Jones wrote, "appears to be settled beyond all doubt, by its appearance in a healthy population after the immigration of foreigners from a leprous country, as in the example of the importation of leprosy into the district of Surinam, in South America, and the origin and spread of the disease among the Sandwich Islanders after an immigration of the Chinese."[51] It would appear from his writings between 1880 and 1887 that Jones had struggled with the problem of trying to disassociate inherited leprosy from the contagious form of the disease.

In the new material that he added to his writings in 1887, it is clear that, for Jones, the issue of leprosy was now ideological. Late in the 1880s, it was generally feared that leprosy was about to become pandemic and would spread to the Western world from the Far East. Jones, who had been rational and humane in discussing Louisiana leprosy early in the 1880s, had by the end of the decade joined the sinophobes and alarmists in warning of the dangers from Asiatic leprosy. "The history of leprosy in the Hawaiian Islands," Jones wrote in 1887, "strongly maintains the doctrine of the contagious nature of this disease, and it is to be earnestly hoped that [this] sad experience . . . may not be repeated in California and Louisiana through the instrumentality of the filthy, vicious, debased, heathen leprous Chinese."[52] If Jones, the scientist, was still uncertain about how leprosy was communicated through contact, as the following quotation reveals, he was anything but uncertain about the Chinese as a source of leprosy:

> The question as to whether the specific form of bacillus found in the lymphatics and sores of the leper can be transmitted through the medium of food, water and clothing, or by inoculation, may not yet be settled; but there are no doubt in the Chinese laundries of San Francisco, New Orleans, and New York, Asiatic men now at work who are in the early stages of the disease; and their practice of taking water in their mouths and spitting it out on the clothes they iron, is more than ever disgusting when considered in connection with the possible transmission of disease by this means.[53]

Jones's recommendation for managing "uncivilized heathen, barbarians affected with leprosy" was that they "should be either rigidly isolated, or else returned to their native countries. . . . The bodies of deceased lepers should be destroyed by fire."[54]

Jones was born in Georgia and had served as an officer in the Confederate Army during the Civil War. He had seen his southern way of life destroyed by armed conflict, by divisive racial issues, and by the abolition of slavery. For Jones, the threat of Chinese leprosy and Chinese immigration transcended the field of medicine. The Chinese symbolized an awesome biocultural danger to Western Anglo-Saxon civilization:

> At the present day Louisiana is threatened with an influx of Chinese and Malays, with filth, rice [sic] and leprous diseases. An inferior and barbarous race transferred from the burning heats of Africa has already been the occasion of the shedding of the blood of more than one million of the white inhabitants of the United States, and in the shock of arms and in the subsequent confusion and chaos attending the settlement of the question of African slavery, the liberties of the country have been well nigh destroyed, and it is but just that patriots should contemplate with dread the overflow of their country by the unprincipled, vicious and leprous hordes of Asia. The

contact of a superior with an inferior race must lead eventually to two results: The annihilation of one or the other, or the amalgamation of the two. The mixture of the blood of a noble race with that of one of inferior mental and moral constitution may depress the former to the level of the latter, but can never endow the brain and heart of the African and Asiatic with the intelligence, independence, love of liberty, invention and moral worth of the Anglo-Saxon race.[55]

In attacking the Chinese so unmercifully, Jones revealed that he was far more national in his outlook than were most of his fellow physicians in New Orleans. Although they too showed concern about leprosy, they nevertheless failed to become denunciatory or so enraged about the Chinese as were Jones and the rest of the nation. In this they were probably responding to their own sectionalism and to the fact that few Orientals had come or were even about to come to the Deep South. A grand total of 535 was recorded for all of Louisiana in 1893, of which only 300 were in New Orleans.[56]

NEW ORLEANS'S RESPONSE TO THE "REDISCOVERY" OF LEPROSY

Blanc's reporting in 1888 of large numbers of leprosy cases at Charity Hospital made some in New Orleans more conscious of leprosy than they had been before. The Blanc data forced home the point that leprosy, formerly assumed by many physicians to occur only in "individuals of foreign birth, or of immediate foreign extraction," was in fact endemic in Louisiana. They further showed that Louisiana was the only endemic area in the United States, and that the disease predominated among white citizens of the city.[57]

In acknowledging leprosy as an indigenous disease, the people of New Orleans were faced with yet another public health issue. Some began to see lepers everywhere—on the streets, in restaurants, at the theater, among prisoners in the dock, among the well-dressed and the shabby, in both the poor and the affluent sections of town.[58] Noting that the American Dermatological Association had reported a total of fifty-two cases of leprosy in the entire United States for the period from June 30, 1878, to January 1, 1893, Dr. Isadore Dyer commented in 1894: "I warrant that there are twice that number in New Orleans today."[59] But when a "Northern paper" reported a rumor that Louisiana harbored 250 lepers, the president of the State Board of Health quickly denied the allegation. He did acknowledge, however, that "there is no law to provide [for isolation] and no appropriation to execute the law," were there one.[60]

Sensitive to its tarnished reputation in matters of public health, the city, and the state to a lesser extent, alternately viewed leprosy as a "burning question" or else responded with supreme indifference. Calls for action flared up in the local press and in the *New Orleans Medical and Surgical Journal* from time to time and then as quickly subsided. Always hovering in the background, however, was the criticism that the city's leaders had neglected to respond in the face of past epidemics of yellow fever. And if the officials of New Orleans were not always prepared to be open about this, then others were. In an editorial in the *New Orleans Medical and Surgical Journal*, in 1891, Dr. H. S. Orme, president of the State Board of Health of California, was quoted as saying that in some places "alarming numbers [of lepers] occasionally come to light. Just now the point most threatened is New Orleans, for no legal barrier stands to protect the great city which, after a long and dreadful struggle, has lately gained the mastery of tropical yellow fever by quarantine."[61] Yellow fever was very much on the minds of the people of New Orleans, and many feared a possible connection between it and leprosy. Dr. Joseph Holt, a former president of the Louisiana State Board of Health, in a newspaper interview in 1894 sought to calm public apprehension. In commenting on the uncertain question of the transmission of leprosy, he said: "I am aware that some exceptional cases, involving inoculation of an accidental kind are reported, but I attach no value whatever to the danger of such conveyance through mosquitoes and sand flies, which can only be regarded as a terrifying suggestion."[62] The denial by physicians in New Orleans that leprosy could be transmitted by mosquitoes or other insect vectors would be repeated publicly more than once.[63]

In the same year that the Blanc cases were published, the *New Orleans Medical and Surgical Journal* addressed the question of transmission. Dr. Benjamin Lee stated at a national conference of state boards of health that "Leprosy has always been contagious. Leprosy has always been infectious." To this, a *Journal* editorial responded that "observation and experience in the well-known habitats of the disease—India, West Indies, China, Sandwich Islands, Norway—give weight . . . [to the] belief that leprosy is not infectious and contagious in the ordinary meaning of the terms. . . . [The] disease is hereditary and inoculable; in plainer terms, . . . it is transmissible in the same manner, and by the same means as syphilis."[64] Returning to the question of the incidence of leprosy in New Orleans, the *Journal* wrote that although new cases of the disease were constantly coming to medical attention, "a notable fact about most of these cases is that they are of long standing.[65] . . . The point which we would make in connection with these facts is that if leprosy were infectious there should be more cases of recent origin, as the result of the unrestricted intercourse of the lepers with the people in this city."[66] Although members of the New Orleans Medical and Surgical Association disagreed with Lee about the infectious and contagious nature of leprosy, they did agree that "the importation of lepers should cease, and that those already here should be rigidly segregated in hospitals especially erected and set aside for them."[67]

A turning point came early in the 1890s. The question was no longer whether the disease existed in the state. The mode of transmission was uncertain, but the disease was believed to be incurable, and the isolation of lepers was recommended. The question that remained in Louisiana was how to arrange for their confinement.

If leprosy was a "burning question," as Dyer had called it, then it was so in the minds of only a few members of the medical profession. "Some feeble attempts have been made to interest our law-makers in lepers," noted the editors of the *New Orleans Medical and Surgical Journal* in 1890, "but there seems to be no disposition to make room in the budget for the unfortunate victims of an incurable malady."[68] In editorial after editorial, *Journal* editors complained bitterly about the indifference of the state, the State Board of Health, the state medical society, about the indifference, in fact, of people in general about leprosy, including the physicians and inhabitants of New Orleans itself.[69]

Disappointed in their efforts to arouse local interest in the disease, editors of the *Journal* appealed to the U.S. Government. Noting that leprosy was not confined to Louisiana, that cases existed elsewhere in the United States, and that "Louisiana is too poor to do her duty" and the "people (and the profession) are callous or indifferent," editors of the *Journal* endorsed a plan that would make leprosy a "national question":

> We know of no better means of stamping out leprosy in the United States than to make it a national question and put the lepers in [the] charge of the Marine Hospital Service. . . . Members of the Marine Hospital Service, being under a discipline almost military, could be detailed from time to time to care for the unfortunates. The lepers from all parts of the country could there be gathered together, and in the course of a generation indigenous leprosy in the United States would be a thing of the past.[70]

As to the location of this facility, the *Journal* noted that "Uncle Sam has a great many islands in pleasant climates situated some distance from the mainland, where the lepers could be confined without fear of escape."[71] By the time the *New Orleans Medical and Surgical Journal* urged that lepers be placed under federal jurisdiction, an antileprosy movement was already under way in the United States. The federal government, however, would not act on the matter for another quarter of a century.

ESTABLISHING A STATE HOME FOR LEPERS

In Louisiana, late in the nineteenth century, two men—physicians—stood out in relation to leprosy. Joseph Jones, the public health activist and epidemiologist, brought the disease to local attention. A decade or so after Jones, in the 1890s, Dr. Isadore Dyer set himself a different task: to bring leprosy within the framework of science and medicine. Dyer was a dermatologist and became dean of the Tulane School of Medicine. In 1915, he was to become president of the Association of American Medical Colleges. Dyer envisioned a responsive state government, a responsive citizenry, a scientifically minded medical profession, and a rational leprosy control program. Hoping to eradicate leprosy in the state of Louisiana, Dyer was influenced by the control program developed earlier in Norway. In 1904 he wrote that "the opportunity is now afforded for the State of Louisiana to parallel the results of Norway in the management of an unfortunate evil."[72] The cornerstone of Dyer's program was to locate a leprosy hospital "as nearly as possible in the centre of infection," which meant the southern portion of the state. New Orleans was the logical site for two reasons: (1) The bulk of the known lepers in the state were in the city or nearby, and (2) Such a location would "bring it within . . . easy reach of the medical talent of New Orleans, so that the work of treatment might be carried on in a more completely scientific manner."[73]

Faced with a state legislature indifferent to the idea of providing for the care of lepers, Dyer, along with a few members of the Orleans Parish Medical Society, nevertheless managed to secure state approval and an appropriation of funds between 1893 and 1894. Success was achieved not through arguments based on medical, humanitarian, or public health grounds, but by the use of political strategy.

The state practice of awarding exclusive contracts to favored physicians to operate private hospitals, often for smallpox, had been abolished in 1877; nevertheless, the practice was allowed to continue at the city level.[74] One such facility was owned and managed by Dr. J. C. Beard in New Orleans. There is little reference to this facility until 1893, when a reporter for the *Daily Picayune* heard about a young girl being shipped to the hospital by way of a boxcar marked up on the bill of lading as "freight," at a cost of $20. The reporter visited Beard's "pest-house, as it was called, and found seven lepers housed there.[75] His account of abandon, neglect, and possible starvation subsequently reached the New Orleans grand jury, which investigated the matter and corroborated the newspaper's report. On top of charges of inhumanity, Beard's finances were also questioned. In addition to monies paid to him by the state, at least one inmate was also described as a "pay patient," the others as being "cared for (?) at the expense of the City of New Orleans or of the parishes from which they came."[76]

The grand jury regretted it was not empowered to bring criminal charges against Beard. News of Beard's "pest-house," however, soon reached Dyer through Captain Allen Jumel, a member of the state legislature whom Dyer described as having "knowledge of the conditions at the pest-house derived from one of the inmates whom he had known for many years." In August 1894, Dyer and members of the Orleans Parish Medical Society forced the state legislature to remove the contracting physician "for cause." Members of the medical society noted that a little known bill had been introduced at the state legislature earlier, in 1884, that proposed a contractual arrangement for a physician to assume charge of lepers for a consideration of $10,000 a year. They used Beard's removal and this earlier bill as evidence that the state had already committed itself to providing funds and thus should now establish a proper agency for the care of lepers in the state.

A State Board of Control for the Leper Home, "whose duty it shall be to provide for the proper care, treatment and maintenance of all persons in the State of Louisiana," was soon enacted into law. The board was organized in September 1984, with Dyer as its first president.[77] During his tenure as president of the board of control, as well as afterward, Dyer would experience many disappointments. From the moment the board was created, Dyer wrote in his first annual report, "obstacles were thrown in the way of the Board's effort to fulfill the high duty imposed upon them."[78] The most serious obstacle was the failure of the board to obtain a site for the hospital in or even near New Orleans. Various locations were considered and then, as the *Daily States* noted in 1894, "the 'blocking' game commenced. Every site the board got options on was ultimately cut from under the feet of the men who were devoting their valuable time, without a dollar's recompense, in the cause of suffering humanity."[79]

At a meeting before the City Health Committee, opponents argued against locating the hospital within city limits on the grounds that "there would be a great danger of contagion." Dyer argued that "although leprosy was an incurable and insidious disease, it was not infectious; that the disease could only be communicated by inoculation, and from two to ten years were required for its development." The observation that the disease was characterized by a long incubation period unsettled some listeners. Others in New Orleans, however, found slowness a comforting trait, one attuned to a style of life they found compatible. However, "the principal objection to the hospital," all opponents agreed, "was that it was proposed to burden Orleans Parish with all the lepers of the State."[80]

The city, Dyer noted bitterly, did not come to the board's aid. But the city alone had not failed Dyer. "If now failure results," Dyer wrote, "it can alone be attributed to a lack of support on the part of those in government power, of a board willing and anxious to drive home the wedge of success with successive blows, directed at an apathetic public, a disinterested coronery system, and a timid medical profession."[81] Dyer, however, was not easily dissuaded, and with the help of Jumel he quietly obtained a five-year lease on Indian Camp Plantation in Iberville Parish, some 85 miles above New Orleans. The location was "desirable in every way," Dyer noted, "except from the point of accessibility."[82]

Dyer had moved quickly. Turned down by the city for a property on Gentilly Road in New Orleans early in November, he not only managed to lease Indian Camp at $750 per year, but on the evening of November 30, 1894, the first transfer of patients from Beard's pest-house to Iberville Parish was accomplished. Dyer, however, only intended Indian Camp to be a temporary arrangement until a more suitable site closer to New Orleans could be obtained, and in March 1901 he informed the governor that the board was ready to submit two new proposals for consideration. A site on the west bank of the Mississippi River opposite the town of Kenner fell within the means allowed by state appropriation. With the governor's approval, the property known as the "Elkhorn" place was duly acquired by the state in April 1901 for the purpose of building a hospital.[83]

No hospital for lepers was ever built at Elkhorn. After the board had the property surveyed and was beginning to construct a facility, "a storm of protest burst forth from the excited fears of some of the people of Jefferson and St. Charles [parishes]." There was "much heated talk," and the board agreed to hold a meeting on May 22, 1901, with delegates from these parishes.[84]

From the account of the meeting published by the board of control, it appears to have been a long one and not at all friendly. Opponents of the proposal raised three objections: (1) "The disease was so contagious that the presence of a Leper Home would be a menace to the neighborhood since the disease could be spread through the atmosphere and carried by mosquitoes and flies"; (2) "The Act originally creating the Home designated *isolation*, which . . . could be attained only by establishing the Home upon some lonely island or in some locality far removed from any inhabited section of the country"; and (3) "The value of property in the neighborhood of a Leper Home would be depreciated and . . . great financial loss would be felt by the people."[85]

Various members of the board of control, the State Board of Health, and the New Orleans Board of Health defended the proposal. Dyer addressed the issue of contagion and based his thesis on the lessons learned about leprosy in Norway. He emphasized the importance of checking the spread of the disease through locating leprosaria in hyperendemic areas and the low, almost nonexistent rate of spread from leprosarium to community. He also denied that there was any scientific evidence to indicate that mosquitoes or other insects could transmit the disease.[86]

The issue of isolation overlapped with that of contagion. It was pointed out that the various ordinances and acts passed since 1892 had specified the isolation of patients "within the city of New Orleans." Dr. C. J. Edwards expanded on Dyer's thesis and reported on the experience of New Brunswick, Canada. When a leprosarium was first located on an island 40 miles from the center of infection, the disease continued to spread. But when the leprosarium was relocated to the center of infection, where it was visited daily by people from the outside for thirty years, "not a single case has spread from the institution nor has any person living in the place and caring for the patients ever been infected during that long space of time."[87]

The argument that property values in the neighborhood would depreciate brought forth from the board the observation that far from depreciating in value, "the ground actually used for the Home [Indian Camp] had risen in price over $4,000.00 in 5 years; and for the past two years there had been an eager demand by at least six of the neighbors to rent the portion of ground not used by the lepers." Thirty-one responses received from neighbors living in the vicinity of Indian Camp, who earlier had objected to the leprosarium, were presented at the meeting. Their statements provided testimony "that the Leper Home has neither been a public nuisance nor a menace to the health of the people or the value of their property . . . but that, on the contrary, has even been of some financial benefit to the trade of the Parish."[88]

The meeting between the two factions ended without a definite decision on either side. The board agreed to take the protests under advisement.

The protesters, however, had their own answer to the board of control, and on that evening the buildings at Elkhorn were burned to the ground.

After the events of that night, the board of control had little choice left, and on December 21, 1905, the state purchased Indian Camp. Although it was the last choice, it became the permanent site of the Louisiana Home for Lepers. Fifteen years later, on January 3, 1921, again as the last choice, it would become the permanent location of the first and only federal leprosarium in the continental United States.

With the burning of Elkhorn and the subsequent decision by the state not to look for another site but to purchase Indian Camp instead, Dyer's hopes of creating a "model sanitorium" in Louisiana were effectively dead. But Dyer's chances of succeeding had begun to deteriorate seriously before these events. From the start there were money squabbles with the state for repairs and construction at Indian Camp. There was the remoteness of Indian Camp itself, along with problems of obtaining adequate medical and nursing personnel and of overcoming the reluctance of patients to submit to hospitalization in far-off Iberville Parish. Dyer had hoped to solve this latter difficulty through legislation and police powers compelling the commitment of lepers, as he had read was the practice in Norway, but the legal machinery was denied him.[89] Dyer had also hoped to enlist the aid of coroners in each parish in an effort to obtain reliable epidemiological data on the number of lepers in the state, but "this was barren of result and even of acknowledgment, save in two or three instances."[90]

Despite considerable statewide indifference and the remoteness of Indian Camp, Dyer nevertheless managed to solve two formidable problems in the running of a hospital: that of providing medical and nursing care. Within a few weeks of the opening of Indian Camp, Dyer secured the services of Dr. L. A. Wailes, who acted as resident physician, nurse, priest, servant, and disciplinarian until he resigned a year and a half later, at which time Dr. E. M. Hooper replaced him briefly. The problem of nursing care was solved in March 1896, when the Order of the Daughters of Charity of St. Vincent de Paul (commonly referred to as Sisters of Charity) agreed "to furnish members of its community who shall be responsible for the domestic arrangement, and all this entails; who shall supervise the household, culinary and laundry arrangement, who shall attend to the nursing of the patients resident in the Home, for which last they shall be responsible to the Resident Physician, and through him to the Board."[91]

One month after the contract was signed, four Sisters of Charity arrived at Indian Camp to take up their duties. With the Sisters now in residence, the state gradually withdrew its promised support to develop the Home into a hospital and instead became content to have it conducted by the Sisters solely along custodial lines. The Home was merely made comfortable enough to attract lepers and thus remove them from public notice.[92] Differences within the board of control over the definition of policy resulted in Dyer's resignation in June 1896. In 1900, at a meeting of the American Dermatological Association, Dyer spoke of the division that existed within the board as a state agency:

The conditions in Louisiana . . . are largely due . . . not so much to the lack of desire on the part of those who are interested in leprosy, as [they are] to the political color of the Board in control. The Home that was first started in Louisiana had every evidence of being successful in dealing with leprosy. The law is explicit and comprehensive in its details, but the Board as it is at present constituted is opposed to the spending of any amount of money in the attempt at cure of lepers, who are looked upon as incurable, and are simply sent to the present asylum to die. On this account, of course, the leper is unwilling to go, and the physician with a conscience is unwilling to have him sent.[93]

On the same day that Dyer resigned, two other members of the board also tendered their resignations, followed shortly afterward by Hooper. As president of the board Dyer had attempted to treat leprosy using a variety of medications then thought helpful, such as strychnine, chlorate of potassium, ichthyol, salicylate of sodium, arsenious acid, and chaulmoogra oil.[94] With the resignation of Dyer and the others, the office of resident physician was abolished; the new board construed the purpose of the institution to be an asylum and refuge for patients and not a hospital. Medical treatment for leprosy was relegated to a subservient position. Domestic care and the dressing of sores was all that remained. Some patients continued to treat themselves, but without medical supervision.[95] Between 1896 and 1902 the state appropriated no more money than had previously been set by law. No provisions were made for medical care or research. Dyer's efforts to make the Home a hospital for the eradication of leprosy in Louisiana had been checked once again.

When it became apparent that Indian Camp was likely to become the permanent location of the Leper Home, the state grudgingly accepted the responsibility. Conditions improved slightly as more money was appropriated for its upkeep. Dyer, who was now honorary consultant to the Home, managed to secure the assistance of Dr. Ralph Hopkins, who visited the colony regularly from 1902 until 1921. With Hopkins in attendance, Dyer was able to reinstate systematic medical treatment, eventually claiming improvement in individual cases and even cures. The mainstay of the "Dyer method" of treating leprosy consisted of

a daily hot bath, raised to the highest temperature of endurance (usually not over 110° Fahr.); a three times a day strychnin pill (1/60–1/40 of a grain); . . . chaulmoogra oil (crude as it can be had in fluid form) [given] three times a day . . . before meals . . . beginning with three drops and running the dose up to the tolerance of the patient, usually from 50 to 80 drops, tho some patients take as much as 120 drops, or more, at the dose. The oil is best taken in capsules, though it may be mixed with cod liver oil, olive oil, or may be taken in milk or with milk of magnesia in a shaken mixture or emulsion.[96]

Throughout most of the years that the Leper Home was a state institution, there was a running battle between the board of control and the Sisters of Charity, on one hand, and the state legislature, on the other, over the future of the Home. Money to adequately fund the institution, to make repairs, and to aid in the construction of improved facilities was never sufficient. Although the state legislature from time to time increased the maintenance appropriation, it made no provisions to change the status of the Home. Funds for medical expenses were held to a bare minimum, despite Dyer's claim that some patients were being cured. Although there was a strong interest in leprosy research at the Tulane School of Medicine, no state funds were made available for research of any type. The morale of the patients and the Sisters was often low. An increasing number of patients absconded from the Leper Home, and the Sisters often made appeals for private donations.

The failure of the state legislature to adequately fund the Home was not, however, a failure directed at lepers alone. According to Charles H. Calandro's study of the financial structure of the Leper Home, the state acted in a similar fashion with the seven other state-supported institutions. The period between 1877 and 1920 was marked by governmental conservativism in Louisiana. Still nursing its post–Civil War Reconstruction wounds and its past "political excesses," the state "was hesitant to support liberal legislation for fundamental reforms, and, as a result, state-supported humanitarian institutions in Louisiana witnessed little change in legislative appropriations during the first decade of the twentieth century."[97] Among the eight state institutions—including homes for the blind, the deaf and dumb, the mentally retarded, and the insane, along with Charity Hospital, the soldiers' home, the state penitentiary, and the Leper Home—the latter received the smallest increase in appropriations.[98]

Speaking of conditions at the home in 1914, Joel J. Prowell, president of the board of control and ideological descendant of Dyer, continued to chastise the state legislature: "Twenty years have passed. In those twenty years much of hardship, privation and even misery have been experienced by the unfortunate inmates and the self-sacrificing Sisters in attendance on them. During most of those years the Sisters of Charity and not the State of Louisiana bore the greater share of the burden."[99] Serving without compensation and receiving a small sum per annum for clothing and other incidental expenses, the Sisters, in the absence of a resident physician, were in complete charge of the Leper Home. During the years that it was a state institution, they "ran the show without interference, instituting a curious blend of tender care and iron monastic discipline."[100]

Letters written by the Sisters, preserved by Sister Hilary Ross, describe the primitive conditions at the Leper Home during the early years of its existence. Judging from the letters, one can only wonder—if the choice had been theirs alone to make and not one decided by "calling" and by the director of the Sisters of Charity in Emmitsburg, Maryland—whether, under the circumstances, they would have come at all, much less stayed on. Their loyalty to Dyer and his ideals is evident, their annoyance and frustration with the state legislature considerable.[101]

The response in Louisiana to leprosy was influenced by its past history and ongoing experience in handling (and mishandling) other major health issues. Little in the public health history of the city or the state before the yellow fever epidemic of 1878 argues for prompt and rational action in responding to the discovery of just a few more cases of yet another disease. Interest in leprosy was sustained by a handful of physicians and officials eager for a new beginning. The fact that the state did what it did in 1894—establish a leper home, the first and ultimately the only institution of its kind in the continental United States—does not argue for extraordinary motivation, however. The original plan to construct a medical and research hospital showed promise that, in terms of public health and social reform, New Orleans was, at least, trying to do the "right thing" at last. The fact that the plan did not succeed and that in its place the state chose only to maintain a rundown, rather miserable leper colony, located in an isolated area 85 or so miles upriver from New Orleans, without proper medical care, where lepers were kept out of public reach and out of sight, was consistent, however, with the failure of the state to move forward with other social reforms at the turn of the century.

The model of medical treatment, patient care, and research that Dyer had in mind was not fulfilled. A conservative state government opposed to reform and convinced that leprosy was a hopeless disease—intensely contagious, incurable, and inevitably fatal—was content to have the Home remain a neglected asylum. Here, patients came to feel that the public viewed them as criminals, to be deprived of liberty and freedom.[102] Later, the U.S. Government, through the U.S. Public Health Service and with the help of leprosy alarmists and sinophobes, would implement a policy similar to that which had evolved in Louisiana—a policy of isolation and confinement that reinforced the fear of leprosy and its stigma.

4

Norway: The "Enlightened Kingdom"

Earlier in the nineteenth century, before Dr. Joseph Jones began his epidemiological investigation of leprosy in Louisiana and Dr. Isadore Dyer struggled unsuccessfully to bring medical knowledge and modern care to the treatment of the disease, two major foci of leprosy activity had already come to Western attention. In Norway, increasing attentiveness to rural populations in that country revealed that the disease existed among farmers and in remote fishing villages. In Hawaii, attention centered on a group of islands that were becoming important commercially to the United States and whose political significance reflected U.S. involvement in the Far East. In Norway and in Hawaii, leprosy rates were substantial. In both countries the disease attracted considerable public attention, but in each case the outcome was different.

Norwegian awareness of leprosy began early in the nineteenth century and coincided with the growth of nationalism and increasing concern about the social and economic problems that the country faced after the Napoleonic Wars. Norway did not become fully independent from Sweden until 1905, but the rise of Norwegian nationalism had begun almost a century earlier with internal autonomy and the writing of a Norwegian constitution in 1814. The collapse of the Napoleonic system was followed in Europe by the emergence of new forms of national expression. Norway took pride in its past greatness, in achieving a new, popular language form, and, as one Norwegian historian has put it, "in the idolization . . . of all things specifically Norwegian."[1] Norwegians think of 1814 as having "an almost mystical significance. A sense of national unity pervaded the people."[2]

Throughout Norway economic conditions were severely depressed during the post-war years. The war had left Norway with a large merchant fleet, but the power of Great Britain interfered with Norwegian trade. Timber had been a major export. The sawmill industry along Norway's southern coast was particularly hard hit, and timber merchants were further disadvantaged by the imposition of new high foreign tariffs. A drastic reduction in timber prices followed. Profits were nonexistent and unemployment rose. "Bankruptcies were the order of the day."[3]

Along Norway's western coast, economic conditions were slightly better. The northern and western fishing industry rebounded faster than the timber market. Bergen—the one true urban center—recovered slightly more quickly than other cities, and Stavanger, whose economy was based on herring, grew rapidly, doubling its population in a single generation. Oslo, on the other hand, remained "an empty harbour."[4]

The real hardships were to be found in the rural farming communities and in the fishing villages. There, living conditions remained primitive, severe, and unsanitary. Scabies, worm diseases, rickets, chronic rheumatism, pulmonary tuberculosis, scrofula, and syphilis were common afflictions.[5] Post-war poverty in Norway was further aggravated by a rapid increase in population, which doubled the number of cotters (tenant farmers) and tripled the number of laborers.[6] Population growth intensified the use of land as a means of obtaining a living. In some parts of Norway, as in Ireland, potato cultivation was increased to alleviate starvation. For many people in both countries, emigration to the United States was the only option available, and in the early 1820s the first Norwegian party sailed for America.

The Constitution of 1814 declared Norway a "free, independent, and indivisible realm," embodying the new egalitarian principles of political liberty prevailing throughout Europe and the United States. Norway's sense of national purpose was influenced by the French revolutionary constitution of 1791, by the U.S. Constitution, and generally by the British system of liberalism. Almost immediately Norway abolished all titles of nobility and ended the practice of corporal punishment and the mutilation of prisoners.

Of greater significance, however, was the emergence in Norway of the peasantry as a powerful political force. Peasant interests centered less on external relations with other countries and more on the internal administration of the country. Peasants agitated for a reduction in government expenditures, especially in the salaries, pensions, and numbers of government officials. They demanded—and obtained—full powers of local self-government. The result of this reorganization of the internal political structure of Norway was that "the peasants of the next generation came—long before the equivalent class in other nonindustrial countries—to be the controlling factor in the life of the nation."[7]

As economic conditions in Norway improved, many nationwide reforms were introduced. Changes in the penal system led to the discontinuance of forced labor among prisoners and to the abolition of capital punishment. A model prison was built in Oslo. By midcentury a modern asylum for the mentally disabled was added. Compulsory schooling from the age of seven until the age of confirmation was established in all towns by 1848, twenty-two years in advance of a similar program in England. In 1860 this program was extended to all country districts. A school was built wherever thirty children were able to attend, with the result that secular teachers gradually displaced the clergy as leaders of rural communities.

It was in Norway at midcentury that the concept of the community as a unit of social science research was first realized—in the work of Eilert Sundt. At the time P.G.F. Le Play was pioneering the use of social surveys in studying labor conditions in France and William Lloyd Garrison and John Greenleaf Whittier were absorbed in abolishing slavery in America,

Sundt was traveling throughout rural Norway, living with peasants and wandering gypsy groups. His community studies of gypsies influenced the Norwegian Parliament to cease penalizing them for their nomadic way of life. Sundt was interested in rural poverty, labor conditions, and population studies. His work in rural areas revealed to the rest of Norway the rich cultural fabric of peasant life. Sundt's foremost aim, however, was to improve the living conditions of peasants, and toward this goal he was a supporter of ideas and programs concerning sanitation, education, and the value of cooperative societies.[8]

NORWAY DEALS WITH LEPROSY

The history of leprosy in Norway in the nineteenth century is part of the history of Norwegian nationalism. The awareness that leprosy existed in the country among impoverished peasants arose through the increasing national attention that was now being paid to the social, economic, and health conditions that prevailed throughout the countryside. The extreme hardship suffered by the rural poor was first brought to public notice by J. E. Welhaven, pastor to the St. Jørgens Hospital in Bergen, in a report published in a medical journal in 1816, only two years after the drafting of the Norwegian constitution.[9] St. Jørgens was originally established in the fifteenth century as a leprosarium. Patients with other diseases were later admitted, but at the time when Welhaven was pastor, it was primarily a leprosy asylum for the poor from western Norway. Welhaven's account of conditions at St. Jørgens gives the impression that the hospital had become little more than "a graveyard for the living."[10]

The initial step taken in Norway with regard to leprosy was to establish the dimensions of the problem. Thus, in 1832, Dr. J. J. Hjort was commissioned to survey leprosy in the various districts of the country and assess what could be done for those with the disease. Hjort's survey, though incomplete, established a precedent for future epidemiological surveys. His recommendation that hospital beds were needed for the care of patients with leprosy was soon implemented.

In 1836, a second leprosy census was completed, this time under the supervision of local parish ministers. A total of 659 persons were identified as having leprosy, corresponding to a prevalence rate of 5 per 10,000 population.[11] In the years that followed, successive leprosy censuses were undertaken: in 1845, in connection with a general population count; again in 1852, conducted by the district health officers; and culminating in 1856, with the establishment of a national leprosy registry, the first of its kind ever developed in relation to a specific disease. The registry was designed to coordinate epidemiological data with public health activities in an effort to understand the cause of leprosy. The registry is still in operation in Norway today.

Although succeeding censuses added methodological refinements, the 1856 registry was workable. Some overdiagnosis occurred during the first

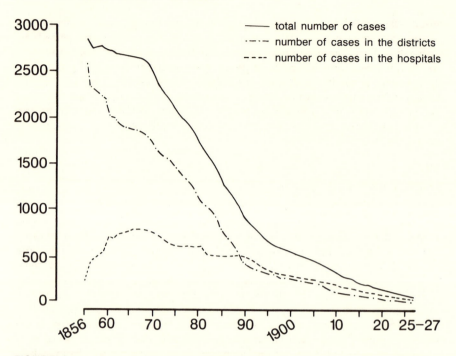

FIGURE 4.1
Course of Leprosy in Norway from 1856 to 1927

Source: Adapted from Lie, H. P. "Why Is Leprosy Decreasing in Norway?" *Transactions of the Royal Society of Tropical Medicine and Hygiene* 22, no. 4, 1929: Table 1, 360.

few years in regions of the country where the prevalence of leprosy was high, and some underdiagnosis occurred in areas of low prevalence. In the early years of registration, overdiagnosis was often the result of misdiagnosing acne vulgaris, scabies, and other common skin disorders as leprosy. Irgens and Bjerkedal, in a 1973 review of the national leprosy registry from 1856 to the present, noted that despite these failings, "accurate and reliable information about almost every leper in the country was achieved in the first years of registration."[12]

Because of improved methods of case finding and increased skills in differential diagnosis, the census of 1856 showed more cases of leprosy in the country and in different places than had been reported earlier. In 1836 the prevalence had been estimated to be 5 per 10,000 population, and in 1845 it was placed at 8 per 10,000. In 1852 it was estimated to be 11 per 10,000, with rates as high as 700 per 10,000 in parts of the hyperendemic western districts.[13] By 1856 the estimated prevalence had again climbed, to become the peak year in modern Norwegian history. Since 1856 rates have continued to decline (see Figures 4.1 and 4.2) to the point where by 1973 only four persons born in Norway were known to have the disease.[14]

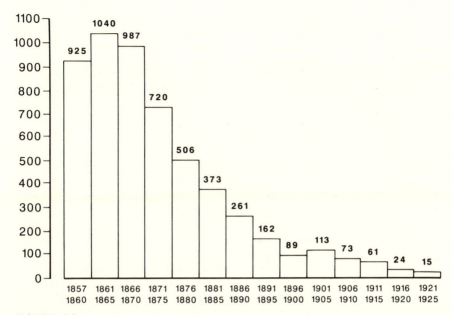

FIGURE 4.2
Number of New Cases in Five-Year Periods from 1857 to 1925

Source: Lie, H. P. "Why Is Leprosy Decreasing in Norway?" *Transactions of the Royal Society of Tropical Medicine and Hygiene* 22, no. 4, 1929: Table 2, 361.

Even before the census of 1845 was completed, a parliamentary decision to promote clinical and pathological studies of leprosy was reached. Norway's aim was to obtain exact knowledge of the disease. Research—in the laboratory, in the hospital, and in the field—was to become the cornerstone of Norway's approach to the management of the disease.

In 1839, Daniel Cornelius Danielssen, then a physician at St. Jørgens, was encouraged to continue his clinical investigations, and C. W. Boeck was awarded a travel grant to study leprosy in Europe. The two men published reports on leprosy in the early 1840s, and on the basis of their research the Norwegian government established a leprosy research center in Bergen. Lungegaard Hospital, with beds for ninety patients, was completed in 1849, and Danielssen became its first chief physician. In 1847, Danielssen and Boeck published a two-volume work, *Om Spedalskhed* and *Atlas Colorié de Spedalskhed*, which dealt with postmortem findings and clinical studies. It was reprinted a year later in a prize-winning French edition, *Traité de la Spedalskhed ou Elephantiasis des Grecs*. The eminent German pathologist Rudolf Virchow was later to call this work "the beginning of the biologic knowledge of leprosy."[15]

Surgeon-Major Henry Vandyke Carter, who would visit Norway in 1873 at the request of Her Majesty's Home Government in India, provided a description of the leprosy research center at Lungegaard Hospital:

I have lastly to mention the *Lungegaards-hospitalet*. This is an institution adapted for the clinical study of leprosy, and for the cure of the disease, so far as may be accomplished under the more auspicious conditions. The patients, who are selected subjects, are either young in years, or but recently affected by their malady; or in other respects seem fit for special treatment and promising cure. . . . They were 78 in number at the close of 1870. . . . The hospital is thoroughly provided with the *matériel* necessary for every variety of curative procedure, and for all kinds of scientic research. The supply of drugs is unrestricted, and the library and laboratory are freely maintained by Government in an efficient condition.[16]

The research investigations undertaken by Danielssen and Boeck on leprosy had two far-reaching consequences. Their studies of morbid anatomy led to the classification of leprosy into two principal types, the tubercle (nodular) and the anesthetic. This typological distinction, as Yoshio Yoshie, director of the National Institute of Leprosy Research, Tokyo, noted more than a century and a quarter later, is "still shedding light on the medical science of leprology."[17]

A second aspect of their work dealt with the cause of leprosy and its transmission. The view held by Danielssen and Boeck was that leprosy was for the most part inherited, with about one-eighth of all cases attributable to "spontaneous outbreaks," due to unsanitary and severe environmental and living conditions. In the course of his work, Danielssen, like many future investigators, repeatedly inoculated himself and others with leprous tissue but never succeeded in transmitting the disease. This failure reinforced his view that leprosy was an inherited condition, a "congenital dyscrasia," as it was termed.

However, even at the time of the publication of *Om Spedalskhed*, not all scientists agreed with Danielssen. Some still favored a miasmatic theory; among others there was a growing suspicion, but little direct evidence, that the disease might prove to be contagious. Nonetheless, heredity was to remain the dominant medical view for years to come, owing in part to the scientific stature of Danielssen and Boeck but, more important, to the absence of any convincing alternative explanation.

The logical strategy of a hereditary position, in terms of disease control, would be to prohibit known lepers from reproducing. Such a prohibition had, in fact, been proposed earlier by Danielssen and Boeck and endorsed, in 1851, by the permanent medical committee of the Department for the Interior.[18] The success of such a control scheme depended, however, on the effective implementation of two component programs. The first was to ban all marriages among lepers and their descendants "in the first and second degree."[19] Such a ban necessitated detailed knowledge about all lepers and their families throughout the country. To collect this information was one reason that the 1856 national leprosy registry was started, and an extensive administrative apparatus was assembled to secure the information. The second step in the control scheme was to establish a series of nursing homes throughout the country, where patients would not only receive medical treatment but where they would also be sexually isolated.

The proposal to prevent lepers from marrying was never implemented. The idea had aroused considerable debate, and according to Richards,[20] indications arose as early as 1845 that Parliament would not go along with the suggestion. However, the other recommendation, that nursing homes be established for lepers, was implemented. Between 1854 and 1861, hospitals to house a total of 680 patients were either constructed or enlarged, in addition to the 250 beds already available at St. Jørgens and Lungegaard. Carter provides a brief description of these facilities as they existed in 1873.

The Trondhjem Asylum, known officially as the *Reitgjerdets Pleiestiftelse*. At the high latitude of this ancient capital of Norway . . . a leper hospital has, it is said, existed from the thirteenth century, but first was made a regular establishment in 1612, when one division was set apart for lepers. The asylum was finally much enlarged in 1861, and at the end of the year 1870 contained 226 inmates.

At Molde, somewhat south of Trondhjem . . . is situated the asylum known as the *Reknaes Hospital* and *Pleiestiftelse*. It was erected in 1713 for the reception of lepers from Romsdal (a highly picturesque but much infested district), and it was afterwards enlarged, also in 1861; at present its inmates amount to about 150.

At Bergen, a town itself free from the complaint, are situated two other asylums appertaining to the districts north and south of the locality. To the north of Bergen, especially, does leprosy prevail, and here is the worst of all known districts. *St. Jörgens Hospital* I have already named as one of the oldest institutions known in the country; in 1654 it was converted into a refuge for the affected from Bergen town and district, and it is yet maintained, having, in 1870, 62 inmates. The present building is an antiquated one; every patient has a small chamber or berth for himself, and there are corridors with a large central space. It is contemplated to make certain changes in this establishment.

Adjoining the last, and in the eastern outskirts of the town, is the asylum, altogether a new structure, known as *Pleiestiftelsen No. 1*. This was opened in 1857 for the reception of sick from the neighbourhood, and from the south; it is the largest in size, and in 1870 had 225 inmates. . . .

I have lastly to mention the *Lungegaards-hospitalet*.[21] [This facility was described earlier in this chapter.]

An important feature of the Norwegian leprosy control program was to locate medical facilities in those parts of the country where the disease was prevalent. This practice had a number of advantages. It integrated treatment and care with surveillance and patient registration and made it unnecessary to remove patients to long distances from the districts in which they lived. The earlier report of 1838 recommending the creation of nursing homes had also not suggested that lepers be totally segregated. The second clause of the report stated that "other cases of skin disease may also be admitted into [the] hospital, should there be room."[22]

Norway's leprosy control program was expensive. Carter recorded that Norway spent nearly one-fiftieth of its national revenue, "if not more, on the single object of ameliorating the condition of the leprous poor."[23] Each facility, Carter wrote, "comprises a resident director, apothecary, steward, and full staff of servants."[24] Carter, who had experience with leprosy in India, had high praise for Norwegian physicians and the quality of scientific care that Norway employed in the management of the disease: "At the present day in no other part of the world, as far as I am aware, are there equally complete, well- conducted, and successful leper-asylums as in Norway; and the physicians in charge are often eminent men, versed in modern science and of European repute."[25]

Thus, within the span of less than a quarter of a century, from 1832 to 1856, Norway, a small, impoverished, but forward-looking country, had already conducted four nationwide leprosy censuses, established a permanent national leprosy registry, funded a research center for clinical study at Lungegaard Hospital, laid plans for the completion of four inpatient treatment centers, sent Hjort and Boeck abroad to study the disease in other European countries, put into operation a national leprosy control scheme, and formulated an accepted theory of the pathogenesis of the disease.

But the theory that leprosy was a disease of heredity was somewhat fragile scientifically at the time that Danielssen and Boeck had endorsed it. By the middle of the nineteenth century the existence of bacteria was widely accepted. Anton van Leeuwenhoek definitely saw and described bacteria as early as 1683. In 1786 Johann Ernst Wichmann described the itchmite that causes scabies, and in 1837 Agostino Bassi found the muscardine of silkworms to be due to plant parasites. At about the same time Charles Cagniard de la Tour and Theodor Schwann demonstrated that fermentation is due to the action of small organisms—yeasts.

Observing bacteria and other microorganisms under the microscope was one thing; proving that bacteria could be the cause of specific diseases was something else. Bacteriological theory was advanced deductively by the anatomist Friedrich Gustave Jakob Henle, who in 1840 formulated the thesis that living organisms—*contagia anamata*—were the cause of contagious and infectious disease. More important, he "indicated the principles upon which experimental proof of his ideas would be based."[26] George Rosen, who translated Henle's article into English, also summarized Henle's main theoretical argument:

> In cases of infectious diseases the morbid matter apparently increases from the moment it enters the body, leading to the conclusion that it must be organic in nature since only living organisms have such faculties. The fact that a certain period of incubation usually precedes the outbreak of the disease also supports this conclusion. Having thus made it logically plausible, that the causative factor in infectious diseases is a living organism, the nature of the as yet unknown parasite must be considered, and here Henle, basing his theoretical considerations on the observations of Bassi and Audouin, who, in their researches on the muscardine—an infectious disease of the silkworms, had found the cause to be a fungus, comes to the conclusion that it is very likely a member of the plant kingdom.[27]

The conditions that Henle postulated—constant existence of the parasite—created bacteriological problems that were difficult to solve. It was not until the work of Robert Koch in the 1870s and 1880s that a scientist was able to fulfill Henle's theoretical conditions and furnish definite proof substantiating the argument.

In terms of disease theory, the years between the publication of *Om Spedalskhed* in 1847 and Hansen's discovery of *Mycobacterium leprae* in 1873 were years of scientific ferment. In Norway, as Carter observed, debate about the pathogenesis of leprosy was the order of the day.

> Respecting the *causes* of leprosy . . . I have not during my tour in Norway found less debate there than elsewhere. The early advisers of Government laid stress on hereditary transmission as the paramount cause of leprosy, and Drs. Danielssen and Boeck, at least, still hold that view; it was, too, my own conclusion, independently formed. But I have been conversant with medical men who believe in the endemic origin (miasmatic)—the contagious, the dietetic, hygienic, and the climatic source of the disease. The more erratic views I need not allude to.[28]

In terms of disease theory, Singer and Underwood have described the period following midcentury as "very confused."[29] Not only were ideas debated intensely, but, more important, a new generation of scientists was being spawned who were maturing on the new explosive social and intellectual ideas that were coming to fruition in Europe. Koch was a student of Henle at Göttingen, and Hansen described his own awakening on first discovering Darwin's *Natürliche Schöpfungsgeschichte*.[30] Late in the century two generations of scientists would battle over the issue of disease theory: older men who had studied the course of epidemics through observing their history and geography and, now, a new generation prepared to find different answers to old questions under the microscope and in the laboratory. The competition of ideas and generations created an atmosphere of scientific tension, a tension that was soon reflected in decisions concerning the making of leprosy policy.

Social policy and control programs in the management of leprosy in Norway hinged on scientific knowledge of causation. However, even before Hansen observed *Mycobacterium leprae* and concluded that the microorganism was the likely causative agent in leprosy, there were already enough discomfort with the theory of heredity and enough events relating to leprosy in other parts of the world to force Norwegian scientists to look more closely at the available data. The national leprosy registry set up in 1856 had not only established a nationwide administrative system for the surveillance and examination of patients, it had accumulated a baseline of epidemiological information that was almost immediately used to study the cause of the disease. Work by O. G. Høegh, begun as early as 1857, and by J. L. Bidenkap was already supportive of the hypothesis that leprosy was an infectious disease.[31] It remained for Hansen, in 1873, to discover the bacteriological evidence.

THE PIONEERING WORK OF HANSEN

Gerhard Henrik Armauer Hansen was born in Bergen in 1841. He completed his medical training at the University of Christiana (University of Oslo) in 1867 and then interned at the state hospital in Christiana. Following his internship he left for the Lofoten Islands, far to the north, to serve as a doctor at the cod fisheries. On his return to Bergen, Hansen obtained a position at Lungegaard Hospital, where he first came into contact with leprosy patients. Hansen wrote of his early experience at Lungegaard:

> I suffered terribly. I had never seen so much misery concentrated in one place.
> Gradually, though, as I commenced handling the patients, my aversion
> disappeared and was replaced by a great desire to learn the illness in detail.
> As I commenced *post mortems* my interest grew deeper. Pathological anatomy
> was my greatest interest in life and here I discovered many things about it I
> had never seen before. I suspected that some were entirely new to medical
> science. The result was that after a few months I eagerly looked forward to
> dealing with my ravaged patients.[32]

Hansen's studies at the University of Christiana on the anatomy of lymph nodes had earned him a gold medal and were useful in his first scientific paper on leprosy, a general pathological description of the disease, published in 1869.[33] In the spring of 1870, Hansen obtained a travel grant to work in the laboratory of Max Schultz, in Bonn, but he found the stay in Bonn to be of limited value.[34]

On leaving Bonn, Hansen traveled—to Heidelberg, Dresden, Berlin, and Venice. Of Vienna he wrote that "one of the most important occurrences in my life happened." He had discovered the writings of Charles Darwin, whose work, according to Hansen, was completely unknown in Norway.

> [W]hen I came upon a copy of "Natural Evolution" fate was at my elbow. The
> title itself challenged everything I had been taught about creation. . . . Never
> had I read anything like it. The whole world stood out in an entirely different
> light than that which I had known. All I had been taught as a child collapsed
> as something unreal. The track on which my thought had formerly moved
> suddenly terminated and everything beyond was out of focus. . . . Later, after
> I had returned to Norway, I studied the works of Darwin in depth. They
> became the foundation of my outlook on life. It was a time in which I came
> into the full realization of how a country like mine had remained so far
> removed from significant developments in the outer world. As a student I had
> never heard a word about this man Darwin and his work, either at the
> university or in my circle of acquaintances. As far as I know, I was the first
> man to bring the scientist and his teachings to the attention of the Norwegian
> people when I wrote a series of articles for the Bergen Post.[35]

Hansen belonged to the younger generation of scientists that was emerging at the time. His proficiency in the use of the microscope was already evident. He is known to have been well acquainted with the work in Norway of

E.F.H. Winge and H. Heiberg, who were investigating chainlike threads, microorganisms later identified as streptococci, found in the heart valves of patients who had died of sepsis. Hansen's commitment to a theory of contagion in the transmission of leprosy was already firm in the early 1870s. Using analogies from other known contagious diseases, particularly syphilis, Hansen's underlying premise was that leprosy was a specific disease, a distinct nosological entity with a clearly definable cause, and not, as others before him had assumed, a degenerative condition resulting from various causes.

During the next few years, Hansen continued to work in the laboratory, in the hospital, and in the field. For two years, during the summer months, he traveled through the western districts of Norway to observe leprosy and conduct field investigations. In a report issued in 1873 and reprinted in abbreviated form in a Norwegian journal the next year,[36] Hansen mentioned for the first time the observation of bacteria-like formations found in leprous nodes resembling, he noted, "Klebs's pictures of zoogloeic masses."[37]

In 1875, Hansen was appointed chief medical officer for leprosy in Norway. Convinced that leprosy was a contagious disease, he set about to make changes in the Norwegian leprosy control program. In Norway, at this time, the seclusion of patients in their homes or in hospitals was based on a voluntary system. Hansen proposed that the system be changed to permit the enforced isolation of the most contagious cases, including even those persons whose general condition was otherwise good. The argument for enforced isolation devolved on calculations extrapolated from the national registry estimating the number of cases expected in the various districts in the years that followed. The prevalence of leprosy in Norway was expected to decrease, but not as quickly, Hansen argued, as it would if legal measures were taken.

Before 1877, at which time the Act for the Maintenance of Poor Lepers was passed, there were no laws in Norway that compelled lepers to enter a hospital; the "majority either came voluntarily or were driven to do so by their poverty."[38] The 1877 Act related to reforms in the boarding-out system, an established welfare measure for the support of the indigent of a parish. Those parishioners who could not support themselves were sent in succession to different farms to work. The Act declared that thereafter impoverished lepers who were unable to work and thereby maintain themselves would be hospitalized. The Act passed Parliament without much opposition.[39]

In 1885 the Act on the Seclusion of Lepers was passed, superceding the Act of 1877. Unlike the 1877 Act, however, the new bill gave rise to intense debate. Critics of the bill viewed enforced isolation as a burden that should not be imposed on persons who already had enough problems. They further argued that the bill was unnecessary because leprosy was already decreasing: The number of new cases by five-year periods had declined from 1,040 in the years 1861–1865 to 373 by 1885 (see Figure 4.2). The bill passed nevertheless, supported by Hansen's argument that the number of new cases declined most rapidly in those districts of the country where the hospitalization of lepers prevailed. Although the theory of contagion was gaining acceptance in Norway at the time, the danger of contagion was assumed to be slight, and intimate contact over a long period was believed necessary for transmission to occur. Despite passage of the bill and a belief in contagion, isolation measures in Norway remained relatively mild. Hospital patients had full freedom of movement, the main requirement being that they spend the night in the hospital.[40] In 1884, Dr. Henri Camille C. Leloir, author of *Traité Pratique et Théorique de la Lèpre*, visited Norway and, according to Roose, stated that "when visiting Norway . . . he found that the lepers entered and left the hospital just as they pleased. They manufactured various articles which were sold in the streets, and even mended boots and shoes. He saw at Bergen lepers standing in the market-place, offering eatables and other objects for sale."[41]

The cause of the decline of leprosy in Norway during the second half of the nineteenth century has been the subject of much debate. Although the Norwegian epidemiological data supported a correlation by districts between the hospitalization of the more infectious cases and a decline in the incidence of new cases, the effectiveness of isolation in reducing that incidence remains an issue that is still being investigated. Historically, the tendency has been to credit isolation with playing an all-important role in bringing about a decrease in the disease. H. P. Lie, who succeeded Hansen in 1912 as chief medical officer for leprosy, presented a retrospective analysis of the Norwegian data to the Scandinavian Dermatologists Society in 1928 in which he acknowledged the importance of economic progress in the country and improvements in hygiene and sanitation since 1856 in causing a decrease in the prevalence of leprosy in Norway. He concluded nonetheless that "*isolation* . . . played a considerable role" in bringing this decline about.[42] Not all observers, even at the end of the nineteenth century, were equally convinced, however. W. J. Collins, a British doctor of public health who visited Norway in 1889, wrote:

> To attribute the decline of leprosy in Norway to compulsory isolation is entirely erroneous. In the first place, no such powers exist or are likely to be sanctioned by the Norse democracy; if they did exist, it would be impossible without further accommodation to segregate even the reduced number of lepers in Norway at the present time. . . . It is not that segregation is stamping out leprosy in Norway, but the increased material prosperity of the people . . . and the opportunities . . . for better and more varied subsistence, which have doubtless effected beneficent changes in this direction.[43]

Recently, Lorentz M. Irgens, head of the Institute of Hygiene and Social Medicine, University of Bergen, used the same body of data available to Lie—the national leprosy registry—to reanalyze the epidemiology of leprosy in Norway with reference to the role of isolation:

> In the first period [1856–1875] the epidemic was at its peak, with relatively high prevalence rates. Under such circumstances the present findings suggest

that an effect of isolation may be expected. The second period [1876–1895] covers a situation of rapid decline in the epidemic. Under these circumstances isolation would seem to have had little effect. In the third period [1896–1920] the epidemic is at an end and an effect of isolation can apparently not be expected.

This means that the answer to the question of whether there is an effect of isolation is neither a definite yes nor a definite no. It all depends on the epidemiological situation.[44]

Legal measures in Norway compelling the seclusion of lepers were enacted midway during Irgens's "second period," 1876–1895, when the epidemic was in rapid decline and where the effects of isolation were negligible. Furthermore, the seclusion of lepers was never firm in Norway, neither before the Act of 1885 nor after it, and the number of lepers hospitalized was never large (see Figure 4.1). Only in 1890 were more patients in hospitals than outside of them, and of those hospitalized many, Lie wrote, "lay in hospital only a relatively short time during their illness. Some came in only to die, after having lain ill at home for many years."[45] While the Act of 1885 provided that "all leprosy patients must either be isolated in separate rooms in their homes, or admitted to hospital, if necessary with the help of the police,"[46] seclusion in hospitals was not rigidly enforced. Many patients remained at home, where "indifference," Lie noted, "[to the law] must have been very great. . . . Thus we see that, of the lepers found to exist in 1856, no less than 70 had got married, notwithstanding that they had presented unmistakable signs of leprosy."[47] Home isolation, Irgens and Bjerkedal wrote, historically was "in many cases illusory."[48]

Norwegian history shows little evidence that a diagnosis of leprosy was especially discrediting. In his memoirs, Hansen commented that "the Norwegian state had always handled its leprosy victims humanely."[49] More recently, Irgens wrote:

> The isolation enforced in Norway was in practice definitely mild. "Isolated" hospital patients in the city of Bergen were allowed to go to the markets for shopping. They were also allowed to return to their homes in the districts on leaves of a duration of several weeks; this I documented in the leprosy registry which has now been transformed to a EDP-file. Furthermore, handicraft produced in the leprosaria was very popular among the citizens of Bergen; wool was delivered at the hospitals and the finished products were brought to the homes around in the city. These facts should indicate a practice of mild isolation (and not strong public stigma).[50]

Leprosy, like other diseases in Norway, was unwelcome to be sure. But like other conditions of hardship and poverty, the disease was more a part of life than an "undesired differentness."[51] And although the Act of 1885 contained the provision that, if necessary, isolation could be enforced with the aid of the police, there was throughout the nineteenth century in Norway sufficient public, professional, and parliamentary concern for the civil liberties of lepers to mitigate the imposition of restrictive or punitive measures. The proposal in the early 1850s to forbid lepers to marry was rejected by Parliament, as those "outside the medical profession" opposed the bill "with great animosity."[52]

Norway's concern for the basic freedom of its leper population extended to the care and treatment they received in hospitals, reaching into high places and affecting high officials, among them Hansen himself. In 1880, by order of the Ministry of Justice, Hansen was permanently relieved of his duties as doctor at the leprosy hospital in Bergen, a position he held in joint tenure as chief medical officer for leprosy in Norway.

The circumstances under which he was charged and later convicted have recently been reviewed by Knut Blom, Justice of the Supreme Court of Norway.[53] Hansen, like many scientists before his time and since, had tried to induce the leprosy bacillus to grow in vivo, human or animal, through inoculation. Following the description of *Mycobacterium tuberculosis* and the conditions laid down by Koch for the recognition of a bacillus as the cause of a specific disease, Hansen began a new series of studies. One of these studies, on November 3, 1879, involved the inoculation of material taken from a leprous nodule into the eye of a 33-year-old woman, Kari Nielsdatter Spidsöen, who was hospitalized with leprosy. Because the woman already had leprosy, Hansen's purpose was to determine whether a more malignant form of the disease could be produced through inoculation.

The operation had no effect on the patient's leprosy, somewhat weakened the sensitivity of the connective tissue of her eye, and caused some initial pain and emotional distress. The matter was brought to public attention by a pastor who served at the hospital. The charge against Hansen was that he performed the experiment without first obtaining the patient's consent and without informing her of the purpose of the procedure. Hansen did not deny the charge, noting that he deliberately had not asked for permission because he had not expected it would be granted.[54]

This incident is offered here not as a sidelight on Hansen's professional activities. As Justice Blom wrote, it demonstrates that the Norwegian people were prepared to "champion the patients' cause."[55] The issue was not just Hansen's scientific indiscretion, but rather, as the chief magistrate noted at the trial, that his actions had so undermined patient confidence in Hansen as to interfere with his medical duties. Hansen's popularity with leprosy patients was never high, for he held strident views about the need for isolation, "forcibly imposed if necessary." As an atheist premised on scientific rationalism in an otherwise devoutly religious country, he held the view that "one was oneself to blame" for contracting the disease—an opinion he deemed "more worthy" and demanding more "moral courage than casting the blame on providence or fate."[56]

The outcome of the case had no appreciable effect on Hansen's stature. After a four-hour hearing he was fined 90 kroner in court costs. The joint positions he held as leprosy doctor at the hospital and as chief medical officer for leprosy in Norway were divided into two positions. The former position was abolished, and Hansen continued to retain his major post for the remainder of his life. He died in 1912, thirty-two years after the incident, at the age of seventy-one. Within the framework of the next 100 years of difficulties in further unraveling the biomedical mysteries of *Mycobacterium leprae*, Hansen's bacteriological accomplishment in the 1870s commands an awesome respect today.

NORWAY AS A ROLE MODEL

Although a relatively minor country among the more powerful and ambitious Western nations, Norway achieved a position of scientific preeminence in the field of leprosy in the nineteenth century. In pursuing the disease Norwegian scientists did not confine their investigations to Norway alone. In the years 1863, 1869, and 1887, three eminent Norwegian leprologists traveled to the United States to study leprosy in Norwegians who had emigrated to the United States and settled in the Upper Mississippi Valley. The purpose in each case was to explore further the question of the cause of leprosy. Each man held divergent views. J. A. Holmboe was a believer in the theory of spontaneous origin. Boeck held to heredity. Hansen sought further confirmation to disprove the hereditary view. Each man, according to Lie,[57] emerged from his inquiries convinced of the essential correctness of his own position. The investigations in the United States contributed little of direct significance to the debate about cause. However, they intensified interest in the disease and concern for the welfare of leprosy patients in the Upper Mississippi Valley among physicians who themselves were of Scandinavian descent.

Scandinavian immigration to the United States was relatively low at first. Only 77,874 Norwegians had arrived in the forty-year period from 1825 to 1865. After the Civil War, however, immigration increased substantially, and an exogenous focus of leprosy appeared in the Upper Mississippi Valley, particularly in Minnesota, Wisconsin, and Iowa. Scientists in Norway were aware of the emigration of Norwegian lepers. In a paper summarized in an 1888 edition of Rudolf Virchow's archives under the title "The Heredity of Lepra," Hansen attested to the fact that "160 lepers have come into the states of Wisconsin, Minnesota, and Dakota."[58] Danielssen, in 1852, is reported as having told *The New York Times* that "the disease will show itself among those emigrants; for he knows leprous individuals who have gone to the United States."[59]

Norwegian medical interest in their emigrating countrymen was not confined to leprosy alone. As early as 1857, Dr. Joachim A. Voss had traveled to the United States specifically for the purpose of studying the effects that migration and a changed environment had on the medical and health conditions of the immigrant population.[60] In fact, throughout the period of Norwegian emigration there was a continuous and sustained interest, both in Norway and in the United States, about life and events taking place in each country.[61] One consequence of the interchange that was maintained between those who remained behind in Norway and those who had emigrated was that the same calm and rational attitude toward leprosy that prevailed in Norway also prevailed among the settlers and among physicians of Scandinavian descent. Many of these physicians came to occupy prominent positions in the state boards of health in the Upper Mississippi Valley.

Norwegian achievements in leprosy research and in managing the disease were recognized by other European nations. The eminent German pathologist Rudolf Virchow visited Danielssen in 1859. In 1873, Her Majesty's Government in India sent Surgeon-Major Henry Vandyke Carter to inquire "into the mode in which that pest is dealt with in the enlightened kingdom of Norway."[62] One of Carter's purposes was to see what in Norway's approach could be adapted to conditions in India, where leprosy was also hyperendemic. However, despite European recognition and despite all its scientific and public health accomplishments, Norway's experience with leprosy was overshadowed, late in the nineteenth century, by leprosy-related events then occurring in other parts of the world.

The late nineteenth century witnessed a remarkable transformation in the patterning and magnitude of world migration and in the "opening up" of new lands in foreign territories. Spurred on by Western imperialism, by colonialism, and by structural changes in European societies, great segments of humankind were on the move. Everywhere, people were coming into direct, firsthand contact with cultures in other parts of the world. Accompanying this mass movement of people was an increase in the means of transportation and communication. Events occurring in far-off places were converted into news at home in what, at the time, seemed like record pace. International interest in leprosy grew as more and more cases of leprosy were reported among alien races in foreign countries and territories now being brought within the expanding colonial orbit.

Among events in other parts of the world were reports of an increase in leprosy in Hawaii in the early 1860s, believed to have been introduced into those islands by immigrant Chinese laborers. The outbreak in Hawaii prompted Great Britain, in 1862, to conduct an investigation of leprosy in all of its foreign colonies.[63] In that same decade there was also a study of leprosy in Dutch Guiana.[64] The French, unlike the British, leaned firmly toward a view that leprosy was a contagious disease—a position that Hansen acknowledged in 1872 had influenced his own thinking.[65] Following events in Hawaii, British administrators in India became preoccupied with containing the disease on that subcontinent. Throughout the Western world the thought that China might export leprosy along with "coolies" became a frightening obsession at a time when an ideology of a "yellow peril" was beginning to crystallize in Europe and the United States.

Sanitary conferences to standardize quarantine procedures and to control the spread of epidemic diseases were initiated among Western nations during the period of mass migration. The first such series of meetings was held in 1851, and by the end of the century sanitary conferences were an institutionalized part of international relations. The first congress to specifically address the spread of leprosy was held in Berlin in 1897. It was sponsored by the Emperor of Germany, presided over by Virchow, and attended by representatives from at least fifteen Western nations. The cause of leprosy, its mode of transmission, and, above all, the management of lepers were uppermost in the minds of the leprologists and government officials who attended the meeting. The fear late in the century was that leprosy would spread, principally from the Far East. China was regarded as the main source. That the First International Leprosy Congress was held in Berlin was perhaps symbolic. Only two years earlier Kaiser Wilhelm II, in a cartoon drawn in 1895, gave popular coinage to the phrase "yellow peril." The cartoon, published in the *Review of Reviews* early in 1896, depicted the nations of Europe as mail-clad Valkyries standing high upon a rock beneath a radiant cross. Before them stood the Archangel Gabriel, sword in hand, pointing toward a horrible spectacle in the East. High in the smoke of the burning cities of Europe, a Chinese dragon emerged bearing a seated Buddha on its back. Beneath the cartoon the Kaiser wrote: "Nations of Europe! Join in Defense of Your Faith and Your Home!"[66]

At the time of the leprosy congress, scientists were still divided in their opinion about the cause of leprosy and decidedly pessimistic about other biomedical features of the disease. Although Hansen's work had convinced many scientists that leprosy was a germ disease, there were still much uncertainty and little exact knowledge at the time to explain how the disease behaved. The theory of heredity was still alive in the minds of some, although it was noted to be losing ground "in comparison with the new generally accepted theory of its contagiousness." Treatment, it was observed, "has only had palliative results up to the present time." Serum therapy "has so far been unsuccessful." Leprosy, the conference concluded, was "virtually incurable."[67]

By the time the first congress of leprologists met in Berlin, the number of new cases of the disease had already decreased appreciably both in Norway and in Hawaii. In Norway, where the disease had been endemic, the number of new cases by five-year periods had declined from 1,040 in the years 1861–1865 to only 89 cases in the years 1896–1900 (see Figure 4.2). In Hawaii, where the consensus was that leprosy had been recently introduced to a virgin population by immigrating Chinese laborers, the number of new cases had also decreased—by more than half for the ten-year interval between 1886–1890 and 1896–1900, from 1,310 new cases to 513.[68]

Quarantine and isolation were accepted measures for the control of epidemics late in the nineteenth century. Many scientists believed that quarantine would be equally effective when applied to leprosy, despite the fact that leprosy was known to be a chronic disease with a long incubation period. Despite the absence of field-based epidemiological surveys and the lack of corroborating evidence, government officials and leprologists never-theless pointed to Hawaii and the leper colony at Molokai as proof that the disease was reduced with the practice of segregating lepers. In Norway, however, the situation was different. Here excellent epidemiological data had existed since 1856. Although Hansen used this material to demonstrate a correlation in the reduction in the incidence of leprosy in those districts where patients were hospitalized, isolation was never practiced systematically and was not introduced into Norwegian law until after the epidemic had peaked. Even then, it was never vigorously enforced.

The idea of isolating foreign lepers, however, strongly appealed to the officials of imperialist nations who feared the disease might spread to Western shores as a result of increased contact with colonial populations. In 1897, at the First International Leprosy Congress, the following resolution was introduced: "In countries in which leprosy forms foci or has great extension, isolation is the best means of preventing the spread of the disease. The system of obligatory notification and of observation and isolation, as carried out in Norway, is recommended to all nations with local self-government and a sufficient number of physicians."[69] The resolution, proposed by Hansen, was passed by the congress on the grounds of "the serious and detrimental effects which [leprosy's] existence in a community causes, and considering the good results which have followed the adoption of legal measures of isolation in Norway."[70] Thus, history records that in advocating isolation in the management of leprosy, the congress erroneously offered Norway's program as the model.

Starting early in the nineteenth century Norway perfected a rational, basic medical science approach to the eradication of leprosy. The history of leprosy in Norway was a model of collaboration between research and public health practice. The model was both scientific and humane. The interplay of research and public health resulted in a number of outstanding scientific achievements and produced little, if any, lepraphobia in Norway.

Leprosy had declined in two major foci of disease activity without benefit of systematic isolation, and no new epidemics on the scale of the one in Hawaii had come to Western attention in more than thirty years. Nevertheless, at the end of the century, officials of imperialist nations were exceedingly apprehensive that the disease posed a major threat to Western civilization. Notwithstanding Norway's accomplishment in reducing the incidence of the disease, all that the Western world apparently heard at the end of the nineteenth century was the single idea—enforced isolation.

5

Hawaii: An Imperialist Solution

Leprosy was first recorded as a public issue in the Kingdom of Hawaii early in the 1860s, when, according to Dr. A.A.St.M. Mouritz, a longtime resident of the islands and former physician to the leper colony at Molokai, "the rapid spread and great increase of leprosy began to alarm the community."[1] The term "community" did not presume to include the 58,000 Hawaiians then living on the islands; nor did it refer to the nearly 1,000 Chinese in Hawaii at that time. Rather, the term referred exclusively to the small group of American and European residents who by the middle of the nineteenth century held positions of prominence in the political structure of Hawaii and occupied almost all of the important bureaucratic offices in the kingdom.[2]

Leprosy came to Western attention in Hawaii at a time when Norway was applying scientific methods in the study of the disease and had already implemented a humane treatment program. Although leprosy was known to exist in other regions of interest to the expanding Western world, such as India and the Far East, the approaches that evolved in Norway and Hawaii emerged as the two most important and also the most thoroughly contrasting models developed by Western nations in managing the disease. In Norway, science and medicine were combined with public health. This rational approach resulted in a number of scientific accomplishments, and it produced little fear of the disease in Norway and no stigma. In Hawaii the course of events took a totally different direction. Attitudes and policies flowed directly from Western imperialism and thus engendered a negative image of the disease. In Hawaii lepers acquired a discredited status. American and European residents in Hawaii feared the disease, and lepers were banished to the island of Molokai. This practice in Hawaii of segregating lepers initiated the modern use of isolated leper colonies, and by the end of the century Molokai became the Western model for controlling the disease worldwide.

Originally Hawaii's inhabitants were Polynesian. U.S. involvement in the Hawaiian Islands followed the classic colonial pattern of Western commercial and territorial expansion that spanned the nineteenth century. The road from a Polynesian society to U.S. statehood was a long and complex historical process in which the Polynesians had relatively little voice compared with the political involvement of the citizens of Western nations. By agreement among Western powers competing in the Pacific Ocean and in the Far East, the indigenous Polynesian monarchy became the Kingdom of Hawaii in 1840. A quasi-independent entity at best, the Kingdom of Hawaii lasted until 1894, when the Republic of Hawaii was created. Well within the U.S. sphere of influence, the Republic of Hawaii became a U.S. territory in 1900, and it remained so until statehood was granted in 1959.

The Hawaiian Islands first came to Western attention with the voyages of Captain James Cook at a time when maritime ascendancy in the Pacific was passing from the Spaniards into the hands of British and American traders. In an effort to replace markets lost as a result of American independence from Great Britain late in the eighteenth century, the Americans attempted trade with China, voyaging, as early as 1784, to the Far East by way of the Cape of Good Hope and the Indian Ocean. Cook's observations on his last voyage of the avid interest of Chinese merchants in furs soon reached the ears of American merchants. By 1786 not only was a new and prosperous trade under way, but a new trans-Pacific trade route was established that linked the New England seaports and the West Coast fur centers with Canton. In time the trans-Pacific sea-lanes became part of a complicated trade and economic network. The Hawaiian Islands, located conveniently in the path of vessels bound for China, were a vital link in this vast and complicated network known as the great "caravansary" of the North Pacific. The supply of American furs for the China trade was not inexhaustible, nor was the market. Profits could be high but were almost always uncertain. Rivalry was keen, and many voyages failed to produce a return on investment.

Yankee merchants were always on the alert for new trade items, and early in the nineteenth century they added Hawaiian sandalwood to their list. In the process they developed a new market, one that directly linked Canton with Hawaii. Sandalwood was in great demand in China as incense and in the making of delicate furniture, and a seemingly unlimited supply of it grew in Hawaii. Almost from the beginning, Hawaiian chiefs and rulers had been receptive to Western visitors and eager to participate in Western mercantile practices. In 1812, when the first large shipment of sandalwood was sold successfully in Canton, Western sea captains persuaded King Kamehameha I to grant them a three-year monopoly on selling sandalwood. This monopoly was granted, but not before the captains agreed to pay the king one-quarter of its market value. As long as supplies lasted and profits were made, Western traders sought increasing quantities of sandalwood and the Hawaiian monarch and chiefs increasingly diversified their terms of exchange. During the prosperous years of the trade, profits flowed both to the traders and to high-ranking Hawaiians. It is estimated that in 1821 about 30,000 piculs of sandalwood—nearly four million pounds—were shipped to China in that year alone.

The sandalwood trade flourished until the late 1820s, by which time the forests were beginning to show signs of overharvesting. Although riches flowed to some, the sandalwood trade severely disrupted the indigenous Hawaiian economy. More was involved than the depletion of the forests.

Sandalwood harvesting was labor-intensive and represented "a new, non-traditional source of wealth independent of the food surplus trade . . . [and thus made available] more goods and power to the [Hawaiian] chiefs."[3] In the feverish years of the trade, farming was often neglected, fewer fields were placed under cultivation, and hunger and famine among commoners occurred frequently. More to the point, however, is that the intensified Western contact with Hawaii brought about by the sandalwood trade "had a fatal impact on the Hawaiians . . . [bringing] previously unknown diseases, firearms, gun-powder, and alcohol."[4]

The trade in sandalwood also had a direct effect on the stability of the Hawaiian kingdom. Although Hawaiian leaders accumulated stores of wealth in the form of goods and possessions acquired in the course of dealing in sandalwood, they also acquired enormous debts. Before his death in 1819, King Kamehameha I, for example, had acquired, but not paid for, no fewer than six large sailing vessels. It is estimated that by 1821, Hawaiian chiefs owed European traders some 20,000 piculs of wood; the value of this debt rose to about $300,000 by 1824. The debt was vexatious to all parties. However, in time it worked to the advantage of the traders and provided leverage by which the Americans, through diplomacy, threats, and negotiation, were able to make further inroads on the economy and politics of the islands.

The development of the trans-Pacific trade also had a disintegrating effect on native Hawaiian culture and social structure. As historian Harold W. Bradley has noted, "with that development it required no prophetic genius to foresee that the age-old isolation of the Hawaiian Islands was at an end."[5] Hawaii was soon drawn into the web of Western maritime commercial rivalries and politics. By the middle of the nineteenth century, Hawaiian monarchs, though retaining their throne and titles, nevertheless exercised less and less power in their own country.

Contributing to this loss of power was the influence of Western contact in producing a decline in the Hawaiian population. From an estimated high of about 250,000 in 1778, the Hawaiian population fell to 53,900 in 1876. Among the leading causes of this decrease in population were a decline in fertility and an increase in infant mortality produced by (1) diseases introduced by early Western visitors, especially syphilis and gonorrhea, and (2) the disruption of the ancient social system and "the discarding of the old *kapus* (taboos) that controlled kinship and dietary patterns [reducing] protective measures and [increasing] the susceptibility of Hawaiian infants to disease."[6] In addition, a host of other infectious diseases occurred for which the islanders had neither natural immunity nor medical knowledge. An epidemic in about 1804–1805, believed to have been cholera, caused between 5,000 and 15,000 deaths.[7] Influenza, mumps, smallpox, whooping cough, scarlet fever, and tuberculosis were among the other prevalent, and at times epidemic, diseases that increased Hawaiian mortality.[8] Nevertheless, after midcentury, leprosy—although a nonkiller—was to become Hawaii's most infamous disease.

Emigration also reduced Hawaii's population. Young men joined the crews of trading ships. Some left feeling oppressed by the new land laws that were enacted as Westerners became more entrenched in Hawaii.[9] By 1850, 4,000 Hawaiians had left the kingdom, a number that "amounts to almost 5 percent of the total Hawaiian and part Hawaiian population at that time, and 12 percent of all Hawaiian males 18 years of age or more."[10]

Early in the 1820s, at the height of the sandalwood trade, two new elements of U.S. civilization, both emanating from New England, descended on the islands: (1) the whaling industry, which boosted the prosperity of the kingdom as a commercial center, and (2) the arrival of the first missionary families, a group that would eventually play a major role in the transformation of the social and political institutions of Hawaii.

The number of whaling vessels to visit Hawaiian ports steadily increased after 1820. Until the 1860s, when a plantation economy evolved, whaling remained the cornerstone of Hawaiian economic prosperity. Whaling increased the opportunity for the sale of American and European goods. Buyers could be found not only among the wealthier Hawaiian chiefs and visiting mariners, but also among Hawaiian commoners, who were beginning to find less expensive items now within their means.

The first group of missionaries included two young graduates of Andover Theological Seminary (Hiram Bingham and Asa Thurston), two teachers, one physician, one printer, and one farmer, along with all of their wives and three Hawaiian converts. They left New England in October 1819 and arrived in Kailua, Hawaii, at a time when traditional Hawaiian society was undergoing radical internal change. The arrival of this first group was part of a well-planned overseas missionary program launched by the New England Congregational and Presbyterian churches in 1810 and organized by the American Board of Commissioners for Foreign Missions.

The political influence of the United States in Hawaii is generally attributed to the work of American missionaries. At first, members were in a strict sense *amici curiae*, remaining in the background, teaching, and offering general counsel to Hawaiian monarchs and chiefs. Evangelism was their primary purpose; politics was not mentioned. However, their formal instruction to "raise up the whole people to an elevated state of Christian civilization"[11] gave more than a hint of the breadth of programs to come.

The most tangible accomplishments of the missionaries were the establishment of schools, the creation of a Hawaiian alphabet, and the printing of pamphlets, books, and, eventually, newspapers. In these efforts, which could not help but alter Hawaiian thinking, the missionaries received considerable support from Hawaiian leaders, as well as from resident foreigners with families who were pleased that their children would not be without formal Western schooling.

Formal schooling, initiated for the chiefs and their children and those of the foreign advisers, eventually offered primary and secondary education and manual training to a large portion of the Hawaiian population. By the late 1830s, however, the educational system had grown beyond the capabilities of the small group of American missionaries. Financially disturbed conditions in the United States limited U.S. support for Hawaiian education. In addition, French Catholics, eager to gain a foothold in Hawaii, posed a formidable threat to the sagging U.S.-supported system. France had more than a passing interest in Hawaii. Although French missionaries were expelled in 1831, owing largely to American pressure, they returned in 1836. In 1839 the Hawaiian government placed France on an equal footing with other Western nations.

In 1840, a solution to the problem of how to save Hawaiian education as an American enterprise was worked out. The plan involved turning the system over to the Hawaiians. American missionaries felt relatively comfortable in offering this transfer. It released them from underwriting the cost of maintaining the schools, but because their influence in island affairs was great, the transfer was expected to have little effect on their control of educational policy. The belief that the schools could safely be turned over to the Hawaiians and Hawaiian acceptance of this responsibility show just how much things had changed in Hawaii since the American missionaries had arrived twenty years earlier.

American and European residents were well received in Hawaii. Although influential in Hawaiian internal affairs, their position there remained somewhat precarious. Legitimatization of their presence was the one concern that united the heterogeneous community of foreign residents. That community was basically split along lines of national loyalties. It was further divided between the ideals of reform-minded missionaries and the aspirations of traders and men of commerce. Despite differences in purpose, both groups were foreigners in an alien world, and their special interests were regulated more by good will and amicable relations with Hawaiians than by any international system of rules and regulations. Over time, a number of issues strained relations between the Westerners and Hawaiians. These issues included the question of debts incurred by Hawaiian chiefs, the desertion of sailors, the expulsion of Catholic priests, the pressure by maritime powers for commercial and religious parity in Hawaii, and the resident status of the foreigners, especially as it pertained to land tenure. They remained unresolvable until common ground in international order was devised.

The system that was designed was basically Western in structure. The strategic importance of Hawaii was too grave in the early 1840s for any of the Western powers to risk forcibly seizing the islands, as France had attempted to do in 1839. One solution was the creation of a sovereign Hawaiian nation; this solution was equally sought by many Hawaiians. Thus, in 1840, a Hawaiian constitution was drawn up that dissolved many traditional institutions. Framed with the help of missionary advisers, it codified previous reforms and acts and added new legislative machinery. Within three years, the independence of Hawaii as a sovereign kingdom was recognized by the United States, Great Britain, France, and Belgium.

Westerners had long known that a variety of marketable crops could be grown in Hawaii. In fact, some small-scale manufacture of sugar and molasses had been going on since 1819. Until the 1830s, however, foreigners were reluctant to consider investing capital in large agricultural ventures. The most serious obstacle in Hawaii to agricultural development rested with the traditional land tenure system, whereby title was vested in the king or major chiefs, with tenants subject to eviction at any time. In 1835, after fluctuations in the whaling industry, the foreign community pressured the Hawaiian monarch into agreeing to lease a valuable tract of land on Kauai to a foreign firm. Further changes in land policy followed, aided by visits to Oahu in 1836 and 1837 by foreign warships. By 1840, land was being leased to the highest bidders for terms of twenty-five years, and in 1841, following the restructuring of the Hawaiian government, the Hawaiian legislature authorized the lease of land to foreigners for periods of up to fifty years.

With these changes in land policy, the way was now open for development of large-scale agriculture. Sugar appeared to be the most promising crop. In 1852, there were 1,650 acres on seven of the largest plantations already under cultivation. A year later, the number had risen to 2,750 acres.[12] Sugar production in 1852 amounted to 730,000 pounds; the amount rose to more than 27 million pounds in 1866.[13] In Hawaii, agricultural development was begun chiefly by Americans and controlled ultimately by U.S. interests.

American expansion into the west and northwest of what is now the United States, and the discovery of gold in California in 1848 and in Australia two years later, helped boost Hawaiian agriculture by opening new and closer markets. Capital investment came from the United States and Europe. Machinery was ordered from abroad, and foundries and machine shops were started locally. Land being sold for one dollar an acre in 1849 brought five dollars an acre one year later. Hawaii supplied the land and the climate. Western nations provided money, management skills, and expertise in agricultural technology. Only labor was to come from another part of the world, namely Asia.

Plantation labor in the large numbers needed and under terms agreeable to estate managers was not forthcoming from Hawaiian commoners. Estate labor was an innovation in the Hawaiian social economy, one totally at variance with Hawaiian notions of work relationships. Although highly regarded as sailors and considered competent enough when it came to doing simple tasks on shore, Hawaiians were judged to be completely worthless for plantation work. For agricultural development to succeed in Hawaii, new and large sources of labor were needed. American and European laborers were unwilling to migrate, other South Sea islanders were considered unacceptable, and the importation of Negroes was opposed by Hawaiian planters.[14] In a plantation economy the terms of employment were an important consideration. From the point of view of management, contract labor was essential. Thus, in 1851, the importation of Chinese coolies began. With 180 arriving that year, followed by another 100 a year later, it was hoped that this was the beginning of the solution to the labor problem.

Replenishing the labor supply was not the only population issue that Hawaii faced at midcentury. A decline in the native population, noted for

TABLE 5.1
The Nationalities of the Population at All the Census Dates from 1866 Onward

Nationality	1866	1872[a]	1878	1884	1890
Natives	57,125	49,044	44,088	40,014	34,436
Half-castes	1,640	1,487	3,420	4,218	6,186
Chinese	1,206	1,938	5,916	17,937	15,301
Americans		889	1,276	2,066	1,928
Hawaiian-born of Foreign Parents		849	947	2,040	7,495
English		619	883	1,282	1,344
Portuguese		395	436	9,377	8,602
Germans	2,988	224	272	1,600	1,434
French		88	81	192	70
Japanese		--	--	116	12,360
Norwegian		--	--	362	227
Other Foreigners		364	666	416	419
Polynesian		--	--	956	588
TOTAL	62,959	56,867	47,985	80,578	89,990

[a]This was the first census at which the complete division of nationalities was noted.

Source: Thompson, J. Ashburton. "Leprosy in Hawaii: A Critical Enquiry." Mittheilungen und Verhandlungen der internationale wissenschaftlichen Lepra-Conferenz zu Berlin, 1897. (A Hirchwald: Berlin, 1898), Part 3, Table 5, 273.

several decades by foreign observers, gave rise to the speculation that this decrease would eventually nullify any possibility for Hawaiians to play much of a role in the future development of the islands. From an estimated 130,000 Hawaiians in 1832, the indigenous population had decreased to 40,000 by 1890—a figure that included more than 6,000 persons each of whom had one parent who was non-Hawaiian.[15] On the other hand, the foreign community had increased, from an estimated 2,000 people in 1853 to nearly 50,000 in 1890. Thus, ten years before U.S. annexation of the islands, the foreign population already exceeded the number of native Hawaiians.[16]

Until the 1850s the foreign population in Hawaii predominantly comprised Americans and Europeans, with only a handful of Chinese, Japanese, and natives of other Pacific islands. After the rise of the plantation economy, however, the composition of the foreign population underwent a dramatic shift, first with the arrival of large numbers of indentured Chinese male laborers and then, late in the century, with Japanese immigration. Table 5.1 shows the changes that took place in the population of Hawaii from 1866 to 1890. In 1866 the Chinese constituted only 2 percent of the total population. This figure rose slightly to 3 percent in 1872, to 12 percent in 1878, and to 22 percent in 1884. By 1884 there were almost as many Chinese on the islands as all other foreigners combined.

By the 1880s the question of whether Hawaii would eventually be annexed to the United States was no longer moot. It was only a question of when and under what circumstances. Although there were many U.S. foreign policy debates later in the century about the place of and need for the Hawaiian Islands, the growing Chinese population in Hawaii and the imperialistic stirrings of China were of grave concern to U.S. diplomats at a time when, in the United States, sinophobia and yellow peril were developing as ideological issues.

A special concern to U.S. diplomats based in Hawaii was that "the Hawaiian nation was dying by slow degrees . . . [that] nearly one-fifth of the population was already Chinese and at the rate they were entering the kingdom they would have more than a majority within the next decade [the 1890s]."[17] In discussing the presence of the Chinese in Hawaii, U.S. policy advisers no longer commented on their admirable qualities as laborers and field hands; instead they were alert to the idea that beneath the surface of international affairs lurked the possibility of a strong alliance between the Hawaiian Islands and China. Tate noted that early in 1880 the Hawaiian King Kalakaua

> personally liked and encouraged this [Chinese] immigration. . . . Coupled with Kalakaua's dream of a Polynesian Confederacy, [James M.] Comly [U.S. resident minister in Honolulu] . . . suspected there was "a longing for a splendid alliance with the great oriental Empire of China." That country, [Comly] was certain, was adopting a new and more aggressive foreign policy. The Chinese had quietly come into possession of a fine, modern navy; they were rapidly building ocean steamers for their foreign trade; they had accumulated immense stores of arms and ordinance, and were beginning to look about them. The Hawaiian Islands, comparatively insignificant politically, "in the hands of a small rabble of shiftless Kanakas" [Comly warned], "would afford homes and subsistence for more than a million Chinamen, and would become an extremely important neighbor to our Pacific Coast."[18]

If the Chinese were unwelcome by Westerners in Hawaii in the 1880s, they had been more than desired two decades earlier. In the early 1860s Hawaiian officials had formally addressed two aspects of the depopulation crisis: the needs of agriculture and the preservation of the race. The first issue addressed the increasing need for agricultural labor. The second addressed the need for permanent immigration to replenish the declining Hawaiian population. Accordingly, on December 30, 1864, a Bureau of Immigration was created.

Replenishing the declining Hawaiian population was never approached systematically. Various nationalities were considered to be appropriate "reproducers"—Portuguese, Swedes, Italians, Germans, and those regarded by nineteenth-century typologists as racially cognate to the Hawaiians, including Pacific islanders, Malayans, and Japanese. But between 1863 and 1872 only 200 immigrants were brought to Hawaii for reproduction purposes.[19]

The question of importing foreign labor, however, turned out to be more manageable, and in 1865 Dr. William Hillebrand, a German-born physician, was appointed by the king as commissioner "to procure, contract and import into this Kingdom Labourers, from such countries in Asia, as can best supply them."[20] Laborers from China were given priority, and Hillebrand was instructed first to secure about "500 coolies," then to travel through the

East Indies to determine the availability and worth of other sources. Hillebrand spent several months in China and India obtaining information about the conditions under which laborers might be hired. In September and October 1865, the first immigrants to arrive as a result of Hillebrand's efforts included 522 Chinese, among them ninety-five women and three children. They were engaged as laborers for a period of five years; their wages consisted of four dollars a month, a two-dollar bonus on the Chinese New Year, and food and lodging.[21] During the next several decades, Chinese labor was continually sought. The Chinese were desired not only for their work habits, but also, as the Hawaiian Planters' Labor and Supply Committee noted in 1883, "because . . . [China] is the only available source from which we can secure an adequate supply of labor at reasonable rates."[22]

Besides ministering to the labor needs of Hawaiian planters, Hillebrand also ministered to the needs of the sick. He was appointed physician to Queen's Hospital when it opened in Honolulu in 1859. Hillebrand is credited with having observed leprosy among the Chinese in Honolulu as early as 1848[23] and with popularizing the idea that leprosy entered Hawaii along with this earlier group of Chinese immigrants.[24] Nonetheless, his observation and belief did not deter him in his later role as labor procurer.

Of all the diseases known to have visited Hawaii from the early days of Western contact, with some (e.g., tuberculosis) lasting well into the twentieth century, leprosy alone elicited alarm among the Western residents of Hawaii, as in similar outposts of the colonial world. Leprosy was officially brought to public notice by Hillebrand when, in 1863, in the annual report of Queen's Hospital, he called the attention of the trustees "to the rapid spread of that new disease called by the natives ma'i Pake [or] . . . the true Oriental leprosy."[25] Western sensitivity to the presence of leprosy in Hawaii, however, had already preceded Hillebrand's announcement. News of the disease, Thompson wrote, "was purposefully omitted from the newspapers which began to appear regularly considerably before 1863 . . . for fear of injuring the commercial development of the [islands]."[26] After Hillebrand's report, the matter was brought up at a meeting of the Board of Health, and on January 3, 1865, a bill "to prevent the spread of leprosy was enacted into law by the Hawaiian legislature."[27]

As the issue of leprosy was erupting in Hawaii, the attention of the administrators of Great Britain's entire colonial empire was aroused in 1862 when the governor-in-chief of the Windward Islands, anticipating a possible increase of the disease "in these Colonies," called on the secretary of state for the British colonies to conduct an investigation "of the character and progress of the disease."[28] On receipt of this request, the British Colonial Office instructed the Royal College of Physicians to conduct a survey of leprosy in "all the Colonies of the Empire." A list of questions was distributed and replies were received from "the West India Colonies . . . from New Brunswick . . . the Ionian Islands . . . several places in the Turkish Empire; from Sierra Leone, Tunis . . . Cairo . . . Tabreez, Ceylon, Hong Kong, China, and Kanawaha."[29] The data constituted the first international epidemiological survey of leprosy ever undertaken. Completed in 1863, the survey was published four years later.

The report of the Royal College of Physicians endorsed the view then prevailing in Norway and in Europe that leprosy was hereditary and stated there was "no evidence that . . . would justify any measures for the compulsory segregation of lepers."[30] The British Colonial Office approved the recommendations, and in 1863 a circular was sent "to the Governors of all Her Majesty's Colonies, expressing an opinion that any laws affecting the personal liberty of lepers ought to be repealed; and that in the meantime, or, if they shall not be repealed, any action of the Executive Authority in enforcement of them, which is merely authorized and not enjoined by the law, ought to cease."[31]

The reaction in Hawaii was far sterner than that of the Royal College of Physicians. The law enacted in 1865 cited the spread of the disease and the "well-grounded alarms" that it had excited as reason for the passage of the bill. The Hawaiian bill authorized these measures:

> Section 1. . . . to reserve and set apart any land or portion of land now owned by the Government for a site or sites for an establishment or establishments to secure the isolation and seclusion of such leprous persons as, in the opinion of the Board of Health or its agents, may, by being at large, cause the spread of leprosy.
> Section 3. . . . it shall be the duty of every police or District Justice, when properly applied to for that purpose by the Board of Health, or its authorized agents, to cause to be arrested and delivered to the Board of Health, or its agents, any person alleged to be a leper within the jurisdiction of such police or District Justice; and it shall be the duty of the Marshall of the Hawaiian Islands and his deputies, and of police officers, to assist in securing the conveyance of any persons so arrested to such place as the Board of Health, or its agents, may direct, in order that such person may be subjected to medical inspection, and thereafter to assist in removing such person to a place of treatment, or isolation, if so required by the agents of the Board of Health.
> Section 5. The Board of Health, or its agents, may require from patients such reasonable amount of labor as may be approved of by the attending physicians.
> Section 6. The property of all persons committed to the care of the Board of Health for the reasons stated above shall be liable for the expenses attending their confinement, and the Attorney General shall institute suits for the recovery of the same when requested to do so by the President of the Board of Health.[32]

Little time was lost in Hawaii in implementing the Act of 1865. During that year, four of the six members of the Board of Health, including its president, were Westerners. Kahili Hospital and Detention Station, located about two miles from Honolulu, was opened in November 1865 to receive light cases of the disease and to serve as a holding area for severe cases of leprosy. Meanwhile, on September 20, 1865, the board purchased land on the north side of the island of Molokai for the isolation of those suffering from incurable cases of the disease. On January 6, 1866, the first group of lepers was shipped to the settlement of Kalaupapa.[33] A total of 142 lepers was sent there in the first year.[34]

The policy of rigid isolation endorsed in Hawaii in 1865 is difficult to defend on medical grounds. Those who passed the Act of 1865 assumed that leprosy was contagious, but that premise had little foundation in the established medical and scientific wisdom of the day. At midcentury, leprosy was not a disease about which most physicians were knowledgeable. Even in Norway during this same period, where the medical establishment was more familiar with leprosy, physicians tended to overdiagnose in regions where the disease was believed to be hyperendemic. In Hawaii, a diagnosis was more difficult to achieve. Given the mechanisms through which information about lepers was passed along to the authorities—including the use of government spies[35]—a considerable margin of error must be allowed as to the accuracy of diagnosis among the many Hawaiians suspected of having leprosy. In the energetic antileprosy campaign of 1873, of nearly 1,200 persons first thought to be lepers and later examined at Kahili Hospital, more than half were ultimately declared to be false-positives.[36]

In Hawaii, as in other parts of the world, it was not uncommon for physicians to have difficulty in differentiating leprosy from syphilis. The two diseases have not only been linked historically but are also linked clinically and in laboratory findings. Leprosy has been called a disease of considerable dermatological mimicry: "the skin lesions of tuberculoid leprosy are as protean as those of cutaneous tuberculosis or syphilis."[37] The diagnostic difficulty in differentiating leprosy from syphilis persists to this day, as one of the characteristics of leprosy is that it may yield a false-positive Wasserman-test result, which, according to Fasal and Arnold, may be "roughly 50 percent in ordinary lepromatous cases, and said to be 100 percent in Lucio's pure diffuse form."[38]

In the second half of the nineteenth century, physicians living in Hawaii constantly confused the two diseases, sometimes to the point of believing that leprosy developed out of syphilis. Dr. John Ashburton Thompson, no casual observer of the leprosy scene in Australia and Hawaii, cited the case of Dr. Edward Hoffman, appointed in 1865 as physician to the Kahili Hospital and Detention Station, who seven years later remained unable to distinguish between the two diseases.[39] Mouritz discussed the radical position of Dr. George L. Fitch, physician of the leper settlement from 1882 to 1884. Fitch was a leading proponent of the theory that "leprosy was the fourth stage of syphilis,"[40] and he endorsed the practice of inoculating patients with syphilis serum in order to drive out their leprosy.

The Chinese were blamed by Hillebrand earlier in the century for bringing leprosy to Hawaii. Although this indictment was criticized by Thompson in 1896,[41] it was accepted as a fact late in the nineteenth century and is still held by some as a probable hypothesis today.[42] But the belief that the Chinese were bearers of the disease was, remarkably, never raised as an argument for restricting their immigration to the islands as long as they were wanted as laborers. It was mostly the Hawaiian people who were disgraced as lepers, detained, and then exiled to Molokai. In the fifty-year period from 1866 to 1905, more than 5,800 persons were sent to the leper settlement.[43] For the five-year period from 1881 to 1885, when 778 lepers were segregated, 97.3 percent were Hawaiian or part-Hawaiian; 1.8 percent were Chinese; 0.26 percent were Portuguese; and 0.64 percent were "others."[44]

Figures for the five-year period from 1901 to 1905 show a slight demographic shift in the composition of those exiled: 83.5 percent Hawaiian or part-Hawaiian; 6.8 percent Chinese; 3.2 percent Portuguese; 2.2 percent Japanese; and 4.3 percent "others." This relatively minor shift in ethnicity caused much concern both in the foreign community and in the United States. Walter R. Brinckerhoff, director of the Leprosy Investigation Station on Molokai, concluded "that leprosy is becoming more and more a disease of all inhabitants and is no longer almost entirely confined to the native race."[45]

Nine years earlier, in 1896, Thompson learned that between thirty and forty Caucasians had already been sent to the leper settlement, while others had left the country on learning they had the disease. However, no official report of the number of Europeans who had contracted leprosy had been recorded, in order "to avoid embarrassment on both sides—that of the [Hawaiian] Government and [their] own."[46] The year 1905 is important as the year when the movement in the United States to establish a national leprosarium was officially initiated as the U.S. Congress debated the need for a place to confine lepers living within the continental United States.

The negative response to leprosy and the strategies designed to contain the disease in Hawaii were the products of the foreign community. The Western response to leprosy was neither shared nor welcomed by most Hawaiians. In time, Hawaiian leprosy policy was to arouse considerable resentment and anger among the native population, triggering acts of open hostility and violence. Numerous observers have commented on the lack of fear displayed by Hawaiians toward leprosy. Others have contended that this lack of aversion merely reflected Hawaiian fatalism, whatever the disease, whether bubonic plague, cholera, tuberculosis, or leprosy. The Hawaiians lived intimately with lepers, married them, and engaged in no visible form of ostracism. They were known to hold the *haole* (white) attitude toward leprosy in contempt. Hawaiians responded unfavorably to the banishing of lepers, to conditions at Molokai, and to those who believed that such a policy was needed. As noted by Mouritz,

the Hawaiians view with . . . contempt the fears of the foreigners, and . . . think that the law of segregation is a special device aimed at them only to cause trouble, injustice, and break up their homes. The Hawaiians mostly view the segregation of their lepers as a tyrannical act. . . . It has been said in my presence by Hawaiians of the better class, "Hawaii is our country, it belongs to us, or at least it did until the haole got possession of most of it. If the haole is afraid of leprosy let him go back to where he came from."[47]

If Hawaiians saw the segregation of lepers in political terms, the foreigners only saw Hawaiian attitudes as furthering the spread of the disease. Dr. George W. Woods, quoting from his own report of 1876, indicted the social habits of the Hawaiians for spreading leprosy. Among their faults, he noted, were

> large families crowded together in small houses and having the same mats and blankets; the eating of poi with their fingers, all seated around and helping themselves from the same calabash; the drinking of kava in the Hawaiian manner, infused by mastication, and passing the pipe from mouth to mouth, a common Hawaiian custom. To this we may add absolute fearlessness and absence of any disgust for the disease in its worst form and the licentious habits of the race.[48]

In 1909, bacteriologist Robert Koch visited Hawaii, and Mouritz described to the famous doctor those native practices that so worried foreigners. Two aspects of Hawaiian daily life were mentioned: that "healthy Hawaiians will eat, drink, sleep, and live with a leper voluntarily, and without fear . . . [and] a healthy Hawaiian man or woman will marry a leper, although there are plenty of well men and women in sight."[49]

Hawaiian attitudes toward leprosy help explain the role and position of *kokuas*. Variously translated as assistants, nurses, or helpers, kokuas were the healthy husbands, wives, or partners of lepers who voluntarily accompanied them to the Molokai settlement; the kokuas would live there, care for the sick, and share in the hardships of colony life. It is estimated that 225 kokuas lived at the leper settlement in the early 1880s. Although they were generally condemned by the foreign community as seeking "a lazy, free from care existence," R. W. Meyer, superintendent of the leper colony and agent of the Board of Health, noted the important role they played in running the settlement and providing the colony with a form of free labor: "These people called kokuas, or assistants, are absolutely necessary to live at the Settlement, for the performance of the work connected with the slaughtering of animals, receiving and distribution of food, preparing food and providing fuel, local police, messengers, etc."[50]

The number of lepers sent to Molokai between 1866 and 1905 varied considerably, year by year (Figure 5.1). The variations reflect vicissitudes in enforcing the law. The formal machinery for the detection and apprehension of lepers remained essentially the same over the years. Police officers and their deputies, medical practitioners where they existed, private citizens, and for a time native tax assessors were mandated under law to report cases of leprosy they saw, knew of, or heard about.[51] Failure to comply with the law was a misdemeanor and carried a fine of not more than one hundred dollars.[52] In the early years of the control program, when there were few physicians in Honolulu and even fewer, if any, on the other islands, suspects would be rounded up and,

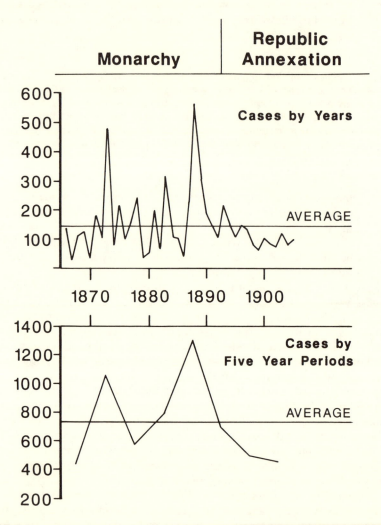

FIGURE 5.1
Leprosy in Hawaii: Cases Segregated by Years: 1866–1905

Source: Brinckerhoff, W. R. "The Present Status of the Leprosy Problem in Hawaii." *Treasury Department. Public Health and Marine-Hospital Service of the United States* (Washington, D.C., 1908): Plate 1.

having been collected at the chief landing-places, were transmitted to Honolulu either by the first vessel offering, or else, if the number were sufficiently large, by a special vessel chartered to make a round voyage from Honolulu. . . . At first their cases were decided by [Dr. Edward] Hoffman acting alone . . . [and] if deemed to be lepers, they were kept there until a sufficient number had accumulated, and were then transmitted to the Settlement; if not, they were returned to their islands as opportunity occurred.[53]

Natives could resist the process relatively easily during the early days of the control program, especially on smaller islands and in villages in remote and inaccessible mountains and valleys. In time, however, it became easier to apprehend lepers, first with the appointment in 1870 of traveling physicians hired by the Board of Health to visit the remoter areas of the archipelago; then with the establishment of a regular interisland shipping schedule in 1876; and later with the arrival of Portuguese laborers, whose contracts stipulated they be provided with medical care at the plantations where they worked.

In general, Hawaiians resorted to passive means of concealing lepers to avoid apprehension, but cases of violent opposition to the law did occur. Thus Mouritz reported about a dozen cases of lepers resorting to firearms to defend themselves against deportation.[54] One of the more serious incidents took place in July 1893 at Kalalau on the northwest shore of the Island of Kauai. Deputy Sheriff L. H. Stolz, who was determined "to tackle the leper problem in Kalalau," was shot and killed by a young Hawaiian leper he was stalking. On receipt of the news that a number of lepers in Kalalau Valley were well armed, the Hawaiian government sent in a squad of about twenty-five soldiers, along with a portable field gun, to bring in Stolz's assailant. The terrain favored the leper "guerrillas." Three soldiers died before the authorities admitted defeat and ordered the squad back to Honolulu. In September 1897, also on Kauai, Dr. Jared Smith was shot to death to prevent him from signing an order to deport a young girl he believed to have leprosy. The murderer was apprehended, tried, convicted, and hung.

Island politics played an important role in whether the segregation of lepers was pursued efficiently or with indifference. Both Mouritz and Thompson mentioned the effect local elections had on the policy of segregation. The "prosecution" of lepers began to be conducted in "a more businesslike manner," Thompson noted, "when the royal prerogative . . . began to be checked. [Thereafter] more continuous, steady, and equal efforts were made to isolate all detected lepers."[55] Mouritz likened the apprehension and segregation of lepers to a "political football," depending on the faction in power. He noted that, during those years when Hawaiians were politically influential, in order "to placate [Hawaiian] voters . . . the enforcement of the segregation law has been purposely allowed to lapse temporarily."[56]

The first energetic effort to carry out the leprosy segregation policy of 1865 was put into effect in 1873. Between 400 and 600 people were sent to Molokai in that year, including Peter Y. Kaeo, a member of the House of Nobles and a cousin of Queen Emma, as well as six foreigners, among them William P. Ragsdale, who was well known for his service as interpreter to the legislature.[57] This antileprosy campaign occurred during the brief reign of King Lunalilo (January 8, 1873, to February 3, 1874) and was encouraged by Dr. George Trousseau, a member of the new Board of Health appointed by the king.

King Lunalilo was eager to conclude a commercial treaty of reciprocity with the United States favorable to Hawaiian sugar. A treaty was desperately needed to bolster an economically depressed agricultural base, but some plantation owners were holding out for annexation to the United States or some other great power. To accomplish his purpose, Lunalilo offered to cede Pearl Harbor to the United States and was willing to ease restrictions on the sale both of liquor and of land on the islands.* In a population as politically divided as Hawaii was at this time, any unpopular law that affected the Hawaiian people was bound to surface as a political issue. According to Bradley, the leprosy campaign of 1873 was an effort to consolidate the support of the resident Americans. Lunalilo "exercised little or no authority on his own initiative and allowed Americans (with some connection with the so-called missionary class) to make policy. In view of the missionary attitude toward lepers, it perhaps is not surprising that a greater number of lepers than usual were exiled to Molokai."[58] According to Kuykendall, the "natives" strongly opposed the segregation of lepers. They held a meeting on March 31, 1873, in Kaumakapili Church, where it was reported "that some inflammatory, not to say seditious, speeches were made." Opposing the natives on the issue of segregation were the voices of the establishment, the local but foreign-controlled press, the Hawaiian Evangelical Association, and King Lunalilo.[59]

In addition to politics, there were also charges of government corruption in implementing the segregation law, according to Bradley:

> There were charges in the early 1880s, and especially about 1882–1884, that the government of King Kalakaua and Prime Minister Walter M. Gibson was especially corrupt. These charges were made openly and repeatedly in the newspapers and elsewhere, and among the corrupt acts with which government officials were charged was the acceptance (or, in some cases, the enforcement) of bribes to permit lepers to remain at home instead of being sent to Molokai.[60]

Some of the tumult surrounding leprosy in the early 1880s was revealed in a libel suit brought by Dr. George L. Fitch against *The Saturday Press*. In a report of the proceedings published by *The Saturday Press* in 1883,

> the libel suit against the proprietor of the Saturday Press was brought by Mr. Fitch ostensibly as a defense against the language of that journal. In reality,

---

*The sugar agreement was not concluded until 1876. In 1887, when it was renewed, Pearl Harbor was leased to the United States, thirteen years before Hawaii became a U.S. territory.

the suit was an effort to crush or at least silence the Press for its plain, direct, unsparing and convincing exposure of the criminal mismanagement of leprosy in these islands by the Hawaiian Board of Health, of which body Mr. Gibson and Mr. Fitch were the officials chiefly responsible.[61]

The trial lasted two days and attracted wide attention, drawing "almost, if not quite the entire bar of Honolulu, including the attorney-generals, *de jure* and *de facto*."[62] Although the suit was initiated against *The Saturday Press*, the trial quickly turned into an indictment of Fitch, both as an administrator and as a leprologist. A large number of witnesses were called, among them island physicians, pharmacists, and lepers. At issue were Fitch's theory of the relationship between syphilis and leprosy, his belief that at certain stages leprosy was not contagious, and his belief that, in some instances, it was curable—hence, the propriety of discharging patients from Molokai back to the community.

Although the state of knowledge about leprosy early in the 1880s was unsettled, the political issue at stake in Hawaii was clear. The issue was summed up in the judge's charge to the jury, wherein he noted that "if by any means, these islands should become a plague spot, the effect would be more important upon the future of the nation than the withdrawal of the reciprocity treaty [with the United States]."[63] By disseminating the belief that leprosy and syphilis are identical, the judge noted further,

> the result would be that those who are living pure and moral lives would become careless as to the exposure of themselves or their children by mere contact with lepers—believing sexual intercourse, by which syphilis is commonly taken, to be the only way in which they could take leprosy. . . .
> So, if Doctor Fitch should persuade people generally that leprosy is curable, people would become indifferent, and say: "I have the means of employing a physician; it matters not if I take leprosy. I can be cured."[64]

Fitch's suit against *The Saturday Press* was dismissed. Following the judge's charge to the jury, the twelve foreign jurymen returned a verdict of "not guilty, two dissenting."

As Hawaii came closer to consolidating its economic and political future with the United States, the number of lepers segregated at Molokai increased, reaching a second peak in 1888 (Figure 5.1). Leprosy remained a political issue until annexation secured the islands to the United States. As late as 1898, articles bearing such titles as "Shall We Annex Leprosy?"[65] appeared in American magazines.

*   *   *

The history of leprosy in Hawaii is important less for its views about how the disease is transmitted than for its policy of exiling lepers. The role of Hawaii in trans-Pacific relations must be considered in evaluating the perspective toward the disease that developed on the islands during the second half of the nineteenth century. In Norway the approach to leprosy was influenced by nationalism, by the fact that its lepers were impoverished Norwegian farmers and villagers, and by the scientific advances then evolving in Europe. Hawaii, on the other hand, radiated in other directions. It was influenced by the West, notably the United States, but also by the Far East. The influences on the foreign community in control of island affairs also came from more than one direction. Their loyalties and background were Western, preponderantly New England Presbyterianism. Their activities and ventures began with missions and evangelism in the early days but grew to maturity with commerce and profit. Their value was utility; their approach, pragmatism.

Unlike encounters in many other parts of the world, the Europeans and Americans who journeyed to Hawaii and settled there generally spoke benignly, though patronizingly, of the Hawaiian people. Some found them "lazy," "indolent," and "immoral"; others, "amicable," "fun-loving," with a "simple intelligence." During the years of religious revival on the islands, missionaries praised the Hawaiians for their Christian potential. Some spoke of the Hawaiians with great respect, especially when contrasting them with other Pacific islanders, some of whom were less receptive to Westerners. But whatever the spectrum of opinion regarding the Hawaiian character, all foreigners, in the years following midcentury, were coming to a single conclusion: that, as a people in their own land, Hawaiians were rapidly becoming a population without much *social utility*. The argument that the Kingdom of Hawaii was moribund and that the Hawaiian people were decadent was extensively used during the 1880s by U.S. advisers and diplomats eager to see Hawaii safely in U.S. hands.[66]

The opinion that leprosy was contagious and thus threatening to members of the foreign community and their future on the islands, coupled with a characterization of Hawaiians as lacking in social utility, makes the decision to banish Hawaiian lepers explicable within a framework of Western political expediency. Expediency alone, however, represents only a partial answer to the question of why enforced segregation was the single, unchallenged solution considered at the time. It must be remembered that the nineteenth-century attitudes of the people of imperialist nations toward native populations were strongly shaped by ideas of racial inferiority. The ultimate fate of those perceived to be inferior and expendable was often harsh. Sometimes they were banished to reservations, as with the American Indian; sometimes to the island of Molokai, as with lepers in Hawaii.

In societal decisions involving the disposition of people, the status of those being disposed of is reflected not only in the decision to dispose of them and the manner in which that disposition is carried out, but also in the accommodations that are provided. In Norway, the establishment of hospitals and nursing homes in districts of leprosy prevalence and the concern for the human liberties of patients indicated a humane approach to the disease. In Norway, leprosy was a social and medical issue. In Hawaii, and later in the United States, the fight against leprosy was a fight against undesired people.

The island of Molokai, one of the smaller islands in the Hawaiian chain, is 23 miles from Honolulu. Ten square miles of the island were set aside for the leper settlement, an area of land "in the form of a tongue . . . three sides of which are washed by the ocean, whilst a steep and lofty mountain chain some 3,000 feet high, cuts the settlement so entirely from the rest of the island that there is no egress or ingress possible except by boat, or by a narrow trail which crosses the mountain at a height of 2,100 feet."[67] Hawaiian lepers were sent to Molokai, it has been noted, "not as patients, but as colonists." Land was set aside for them, and other than having a few essentials provided for them by the government, "they were left to fend for themselves."[68]

It was expected in Honolulu that the cost of purchasing the land would be the principal expenditure required in the exiling of lepers, that the stronger and healthier members of the settlement would cultivate the land and grow the food, and that with the exception of some clothing and perhaps some meat, the Board of Health would be spared any further support of the "colonists." "To its great surprise," Father Yzendoorn wrote, quoting from an early report of the Board of Health, "a Frenchman by the name of Lepart, who lived in the settlement, informed the Board, in the month of September, 1866 . . . that supplies must be sent from Honolulu, as the settlement would be able to produce but little from that time forth."[69] Aside from the need for supplies, conditions at the colony were "unspeakably unhygienic." This observation was echoed in the descriptions of both early residents and visitors, by the sick as well as by a number of those whose duty it was to minister to the patients.[70]

In time, conditions at Molokai changed; sometimes things improved, sometimes they only became different. In 1873, Joseph Damien de Veuster joined the colony as its resident priest—a move that, a decade and a half later, was to have a profound effect on leprosy history. Damien, who remained at the settlement until his death, was of considerable help in improving living conditions at the colony and a source of considerable nuisance to authorities in Honolulu, to whom he appealed for support on behalf of the lepers. Among Damien's chief complaints was the lack of an available supply of fresh water close to the settlement. Housing, he noted, was woefully inadequate: "nothing but small, damp huts." The winter was cold and Damien wrote: "On my arrival I found the lepers in general very destitute of warm clothing. So far they had received from the administration a suit of clothes and a blanket; but . . . in a few months nothing remained but rags."[71] Damien's own housing, when he first arrived, was no better than that of the lepers'. "I myself was sheltered," he wrote, "during several months under the [settlement's] single pandanus tree."[72]

Between 1866 and 1873 the settlement was without medical care of any sort, according to Damien:

I remember well that the poor people were without any medicines, with the exception of a few physics and their own native medicines, from which, I judge, it had been the same from the inauguration of the Settlement. It was a common sight to see people going around with fearful ulcers, which for want of a few rags, or a piece of lint and a little salve, were left exposed to dirt, flies, and vermin. Not only their sores were neglected, but anyone getting a fever, diarrhoea or any other of the numerous ailments that lepers are so often heir to, was carried off for want of some simple medicine.[73]

R. W. Meyer, a former superintendent of the settlement, noted that before 1878 a physician from Maui would visit the colony "two or three times a year . . . for a few hours and return." But, Damien recorded, "we had no doctor during this second period [1873–1880s]."[74] All that was available was a "white man [Mr. Williamson], a leper himself, who had been an assistant to the doctors at the Kahili hospital. He had quite a practical knowledge of simple medicine."[75]

The failure to supply medical care to the leper settlement was not due to the absence of such facilities elsewhere in Hawaii. Acts of 1855 authorized the establishment of hospitals on the principal islands, and the sum of $5,000 was appropriated for hospitals in Honolulu and Lahaina.[76] Foreign governments already had hospitals in Honolulu for seamen, and there were small private hospitals for foreign residents. Queen's Hospital, a charitable institution for poor Hawaiians, was opened in 1859, and within three years "more than 6,000 persons had applied for treatment and more than 16,000 prescriptions had been furnished."[77]

Nursing care did not reach the lepers of Hawaii until Mother Superior Sister Marianne and six sisters from the Franciscan Convent of Saint Anthony, Syracuse, New York, arrived in Honolulu in 1883. For the first five years they were assigned to Kakaako Hospital, a receiving station for lepers that had been opened in 1881, six years after the closing of Kahili Hospital. In November 1888, the sisters were transferred to the Bishop Home in Kalaupapa, an institution founded for young leper girls and single women by Charles R. Bishop, banker, minister, philanthropist, and husband of Hawaiian Chiefess Bernice Pauahi.[78]

The belief in Hawaii that leprosy was contagious was accompanied by the thought that the disease might be communicated through vaccination. Vaccination became a general practice in Hawaii at the time of the smallpox outbreak in 1853, when thousands of the Hawaiians were carried off by this epidemic. Owing to shortages in the supply of bovine and calf lymph, the mode of vaccination was "arm to arm." The belief that leprosy might be transmitted through the medium of arm-to-arm smallpox vaccination seems to have been held by both laymen and physicians alike well into the 1880s. Mouritz noted that during the smallpox epidemic of 1880–1881, which was introduced into Honolulu from San Francisco and caused 252 deaths, foreigners reported "that as soon as the operation was performed the party vaccinated was thereafter as soon as convenient, subjected to suction of the wound by the parent's mouth, or other person, in order to avoid the germs of leprosy."[79] Dr. Edward Arning, a German physician investigating leprosy in Hawaii from 1883 to 1885, concurred in the vaccination theory, noting that "the unusually rapid spread of the disease [leprosy] may possibly be attributed to the great amount of indiscriminate vaccination which had been carried on in these islands."[80]

In Hawaii, many efforts were made to test the vaccination hypothesis. Experiments were chiefly carried out using healthy kokuas living at the leper settlement. Mouritz, who was physician at Molokai, selected fifteen kokuas, ten males and five females, and inoculated them with leprous matter. These inoculations were conducted between 1884 and 1909. "Every case was a FAILURE," Mouritz reported emphatically, "and produced no results."[81]

The case of Keanu, however, was different. A convicted murderer, sentenced to death for killing a Japanese man, Keanu had his sentence commuted to life imprisonment on the condition that he "submit to inoculation with leprosy."[82] Keanu was confined in the Oahu jail; in September 1884 he gave written consent to Dr. Arning to conduct the experiment. In his report to W. M. Gibson, president of the Board of Health, dated November 14, 1885, Arning stated that he had "made a most searching inquiry as to any leprous taint in his [Keanu's] family, and a close examination of his own body" and was satisfied that "no trace of the disease could be found."[83] Others, however, were unconvinced. According to Mouritz, Dr. S. B. Swift, who resided at the leper settlement from 1888 to 1892, "made known the fact that Keanu's relatives were affected with leprosy, and that he had lived in the same house with these leper relatives." Keanu developed leprosy after the inoculation. According to Mouritz,

> Twenty-five months after [the inoculation], October 1886, Keanu showed the maculation of nodular leprosy all over his body, the nerves and lymphatic glands near the seat of the wound also showed implication. The infection in the various selective seats of the body peculiar to leprosy became apparent (ear lobes, helix, cheeks, forehead, supraorbital alopecia, etc.), in the year 1887; in the fall of that year, some three years after inoculation, Keanu was a confirmed leper. . . .
> I [Mouritz] examined Keanu in February, 1888, at the request of the United States Minister, G. W. Merrill, at the Oahu jail; the details of this examination were forwarded to Washington.[84]

Regardless of the merits of the experiment, Keanu became a celebrated case, and the news spread that leprosy was, indeed, contagious through inoculation.

The events surrounding the contracting of leprosy by Father Damien, and his subsequent death in 1889, however, had a far more explosive impact and triggered fears that leprosy was an imminent threat to the white Western world. Of Damien's death, Mouritz wrote:

> When Fr. Damien fell a victim to leprosy and later succumbed to the disease, his semi-tragic death created a marked change and revulsion in the opinions previously held about the *noncontagiousness* of leprosy. A certain element of the British public became alarmed when they learnt of the case of Fr. Damien; rushed into print, and almost hysterically proclaimed leprosy to be an imperial danger and menace.[85]

Damien was born at Tremeloo, a small village near Louvain, Belgium, on January 3, 1840. He arrived at Honolulu on March 19, 1864, and died at Kalawao, Molokai, on April 15, 1889, at the age of forty-nine years, three months, and twelve days. It was on the first Sunday in June 1885, so the story goes, that Father Damien first announced to his congregation that he was one of them, that he too was now a leper.[86] The fact of Damien's leprosy, however, had been known earlier; it was traced positively by Damien himself back to 1876[87] and reported by Mouritz to have been "plainly visible in the year 1884."[88] In the last years of his life, Damien received many visitors, and much was written about him—some scurrilous, some much too praising. The news traveled fast and far that the Belgian Catholic priest had contracted the disease in the course of living among Polynesian lepers in the Sandwich Islands.

The death of Damien had an immediate impact on the British empire in particular. Jonathan Hutchinson, who had vigorously expounded fish-eating as a cause of leprosy, moderated his views and, writing from Great Britain, noted ten years before Mouritz that the fate of Damien had sharply altered Western opinion. In 1906, Hutchinson wrote that "the case of Father Damien had great influence in impressing popular opinion in favor of contagion. Everyone heard or read about it, and everyone believed that the devoted priest had, in the course of his zealous ministrations in a leper home, acquired the disease by direct contagion."[89] The colonial world also noted Damien's fate, and in 1889 the National Leprosy Fund, sponsored by the Prince of Wales, was formed as a memorial to the Catholic priest. The first meeting was held on June 17, 1889, a mere sixty-three days after his death. An Executive Committee was formed and "at a meeting on June 30th, resolved on the erection of a memorial to Father Damien at Molokai, the formation of a fund for indigent British lepers in the United Kingdom, the endowment of two Leprosy Studentships, and finally the appointment of an Indian Leprosy Commission."[90]

The mandate of the Indian Leprosy Commission was to survey leprosy in India and formulate policies on the management of the disease in that subcontinent. The commission was composed of one member each from the Royal College of Physicians, the Royal College of Surgeons, and the Executive Committee of the National Leprosy Fund, together with two delegates from India. Their report, drafted in 1891, dismissed heredity as a cause of leprosy, noting instead that

> although they consider leprosy an infective disease, caused by a specific bacillus, and moreover also a contagious disease, they are of the opinion that there is not sufficient evidence that leprosy is maintained or diffused by contagion; indeed under the ordinary human surroundings the amount of contagion which exists is so small that it may be disregarded, and no legislation is called for on the lines either of segregation, or of interdiction of marriages with lepers. . . .[91]
>
> In conclusion, the Commissioners believe . . . that neither compulsory nor voluntary segregation would at present effectually stamp out the disease. . . .

The Commission agree with most authorities in believing that the decline of leprosy in Europe has been due principally to improved hygienic habits and surroundings, and increased material prosperity.[92]

On receipt of the above recommendations, a special committee of the National Leprosy Fund was appointed to review the report. The members of the special committee were the undersecretary for India, chairman, a nominee of the Executive Committee of the National Leprosy Fund, and two members each from the Royal College of Physicians and the Royal College of Surgeons. In a strongly worded dissenting opinion, members of the special committee pointedly disagreed with the original report, holding instead to a much harder line on contagion. Furthermore, they strongly objected to the report's adverse recommendations about segregation. With respect to segregating lepers, the special committee noted that [they] "entertain a precisely opposite opinion, and would be sorry if the Government of India were encouraged by the *Report of the Commission* to refrain from taking the necessary steps in the direction of such segregation of lepers as may be found possible."[93]

A hard line on contagion, which had been emerging for some time, now coupled with a hard line on the segregation of lepers, gained considerable momentum with this reversal by the special committee of the more moderate views of the commission's report. When the commission's report was published in 1893, the dissenting report was part of the document. International endorsement of these more strident views soon followed, and in 1897 the First International Leprosy Congress, held in Berlin, took the position that "every leper is a danger to his surroundings," and resolved that "isolation is the best means of preventing the spread of the disease."[94]

Hawaii became a territory of the United States in 1900, and in 1959 it became the fiftieth state in the union. In 1909, the U.S. Government assumed control of the leper settlement at Molokai. But the fate of Hawaiian lepers was still a severe one ten years after statehood had been achieved. For more than 100 years, from 1865 to 1969, it remained the legal policy in Hawaii that lepers could be isolated at Kalaupapa, involuntarily, for life. Only in 1974, after years of controversy, indecision, and politicking, and long after policies favoring outpatient treatment had been endorsed by the World Health Organization and implemented throughout the world, did Hawaii relax its restrictions. The state finally ruled that in the future all new cases of the disease would be treated as outpatients.[95]

However, until this decision was reached, segregation for life remained official policy—a banishment reinforced by the physical geography of Molokai itself, where rocky shores, turbulent surf, and treacherous landing were designed by nature more to exclude visitors than to welcome them. Today, traffic in and out of the island can be made by air. Although tours of the settlement could be arranged with special permission, until recently visitors were still enjoined from engaging in even the briefest form of personal contact with patients at Molokai, including that of shaking their hands.

PART 3

The Period of Alarm: Turn of the Century

6

Changing American Images of the Chinese

The discovery of leprosy in Hawaii and the events that followed occurred at the height of late nineteenth-century Western imperialism. This period witnessed a remarkable transformation in the pattern and magnitude of world migration and the "opening up" of new lands and territories. Not only were Europeans relocating abroad in large numbers, but large numbers of Asians, particularly the Chinese and Indians, were moving south and eastward to Australia, Hawaii, and the United States. Certain races and peoples, notably the Chinese, other Asians, and Negroes—the yellow and black races—were being identified as leprosy-prevalent populations, and more and more cases of the disease, both real and imagined, were being reported from abroad. Leprosy was believed to be increasing at an alarming rate, and the fear was developing that Europeans had "ceased to show the immunity from its attacks which was once thought to be their privilege."[1]

European discovery in foreign lands of "new" diseases, and of familiar diseases in new and different forms, among peoples of different sizes, shapes, and colors renewed an interest in the pursuit of medical geography. Mapping of the geographical distribution of diseases had flourished in Europe from the middle of the eighteenth century until late in the nineteenth century, when spectacular discoveries in bacteriology "seemed to make . . . further research in other directions . . . superfluous."[2] The systemic writing of the history of disease was an even earlier development and "may be said to have begun in the eighteenth century with such monographs as that by [Johannes] Kanold on the history of the plague, by [Jean] Astruc on syphilis, by [Johann Gottfried von] Hahn and [Paul Gottlieb] Werlhof on smallpox, by [Rudolph Augustin] Vogel and [Joannes Christianus Gottlieb] Ackerman on dysentry, by [Christian Gottfried] Gruner on the sweating sickness, and by [Philipp Gabriel] Hensler on leprosy."[3] The crowning point of a historical and geographical synthesis to an understanding of diseases was achieved with the publication in the 1860s of the first edition of August Hirsch's *Handbuch der historischen und geographischen Pathologie.*[4]

Although the practice of medical geography came to a standstill in the 1880s with regard to the mapping of European diseases, it continued "to exist under the name Tropical Medicine. By tropical medicine was actually meant Colonial Medicine, i.e., that branch of medicine dealing with diseases that for the most part were not tropical *per se* but were prevalent in tropical colonies and which therefore were of intense practical interest to colonial powers."[5]

According to the canons of conventional medical history, leprosy was a prevalent disease in Europe and Great Britain during the Middle Ages. According to others it was more properly a generic term used loosely to cover a wide assortment of observable cutaneous conditions. The use of vague generic terms, such as "plague," "fever," "wasting," and, of course, "leprosy," to cover a variety of now distinguishable clinical entities was a common occurrence until about the sixteenth century, when a more modern approach to the concept of disease was formulated. Many new diseases, consequently, were "discovered" at this time, as "reoriented observers" using more refined methods of observation "began describing diseases as though they were altogether novel."[6] From such arguments Charles Creighton strongly admonished historians in the 1890s against even attempting to trace the origins of leprosy in British antiquity[7]; and August Hirsch expressed his conviction that it was not leprosy, but probably syphilis, that the returning Crusaders brought to Europe.[8]

With the epidemic in Hawaii, leprosy—known to Europeans primarily as a disease of the past—was now observed in the flesh, so to speak, among strange peoples in far-off lands recently secured through the domination of Western imperialism. Among the major epidemics that had accompanied the growth and expansion of the Western nation-states, Europe got as well as it gave and was exporter and victim alike of transnational and transoceanic afflictions. Leprosy, however, was the sole major disease that "inferior" peoples could bestow on the "civilized" West.

The fate of Father Damien in Hawaii had an enormous impact on Western thinking about leprosy. Damien, however, was not the only Westerner to become a known leper while abroad. Other Europeans in Hawaii, priests and laymen alike, were also known to have contracted the disease on the islands or elsewhere in their travels. But they were personages less celebrated than Damien. Some returned quietly home, where little was ever to be known about their past lives and adventures. Damien, on the other hand, was special. From 1873 until 1889 his whereabouts were public knowledge, first locally, later worldwide. For sixteen years, as everyone was to come to know, he had lived intimately among the lepers at Kalaupapa. Some were later to say, too intimately. It was this fact about Damien—his residing in close contact with lepers—that worried the people of the West. Those from Western nations who previously had regarded themselves as "privileged" and immune now expressed concern about the risks of settling abroad and living among natives, no matter how carefully or cautiously. Hutchinson noted,

No one at the present time [1906] residing in England fears to become a leper, whereas any trader or missionary going to India, the West Indian Islands, Iceland, China, the east coast of Norway, the Sandwich Islands, or even South

Africa, and living as do the poorer classes in these districts, encounters a not very inconsiderable risk, which risk is not wholly removed by living a very careful life, nor by the utmost care as to cleanliness, and immunity from every species of hardship.[9]

Those who had always "known" that leprosy was "contagious" were not at all modest about publishing reminders that they had known this fact all along. C. N. Macnamara had published a book in 1866 entitled *Leprosy a Communicable Disease*. It received little attention at the time and then was out of print for some years. He reissued the work in 1889, noting in the preface to the second edition that "as interest has lately been excited in this country [Great Britain] regarding Leprosy, largely in connection with the history of Father Damien's life and death, it seemed possible that the evidence I had collected as to the nature of Leprosy might be useful to those working at this subject."[10] Macnamara's interest in leprosy in 1866 was not parochial. Even at that time, among his other sources of information, Macnamara was in correspondence with Hillebrand in Honolulu.[11] Macnamara's view of the means by which leprosy was communicated from one person to another—"it is contagious in the same way that syphilis is understood to be contagious"[12]—revealed a tendency not uncommon at the time to cast a shadow of sexuality over the transmission of the disease. That overtone of sexuality was used by Dr. C. M. Hyde—a Protestant clergyman—and others to vilify and demean Father Damien.[13] Furthermore, that overtone was of deep concern to all colonizing nations troubled about the issue of racial contact and race mixture.

The period of the late 1880s and early 1890s, especially the years 1889–1891, were the peak years of alarm in Great Britain (Figure 6.1). More and more real and alleged cases of leprosy were being reported from abroad, and more and more stations within the colonial orbit were becoming agitated about whether leprosy was, in fact, already present among them—and, if so, whether it was also increasing locally, as was being reported elsewhere. At the same time, more and more information about the disease, its presence, and its spread was being disseminated worldwide. Opinions, rates, and estimates varied, but the alarmist consensus of the time was that the disease was steadily increasing and, in fact, was about to become pandemic.

The fear, of course, was that the disease would spread to the centers of Western civilization. Sir Morrell Mackenzie, who was "discovering" more leprosy in Europe and in the United States, in an 1890 article, "The Dreadful Revival of Leprosy," clearly stated the threat to Europe:

The facts . . . represent an unspeakable amount of suffering to many races whose destinies we have taken into our keeping, but besides this they indicate a possible danger to ourselves. Leprosy has before now overrun Europe and invaded England, without respecting the "silver streak" which keeps off other enemies; and it is perfectly conceivable that, under certain circumstances, it might do so again.[14]

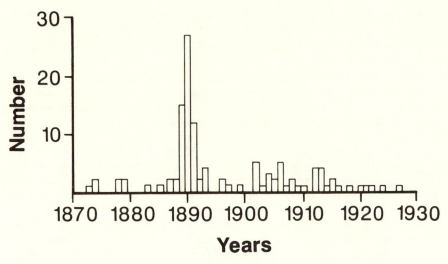

FIGURE 6.1
Number of References to Leprosy in Index to the *London Times*, 1870–1930

Source: Gussow, Zachary, and Tracy, George S. "Stigma and the Leprosy Phenomenon: The Social History of a Disease in the Nineteenth and Twentieth Centuries." *Bulletin of the History of Medicine* 44, no. 5, 1970:436. Reprinted by permission of the Johns Hopkins University Press.

Sir Morrell's work was circulated widely in medical circles both in Europe and in the United States through being printed in *Wood's Medical and Surgical Monographs*. In the United States, there were even gloomier prophets, like the Reverend L. W. Mulhane, who in his 1896 book, *Leprosy and the Charity of the Church*,[15] warned of the imminence of the leprosy "menace." Dr. Leonard F. Pitkin expected to find "within the next ten years at least 250,000 to 500,000 lepers included among the inhabitants of the United States."[16] India was expected to contribute an additional untold number of cases, according to Dr. A. W. Hitt, a believer in the transmission of leprosy through vaccination. In a paper read before the Chicago Medical Society, September 29, 1897, he told his audience:

> I know of several cases where children have become infected by being vaccinated with the lymph taken from the arms of lepers. Mr. William Tebb, in his interesting book on the recrudescence of leprosy, reports a case in which about 60 school children out of a class of 150 who were vaccinated with lymph taken from the arms of infected persons were attacked by leprosy. From 3,000,000 to 6,000,000 children were vaccinated in this way every year in India. Who can tell what the results will be?[17]

Writing about the danger in areas in and abutting the Pacific Ocean, James Cantlie, in his prize-winning essay on leprosy, issued another warning:

"A whole ocean is threatened. It has been crossed by leprosy already. Hawaii was the stepping-stone to California, and California is a new and dangerous centre for the distribution of the disease."[18] Then, of course, there was Henry P. Wright, rector of Greatham. The title of his book *Leprosy an Imperial Danger*,[19] thoroughly conveyed the spirit of the alarm. Everywhere the civilized world was seen as being under attack, even countries whose "civilized" status was sometimes questioned. "It is spreading to an alarming degree in Russia," noted Sir Morrell Mackenzie.[20]

The number of Westerners alleged to have contracted the disease as a result of assisting lepers was said to be increasing. Mackenzie contested the thesis that was argued in the 1867 report of the Royal College of Physicians "that attendants on lepers are never attacked," noting that "its own report contains several instances in which persons who had the care of lepers contracted the disease." In addition to the well-known case of Father Damien, Mackenzie offered a list of other less well-known victims: "Dr. Hoffman, the medical officer of Molokai [and] Damien's colleague . . . Dr. Robertson, medical superintendent of the Curieuse leper establishment, Seychelles . . . several cases . . . recorded by Hansen, and Father Etienne . . . Dr. Goddard, a young French physician . . . who took up abode in a lazar-house, in Palestine. . . . Other cases are reported from South America." Besides Westerners, Mackenzie added, we also "have the crushing fact that, out of sixty-six kokuas, or helpers, on the island [Molokai] in 1888, twenty-three were known to have contracted the disease, while in eleven more its existence was suspected."[21]

Mackenzie's attack on the 1867 report of the Royal College of Physicians was, more to the point, an attack on those who in 1890 required convincing that leprosy was a serious disease. Although the evidence was mounting that leprosy was contagious, the view was not unanimously held. Some still called leprosy a "telluric" disease—one of those arising from the earth or soil in the old typology attributing diseases to earth, air, fire, or water. Some clung to the idea that diet was somehow responsible, whereas others voiced the argument that the anaesthetic form ("tuberculoid" leprosy in a later classification) was not contagious. Furthermore, there were many differences of opinion regarding the question of just *how* contagious leprosy was and *how* it was transmitted.

Leprosy did not spread pandemically throughout the Western world. The alarm of pandemicity and the fear of leprosy itself, however, rode through Western nations on the tidal wave of the forces of racism and the yellow peril. "Racism" is the more generic term for Western views and structures expressive of the ideology of human biosocial inequality. The yellow peril, which reached its height at about the same time as the doctrine of racism, was addressed particularly to the peoples and nations of the Orient, but most specifically to the Chinese.

In advancing the tenets of racism, Western theorists left no avenue of human potentiality and human activity untouched. There were biological arguments, population arguments, and economic and social arguments. There were cultural arguments and military arguments, and there were also sexual, medical, and disease arguments. Late in the nineteenth century, the United States received the largest and most diverse portion of migrating humanity seeking refuge, settlement, and liberty. The United States also offered the broadest possible arena in which to exercise the practice of racism. Although "undesirables" from southern and eastern Europe and from some of the other less favored parts of the earth were grudgingly admitted into the United States after the period of "free immigration" ended, the U.S. Government remained adamant in its racial stance with regard to both Negroes and the Chinese.

The concept of yellow peril and the peculiar Western image of the Chinese constitute a strange chapter in human history. The persistence of the image is as unfathomable as the alleged attributes of the people of the Celestial Empire themselves. It cannot be taken for granted that this period in Sino-Western relations is well known or that the enormity of the vilification of the Chinese is even remembered. It is difficult to realize today that the Chinese were not so very long ago irrationally feared, hated, and persecuted in the United States. In 1882, under the Chinese Exclusion Act, they alone were handed the final debasement of being legally barred from entering the country.

The enormity of American fear and denigration of the Chinese is highlighted by yet another fact—how long and how thoroughly that period has been ignored by American historians. The subject of Chinese exclusion and the awesome stereotype held in the United States toward all things Chinese have received limited monographic coverage. Mary Roberts Coolidge's 1909 work, *Chinese Immigration*,[22] remains the standard account of Chinese exclusion. Little of substance was added until the publication of Gunther Barth's *Bitter Strength* in 1964.[23] Barth's work, however, stops at 1870, more than a decade short of the first exclusion law, and focuses almost entirely on anti-Chinese sentiment in California.

It was 1969, a full sixty years after the publication of Coolidge's work, before a full-scale historical description of U.S. exclusion of the Chinese appeared. Stuart Creighton Miller's *The Unwelcome Immigrant*[24] covers the period from 1785 to 1882. Miller's study is important because it documents that American persecution of the Chinese in the late nineteenth century was not a sectional phenomenon limited to California but was, in fact, the national attitude throughout the United States. This thesis renders the actions of the federal government in excluding the Chinese more comprehensible than the position that Chinese exclusion was due to a California "conspiracy."

The conventional historiographic view of the American image of the Chinese during the early days of the China trade, generally from 1785 to 1840, has been that Chinese civilization was held in high esteem by Americans. Before the first Anglo-Chinese conflict in 1841 (the so-called "Opium War"), American opinion of China is said to have been characterized by "respect," "admiration," "awe," and even "envy." This interpretation was later reflected in the writings of diplomats. The Opium War, however, is claimed to have changed this attitude altogether. The events of the war drastically reversed American opinion, to be followed by an "age of contempt" that lasted into the twentieth century.

In his superbly researched study of Chinese immigration and exclusion, Miller was severely critical of past conceptualizations of the American image of the Chinese as ever having been positive in any way. By digging deeper than most historians, using a larger sample of archival materials, and asking different questions, Miller was able to pierce the facade of the formal, flowery pidgin-language that passed for communication between the early American traders and Chinese merchants. The vernacular form of speech misled listeners into the belief that only friendly thoughts characterized the attitudes held by both groups toward each other. In his survey of the traders' reflections, Miller found no trace of racism—which is as it should be, for the doctrine of racism did not crystallize in America until the post–Civil War era. In its place, however, he found an unmistakable tendency toward derisively dismissing all things Chinese as ludicrous and anything but admirable.[25]

The early traders were not the only group of sojourners to send impressions of the Celestial Empire back to America. In the late eighteenth and throughout much of the nineteenth century, two other groups of opinion makers furnished the United States with a first-hand description of China—diplomats and Protestant missionaries.

The diplomat-authors, whether American or European, who visited and later wrote about China during the fifty-five years from 1785 to 1840, differed from the early traders in a number of ways. Their background and training tended to be aristocratic. In general, they were articulate and well educated. The nature of their business in China provided them with a broader view of the country and allowed them access to interior provinces not frequented by traders, nor by missionaries as yet. Their superior experience and articulateness were not lost on American editors, who, Miller noted, considered that "ten books on China that were the by-products of European embassies to that nation were more important than the accounts of the less literate and prestigious trader."[26] Scarcely an article was written about China before 1850 that failed to cite one or another diplomat-author as the authority. Despite the many differences that existed between the diplomat-authors and the traders in background, training, and education, however, Miller found that in their views about China the two groups paralleled one another, sharing many negative opinions in common.[27]

The Protestant missionaries arrived in China a bit later than the traders and diplomats. Although their numbers were relatively few before 1840, their influence on American public opinion proved in the long run to be the most influential and lasting. The strength of the missionary influence in shaping the American image of the Chinese was due, in part, to the missionaries' voluminous reportage. Unlike the traders and most diplomats, missionaries generally became fluent in one or more of the Chinese languages. Missionary writings tended to be popular or semi-popular and received a wide circulation in the United States. Missionaries did not have to rely solely on a lay press for distribution. A large religious press, as well as the more personal forum of the pulpit, was available to them for spreading news of their work abroad.

The strength of the missionary influence on American thinking rested not only on the volume of the news they sent back and on the efficient manner with which their views were disseminated at home, but also on the emotional quality with which they expressed their views. As the latest of the opinion makers, they had inherited the earlier negative views of the traders and diplomats, which had already prepared the ground for a missionary denunciation of the Chinese.

That denunciation was total; it was emotionally conveyed through a "moral indignation" about all things to be found or seen in China. In many ways the missionaries were more parochial than the traders, and certainly more so than the diplomats, who displayed some respect for "China's religious toleration and general religious indifference."[28] The missionary focus "on paganism impugned all aspects of Chinese society and led to a . . . pronounced assault on the moral and intellectual characteristics of the people and their character development."[29] In several ways the goals of the missionaries in China were far more grandiose than those of traders, who sought profit and markets, or those of diplomats, who sought negotiating stances and favorable positions of power. The missionaries sought an absolute: the perfect conversion of heathens and pagans to Christianity, a conversion within which the concept of "civilization" itself was argued. Either civilization paved the way for Christianity, or without the benefit of Christianity there would be no civilization. The missionaries argued the latter course, but the more they confronted the Celestial Empire, the more frustrated—or episodically, over-optimistic—they became about the eventual conversion of China to the ways of New England Christianity.

China was little inclined to bend in the direction of missionary goals. Such was the magnitude of missionary ethnocentrism, however, that in place of attempting to understand China, as the Jesuits earlier had done, Protestant missionaries translated their perceptions into the calculus of their own ideological framework and concluded that the Chinese were in partnership with the Devil. Supremely convinced that New England gospel of civilization was the highest form of cultural achievement and utterly disdainful of Confucianism and its philosophy, the missionaries found little in China that was not inimical to their own standards and values. Miller wrote,

Nothing Chinese escaped the critical pen of the missionary. Even China's esteemed examination system was reduced to trite penmanship exercises in the rote memorization of Confucian banalities. Often the stinging indictments of Chinese behavior to be found in missionary sources could easily have been written . . . in the heyday of sandlot sinophobia in San Francisco or uttered in the halls of Congress during the exclusion disputes. For example, one passage in an American Board [of Commissioners for Foreign Missions] pamphlet declared, "Underneath a calm and courteous exterior, foreigners have found them cunning and corrupt, treacherous and vindictive. Gambling and drunkenness, though abundantly prevalent, are far outstripped by their licentiousness, which taints the language with its leprosy, often decorates the walls of their inns with the foulest of scenes by them called 'flowers' and lurks beneath a thin Chinese lacker as a deep dead rot in society."[30]

The negative stereotype of China dispatched back to America by traders, by diplomats, and, above all, by the frustrated but indefatigable missionaries prepared the way for the formation of the grossly unfavorable image of China and the Chinese people that emerged in the United States after the Anglo-Chinese War.

The geopolitical phase of Chinese relations with the West had been opened by the Opium War of 1841.[31] The war signaled the piercing of China's autonomy by the merchant nations of the West. The issue at first was trade; beyond that was the issue of the treaty system whereby Western powers gained an increasing series of concessions from a reluctant China. Internal unrest and disorganization within China itself made that nation vulnerable. Great Britain seized upon this vulnerability when the Chinese government attempted to regulate the inflow of opium that Britain had for decades shipped to China from India in exchange for Chinese tea.

Inaccessible to the West since the European Middle Ages and insistent on enlarging its own territory rather than be engulfed, China was ultimately forced to give ground in the face of Western imperialism. In 1842 Hong Kong was ceded outright to Great Britain. Through the treaties of Nanking in 1842 and of Tientsin in 1857, as well as others that followed, dozens of cities, including Shanghai and Canton, were opened to Europeans as "treaty ports." Europeans were allowed to settle and to be immune from Chinese laws and regulations. Western gunboats now patrolled the Yangtse River. The Chinese paid war indemnities and agreed to levy import taxes on European goods not in excess of 5 percent; this practice created a highly favorable trade market for Europe.

A new combined British and French incursion into China took place in 1857, when 17,000 soldiers entered, burned, and looted Peking. This event forced the Chinese to receive foreign diplomats, and the legitimization of European trade in that country was secured. Foreign annexation of huge regions along the outer periphery of China's landmass soon followed. The Russians moved down the Amur River and founded the port city of Vladivostok in 1860; the French consolidated Indochina in 1883; and the British annexed Burma in 1886. By 1898 it looked as if the entire Chinese Empire would soon be partitioned away, much as the European powers, in fact, were already doing in Africa.

News about events in China and elsewhere abroad quickly spread in the United States with the growth of the "penny press." This inexpensive and popular format effectively challenged the older, more respectable Wall Street newpapers in the battle for readers. The penny press was born in the 1830s. By the time its ideological struggle with its Wall Street competitors reached a climax, the United States, "a simple nation," Carl Bode, the cultural historian noted, "when the forties began . . . [had become] a complex one when the fifties ended. The people and the printed word came together."[32] The penny press, a term synonymous in the United States with James Gordon Bennett, thrived on the sensationalism of the day—scandals, adventures, wars. The Opium War provided Bennett with an opportunity to sharpen his paper's competitive manner and to mold its idiosyncratic style, and at the same time to provide readers with copy, real and embroidered, with which to shape American thinking and policies.

The development of an unfavorable image of the Chinese was a process that accelerated and gathered momentum as the nineteenth century wore on. After 1850, American impressions of the Chinese were fed from more than just news accounts of events taking place in China. Of greater interest to Americans at midcentury and in the decades that followed was the fact of Chinese immigration to the United States. By 1880, more than 100,000 Orientals had arrived in U.S. cities and towns.[33] In writing about the Chinese after midcentury, "American editors," Miller noted, "did not always consciously relate the happenings in China . . . to the question of Chinese immigration into the United States."[34] They did not need to, for by 1870 the Chinese, wherever they were—in California, New York, New Jersey, Pennsylvania, Massachusetts—"were uppermost in the minds of Americans; and it would not have been easy to separate reports of barbarity and perversity in China from the Celestial immigrants."[35] The process whereby Americans increasingly viewed the Chinese as undesirable immigrants culminated in the United States with the passage of the Chinese Exclusion Acts later in the century. The legal exclusion of the Chinese was a response that developed in concert with the growing perception throughout the Western world that China was a danger to Western civilization—the "yellow peril."

Yellow peril was to become an absorbing concept that has continued in one form or another well into the present. It encompassed Western fears of the latent strength and growing power of the Asiatic mainland. The yellow perilists first feared China alone. They later came to dread the possibility that either Russia or Japan would upset Western dominance by securing control of China. With the defeat of Russia by Japan in 1905, the yellow perilists turned their attention to the changes that would result from some form of Sino-Japanese collaboration. Finally, after 1915, Japanese imperial expansion alone formed the basis of the fear of Oriental power.[36]

Throughout the active history of yellow peril and its later variant, the "red menace," the Western image of China, Japan, and Russia alternately has been less than favorable, depending on the circumstances of the particular nations involved. China, the first of the Asiatic nations to be feared, received the strongest, and by far the most all-embracing, denunciation. American denunciation of the Chinese was compounded by the fact that fear of the Chinese coincided with the development of American racist ideology, with the emancipation of Negroes and their subsequent institutionalized "inferiority," as well as with the popularization of Spencerian ideas of biosocial evolution.

The doctrine of racism, Haller noted, was to become the social instrument for making America "safe" in order to protect democracy.[37] Evolutionary schemata incorporating ideas of the survival of the fittest had little bearing, Haller wrote, "on the concept of race inferiority and much less upon the derivation of its racist ideas." Yet, although scientists, physicians, and academicians endlessly debated the fine points of racial classification and the relative merits of the races of humankind, the subject of race inferiority itself was beyond critical reach in the late nineteenth century.[38]

The social Darwinists or Spencerians of the late nineteenth century viewed human evolution from a unilinear perspective. They made no distinction between organic and social development and argued that cultural life unfolded in accordance with the same evolutionary principles that operated in the physical world. With this felicity of thinking, they easily bridged the physical and social sciences, from biology to psychology to sociology. In arguing the thesis of Aryan supremacy, American Spencerians sought a social-scientific foundation for creating a social structure in the United States embodying the values and virtues of white, Anglo-Saxon civilization. Pragmatically and ideologically oriented, they sought to restrict from participation in American life those groups who failed the test of Aryan criteria.

In the late nineteenth century three "races" provided the United States with its severest test of assimilation: Negroes, American Indians, and the Chinese. In the framework of the early cultural evolutionists, Negroes and American Indians occupied a low place on the ladder of human evolution, too far down on the scale biologically and psychically to live with civilized man on an equal footing. Cranial capacity, one of the most widely used anthropometric indices, and other osteological measurements placed Caucasians at the top of the evolutionary list, Africans at the very bottom.[39] Racial "progress" was viewed as proceeding at different rates. Caucasians advanced geometrically, whereas the "lower races" progressed at a simple arithmetic pace, if, indeed, they were capable of progressing at all. Although according to some rankings the American Indian stood higher on the scale of evolution than the Australian, Polynesian, and African, others placed the American Indian at "the zero of human society," from which "there was no hope of elevation."[40]

In terms of evolutionary development, of the three groups directly confronting America's evolving supremacist ideology, the Chinese posed a peculiar dilemma for theorists.[41] Anthropometry did not prove as helpful in arguing the case of Chinese inferiority as it did in demonstrating physiological differences between the Negro and the Caucasian. Given the massive data accumulated during the Civil War comparing body measurements of white, black, mulatto, and American Indian males in the service of the armies of both the North and the South, "scientists," Haller wrote, "found it easier to argue Negro inferiority from facial angle, prognathism, and brain weight than to argue the inferiority of Indian, Chinese, and Malayan using the same devices."[42]

Spencerian sociologists, noting the Chinese proclivity for hard work, their intellectual ability, and their capacity to adapt to the range of environmental conditions that China's vast territory demanded, were also hard put to condemn the Chinese on sociological grounds. China's history, empire status, and emphasis on education in government also had to be considered by the historical sociologists of the day. In the absence of comparable anthropometric and sociological evidence, Spencerian theorists indicted the Chinese as inferior on the basis of judgments of contemporary Chinese social behavior.[43]

In the case of the Chinese, the Spencerian theorists said, evolutionary stagnation was the result of an absolute adherence to tradition and custom. China was a backward nation, "a fossilized representative of an antique system, physically active but mentally inert," wrote Charles Morris in 1902.[44] The Chinese were possessed of a pointless belief in ancestor worship and exhibited characteristics that persisted long after their usefulness had vanished. They retained a simple, monosyllabic language that lacked a word for "liberty." Furthermore, they displayed a propensity to save and a willingness to live on so little that they had an undesired advantage in the world of Anglo-Saxons, who had come to demand more from life. In short, they possessed character traits so conservative as to make them unable to assimilate to the progressive nature of Western civilization. According to sociologist Gerrit Lansing, the Oriental's traditional blind dependence on authority would assuredly erode America's struggle to preserve freedom, independence, and individualism for its people.[45]

The intellectual response to Herbert Spencer's ideas was considerable. In addition to attracting many disciples, his books sold splendidly, even more so in the United States than in England. By the end of the nineteenth century more than 300,000 volumes had been sold in the United States alone.[46] Spencerian ideologists ultimately provided the conceptual framework for racial distinctions and enunciated the rationale on which restrictive immigration policies were formulated. But in the years after midcentury it was the penny press and the popular monthly magazines, along with the daily newspapers, that carried the message accentuating American fears, suspicion, and contempt of the Chinese.

With the arrival of the first Chinese immigrants to the United States at midcentury, the earlier negative themes about the Chinese character developed by traders, diplomats, and missionaries continued to appear in U.S. newspapers and magazines. Soon, however, newer themes began to emerge

that owed little or nothing to developments in China . . . [but] owed much to certain key phenomena inside the Unites States. . . . Chief among these newer critical themes were the fear of slavery, the emphasis on racial differences, and the menace of loathsome, contagious disease. . . . For one thing the Chinese arrived in the middle of the slavery controversy and were never able to shake the "coolie" label. They also arrived during the period when the work of Holmes, Lister, and Semmelweis made Americans more conscious of the relationship between dirt and disease. By the time the first exclusion law was enacted, these fears had advanced to the more sophisticated level of "Chinese germs."[47]

The Spencerian Darwinist doctrine of the survival of the fittest enabled white Anglo-Saxons to see themselves in the most self-congratulatory terms. The doctrine convinced its adherents that natural selection worked. It had placed Caucasians at the top of the evolutionary ladder, where, through the enlightened processes of nature and superior biology, they would remain. The germ theory of disease, however, soon provided a disquieting glimpse into the manner by which an obviously inferior group could vanquish a superior one.

Racial factors in disease became a subject of intense interest to physicians after the midcentury, first as they applied to emancipated Negroes and second, to the Chinese. Under emancipation, the Negro was thought to be doomed to extinction. Physicians "vehemently dismissed the possibility for race improvement and, with a minimum expenditure of rhetoric, they offered a prophetic warning for the race's future."[48] If the Negro did not die off from promiscuity and syphilis, the overwhelming responsibilities incurred with freedom would alone bring the race to the edge of insanity. If not insanity and idiocy, then consumption would kill them off. If not tuberculosis, there was still a long list of other diseases that physicians predicted would bring an end to the race problem.

Chinese diseases, on the other hand, were perceived differently. It was anticipated that the Negroes would succumb alone to those diseases and morbid tendencies to which they were vulnerable; but Chinese germs were seen as posing a threat not only to the Chinese themselves but also to those peoples and lands where they emigrated. Having no natural immunity to new environments would only heighten the disease susceptibility of alien races to epidemic proportions, so one theory of the day argued, thereby adding to the probability that the indigenous population would increasingly become infected.[49]

Early missionary reports had helped to lay a foundation in the American mind that China was overrun with myriad diseases.[50] Chinese diseases were cited early as an argument proclaiming the threat that Chinese immigration posed to the United States. In 1862, Dr. Arthur B. Stout noted in *Chinese Immigration and the Physiological Causes of the Decay of a Nation* that the main threat to society was from the "hereditary diseases," among which he listed "phthisis or consumption, scrofula, syphilis, mental alienation and epidemic diseases," all, in turn, aggravated by the Chinese proclivity for smoking opium.[51]

The threat of Chinese diseases became a favorite theme in arousing American fears and hostility and in emphasizing the terrible danger that Chinese immigration posed to U.S. civilization. Chinese diseases were not perceived to be diseases in the ordinary sense. They were portrayed as more potent and, moreover, incurable. One common journalistic and oratorical device was to describe Chinese diseases as "nameless," or else to refer to them emotionally as "epidemics," "pestilence," and "plague." In arguing the case for Chinese exclusion, Oregon Senator James H. Slater warned the U.S. Senate that the Chinese would "bring with them their filth and frightful and nameless diseases and contagions."[52] By leaving diseases nameless, or even when calling them "the incurable . . . Asiatic scrofula," journalists and orators rendered them more mysterious and more terrifying. Even more menacing, however, was the fact that Chinese diseases were associated with a race of people that Americans increasingly perceived as "morally unclean." Images of filth and pollution were extensively used in congressional debates to describe the Chinese character: They were "debased and degraded," "personally and collectively filthy"; and their "touch is pollution." "Their garments reek with pestilence and decay." With their supposed addiction to opium and delight in perverse sexual habits, their continued presence was seen as poisoning America's bloodstream through the large numbers of prostitutes entering the country.[53]

From the many speeches and articles condemning the Chinese and arguing for their exclusion, it would appear that the sole reason for Chinese immigration into the United States was for the purpose of encouraging prostitution. "Ninety-nine out of a hundred of the females imported are for immoral purposes," California Senator Aaron A. Sargent informed his colleagues in the Senate on July 6, 1876.[54] Themes of prostitution had been advanced in congressional debates during the previous ten years. The same argument was used by William Highy, then member of Congress from the second district of California, in a speech in 1866.[55] Prostitution was an emotional and multifaceted issue to those who sought to exclude the Chinese from the United States. In the late 1860s and early 1870s, Chinese prostitution was linked to criminal behavior and to slavery. The Chinese, Senator Slater argued in Congress in 1882 during the exclusion debate, cunningly evade our laws and display a devilish capacity to organize. "Those who come . . . are of the lowest orders of the Chinese population, largely criminal. . . . They bring no families as a general rule, but numbers of their country women are brought for purposes of prostitution, and are brought and sold among themselves as slaves, and our laws and courts are powerless to prevent it."[56]

West Coast officials in the House of Representatives and in the U.S. Senate were not alone in sounding a national alarm about prostitution and the threat of Chinese diseases. The American medical profession soon joined in reinforcing these fears. In 1876, Dr. J. Marion Sims, president of the American Medical Association, in an official address, warned that syphilis had already reached epidemic proportions, spread by Chinese "slaves." He stated that "ninety-nine hundredths of the Chinese women imported into California are sold and held as slaves—slaves to be used wholly and solely for the purpose of prostitution—and . . . their presence necessarily breeds moral and physical pestilence."[57] Sims told his audience that on the West Coast "even boys eight and ten years old have been syphilized by these degraded wretches." Cholera, at least, he noted, has a permanent home in Asia, "where it is perpetually generated, [and when] transplanted, it flourishes for a while, then dies out. . . . But syphilis . . . always fixes itself in great populous centres, taking up its abode in the haunts of ignorance, poverty, squalor, filth, and vice. From these low conditions of life, it mounts gradually higher and higher, and sometimes to the highest, so that in the end whole communities . . . become contaminated.[58]

The potency of Chinese syphilis, sensationalized in the press and in congressional oratory, was heightened by lurid descriptions of the personal filth of the Chinese, of the horrible human conditions of opium dens and brothels, and of the overcrowded squalor of Chinatowns in San Francisco and New York.[59] The fear of Chinese diseases and other moral perfidies was excited by such nationalist sentiments as that expressed by Senator Sargent when he said, "Can we stand all the vices, all the diseases, all the mischief that infect humanity the world over and retain our American civilization?"[60] The fear was so intense by the late 1870s that the editors of *The New York Times*, although opposed to Chinese exclusion, admitted defeat and predicted that disease fears alone would decide the Chinese question.[61]

Early in the 1870s, leprosy finally joined the long list of grievances accumulating in America against the Chinese. In the process of excluding the Chinese, the United States was expressing its growing racist ideology and simultaneously preparing the way for regulating future immigration. As a "loathsome" disease known to be spreading in Hawaii as a result of the importation of Chinese laborers, and as a pejorative metaphor, leprosy came to be increasingly referred to by American writers and orators in denouncing naturalization policies that permitted the continued immigration into the country of undesirable races. A resolution was offered on January 25, 1870, on the question of the right of individual states to exclude the Chinese, notwithstanding the existence of a treaty between the United States and the government of China. Representative James A. Johnson of California delivered a long, emotionally charged speech in which he summed up the fate that awaited America should such immigration continue:

> If the Hottentot, the cannibal from the jungles of Africa, the West India negro, the wild Indians, and the Chinaman are to become a ruling element in this country, then call your ministers from abroad, bring your missionaries home, tear down your schoolhouses, convert your churches into dens and brothels, wherein our young may receive fatal lessons to end in rotting bones, decaying and putrid flesh, poisoned blood, leprous bodies, and leprous souls.[62]

The early Protestant missionaries in China had helped to create the impression, later sensationalized in America through the mass media, that China was rotten with disease. Miller has noted that their "reports were full of comments on the wretched climate and high incidence of epidemics that had claimed the health and lives" of many a missionary. One medical missionary, according to Miller, "would have it that the Chinese shake hands with themselves upon greeting a person because of the prevalence of cutaneous diseases among them."[63] In emphasizing the medical threat that the Chinese posed, venereal disease was generally implied. However, leprosy was also noted in early reports, although infrequently. Sir John Bowring,

Great Britain's representative to China early in the century, reportedly said that in 1840 Chinese advisers had suggested infecting "British invaders with leprosy, but it was deemed impractical since the effect would not be quick enough."[64]

Unlike venereal disease, leprosy came to Western attention relatively late. The disease first came to international public notice in the 1860s, when leprosy was reported to be spreading in Hawaii. A full-scale alarm did not materialize in the United States and in Europe until the death of Father Damien in 1889. The first law excluding the Chinese from the United States had passed seven years earlier, but Western fears of "yellow peril" and of "Oriental" leprosy would persist well into the twentieth century.

The call for the exclusion of the Chinese from centers of Western civilization on the grounds of disease was not limited to America. Great Britain's James Cantlie, writing from his experience in the Far East, dramatically called for the exclusion of the Chinese in order to prevent the "destruction of whole races" through the spread of leprosy. In his prize-winning essay on leprosy, published by the New Sydenham Society, Cantlie wrote:

> [T]here are three homes of leprosy in the Pacific—Hawaii, Fiji, and New
> Caledonia. At once the thought strikes one, Hawaii is practically American, Fiji
> is British, New Caledonia is French. Yet the Americans, the British, and the
> French are not leprous, and cannot have introduced the disease. Leprosy is not
> indigenous in any part of the Pacific, yet there must be some common factor
> in the three centres which has determined its presence. That fact—indeed, the
> only common factor—is the Chinaman, and he *is* leprous. . . .
> If ever there was a case in which strong governments should act strongly it
> is this. . . . There seems but one way to prevent [the spread of leprosy] . . .
> and that is the exclusion or the rigid control of all Chinese coolies. I know the
> good qualities of the Chinaman . . . but when it comes to tainting the
> world—and this is what it amounts to in the end—one would be wanting . . .
> if one did not speak in the most unmistakable terms upon the danger that is
> at our doors in the Far East.[65]

The symbolic image of leprosy that was shaping up toward the end of the nineteenth century fit very well with the collective image that Westerners had already formed of the Chinese. Popular beliefs about leprosy—that it devoured its victims' appendages and that it was fearfully infectious—would appear to represent a view more consonant with the period of ardent sinophobia and the stereotype of the Chinese than was warranted on the basis of medical knowledge. Leprosy was known to have a long incubation period—a fact considerably at odds with popular misconceptions about instant deformity. Medical science also endorsed the necessity of intensive skin-to-skin contact for infection to occur, but this knowledge was far removed from the looseness with which the idea of transmission was popularly interpreted.

The exclusion of the Chinese and the subsequent passage of laws restricting the future immigration of those suffering from "loathsome and contagious disease" did not, however, diminish the thought that leprosy would invade the United States. Late in the nineteenth century, voices were raised that Americans were exposed to a great danger not only from the importation of undesirable people, but also from "foods and merchandise exported to this country from localities where leprous bacilli have . . . taken possession of communities favorable to its spread." Reverend Mulhane, in 1896, warned of the danger from imports grown and handled abroad under unhygienic and "barbaric" conditions:

> Sugar, bananas, and the like . . . have been handled by leprous West Indian negroes. . . . Tea and ginger from China, codfish from New Brunswick, and rags from the countries bordering on the Eastern part of the Mediterranean, have been particularly regarded by . . . dermatologists as of the most dangerous of all the ways in which leprosy may be communicated through the length and breadth of this country.[66]

An even greater fear, however, was expressed about U.S. annexation of foreign territories. Dr. Prince A. Morrow informed fellow dermatologists in 1900:

> Our territorial expansion has created conditions favorable to the increase of leprosy in this country. The danger will come from the exposure of soldiers and sailors who form the army of occupation, of civilians who fill administrative posts in the government of these colonies, and of others who are attracted by considerations of trade and commerce and who are thus brought into intimate contact with their leprous population. Whatever doubt there may be of the contagious activity of leprosy when transplanted to this country there can be no question of its ultracontagiousness in these tropical islands.[67]

The territorial acquisitions uppermost in the minds of American men of medicine at the turn of the century were the leprosy-prevalent Hawaiian Islands, Puerto Rico, Cuba, and the Philippines. Morrow called the Philippines "one of the most important centers of leprosy in the Orient." As much as the Philippines was regarded as a center of leprosy, however, the danger hardly compared with the fact that the islands were in close "proximity to the 'cradle of leprosy' in Kwan Tung [China] and the leprosy-infected countries of Japan." Both these countries were expected to furnish the Philippines with "fresh increments of infected material through immigration of Chinese and Japanese coolies."[68]

To Westerners at the turn of the century, China was the most feared country imaginable and leprosy was the most feared disease. Fear of the Oriental had been part of the Western image of China at least since Genghis Khan, Miller has noted.[69] To this ancient fear was now added the belief that the "Flowery Kingdom has been the breeding-place and nursery of pestilential diseases, cholera, plague, as well as leprosy, from time imme-morial." Only the "traditional exclusiveness" of China had prevented these diseases from spreading beyond where they have domiciled for centuries. An "open door" policy to the West would change this, and Chinese "infectious diseases will lose their endemic character and become pandemic." Already, in modern times, "the Chinese have been the most active disseminators of leprosy. . . . These pig-tailed Argonauts of the Orient in their world-wide migrations in quest of the Golden Dollar have invaded many lands and almost every land they have touched they have tainted with leprosy."[70]

The fear that the Chinese represented a leprosy threat to the United States would remain part of American thinking from the early 1870s until at least the middle of the twentieth century.[71] In California, Denis Kearney, whose sinophobia became legendary, exploited the issue of the Chinese as leprous on the street corners of San Francisco. He went so far as to have his lieutenants drive disfigured Chinamen around the city on public exhibition, "while the fiery Caucasian," as *The New York Times* reported one incident, "launched a harangue at the crowd, pointing to the helpless John as an awful example."[72] California's sinophobia and leprophobia received considerable coverage in eastern newspapers. *The New York Herald* reprinted the testimony of a sailor who caught leprosy in a "Chinese den" and of another who attributed his disease to cigars wrapped by Chinese workers.[73] Dr. C. C. O'Donnell, one of Kearney's ideologues, spurred Dr. James Hyde, the president of the American Dermatological Association, into requesting an examination of the spread of leprosy in the United States. James Gordon Bennett demanded that Congress investigate the disease before it became "naturalized" in California.[74] In other parts of the country sinophobes were freely attributing the spread of leprosy through casual contact with "tawny fingers." Chinese cigar workers in New York City were erroneously reported to the Board of Health as having "Asiatic leprosy."[75] Convinced of the need to take local action in ridding California of its lepers, San Francisco authorities in 1880 began shipping Chinese lepers out of the state secretly for "fear of writs of habeas corpus being obtained by their friends."[76]

Early in the 1890s, physicians in California were having a hard time reconciling their scientific knowledge about leprosy with their sinophobia. Dr. John Foye, who had been asked by Hyde to conduct an investigation of leprosy in California to determine whether it might spread across the country, reported that the disease was "less general than is supposed" on the West Coast and that only one non-Mongolian had it.[77] This report, however, did not calm the alarmists. Nor were they calmed by the knowledge that the disease failed to take root in America when brought to the Upper Mississippi Valley by Norwegian immigrants. The Chinese were regarded as an exception. The exception followed the thinking of the social Darwinists and, in the words of Dr. Douglass W. Montgomery, was based on "the difference in social conservatism between the Aryans and the Mongolians." Dr. Montgomery argued:

> The European, of whatever nation, comes here to form a home, and the more prosperous he is, the more comfortable the home becomes. The Chinaman, no matter how prosperous he may be, lives under mean conditions and saves his money that he may realize his ideal of living in splendor on returning to China. . . . The Chinese in California live practically the same way they do in

China and, as far as social conditions are concerned, leprosy would have an equal chance of propagating itself among them here as there.[78]

As the United States approached the twentieth century and entered the arena of great powers, an enormous cultural transformation had altered the structure and fabric of an earlier America. "The Civil War," Oscar Handlin wrote, "had shaken the polity and industrialization had transformed the economy. . . . Festering beneath the surface [was] a gnawing anxiety about the meaning of Americanism."[79]

On epidemiological grounds, leprosy was an insignificant disease in the United States at the turn of the century. In Louisiana it was only hypoendemic and limited mainly to the indigenous white population of New Orleans and its surrounding parishes. Once the question of the location of the state leper home was settled, the disease ceased to make headlines. Among the Scandinavian settlers of the Upper Mississippi Valley, leprosy had declined to near extinction. Only the Chinese remained. By the end of the nineteenth century, the imagery of leprosy had merged with the symbolism of racism and yellow peril to the point where a distinction between the medical entity and unfavorable populations was effectively blurred.

7

Beginnings of a
U.S. National Leprosarium

Leprosy did not become an issue in the United States, in either Louisiana or the nation, until late in the 1880s, that is, not until the great "cultural transition" in America had already barred the Chinese from entering the country. By then, too, new immigration policies were being formulated, first to select, then to restrict, the future peopling of the United States.

No references to leprosy appear in the *Descriptive Catalogue of the Government Publications of the U.S.* from the date of the first issue on September 5, 1774, until March 4, 1881.[1] The first three items to appear were brief reports on leprosy in Hawaii (1881), Venezuela (1883), and South Africa (1887).[2] The fourth item was a two-page letter from Dr. A. Berger of Tampa, Florida, dated December 29, 1888; the letter was referred to the Committee on Epidemic Diseases, U.S. Senate, on January 5, 1889. Berger noted that he had made leprosy a specialty of his general practice for the preceding nine years and in that time had "found lepers all over the Union; far more than I or any other physician had expected . . . in New York, Michigan, Illinois, British Columbia, California, Missouri, etc., but most of them . . . in the South, Cuba, the West Indies, Key West, . . . [altogether] over one thousand lepers in the United States and Cuba." Pronouncing leprosy "one of the most important national questions of our country," Berger proposed that the U.S. Government "should procure an isolated place, some island far enough from any land to make separation easy and perfect, and should make there a regular leper settlement, like other Governments, according to science and humanity."[3]

Starting in the late 1880s, there was a spate of articles and speeches calling upon the federal government to create a place to isolate all lepers who had found their way onto the shores of the continental United States. Concomitantly, the Surgeon General, with the approval of President Benjamin Harrison, on December 23, 1889, ordered that all lepers attempting to enter the United States be returned to their country of origin or, if detected within three years of their arrival, be deported.[4] This action added to a sense of "crisis," but because its provisions were difficult to implement it merely strengthened the argument for federal intervention in confining lepers internally. These early efforts to single out lepers antedated the Immigration

Act of March 3, 1903, by fourteen years. The 1903 Act was the first detailed law to specifically exclude from the United States "persons afflicted with a loathsome or with a dangerous contagious disease."[5]

The motion calling for federal control of leprosy through the creation of a national leprosarium sputtered along unresolved for the next quarter century until 1917, when a bill, S. 4086, defeated earlier in 1905, finally passed the U.S. Congress. Implementation of the bill was delayed another four years before the Louisiana Home for Lepers came under federal jurisdiction on January 3, 1921.

In his article on the national leprosarium movement, historian Philip Kalisch refers to the federal search for a site on which to locate the institution as a "comedy of errors."[6] Although more congressmen voted in favor of the legislation than opposed it, the documentation reveals that those in favor of it also favored that the leprosarium not be located in their own state. The selection of Carville, Louisiana, the site of a state leper home since 1894, was not a logical or an orderly choice. Described as "rundown" and earlier characterized by Surgeon General Rupert Blue as having "but little to commend it beyond the fact that it would have offered a prompt solution to the question of providing a location,"[7] the Carville home was a late and expeditious compromise.

The problem the federal government faced in securing a site for a national leprosarium was part of the same set of nagging questions it faced in considering whether a national leprosarium was even necessary. In describing the defeat of the 1905 bill, Kalisch depicts the debate in the House of Representatives as a struggle about where to locate the institution.[8] The issue of leprosy in the United States at the turn of the century, however, was more complex than simply establishing agreement on the need for federal control over the disease and finding disagreement only in terms of where to locate the lepers. The issue of whether lepers needed special confinement, or, indeed, any special treatment beyond that already accorded those afflicted with tuberculosis or syphilis, was not decided on medical grounds. Ultimately, the important policy decisions were decided on emotional and ideological grounds that encoded leprosy with the overtones and images of nineteenth-century Western ideas about race.

As early as the Berger memorandum, government officials and leprosy alarmists had already prefigured the stance that the United States would take in the management of leprosy. The model was Molokai. If the federal government was slow in establishing a Molokai of its own in the continental United States, it moved rapidly enough in 1901, at the end of the Spanish-American War, when it created one of the world's largest colonies, for Philippine lepers, on the island of Culion, 200 miles from Manila in the South China Sea.[9] If the true goals were "science and humanity," and not "some island far enough from any land to make separation easy and perfect," then the United States, in seeking to deal with leprosy at home, had another model from which to choose—the approach that had developed in Norway.

In choosing banishment in place of medicine and science, the U.S. leaders effectively reclassified the disease. They removed leprosy from a medical context and made it a social or moral issue. This change in status is implicit in discussions of whether the U.S. Government had the constitutional power to nationalize leprosy. In reviewing the situation in 1894, Surgeon General Walter Wyman noted that "the United States Government can only legislate in accordance with powers expressly delegated by the Constitution, and . . . the latter are only granted when necessary for the general welfare." Wyman, however, saw a solution to the constitutional question by following another procedure:

> The States, however, may make any laws which are not forbidden by the Constitution. . . . This view would discourage the attempt to establish a national leper hospital by the General Government, but it is claimed that the end might be met by one State establishing a hospital and being willing to receive into it the lepers consigned from other States, their expense being paid by the latter, as has been done in a number of instances with regard to jails and penitentiaries.[10]

In discussions late in the nineteenth century about deporting foreign lepers or else confining them internally, the presence of leprosy among Scandinavian settlers in the Upper Mississippi Valley went relatively unnoticed. Norway was well known for leprosy. Between 1857 and 1900, nearly 8,000 cases of the disease had been counted. During the same period more than 200,000 Norwegians had arrived in the United States, and since the 1860s Norwegian physicians had kept this population under observation.[11] Yet the presence of leprosy among Norwegians never frightened the Western world. Norwegian leprosy was never regarded as an "imperial danger."

From time to time, a few attempts were made to whip up a scare by pointing to Norwegian immigration. However, for the most part these efforts were unsuccessful, as the Scandinavian community would quickly mount a defense. Leprosy was not regarded by Norwegians with the same negative awesomeness that overwhelmed those whose point of reference about the disease lay elsewhere in the world. Norway had discovered leprosy in its own backyard, so to speak, among its own countrymen. Leprosy was a disease, no more; it was an unpleasant fact of life, like poverty and illiteracy. It was not an alien phenomenon and, as such, did not provoke an extreme response or demand extreme measures. Thus, in 1889, Dr. Charles N. Hewitt, nonresident professor of public health, University of Minnesota, warned fellow physicians to be on the alert against inexperienced "experts" demanding the deportation of Scandinavian lepers.[12] In a similar fashion, Dr. Chr. Grönvold, an early pioneer in preventive medicine, in a letter to Dr. Franklin Staples, president of the Minnesota State Board of Health in 1890, criticized the alarmist activities of "a Miss Flaven" who had lectured on leprosy in Duluth: "I understand that she has a medical education and intends to go to the Sandwich Islands to take the place of the late Father Damien. She tells the Duluthians . . . that lepers are everywhere in Scandinavian settlements and that Minnesota must, as soon as possible, establish an isolation hospital for them."[13] And when physician Albert S.

Ashmead charged, in an article entitled "Did Norway Send as an Official Representative a Leper to America?"[14] that Norway was ridding its country of lepers by exporting them to the United States, Armauer Hansen himself responded angrily to the accusation.[15]

The presence of leprosy among Scandinavians in the Upper Mississippi Valley was unmemorable even to historians. In fact, August Hirsch, in reviewing the distribution of leprosy in North America in 1885, totally failed to mention the Norwegians at all. He cited only "the wide diffusion of the disease in Mexico, the occurrence of it among Chinese immigrants to California, and two smaller foci, the one in Louisiana and the other in New Brunswick [Canada]."[16] Nor were the Norwegians mentioned more recently in Harold H. Scott's 1939 textbook, *A History of Tropical Medicine*, in his discussion of the historical distribution of leprosy in the nontropical parts of the Western Hemisphere.[17]

The Scandinavian settlers who came to America began arriving in the 1820s. They were part of the "old immigration" that had peopled the United States before that period of U.S. history when Chinese "heathens" were excluded, when the "gentlemen's agreement" limited the entry of Japanese laborers, and when the native philosophy of "Americanism" emerged along with opposition to the "new immigrants" from eastern and southern Europe. Scandinavians were never subject to the extremes of racism that other groups encountered in the United States at the turn of the century. Norwegian leprosy never generated horror and alarm simply because Norwegians were never perceived as a "loathsome" people whose germs were considered culturally and biologically anathema to Anglo-Saxon civilization.

*   *   *

Two months before Berger's letter urging federal control of leprosy and the surveillance of all cases from Cuba and the West Indies, the American Public Health Association passed a resolution "calling upon the Marine-Hospital Service and the State board of health of Florida, and all quarantine commissioners of ports having intercourse with Cuban ports, to exercise the same vigilance with regard to leprosy that is already observed in the case of yellow fever."[18] In December of that year a circular was issued by the Surgeon General "forbidding entry of any vessel to any port of the United States without a certificate . . . that no case of leprosy was found on board . . . or in the case one had been found, that it had been detained at the quarantine station; with a further provision permitting the departure of the detained leper on out-going vessels bound to the foreign country from which the leper last sailed."[19]

The initial impulse of the federal government had been to control leprosy in the same manner it controlled acute infectious diseases: quarantine at the point of entry. Dr. Benjamin Lee, secretary of the State Board of Health of Pennsylvania, however, questioned the effectiveness of the method, noting: "So easy is the concealment of the disease . . . and so numerous are the avenues through which it may gain entrance . . . that we may reasonably look for a very considerable augmentation of the number of persons suffering from this infection. . . . I therefore venture to solicit . . . attention . . . to the question of the domestic quarantine or segregation of lepers."[20]

The idea of domestic quarantine was a hard notion to dislodge in light of the assertion that the United States was threatened on all sides by lepers gaining entry into the country undetected and in light of unsubstantiated claims as to the number already here, to say nothing of the numbers expected in the future. Verbal reports were circulated of the "vice" of "loathsome" foreign lepers. *The New York Times* reported missionary nurse Kate Marsden's description of Russian lepers exiled to Siberia in those terms.[21] These stories, along with pictures of the deteriorated physical condition of lepers in foreign lands, circulated among members of Congress and printed in government publications, further fueled the movement for the internal banishment of lepers.

Not all leprosy watchers, however, were convinced of the need for strict segregation controls. Nor were all convinced that leprosy warranted being singled out for special attention. Some people were far more concerned about tuberculosis. At the same time that Lee was issuing dire warnings to the American Public Health Association and to members of the Pan-American Medical Congress, Dr. Beaven Rake, medical superintendent of the Trinidad Lepers' Asylum and late member of the Anglo-Indian Leprosy Commission, was expressing a contrary view. Rake pointed out that in Norway, Iceland, India, and the Upper Mississippi Valley "there has been a large absolute decrease of leprosy apart from . . . segregation." In Trinidad, where "there is no compulsory segregation . . . the ratio of lepers to the general population has remained practically stationary." In Hawaii, on the other hand, "where compulsory segregation has been enforced for many years, there has been an enormous increase" in the disease. "The accumulated evidence goes to show that leprosy is rather less communicable than tuberculosis, and that if we isolate lepers, we ought *a fortiori* to shut up those suffering from tuberculosis."[22] Jonathan Hutchinson opposed the raising of special funds for leper asylums, as had happened in the case of the Prince of Wales Fund after the death of Father Damien. Hutchinson argued that the money should be used not solely for leprosy but for the study of endemic diseases:

> I do not think that I much approve the idea of collecting money for leper houses. What we have as medical and scientific men to do is to find out the cause and the means of prevention, and we should need all the money we can obtain for researches. In the administration of the "Prince of Wales fund" we felt it to be a mistake to have undertaken aid to asylums. . . . Why not include "Yaws," or why not make it "For the Study of widely spread Endemic Diseases, Especially Leprosy and Yaws."[23]

"Amazingly," Kalisch writes, "the fear displayed by most people lest they and their families become contaminated did not have its counterpart among many leading dermatologists and other medical men. On the contrary, the tendency for these authorities was, if they became concerned at all, merely to react as if leprosy was something less than a case of tuberculosis."[24] The eminent pathologist Dr. William Henry Welch, founder of the School of Hygiene & Public Health at Johns Hopkins and first director of the Institute of the History of Medicine, was among those least concerned. Welch held the view that "leprosy is practically the least contagious of all the infectious diseases"[25] and preferred to regard tuberculosis, whose mortality in the United States alone in the year 1900 was about 2 per 1,000, as a far more serious disease. Dr. William Osler, in a clinical lecture at the Johns Hopkins Hospital, February 2, 1898, expressed equally strong views and noted that attention to the disease was due to the activity in England of an Indian Leprosy Commission and the establishment of a National Leprosy Fund. Osler commented that "the likelihood of the disease progressing in the native American population is very slight. . . . I believe the danger of the disease spreading and becoming in any way a serious menace to the country is entirely fanciful."[26] One case had been at the Johns Hopkins Hospital "since April last," and Osler intended that as "she has improved so much . . . and as she is a free agent, I shall take an early opportunity to discharge her from my care."

New York City health authorities also took a benign view of leprosy. Following a special investigation by the New York Medical Society in 1896, the city of New York refused to segregate lepers or to classify leprosy as a contagious disease.[27] In the years of debate that followed, the attitude prevalent in New York City made some health officials question the need for a national isolation policy. In 1910, at a conference of state and territorial health officers meeting in conjunction with the United States Public Health and Marine-Hospital Service, Dr. F. Y. Porter of Florida expressed his doubts about the necessity of segregating lepers:

> It seems useless, Mr. Chairman, for the United States to be doing anything for this class of sufferers in view of the fact that the city of New York permits them to go at large. . . . Now, if they do that in a large metropolitan city like New York it certainly would cause us to hesitate and think over the question as to whether there is any existing necessity of segregating these unfortunates any more than segregating syphilitics in various stages of development.[28]

Others, however, found the attitude of New York City's leaders disturbing. Dr. Isadore Dyer, who was militant in his demand for national control, complained that those who called leprosy a danger were charged with behaving hysterically. "Such attacks," Dyer argued, "are engaged in by men to whom leprosy is an exotic disease, rarely observed and to whom [there is no] appeal. . . . While leprosy is slowly contagious and probably mildly contagious, its usual horrors argue the danger of neglect. With probably 500 known cases today, how many will there be in ten years, if there is no control?"[29] Dyer was from New Orleans and had been endorsing the idea of a national leprosarium ever since becoming disenchanted with the policy of the state-operated leper home in Louisiana. Since 1903 Dyer had hoped that the federal government would establish a control program based on science and medicine and not merely perpetuate an asylum, as was happening at Indian Camp.

Federal officials high in the ranks of the public health service were also interested in a national leprosarium. When the Congress of American Physicians and Surgeons met in Washington, D.C., in May 1894, leprosy was one of the issues on the agenda. One of the main speakers was Dr. Walter Wyman, surgeon general of the United States Marine-Hospital Service. At the end of his address, Wyman expressed a personal view: "As for myself, I believe that leprosy should be under national control."[30] If the purpose of the physicians and surgeons meeting in Washington, D.C., was to federalize leprosy, then in inviting Wyman to address them, they had little need to further lobby him. Wyman seems decidedly on the side of national control, despite any disqualifying statements about the relative contagiousness of the disease or its prevalence in the United States that he might have made. In a carefully worded address, Wyman argued the paradoxical facts. He said that a national asylum was warranted because

in some States the disease is of so rare occurrence that the erection of a special [state] hospital or place of confinement is scarcely justified, and it is desirable, therefore, that there should be established an asylum to which any of the States might send these unusual but highly objectionable patients. . . . If a national asylum were provided there would be no motive for concealment. Granted that the danger of contagion is small; granted that, in the language of another, a case of leprosy within a family should be regarded with less concern in its relation to the health of the remaining members than a case of tuberculosis . . . the disease spreads chiefly among the lower classes.[31]

Noting that there might be a constitutional question involved in establishing a national asylum, Wyman advised that "its necessity would have to be demonstrated to Congress." He suggested that a leprosy commission be appointed "to make a report on the prevalence of leprosy in the United States and the necessity and proper method of its control."[32]

The establishment of a national asylum had been strongly urged by sundry persons and medical societies since the late 1880s. The taking of immediate preventive measures is explicable as a public health procedure where the issue is a matter of disease mortality or morbidity. On epidemiological grounds, however, the targeting of leprosy was remarkable. The prevalence of the disease in the United States was not known. In fact, the number of cases in the country had never been investigated. What was known, however, was that leprosy existed on a far lesser scale than the more infectious tuberculosis. The question of contagion in leprosy was also uncertain, and if the procontagionists were willing to damn the nonbelievers they were also prepared to accept the idea of infection in the absence of scientifically convincing evidence. "It is purely an academic argument," Dyer wrote in 1920 and earlier in 1903, to contend that leprosy is not contagious "based on the fact that Koch's law is not fulfilled."[33] And on the question of "mild" contagion versus more rampant forms of dissemination, the alarmists were perfectly willing to argue the question both ways. If leprosy was topsy-turvy on medical and scientific grounds, it was anything but tospy-turvy on population grounds. At the turn of the century, the issue of leprosy in the United States was a firm part of the immigration question and of that of the acquisition of foreign possessions.

Wyman had called for a report on the prevalence of leprosy in the United States, and such an investigation was approved by Congress on March 2, 1899. On November 30, 1901, a commission reported that there were at that time 278 cases of leprosy in the country.[34] A second survey undertaken in 1909 proved to be even more embarrassing: It located only 139 cases. This caused Walter R. Brinckerhoff, director, Leprosy Investigation Station, Public Health and Marine-Hospital Service, to comment that "the total number of cases, 139, is trivial in relation to a total population of over 76,000,000 in the area under consideration." The numbers would be of little significance, Brinckerhoff noted, only "if it were not for the popular dread of leprosy."[35]

With the support of Surgeon General Wyman and various medical associations, a bill "to provide a leprosarium for the segregation of lepers and to prevent the spread of leprosy in the United States" was passed by the Senate in 1905 and favorably reported out by the House Committee on Interstate and Foreign Commerce. In a letter written on January 10, 1905, to the secretary of the treasury in support of the bill, Wyman added a few embellishments to his argument heightening the "absolute necessity" for a national leprosarium, extra touches that enhanced the argument for strong controls. The first linked leprosy to the spread of tuberculosis. "Another reason for the . . . segregation . . . of all lepers in the United States," Wyman wrote, "is . . . that one of the recognized terminations of leprosy is by an intercurrent infection of pulmonary tuberculosis." The leper "becomes not only dangerous from the point of view of the spread of his original ailment—leprosy—but is also an agent in the possible spread of tuberculosis."[36] The second touch was Wyman's reasoning in providing "hazard duty" pay to those officers detailed for service at the leprosarium:

> The provision that officers of the Public Health and Marine-Hospital Service when detailed for duty at this leprosarium shall receive the pay and allowance of their grade and one-half the pay of their grade in addition it is believed is reasonable and justified for the reason that such duty will be onerous, dangerous, and mentally and physically unpleasant from daily contact with leprosy, whose lesions and mutilations are not only unsightly, but often disgusting to the last degree.[37]

Section 6 of the bill, in providing hazard-duty pay, perhaps states more clearly than any other words the official government reaction to leprosy. Furthermore, although the final bill did not not contain Wyman's pejorative adjectives, the inclusion of this provision clearly established that the federal government considered leprosy an abomination. Section 6 survived passage of the bill in 1917, and the payment of hazard-duty pay—now termed "incentive" pay—still continues as an active practice for all employees at the USPHS Hospital, Carville, Louisiana.

On March 2, 1905, the bill to establish a leprosarium failed to pass the House of Representatives by a vote of "ayes 36, noes 180."[38] According to Kalisch[39] and Carville historian and celebrated patient Stanley Stein,[40] the bill was defeated on the grounds that no congressman or territorial delegate was willing to establish a national leprosarium in his region. To an extent this was true; certainly everyone present opted that it should be located elsewhere.

The hidden issue involved in the defeat of the bill, however, was far more complicated than an inability to convince members of the House to accept a leprosarium in their part of the country. The defeat of the bill had much to do with the political future of the territories of Arizona and New Mexico. The people of both territories had been actively battling for the preceding eighteen years to gain statehood. The bill presented to the House of Representatives specified that the leprosarium was to be located "within a Territory or insular possession of the United States."[41] The leaders of both territories, but especially of New Mexico, knew they had been targeted. The ensuing debate, though appearing to involve leprosy, was in reality a fight about territorial status. On learning that the U.S. Senate had already approved a bill to establish a leper colony in New Mexico, the territorial legislative assembly wired the speaker of the House "to oppose and defeat it . . . to keep from us this bitter cup, following after our being denied our just right to be admitted as a State of the Union."[42]

The voteless New Mexico delegate, Bernard S. Rodey, certainly did not speak glowingly of leprosy. The thrust of New Mexico's obdurance rested with its leaders' anger and frustration over being denied admission to the Union, an anger only heightened by the sense of ridicule heaped on them as to New Mexico's fitness for statehood. Representative William P. Hepburn of Iowa, who was attempting to ram the bill through Congress, sarcastically put forth the view that "one of the great objectives just now urged to the advancement of some of the wishes of the gentlemen from the Territories is that there is not sufficient population there. Here is a kindly effort to populate at least 1 mile or one-half dozen miles in one of those Territories [Laughter]." Piqued by this stinging barb, Rodey replied, "Mr. Speaker, the Territory of New Mexico has received a great many Pickwickian compliments in times past from the gentleman from Iowa, but none quite equal to this. . . . Put this institution down in New Mexico or Arizona and the unjust and incorrect arguments you have been flinging at us here as to our fitness for statehood will receive double force."[43]

At the opening of the session, Hepburn asked for unanimous passage of the bill. John S. Williams of Mississippi immediately voiced his objection "unless the Territories are stricken out of it," whereupon Hepburn moved "to suspend the rules and pass the bill."[44] The rules were not suspended and the bill was defeated after forty minutes of debate.

Although the bill was defeated mainly over the issue of territorial rights, other issues were raised and statements made that were hardly in support of a national leprosarium, regardless of location. Williams, along with several other representatives, raised the issue of "paternalism." "It is rank paternalism," Williams warned, "it is an absolute disregard of the right of the States, as well as the rights of the Territories. If you are going to establish a 'leprosarium' . . . [why] not make a national any-other-sort-of-contagious-disease hospital? Where is the National Government going to stop after it goes into States and Territories of continental America to the extent of a national leprosarium? Where are you going to draw the line?"[45] John Dalzell of Pennsylvania questioned, "Why should we establish this any more than to establish a national poorhouse?" an idea seconded by Edgar D. Crumpacker of Indiana.[46]

Gilbert M. Hitchcock of Nebraska, speaking in support of the general intent of the bill, countered the argument of paternalism and argued that the government had a responsibility to take care of lepers. He linked the issue of leprosy in the United States directly to American imperialism.

Now, Mr. Speaker, in entering upon a world-power policy, the evil of leprosy is one of the numerous evils which we have brought upon ourselves. It has not been brought upon us by a single State, but it has been brought upon us by a national policy of imperialism, and it is the duty of the nation having entered upon this policy to deal with this evil in the best way possible. . . . I do not think it will be claimed there were many cases in the United States before we acquired the Philippine Islands and other possessions in the Pacific Ocean.[47]

In arguing for responsibility, Hitchcock touched on another important but little mentioned aspect of the bill—the question of eternal banishment: "I think these hundreds of unfortunate beings have some rights which we should consider. Because they are unfortunate by reason of our national policy, I do not think it is proper that we should sentence them to expatriation for life."[48] Hepburn, knowing that the bill was in trouble, tried in his closing argument to salvage victory; at the same time he managed to chastise the territories for their willingness to harbor cases of tuberculosis but refusal to accept lepers:

I say this opposition is a sentimental proposition. . . . The disease of tuberculosis is more dangerously infectious than that of leprosy. . . . These gentlemen from the Territories welcome all people so diseased. Why? Because they can prey upon them; because they are a source of revenue; because the man in pursuit of health who goes into the Territories has money in his pocket.[49]

Defeated in 1905, leprosy legislation languished until 1913 when, for the next four years, a number of bills were introduced in Congress.[50] Congress, however, did not become sufficiently lepraphobic until the 1916–1917 session, when bill S. 4086 passed the U.S. Senate and was signed into law by President Woodrow Wilson on February 3, 1917.[51]

In enacting leprosy legislation in 1917, congressional motivation was no longer based on the fear of hordes of leprous Chinese immigrants entering the country, an argument that had stirred alarmists earlier. The number of cases of the disease in the United States had not appreciably increased. What motivated Congress now was the fear that leprosy would gain entry through Americans acquiring the disease in foreign countries and bringing it home. The earlier involvement of the United States in the Philippines, the Caribbean, and Latin America, and the presence, years later, of leprosy among a few ex-soldiers, made Congress nervous about the number of undetected cases that remained in the country as well as those cases still incubating.

The years between 1913 and 1916, when efforts were made to introduce leprosy bills in Congress, were also the years that Europe was at war. From the time symptoms of leprosy first began to appear in U.S. soldiers who had served in the Far East and in countries to the south of the United States, American leprologists had been expecting an increase in the disease as a result of military service abroad.[52] In pushing the leprosy bill through the Senate in 1916, Senator Joseph E. Ransdell of Louisiana, chairman of the Committee on Public Health and National Quarantine, may well have been looking ahead. For in 1916 the United States was on the verge of another military involvement—World War I—where again U.S. soldiers would be going abroad, fighting, dying, and perhaps even bringing leprosy home with them. In arguing for internal quarantine, Ransdell asserted that "in segregation we have a method of protection which, if utilized, is wholly sufficient to prevent the dissemination of the disease." Ransdell cited the example of the eradication of leprosy from Europe during the Middle Ages and noted the success of "our own efforts in the Hawaiian Islands and the Philippines . . . which previously have been hotbeds of the infection." Segregation, Ransdell also added, is sanctioned by the Bible.[53] The notion that segregation would eradicate leprosy—and that this approach had worked in the past—was an idea that found many supporters. Segregation fostered the belief that a solution to a worrisome problem had been found, and in 1917 isolation exerted a strong emotional appeal.

In calling for the isolation of lepers, however, members of Congress were doing more than seeking a solution to a worrisome problem. They were expressing the mood of the country. U.S. adventures abroad at the turn of the century never reached the scale of acquiring foreign possessions practiced by the European powers. Turn-of-the-century imperialism, Oscar Handlin wrote, was "a temporary aberration of American policy."[54] At the same time that militarists, industrialists, and some intellectuals urged a more aggressive foreign policy, popular sentiment overwhelmingly opposed expanding U.S. interests and territory. Racist thinking in the United States during the first three decades of the twentieth century affected American attitudes about the world and made most Americans "dubious not only of colonialism but of every type of foreign contact."[55] American ties to Europe were stronger, however, than the desire to remain uninvolved in the affairs of the world. The United States, though reluctant at first, was nevertheless belatedly drawn into World War I. From the American perspective the results of the war did not improve Europe or the world in the slightest. If anything, the war and the peace settlement that followed only strengthened the American resolve that it was futile to involve itself with other countries. Once again, the United States withdrew into the familiar and more comforting refuge of isolationism; renewed emphasis was placed on an earlier ideology of "Americanism." Whatever did not conform, Handlin wrote, "was to be excluded."[56]

The ideology of Americanism was a pervasive force in the United States and dominated American thinking well into the 1930s. "Stability" and "purity" were ideal values expressive of what Americans thought their country should be like. The established social order viewed new immigrants to the United States as possessing bodies and souls alien to the style of life favored by those who preferred the older closed communities that had existed in the nineteenth century. The targets were no longer limited to Negroes, Chinese, and American Indians, however. The circle of discrimination was now widely extended to include Catholics and Jews, Italians, Japanese, and Poles. These populations were to be held down "as a sign of the worth of the one hundred percent American."[57]

Under Americanism the country was to be purged of foreign political elements. Dissident radicals of all sorts were assumed to bear loyalty to alien ideologies, and deportation became the fate of many. Criminal syndicalist laws were enforced and resulted in the jailing of political activists. Voluntary associations like the American Protective League, the American Legion, the Ku Klux Klan, and the Daughters of the American Revolution engaged in "witch hunting." The days of the Palmer raids and the origins of J. Edgar Hoover's F.B.I. were not far away. The growth of bureaucratic power since 1900, Handlin wrote,

> had begun ominously to encroach upon the freedom of the individual. The first victims were pacifists, aliens and radicals. . . . The excesses of the wartime sedition acts, of the Red scare . . . evoked a determined counterattack which reached its head in the agitation over the Sacco-Vanzetti case . . . [an] incident [that] revealed that the poor, the foreign-born, and the unpopular could not get a fair trial. . . .[58]

Related to increasing federal control over unpopular political ideas and activities was the attitude that the country must also be purified in terms of what people inhaled, injected, or ingested. The movement to prevent the manufacture, sale, and consumption of alcohol, and the movement to regulate drugs, especially opium and cocaine, were realized within five years of each other. The Harrison Narcotic Act controlling the sale of narcotics was passed in 1914, followed by the Eighteenth Amendment to the U.S. Constitution in 1919 prohibiting the manufacture and sale of alcohol.

Efforts to encourage abstinence in the United States had a long history dating back to the 1830s. The banning of alcohol was seen by the prohibitionists not as a denial of individual liberty but as a means of extending freedom by removing "temptation from men" who otherwise were "incapable of freeing themselves from its corrupting effects."[59] Racial arguments figured prominently in building up a national consensus for prohibition. Alabama Congressman Richmond P. Hobson's assertion in 1914 of the need to keep alcohol away from Negroes summed up much of the thinking of the day: "Liquor will actually make a brute out of a negro, causing him to commit unnatural crimes. The effect is the same on the white man, though the white man being further evolved it takes longer time to reduce him to the same level."[60] Earlier, in 1900, the Reverend Wilbur F. Crafts, in an address to the Ecumenical Missionary Conference, had extended the argument to include all the "child races" of the world.[61]

The Eighteenth Amendment to the Constitution was repealed in 1933. Controversy over narcotics remains. The antinarcotic movement in the United States has a different history from the movement that called for the prohibition of alcohol. The outlawing of narcotics was closely linked to American vilification of Orientals, particularly the Chinese. The connection of opium with the Chinese character was a theme that was repeated over and over again during the period when "yellow peril" was a threatening issue. Although the pharmacological properties of opium had not changed, opinions about opium had changed. In American thought processes, opinions about opium and opinions about the Chinese were interchangeable. Thoughts of one aroused thoughts of the other. Once considered a medical "cure-all," opium was transformed into a panapathogen. In 1915, the lead sentence in a lead article in the *Journal of the American Medical Association* characterized opium as follows: "If the entire materia medica at our disposal were limited to the choice and use of only one drug, I am sure that a great many, if not the majority, of us would choose opium; and I am convinced that if we were to select, say half a dozen of the most important drugs in the Pharmacopeia, we should all place opium in the first rank."[62] The role played by racial factors in creating an anti-opium attitude in the United States earlier in the century has been acknowledged only recently.[63]

In preaching the doctrine of opium as humankind's "deadliest foe," the antinarcotic supporters compared the drug to the ravages of leprosy. In a nationwide radio broadcast entitled "The Struggle of Mankind Against Its Deadliest Foe," delivered at the close of the second annual observance of Narcotic Education Week, Congressman Hobson, prohibition propagandist and publicist in every conceivable way of the danger of narcotics, declared:

Heroin addiction can be likened to a contagion. Suppose it were announced that there were more than a million lepers among our people. Think what a shock the announcement would produce! Yet drug addiction is far more incurable than leprosy, far more tragic to its victims, and is spreading like a moral and physical scourge. . . . Drug addiction is more communicable and less curable than leprosy. . . . Upon the issue hangs the perpetuation of civilization, the destiny of the world and the future of the human race.[64]

By 1917 all the pieces needed for Congress to enact legislation regarding leprosy were set in place. The philosophy of Americanism was being redefined. Political repression and racial discrimination were at a high point. New policies numerically restricting immigration were in the making. Dislocations in Europe caused by World War I and unemployment, and a housing shortage in the United States, aggravated public demand to limit the entry of the foreign-born. The Immigration Act of 1917 was the first of the new bills to be enacted. It codified previous provisions excluding aliens and added a long list of new categories of persons to be excluded. Congress was so determined to impose tighter restrictions that, although it was twice vetoed by President Wilson,[65] the bill passed. Federal legislation banning narcotics had already been enacted three years earlier and the prohibition of alcohol was only two years away. The United States was also on the verge of getting involved in another war. At the Senate hearings on leprosy early in 1916 congressmen heard a great deal about how U.S. soldiers had acquired leprosy abroad in past wars and had brought the disease home with them. Remembering its past experience with the peoples and countries of the Far East, the United States had closed its doors to opium and to the Chinese. Leprosy—another "menace" associated with undesirable foreigners—was itself now on trial.

In the Western imagination leprosy is an "extreme" disease. The fantasy includes exaggerated notions both of contagion and of deformity. Severely deteriorated cases of leprosy are held as representative of all cases of the disease, when in fact the severe cases are comparatively rare. Therein lies the stereotype. An unreal image of leprosy persists. It not only is found among the uninformed but, unfortunately, also has lingered within the medical profession. As late as 1940, an editorial in the *American Journal of Public Health*, entitled an "Unreasonable Fear of Leprosy," commented on the stereotype:

> Although nearly every textbook on medicine and nearly all special articles dealing with the communicability of leprosy carry a statement to the effect that prolonged and intimate contact is necessary for the transmission of the disease, there remains, among the medical profession generally a fear of the risk involved in even slight contact with a leper—an anxiety which is almost incomprehensible. This being true, perhaps it is not difficult to understand the even greater distrust among the general public.[66]

The 1916 Senate hearings produced no debate on the question of whether concern about leprosy was in the national interest. In a sense, the hearings were pro forma. A national leprosy bill had been before Congress each year since 1913. However, only in 1916–1917 did both houses of Congress endorse a bill during the same session, a constitutional requirement for the passage of legislation. Thus, the hearings become important reading less for their influence on leprosy legislation than for understanding the tenor of congressional support for such a bill. In presenting the bill the committee noted that leprosy was a "communicable, loathsome, mutilating, chronic disease" that inspires horror in the public mind.[67] Pejorative descriptions characterizing leprosy in extreme terms were used extensively throughout the hearing's 200 pages of testimony.

There was considerable diversity of opinion among the expert witnesses about the infectiousness of leprosy, its mode of transmission, and whether the disease was curable. However, there was little disagreement about an expected increase of the disease in the United States. Dr. Howard Fox, vice president of the American Dermatological Association, predicted that leprosy would "suddenly increase" and "gain a strong foothold" in the country in the near future.[68] The sources of the increase were expected to be the extraterritorial possessions recently acquired by the United States as well as continued American contact with foreigners, both through immigration and through commercial and military involvement abroad. There was nearly unanimous support for a national leprosy bill among the fourteen witnesses who testified. All twelve in favor of legislation believed that the isolation of lepers would prevent the spread of the disease and eventually eliminate leprosy from the country. The only two witnesses to express little enthusiasm for either the need or the desirability of such an institution were both public health officials. Dr. George W. McCoy, director, Hygienic Laboratory, United States Public Health Service, stated that "there are only a limited number of people in any community who are infectable"; he thought that a national leprosarium might be welcomed by "floating lepers," that is, those who were without means of support and could not be cared for at home.[69] Dr. W. C. Woodward, health officer, District of Columbia, expressed the belief that ordinary pulmonary tuberculosis was a far greater public health threat than leprosy.[70]

From the perspective of congressional legislators, the felt need for a national leprosarium to prevent the spread of the disease within the United States was one consideration. Another issue that legislators considered at the hearings was the justification of having a leprosarium in order to care for U.S. soldiers who had contracted the disease abroad while in the service of their country. The presence of John Ruskin Early in Washington, D.C., at the time of the hearings and the publicity that surrounded him focused congressional attention on both issues.

John Early had served with the U.S. forces first in Cuba from 1898 to 1900 and later in the Philippines until 1902. The likelihood that Early had contracted leprosy in the Philippines was later corroborated by Hasseltine[71] and then by Aycock and Gordon[72] in their studies of leprosy among veterans of foreign wars. Early already showed signs of leprosy in 1908, when he arrived in Washington, D.C., to see the pension board about his recently aggravated malaria which he had acquired while stationed in Cuba. In Washington his face became so acutely inflamed and swollen that he sought out a local physician. The physician was puzzled by the symptoms, but with the information that Early had served in the Philippines, he contacted Dr. William C. Fowler, inspector for contagious diseases in the District of Columbia. Together with two other physicians, they diagnosed Early's condition as leprosy. The fear of leprosy was so strong that Early was immediately "forcibly quarantined in a hastily erected tent down on the marshy bottom adjacent to the . . . Potomac River."[73] There, he was watched over by a twenty-four-hour armed guard.[74]

From that day until his death at the age of sixty-four at Carville on February 28, 1938, John Early warred interminably against his government's treatment of lepers. His own life became a strange combination of odyssey, crusade, fierce indignation, and horror.[75] Later dubbed the "obstreperous mountaineer" by fellow inmates at Carville, John Early was not a man to be hunted down by his countrymen, locked away, or shipped across state lines in a sealed baggage car later to be disinfected. Early became the first leprosy patient activist. His public appearances, his extravagant publicity plans, and the activity, debate, and emotion he stirred were covered by the mass media and soon reached congressional ears. *The New York Times* and *The Washington Post* interviewed Early as well as health officials.[76] Early's name was frequently mentioned in connection with congressional efforts at introducing leprosy legislation.

At the time of the Senate hearings in 1916, Early was once again back in Washington, this time under arrest for coming into the District of Columbia "while suffering from leprosy and without a permit to do so." According to Fowler's testimony, Early was confined in a brick building, windows and doors all barred, on grounds surrounded by an eight-foot barbed-wire fence, with a T-shaped projection at the top of the fence, "so that it would be almost impossible for him to get out."[77] Senator Ransdell, however, thought Early was important enough to be heard regarding the need for a national leprosarium and visited him in his prison a few days before the hearings began. Several days later Early sent the following letter to Ransdell, which was read by Ransdell as chairman of the Committee on Public Health and National Quarantine and inserted into the report of the committee:

Senator RANSDELL
Washington, D.C.

DEAR SENATOR:
    Sunday you asked the question is there enough lepers in the United States to justify a national leprosarium, to which I will answer through the following facts: There are about 500 known cases in the United States that have developed mostly within the past 10 or 15 years. Three of them I have knowledge of personally and was soldiers in the Philippines, and as far as the facts show the disease was contracted there. Therefore, we can readily see that leprosy is spreading in the country to an extent that calls forth sharp local attention and certainly should call forth national. To segregate a leprous person is wise and humane thing to do, but to let matters to drift on in the present road is another thing. As soon as a leper is found, under present conditions, he finds himself out of a home and absolutely unwelcome in the

jurisdiction where he is found. I know of cases where the law has been violated by one jurisdiction shifting a leper into another. Such would cease under national supervision. There is a tendency on the other hand, under existing status, for the local doctor to refrain from reporting cases which would also cease under national care. Leprosy is surely a dread disease, not only in name, but in facts, gnawing away the vitals of the system, in time reduces the strongest to apathy and helplessness. Truly he is a hard sufferer when all conditions are considered. Then, we ought, as a Christian Nation, make provision for him. Remember we are outcasts of society; yes, with human tastes and feelings.

Yours, very truly,

JOHN EARLY.

P.S.—Please pardon mistakes. I had to write in haste.[78]

In his letter to Ransdell, Early, the ex-soldier, did not raise the question of federal responsibility in the instance of a service-connected disability. Early's appeal for care was based on moral, Christian considerations. However, the issue of federal responsibility was never far from committee members' thoughts. In an earlier exchange of views between Dr. Frederick L. Hoffman, statistician for The Prudential Insurance Co. of America, California Senator John D. Works, and Ransdell about the legality of government intervention in leprosy cases where interstate quarantine was concerned, the role of the government in providing care for soldiers who developed leprosy subsequent to their discharge from service abroad was also raised. Works supposed "the Government would have no further responsibility . . . than it would have toward any other American citizen." Ransdell, however, thought otherwise. "Perhaps not," he replied, "but the disease was incurred in the performance of the soldier's duty to the Government and to the people, and, since we do not hesitate to pay a substantial pension to the soldiers of the Civil War, there would seem to be no reason why some Government obligation does not exist in the case of these men."[79]

With the passage in 1917 of a national leprosy bill, it had taken the U.S. Congress approximately twenty-eight years (1889–1917) to digest the idea that a federally sponsored, disease-specific institution for leprosy was warranted. Disease-specific institutions sponsored by the federal government for the general civilian population are uncommon in the United States. In fact, the leprosarium at Carville is the only disease-specific institution for the general civilian population that the U.S. federal government has ever opened. Nothing like this would happen again until 1935, when the federal government opened the U.S. Public Health Service hospital at Lexington, Kentucky, for convicted narcotic addicts.[80] In taking steps to open a national leprosarium—a move that was not accompanied by any effort or intent to establish federal institutions for other specific diseases—the U.S. Congress acceded to the view that leprosy was very special indeed.[81] In according leprosy an institution of its own, Congress accorded leprosy a very special status, one from which it has never fully recovered.

The opening of a national leprosarium was delayed by World War I and the search for a site. Various locations had been considered, but opposition was strong. The old Louisiana State Home for Lepers already existed and was therefore available. Although officially designated as U.S. Marine Hospital No. 66, the leprosarium at Carville was designed less as a hospital and more as a place of confinement. And although federally sponsored hospitals for specific diseases are uncommon in the United States, federally sponsored places of confinement are not. Historically they have included such establishments as reservations for American Indians, quarantine stations for regulating imports and in-migration, Veterans Administration Hospitals for the mentally ill, a host of penitentiaries for federal offenders, and relocation centers for containing Japanese-Americans during World War II.

With leprosy linked to these categories for which federally sponsored places of confinement have been established, it would appear that the disease was being addressed not as a medical problem but as an ideological issue. Leprosy was special in that it was perceived as an affront to the nation. In short, the disease was "un-American."

On February 1, 1921, the U.S. flag was raised over the leprosarium at Carville, Louisiana. Dr. Oswald E. Denney, former director of the leper colony at Culion, in the Philippines, became the first medical officer in charge. Stanley Stein, Carville historian, wrote of the rejoicing that took place among the ninety patients when the "hateful fence dividing the sexes" came down and

> husbands joined wives, brothers met sisters, and mothers could talk to their sons without risking punishment. . . . To emphasize the fact that Carville had become a hospital instead of a "Home," and that the monastic days were over, Dr. Denney organized the first dance on the old plantation since the Civil War.
>
> In addition to elevating patient hopes, Dr. Denney, however, also raised the yellow jack . . . as a symbol of P.H.S. occupancy. Patients screamed at the baleful quarantine symbol and the most vociferous screamer in Carville history, John Early, made inflammatory speeches and wrote to his congressman. The Surgeon General's office reminded Dr. Denney that the yellow jack was the emblem of the Quarantine Branch, not the Hospital Branch of the service, and the . . . flag came down.[82]

Nonetheless, the high barbed-wire fence that surrounded the institution and bore the sign: "U.S. Government Preserve, No Trespassing," remained to symbolize that the leprosarium was "off limits."

Denney, who served as medical officer in charge at Carville from his appointment in 1920 until his replacement in 1936, was not very popular with the patients at Carville. Denney created an atmosphere of strict discipline that was resented and bitterly contested by patients for years. He drew up the draft of rules and regulations covering the prescribed conduct of patients at the newly created federal leprosarium. In reviewing Denney's "Scheme of Regulations for the Apprehension, Detention, Treatment, and Release of Lepers,"[83] A. J. McLaughlin, Assistant Surgeon General, wrote in a memorandum dated February 1, 1922, that "these regulations contain serious defects."[84] Earlier, Dr. George W. McCoy noted that "the proposed regulations might well be dispensed with provided a capable, tactful officer has charge of the station." Section 7, "Provisions for the Enforcement of Discipline," drew the most serious objection from both McLaughlin and McCoy. The latter observed that "this whole section makes one feel that the provisions have been drawn for a penal institution rather than for a hospital."[85]

The rules and regulations later approved by the secretary of the treasury were milder in tone and language.[86] Nevertheless, as Stanley Stein wrote of his arrival ten years after the federal government assumed control, Carville "was still a pretty dismal place in which to spend the rest of one's life,"[87] a place to which patients were sent by special "leper trains," where their mail, both within the colony and outgoing, was disinfected, and where patients were disenfranchised and encouraged to assume aliases.

PART 4

The Leprosarium:
The Twentieth Century

8

The Carville Leprosarium: The Asylum Years, 1894 to Post–World War II

With the passage of Public Law No. 299 in 1917, Congress adopted a national leprosy policy that was based on the premise that leprosy was highly contagious. The policy contained two provisions. One was to segregate lepers in order to prevent the spread of the disease. The other provided for care and treatment through the scientific study of the disease.[1]

The need for a policy of segregation was questionable even at the time that the legislation was enacted. Leprologists working in areas of the world where the disease was hyperendemic had, by 1916, already agreed that leprosy was not highly infectious.[2] Furthermore, segregation was considered by many to be an ineffective and inhumane control measure. Leonard Rogers and Ernest Muir, two of the leading medical authorities on leprosy earlier in this century, noted that such "prophylactic measures have only too frequently failed to stamp out, or even greatly reduce the incidence of the disease."[3] Writing of their experience with leprosy in India before 1920, they advocated that leprosy be treated on an outpatient basis. This method, they noted, had proved successful in a number of places where it had been tried.[4]

There was no evidence presented at the Senate hearings in 1916 to show that the incidence of leprosy in the United States was increasing or that the disease was spreading among native-born Americans. Expert witnesses speculated that the number of cases of leprosy in the country was between 500 and 2,500. However, hard data presented by Dr. Frederick L. Hoffman, statistician and chief witness on the distribution and spread of the disease, accounted for only about 150 cases in 1914.[5] The figure was considered by many to be low, owing to the facts that the disease was not reportable in most states and that physicians generally were too unfamiliar with leprosy to diagnose it. Rumors of the number of lepers loose in large cities—thirty in New York and eighty in Chicago[6]—and expected increases from non-contiguous possessions of the United States served, however, to magnify the threat to those who believed there was one. U.S. military service abroad, chiefly in the Philippines, was one source through which the disease was expected to gain a foothold in the country. But aside from the well-publicized case of John Early, Hoffman could cite only three other cases of the disease in ex-servicemen who had served in the Far East at the turn of the century.[7] His testimony that it was extremely rare for attendants at leprosaria to contract the disease surprised committee members.

Congressional resolve to establish a national leprosarium, however, was too strong to be set aside by the absence of convincing data on the necessity for segregating lepers. Leprosy was more than a disease. It was also an ideological symbol of the danger that the United States faced should it abandon its philosophy of Americanism and its policy of political isolation. In this sense, Philip Kalisch was right in likening lepraphobia to a structural tension in U.S. political life that reflected conflicts within the country.[8]

Congress wrote a national leprosy policy in the language of public health. On the other hand, Congress was motivated by ideological concerns. Whether leprosy was construed as disease or as symbol, both Congress and the Public Health Service acted as if it were anathema, even if it was not always clear which aspect of leprosy was being addressed. The conflict between symbol and disease would affect leprosy policy in the United States in the years ahead and would not be resolved until after World War II. By that time, international events would combine to restructure Western attitudes toward the disease.

The policy that Congress set into motion and that the Public Health Service (PHS) was authorized to implement was limited by the absence of the legal machinery to segregate all the known lepers in the country. Although the federal government had the power to regulate immigration into the United States and had certain powers in matters pertaining to interstate travel, it had no power to force individual states to send lepers to a federal facility other than in cases where the person was also legally deportable. Each state had the power to decide its own health policy and was under no formal obligation to accede to federal wishes. Lepers might be social outcasts, but they were not federal criminals or otherwise without the protection of states' rights. Some state health officials were only too willing to ship lepers out of their jurisdiction. Others, however, thought that there were other health problems more worthy of their attention. Furthermore, the United States had so few lepers in comparison with the numbers of persons having other known troublesome diseases, that difficulties in diagnosis and problems in tracking down patients and transporting them to a national leprosarium posed an enormous logistic challenge, apart from the social protest it could have aroused. Ultimately, the success of incarcerating patients depended on the initiative of local health officials in sending patients to the leprosarium and on the willingness of patients themselves to enter and then to remain at the institution. Certainly, it was not difficult to convince some patients of the desirability of going to Carville on a purely voluntary basis. John Early, in his sickness and despair, had welcomed the idea of a national leprosarium with its promise of care and treatment.

Just as the federal government was limited in its capacity to enforce admissions to the leprosarium, it was also limited in its capacity to compel patients to leave the leprosarium. Nowhere in the rules and regulations governing the leprosarium was anything said about patients having to leave on becoming eligible for a medical discharge. In this respect the leprosarium at Carville is unlike other hospitals and institutions, where decisions about discharging patients are made by members of the staff. When the national leprosarium was founded, stringent criteria for a medical discharge were specified, and it was not expected that many patients would qualify. Leprosy-specific treatment was limited, and what was available was not very effective. Furthermore, there was no appreciable research under way that promised better medical treatment in the future. The expectation that patients would remain at the leprosarium for life—as well as after death—was provided for by Congress. Included in the regulations that were approved in 1922 was a provision whereby patients dying at the hospital were authorized to be buried on the grounds of the leprosarium at federal expense. In the event that families wished to bury their own deceased, removal "in conformity with interstate quarantine regulations and State regulations governing the transportation of human bodies dead from contagious diseases" was required.[9]

In a number of ways, the national leprosarium, like the Louisiana State Home for Lepers before it, was a voluntary institution. The leprosarium offered patients a place of refuge, medical care, food, lodging, and, in later days, a clothing allowance and recreational facilities. The institution also provided patients with tangible evidence that society feared the disease. With public fear held to be a real issue, specific power to discharge patients back to the community was never thought to be necessary. The poor medical condition of most patients in the past, the absence of definitive treatment, and the lack of interest in leprosy research, combined with public stigma, were considered sufficient insurance that most patients would remain. As long as the exile of lepers was public policy, society was prepared to subsidize their total maintenance, asking nothing in return other than that they remain sequestered.

Despite the prison-like atmosphere that the PHS attempted to create in the early days of running the leprosarium, the institution had few really effective ways of preventing patients from "absconding" or of compelling their return. There was always the celebrated "hole in the fence" near the front gate. Besides, the boundaries of the leprosarium were permeable, and surveillance at the federal level was almost nonexistent. Patients who absconded were always accepted back, whether their medical condition warranted it or not. In time, patients found that the voluntary nature of the institution provided them with the opportunity to settle down at Carville as colonizers, permanently so if they chose.

THE NEGLECT OF SCIENTIFIC RESEARCH

With the question settled that lepers were to be isolated, it would be some time before scientific research into leprosy as a disease would begin. The 1916 Senate hearings had envisioned the national leprosarium as a "great workshop" for the study of the disease. However, by the time the PHS assumed jurisdiction of the leper colony in Louisiana in 1921, "the chief purpose of the hospital was to serve as a refuge and sanctuary for the patient." And so it remained until the 1940s, at which time a more effective chemotherapy (which had originated in relation to another disease) became available.[10] Concentrated efforts to expand research did not materialize at the national leprosarium until the 1960s.

Things were no better at the other two leprosaria that the United States sponsored—Molokai and Culion. In Hawaii, Congress had appropriated funds in 1905 for a hospital and laboratories for the investigation of the cause of leprosy and ways to cure the disease. These efforts were short-lived and the investigation station closed eight years later without ever having begun its work.[11] Matters moved no faster at Culion, where scientific work, under the auspices of the Leonard Wood Memorial for the Eradication of Leprosy, did not begin until the 1930s.[12]

The United States was not alone in neglecting research. The failure was inherent in the leprosarium model. In Norway, leprosy research was basic to that country's public health approach. Imperialist nations, however, saw leprosy from a different perspective. For them, leprosy was not a local disease. Rather, it was one that was prevalent in overseas areas among racially "inferior" peoples with whom the West was now increasingly coming into contact. In Norway, moreover, physicians had dealt with leprosy largely believing it was hereditary. The discovery of *Mycobacterium leprae* changed people's thinking in two ways. First, it convinced most scientists and physicians that leprosy was contagious. The second change had to do with the growth of the new science of bacteriology and how it affected ideas about disease control. Norway officials earlier had addressed the question of control epidemiologically and were able to observe declines in the incidence of the disease. The next generation of Western scientists, on the other hand, were then looking exclusively to the laboratory for vaccines to control specific diseases. The failure to find a vaccine for leprosy led scientists early on to conclude that the disease was hopeless. Had they kept the epidemiology of leprosy in mind, the picture they obtained might have been less pessimistic. With the rejection of a public health model, the philosophy of leprosy control soon shifted away from science and thus left the imperialist nations open to adopting leprosaria and isolation as their alternative.

The isolation of lepers in colonies served to diminish Western anxiety. Laws restricting the immigration of undesired populations, and the entry in the 1870s of missionary societies as the principal custodians of leper homes worldwide, further attenuated Western fears and reinforced the idea that the problem was now well attended to. The disease showed no signs of becoming pandemic and was considered contained in Asia, Africa, and other tropical areas of the world. As a "tropical" disease, leprosy no longer constituted a subject of interest to clinical medicine, and the disease was soon placed to rest outside the mainstream of Western scientific concerns, tucked away in the relatively minor subspecialty of tropical medicine.

The step from public health to leprosaria sent leprosy stumbling backward to the Middle Ages. Norway had maintained the disease respectably within the scientific world. With the adoption of the leprosarium model and the enactment of laws compelling the segregation of lepers, the association between leprosy and science came to a standstill. The status of lepers changed. People with leprosy were no longer physically ill people, as in Norway, whose disease was responded to by scientific study. They were now outcasts to be apprehended and detained. With leprosy's ties to science and medicine severed, the leprosaria era revived ancient ideas of extrusion and asylum; this opened the door to an explosion of myths and superstitions about the disease and its sufferers.

THE GROWTH OF THE COLONY

Carville, in its presulfone days, was an asylum where it was more or less expected that patients would remain sequestered for long periods—if not for the remainder of their lives. By 1960 the institution had become a "quasi-open residential treatment community" with a well-developed patient culture that traced its origin back to the late nineteenth century. Contributing to the development of community and culture were (1) the length of time that patients remained at the leprosarium, and (2) the fact that most patients were ambulatory most of the time and led private lives within the large patient "colony" portion of the facility.

The colony at Carville is the antithesis of the type of establishment that Erving Goffman, in his study of asylums, called a "total institution": "A total institution may be defined as a place of residence or work where a large number of like-situated individuals, cut off from the wider society for an appreciable period of time, together lead an enclosed, formally administered round of life."[13] "The handling of many human needs by the bureaucratic organization of whole blocks of people," Goffman wrote, "is the key fact of total institutions."[14] Colonies, as opposed to total institutions, have rarely been studied, and there is, to my knowledge, no sociological definition descriptive of their social character. Leper colonies are only one entry in this classification of special communities; certain penal colonies would be another. Obviously, the term "colony," as it is used here, must be separated from its nineteenth-century imperialistic meaning. The outstanding difference between "colonies" and "total institutions" is that in the former the daily round of life is *not* formally regulated by a bureaucratic organization. In its place, groups of people are left to fend for themselves, with basic human needs being more or less provided. In the absence of a close, formally administered round of life, colony members may, in time, evolve their own distinct subculture and social organization.

In Hawaii lepers were first sent to Molokai as colonists, not as patients. The land on which they were settled was purchased by the kingdom, and, except for a few essentials supplied by the government, the lepers were expected to take care of themselves. It was taken for granted that the healthier members of the settlement would cultivate the land and grow the food and that the Hawaiian Board of Health would be spared any further expense. The assumption of those responsible for the disposal of lepers in this fashion was that the survival of the colonists depended on their energy and direction alone.

At Carville, things were not quite so stark. Dyer had not intended the state home for lepers to be a colony. He had a hospital and research center in mind. However, if the indomitable Dyer had not, in 1896, been able to persuade the Sisters of Charity to come to the leper home, it is questionable whether he could have found other arrangements for nursing care and administration. Notwithstanding the care and the services that the Sisters provided and the "iron monastic discipline" they imposed on the institution, patients at the leper home still had considerable freedom in their daily lives and the time to exercise and develop that freedom. Even the "iron monastic discipline" that Stanley Stein attributed to the Sisters[15] had its limits. Aside from whatever internal controls that the Sisters could manage to implant, patients, as sick people, would not be mistreated. But neither could they be threatened with expulsion from the institution. No jails would take them, no other hospitals or nursing homes would accept them, and the idea of releasing them to the community was not considered. Patients, on the other hand, were not so doubly bound. They could stay if they so chose or they could abscond.

There is some evidence to indicate that patient life at Carville was somewhat more closely supervised during the days when the institution was a state home run by the Sisters of Charity than it was later as a federal facility. True, there were fewer patients when it was a state institution, but there were also fewer caretakers. Perhaps the reason lies with the convent training of the Sisters and with the order, discipline, and sense of higher service that such training teaches. In the early days of the state home there were few helpers and aides, and the Sisters and patients worked together to keep the institution habitable. As managers of the institution, the Sisters were in charge, and the schedule of daily patient events, although by no means totally organized by them, was nevertheless never far from their control. In early letters written by the Sisters at Carville to their superiors in Emmitsburg, Maryland, and to others, and according to Charles H. Calandro's study, "From Disgrace to Dignity: The Louisiana Leper Home, 1894–1921," a certain closeness between the Sisters and the patients shines through.[16] In caring for lepers the Sisters also believed they were serving their Lord in a tradition some would insist had forever been part of the mission of the Church. In living and working so closely among lepers, in Louisiana and elsewhere, the Sisters found that the social distance separating savior from victim was not all that great.

Under federal management, relations between patients and staff became less personal. With the quasi-military structure, the rules and regulations, and the ideology of contagion that the PHS brought with it, the social distance separating inmates from managers increased. Under federal auspices, the style of the institution changed from a "Home," where the Sisters had moved freely among the patients and intermingled with them, to what the PHS sometimes called a "reservation," with the staff living on the "station" and the patients occupying the "colony." It was in this colony that a distinct patient subculture evolved. The formation of a patient community within the colony area of the leprosarium was a satisfactory development insofar as the PHS was concerned. A laissez-faire attitude by the PHS to patient organizations, activities, and enterprises represented an accommodation to the fact that the staff possessed few formal rules or sanctions for the control of patient behavior.

The number of patients in residence at Carville at any one time has never been very high, about 400 at the most. Many patients have been able-bodied and capable. With patients physically separated and formally segregated from their PHS caretakers, and with medical care taking up only a small portion of their time, life in the colony developed its own character. Soon patient organizations began to spring up. In the early 1930s, a former social club evolved into the Patients' Federation and a newspaper was started. In time, other patient-initiated organizations and enterprises followed. By the mid-1960s, although patient participation in colony activities had declined, at least nine clubs, in addition to the Patients' Federation, were still active. Apart from patient organizations, which were both social and political in character, the patients also operated two enterprises and a number of private businesses. The enterprises were *The Star*, the patient newspaper, and the patient canteen, a nonprofit organization that raised money for patient activities and financial assistance for indigent patients.

Individual private businesses flourished. Some patients worked out of their own living quarters, and in time others acquired space within the buildings owned by the hospital. Patients paid no rent and were not subject to local or state licensure regulations. *The Star* noted in 1953 that entrepreneurship at Carville began "long ago" and combined a patient's "need for income with the need of the community for goods and services."[17] In time a variety of shops and services were available within the colony: barbers and hair stylists, dry cleaning establishments, novelty stores, photographers, vendors, cabinetmakers, and repair shops and "fix-it" services for bicycles, shoes, appliances, and radios. While other patients were their primary clients, these private businesses also catered to the families of patients, visitors, leprosarium workers, and, at times, even members of the staff.

One consequence of the development of a patient community was the creation within the institution of a structural division separating the colony from the administration. Residents of the colony, in their contacts with physicians at Carville regarding medical issues, leprosy related or not, came to regard themselves more as "outpatients" than as hospital patients. The question of how to log these events long perplexed the administration. The official approach, as noted in an in-house memo in 1958, was to log these contacts as "inpatient visits."[18] Patients, however, other than at times when they were bedridden in the infirmary, tended to behave otherwise. The administration viewed colony activities and behavior as an adjunct of a life isolated from the wider society. Patients, on the other hand, viewed their activities as evidence of the changes in the institution that they were able to effect. Patients at Carville take great pride in remembering their accomplishments as proof of how they managed to "beat the institutional life."

Patient history attests to the fact that inmates at the leprosarium have been beating the institutional life since the early days when it was a state home. Although the Sisters of Charity made valiant efforts to depict the Louisiana Home for Lepers in "cozy" terms, patients often sought relief from the style in which the Sisters and the State Board of Control chose to run the facility. For married patients where both partners were at Carville, or for couples who wanted to be together, the problem was particularly distressing. The sexes were physically separated. Permission for patients to be married in the chapels at the leprosarium was not granted until 1952. Patient initiative helped to solve some of the dilemmas of friendship and privacy. "Even before 1921," a historical review of patient housing at Carville published in *The Star* noted, "patients were wont to trek to a secluded area of the hospital grounds, where they cooked their meals and enjoyed the companionship of friends. Each individual and group had a special site, inviolate as any home." Campsites in turn gave way to tents and primitive shelters. Some patients eventually made the transfer from hospital-provided accommodations to rustic shacks, for these alternatives "belonged to them and offered a measure of freedom from institutional regimentation."[19] Carville crusader and patient activist John Early is credited by patient historians as having built "one of the first cottages, if not the first."[20]

Purchasing or foraging for materials, patients improved the property, doing "as much of the actual construction as they could within the limits of physical handicap." The more affluent the patient, the more comfortable and attractive the cottage. These first homes built by patients on the edge of the leprosarium were not opposed by the hospital administration. In fact, the PHS supported the effort. Hospital workmen helped with the wiring and the plumbing, and as in the earlier "cook fire days, the hospital supplied retreat-minded patients with 'raw' rations."[21] Eventually the number of cottages increased; a maximum of eighteen was reached by the early 1950s. The cottage development acquired a distinct demographic identity, as well as a life-style of its own. In time the development came to be known variously as Cottage Grove or Suburbia and, euphemistically, as White City. Individual homes sprouted names reflecting their occupants' private visions— Chateau Simon, Lucky Villa, and Wit's End, for example.

Although the national leprosarium was tucked away in rural Louisiana, Carville was not all that isolated from the rest of the nation, and early in the 1930s a series of events took place that transformed the patient body into a politically effective collectivity. In 1931, more than twenty veterans of foreign wars were among the patients at Carville. Dissatisfied with conditions at the leprosarium and in search of more contact with the outside world, these veterans found a sympathetic audience among leaders of the state chapter of the American Legion. Almost immediately, in December 1931, a post of the American Legion was formed at the leprosarium.[22]

One of the issues that brought the American Legion and the veterans at Carville together was a common struggle with the federal government over benefits and pensions for service-connected disabilities. Disturbed that war veterans at the leprosarium "had been neglected by the Government," the *American Legion* magazine made public the fact that "nearly all of the twenty-three [veterans] were entitled to service-connected compensation for their disability, but they received nothing. There were no rulings on leprosy."[23]

The 1930s was the period of the Great Depression in the United States. Throughout that decade, at least 10 million persons—one-fourth of the nation's labor force—were unemployed. Numbering among the many Americans who had lost their jobs, homes, and savings were millions of men who had served in World War I. Beginning in 1919, the newly organized American Legion had made the issue of veterans' war bonuses one of its principal legislative goals. The estimated $2 billion to $4 billion cost of the bonus delayed its passage in Congress and plunged the nation into a bitter political fight. In 1924, a compromise was reached with the powerful veterans' lobby. In place of immediate payment, a twenty-year endowment fund would be established that would pay an average individual bonus of about $1,000 by 1945.[24] Because of the Great Depression however, economically destitute veterans began to demand immediate compensation. Antagonism between veterans and the federal government reached crisis proportions in the bonus marches and the riots that took place in Washington, D.C., in the spring and summer of 1932.

Other national veterans' groups and civic organizations, following the example of the American Legion, established auxiliary branches at Carville and adopted the entire patient body as a "special project." These organizations played a decisive role in forging patient links with the outside world. Such links contributed to the development among patients of a broader perspective about themselves and about leprosy. By admitting patients to membership, these organizations demonstrated that lepraphobia was not universal, and with their backing Carville became a more open institution. American Legion baseball teams arrived to play exhibition games, and the Legion furnished musicians for patient dances. Patient initiative was stimulated. The "What Cheer Club" became the Patients' Federation, and what had started in May 1931 as a light, intramural newsletter became, in time, a major journalistic operation. More important, however, than the entertainment and the equipment that was provided for sustaining a newspaper were the political voice and support that veterans' groups could apply in Washington on behalf of the patients.

The patient world at Carville had expanded. The division separating colony residents from administration now became political as well as physical. The orientation of the PHS was conservative. Patient leaders, on the other hand, became activists and sought reforms. With the creation of the colony newspaper, *The Star,* patients at the leprosarium added their own voice to discussions about issues of leprosy control, management, and ideology. *The Star* addressed the leprosy situation as it existed not only in the United States but in the world at large.

The newspaper started out as a weekly "devoted to the interests of the colony." By the fall of 1933 it had become a crusading journal. In an October editorial entitled "Without the Camp," coeditor Stanley Stein set the stage for the Carville position that the present-day disease and biblical "leprosy" were *not* the same entity. He also emphasized that the public's assumption that they were the same accounted for the fear of the disease and for the superstitions that surrounded it. The position was revolutionary; forty years later, it was adopted by missionary leprologists writing about the historical basis of the stigma. The editorial also took the position that isolation would not eradicate the disease. This position was already endorsed by leprologists working in hyperendemic areas of the world, but not by the PHS.[25] The policy of doing away with leper colonies would not be implemented until after World War II, when international control of leprosy was placed on the agenda of the World Health Organization.

The Star was no ordinary publication. It has been called "a journal of protest" on behalf of leprosy patients in every part of the world.[26] By the 1980s, *The Star* had grown to a circulation of 84,000, and was distributed throughout the United States and in 150 foreign countries. In 1949, it was honored by the Louisiana State University chapter of Sigma Delta Chi and given the award annually bestowed by that professional journalistic society to nonmetropolitan Louisiana newspapers for meritorious community service.[27]

The Star had a shaky time of it during the 1930s, when it folded twice, but not before it began a major campaign to eliminate the use of the words "leper" and even "leprosy" in referring to the disease and its victims. Stein was convinced that the "odious" words reinforced the public's belief that the present illness and the ancient malady were the same entity. Alternative terms had already been suggested by physicians—Hansen's disease, Hansenitis, and Hansenosis—substitutions paralleling the change from "consumption" to "tuberculosis." A number of dermatologists and international leprologists were in agreement insofar as the word "leper" was concerned. In 1931, Robert Cochrane and others had argued the point in Manila at the scientific meeting that gave rise to the *International Journal of Leprosy.*

The Star was reborn in 1941 with a new format and a renewed sense of purpose. Stanley Stein, now totally blind as a result of leprosy, was its sole editor; he held the position until just before his death in 1968. It is perhaps not fortuitous that Stein made the enormous effort to revive the publication when he did. The introduction in 1941 of Promin, a sulfone derivative, in the medical treatment of leprosy elevated patient hopes as never before. Although the results of drug trials using Promin in patients at Carville were not published until 1943,[28] the first indication of positive benefits became noticeable to colony residents in the summer of 1941.[29] The new journal complemented the new chemotherapy. Improved drugs promised relief from the physical disabilities of leprosy. Public and professional education, however, was not part of the PHS mission. *The Star* filled the vacuum and immediately announced that it planned to publish the "real facts about Hansen's disease" and "to contradict the mass of misinformation that is constantly published in even the best newspapers and magazines."[30]

Stein's intention to print the "real facts" and to correct published misinformation took the publication and its supporters on a long odyssey. Early in 1942, *The Star* initiated an educational campaign directed at the secular press, encyclopedias, missionary magazines and agencies, and Bible schools. This phase of *The Star*'s educational campaign lasted into the 1960s. In his opening salvos, Stein cited the "Chinese laundry" stories as "the most classic example of misinformation published." The theme of those tales concerned the instant infection of Caucasians through the casual touch of a Chinese laundryman with leprosy. Stein took missionary magazines to task for "so vividly" overdrawing "the picture of foreign sufferers . . . that the reader's conception of . . . all victims of leprosy is prejudiced by the highly colored report of the disease in foreign lands." He rebuked publishers of encyclopedias for gross inaccuracies and misleading statements about contagion. Missionary agencies working with leprosy were urged to stop using the word "leper," and efforts were made to educate Bible schools to a modern understanding of the disease.[31]

As editor, Stein did more than bring misinformation about leprosy to his audience. He also initiated a staunch campaign urging retractions. In time, books, radio broadcasts, films, and professional journals were added to the list. When *The Star* subscribed to a news-clipping service for materials on leprosy, Stein's correspondence grew voluminously.[32] There were no items of "misinformation" too big or too small for *The Star* to let go unanswered. *The Star* took the obscure "Queens County News" in New York City to task for publishing a Chinese laundry story, and followed up by checking the incident with the department of health in that city. With equal vigor, *The Star* objected to misleading statements about leprosy and about Carville patients made by Dr. Victor Heiser in his best-selling book, *An American Doctor's Odyssey*.[33]

During his long career Stein endlessly battled what he called "the tropistic attraction of leprosy for organized religions, Protestant as well as Catholic." Most missionary magazines, Stein noted, "reek with the word 'leper.'" Stein fought with the American Mission to Lepers to change its name and its policy. Formed in 1906 as an American branch of the British Mission to Lepers, the American organization was the oldest and most active agency in the United States to aid the world's leprosy population. William Danner, secretary-emeritus of the American Mission, was not unsympathetic to *The Star*'s cause, but pointed out that eliminating the word "leper" was opposed by his own fundraisers, who found the word emotionally useful in appealing for donations.[34]

In time, the offending word was phased out of usage. The editorial staff of the *International Journal of Leprosy* took the lead. In 1948, at the Fifth

International Congress of Leprosy, held in Manila, a resolution was passed recommending that use of the word "leper" be abandoned; henceforth they would be called "leprosy patients."[35] Five months later, the American Mission announced its intention to modify its name to the American Leprosy Missions.[36] *The Star* hailed this name change, as well as the change that occurred in 1949 when "Hansen's disease" became the legal name for leprosy in Hawaii, as personal victories.[37] International leprologists meeting in Madrid in 1953 reaffirmed the 1948 resolution. But "implementation of the sentiment," Stein wrote ten years later, "has been . . . sporadic."[38] The British Mission to Lepers still had not budged by the mid-1960s, but the organization made a conciliatory move a few years later when it changed its name to The Leprosy Mission, accompanied, however, by a note on the masthead informing its readers that it was "Formerly the Mission to Lepers." In time, smaller missionary agencies followed suit: In 1967, for example, The Saint Francis Leper Guild became the Saint Francis Leprosy Guild.

The modest success that *The Star* enjoyed in its educational campaign was offset by the indifference with which the newspaper's overtures were received by Bible schools across the country. With Terrelle B. Crum, secretary-treasurer of the Accrediting Association of Bible Institutes and Bible Schools, supplying the list, *The Star* sent copies of its publication and several scholarly reprints on the distinction between the modern disease and biblical "leprosy" to forty Bible schools. In addition to supplying the list and offering his "good wishes," Dean Crum also offered the prophesy that the reply "may run in some instances to the kind of preaching you get which regards leprosy as a type of sin and paints such parallels as prove a hardship in the treatment of the disease."[39]

Only five schools answered *The Star*. The librarian of the Bible Institute of Los Angeles responded pointedly: "I doubt whether it would be significant for you to send us the magazine regularly. We do have a school of missionary medicine, and they are interested in leprosy, of course, but probably not to this extent."[40] That advocates of leprosy reform could expect strong opposition from those organized religious groups having their own special interest in leprosy was the subject of Dr. Frank C. Combes's testimony in 1949 at a Senate subcommittee hearing. Combes, who was professor of dermatology at New York University, told committee members that he was also on the faculty of the National Bible Institute, where he taught hundreds of missionaries about leprosy: "It is surprising how many think that one of their missions in life is to 'care for the lepers,' not in the sense that they would care for an individual with syphilis or tuberculosis. No—leprosy is a thing apart from a purely medical problem. The 'victim' is to be pitied and prayed for."[41]

The greater incentive in dealing with leprosy that came in 1941 with the introduction of Promin and the revitalization of *The Star* as champion of reform had raised expectations that changes in leprosy policy would be forthcoming. But late in 1941 the United States was again at war; before the war was over more than 12 million American men and women served in the war theaters of Europe, North Africa, and the Pacific. World War II and its aftermath embroiled the leprosy world in complex issues over the kinds of changes in policy that should or should not be made.

Wars always made U.S. leprologists nervous, and most agreed that the conditions of war, especially in the highly endemic Pacific areas, would result in an increase of leprosy in the United States. Some predicted modest increases, but others were less optimistic. Aycock and Gordon warned that "an appreciable number of cases of leprosy may be expected . . . [and] based on experience, observations should be continued until about 1982."[42] Under the alarmist heading "Unclean, Unclean!" *Newsweek* magazine quoted Dr. Eugene R. Kellersberger, general secretary of the American Mission to Lepers, as saying that "leprosy will be one of the diseases brought back to this country in the near and far future, as never before."[43] A year later, the *New York Herald-Tribune* quoted Kellersberger as estimating the number would be between 500 and 5,000.[44] Norman R. Sloan, medical director of the Molokai leprosarium, warned Americans that "the experience of the . . . Spanish-American War is likely to be repeated on a larger scale" and listed North Africa, southern Europe, and the Far and Middle East, where Americans were fighting, as geographical areas where leprosy "is abundantly present" and "contagious."[45] The American Legion sounded its own alarm. It noted that in 1943 there were already nine veterans of World War II at Carville and predicted that the number would surely increase.[46] Not all leprologists were pessimistic, however. Dr. Guy Faget, medical officer in charge at Carville, felt that only a small number of veterans would contract the disease on foreign soil.[47]

While Faget did not anticipate a large increase in the number of cases of leprosy from the war, he was preparing, nevertheless, to receive those new cases that did arrive. Mindful that the general public was not well informed about leprosy and that there was "a crying need" to educate people, Faget contributed ten articles to *The Star*, between 1942 and 1943; the series was entitled "What The Patient Should Know About Hansen's Disease." Article 9 reviewed the rules and regulations that governed the operation of the leprosarium. Faget noted that these rules and regulations were approved by the secretary of the treasury in 1922 "and are still applicable at present."[48]

Article 9 had an enormous impact on the Patients' Federation and on the editorial board of *The Star*. *The Star* had initiated a campaign against the rules and regulations in 1932, but the effort was short-lived. Speculation among Carville residents had it that the proposed campaign had been indirectly aborted by the administration.[49] Faget's series, however, opened the door. "When Dr. Faget included the Rules and Regulations . . . in his current series," Stein explained, "he stirred up a veritable hornet's nest. . . . If *The Star* had unearthed these antiques we could be justly censured for not 'letting sleeping dogs lie.'" Most patients, Stein acknowledged, "will agree that under the present regime there has been a more liberal interpretation of some of these rules. . . . [but] we cannot be sure of how they will be interpreted tomorrow even by the present administration or its successors."[50]

Along with their other adversaries, patient activists at Carville now added the PHS to their list. Patients had been quietly encouraging reforms at the national leprosarium for some time. In the early 1940s they broke an important barrier by convincing the administration to permit visitors at the leprosarium.[51] Now they were after more substantial changes, and at the conclusion of Faget's series, *The Star* announced plans to comment editorially on the rules and regulations governing the leprosarium. The series that appeared between May 1943 and March 1944 was entitled "Carville's Bill of Wrongs." Stein acknowledged the need for regulations to safeguard the public in matters threatening the nation's health, but, he noted, these rules "should be based on scientific facts . . . and not . . . on prejudice, tradition and fear." The rules and regulations "defeat their own purpose. . . . It is high time the authorities realize the folly of treating Hansen's disease as if it were a crime instead of an illness."

Speaking for the patients at Carville but also expressing the view of many veterans' groups, Stein totally dismissed U.S. leprosy policy as effective in any way in regulating the spread of the disease through the current system of apprehension and quarantine laws:

> The present system seems to keep about 375 patients inside the leprosarium at all times. It is economically possible to segregate this handful of patients and it gives the impression that all cases of leprosy are segregated, thus humoring the public's phobia and giving them a false sense of protection, whatever the degree of infectiousness may be. The hard facts are these, there are three times as many cases, conservatively speaking, on the outside as on the inside, apparently with no concern on the part of the public or the Public Health authorities, and many of these cases are on the outside because of the very Rules and Regulations which seek to control the disease. Some of these cases, probably a very small percentage, are taking treatment on the QT, but it is more than likely that the large majority of cases, particularly in the early stages when the disease is said to respond to treatment, are getting no medical treatment whatsoever because they fear "apprehension."[52]

As World War II came to a close and as servicemen began to return home, the United States was faced with providing medical services to those injured in the war. Combat had created a whole new population of patients. Existing staffs and facilities within the nation's hospital systems were inadequate. The reorganization of the federal hospital system that took place at the end of the war included leprosy, and within a few years the federal government signaled that it was ready to consider a total review of its leprosy control program.

The review that was initiated in 1946 resulted in temporary setbacks and produced serious controversies in leprosy policy that continued for ten years. In 1956, the PHS finally embarked on a series of changes that brought the treatment and management of leprosy in line with contemporary medical thinking and practice. The struggle took place at Carville and in Washington. It involved both disease ideology and national politics. It pitted Carville patient activists and their war veteran allies against various agencies of the federal government, which were alternately reform-minded, conservative, or indecisive.

A National Advisory Committee on Leprosy, composed of officers of the PHS, state health officials, and leprologists, was formed in the spring of 1946 to conduct a comprehensive review of the national leprosy policy. The need for such a committee had been urged earlier by the American Legion. In November, Dr. R. C. Williams, assistant Surgeon General, came to Carville to discuss the forthcoming meeting of the committee and, according to *The Star*, took the opportunity to express his belief that "this is an opportune time for changing the archaic system now in effect."[53]

The preliminary recommendations of the committee were encouraging. At a meeting held in December, it was proposed that a public health approach to the disease be adopted in place of "the present institutional plan." The control program would be decentralized. Diagnostic and then treatment centers would be set up in those states where the disease was endemic. The policies at Carville for patients receiving treatment at that institution would be liberalized. Outpatient treatment centers were considered a vital component of the new system: Only then would patients voluntarily seek treatment and more cases could be reached in the early stage of disease, when the new drugs were most promising. One of the criticisms of the institutional plan was that by the time most patients arrived at Carville the disease was already well advanced.[54]

Some of the changes under discussion had already been implemented elsewhere. Since 1938, Latin American dermatologists had been making a vigorous effort to have the tuberculoid form of the disease—"neural," in an earlier classification—included in the international nosology of leprosy. This was achieved in 1948. The tuberculoid form was considered to be relatively benign, generally self-limiting, often negative on bacteriological examination, and, many thought, noncontagious for all practical purposes.[55] In Brazil, where there was a far higher prevalence of this form of the disease than in the United States, tuberculoid patients had been allowed to remain free of isolation since the 1940s.[56] Although some leprologists in the United States were recommending that "each case be considered as a separate problem" and stating that segregation "is medically necessary only in extreme cases" and that it is practiced "in most instances . . . to satisfy public opinion," a blanket policy of isolation prevailed nonetheless.[57]

Speaking from the perspective of institutionalized patients, *The Star* staff members welcomed the proposed recommendations and were pleased that a public health approach to leprosy was being considered; they cautiously awaited further developments. Specialized war veterans' groups, on the other hand, particularly the American Federation of the Physically Handicapped, which represented a much wider group of disabled persons, were dissatisfied. In their opinion, the recommendations did not go far enough and dealt only with "comparatively minor matters." Left out of the recommendations were specific proposals for medical research, vocational and rehabilitation training, public education, an expanded program for patient financial assistance, housekeeping quarters for married couples at the leprosarium, and elimination of the common carriers' travel restrictions on persons with leprosy. The Federation found the reason for postponing outpatient treatment centers until some future date unclear.[58]

In July 1947, when Watson B. Miller, head of the Federal Security Agency, visited Carville, he told patients "Now that the balloon is up we hope we can keep it going." Dr. R. C. Williams announced that "the new treatment center for early cases of Hansen's disease at the U.S. Marine Hospital in New Orleans will be launched within six weeks." Proponents of reform felt that major innovations were on the way. The Federal Security Agency was then the umbrella organization of sixteen important federal agencies, including the PHS, and for eighteen years Miller had been the national rehabilitation chairman of the American Legion. Miller also served as chairman of the Legion's own national leprosy committee and was accorded "top billing" in *The Star*'s list of friends. Among his plans, Miller told the group, were efforts "to secure funds for 18 new [patient] cottages [at Carville] . . . and an agreement by the Association of American Railroads" to change the travel restrictions placed on persons with Hansen's disease, "which were formulated more than 35 years ago."[59]

Six months later, however, *The Star* complained that "a year has passed" and that although several recommendations of the National Advisory Committee on Leprosy had been carried out, the "PHS seems hesitant to take 'full steps' toward their objectives." Those recommendations that were implemented were mainly administrative and applied to liberalizing patient leaves and vacations and to authorizing funds to return deceased patients home. Although the new practices elevated patient morale, they had little effect on the overall structure of the leprosy control program.

A pilot program for an outpatient leprosy clinic in New Orleans was announced in the *New Orleans States* newspaper in 1947.[60] The newspaper applauded the decision in an editorial, but the Louisiana State Medical Society went on record "as opposing any relaxation of standards used in diagnosis of leprosy and confinement of its victims." The state society also opposed any research in connection with an outpatient center and any reduction in isolation requirements before patients were released.[61] It was not until the early 1950s, when the Louisiana State Medical Society reversed its position, that an outpatient clinic was established in New Orleans. A second such clinic, in San Francisco, was not opened for another ten years.

Despite complaints about the pace with which the PHS was moving, two changes took place at Carville in the summer and fall of 1948 that made local history. The first was symbolic and involved the removal of three strands of barbed wire from the top of the fence in front of the hospital. The second had far-reaching implications: A new medical discharge policy was announced. Since 1922, PHS policy had called for three types of discharges: cured, arrested, or latent. In reviewing the history of patient discharges, *The Star* noted that only the arrested category had ever been used. The requirements for discharge as an "arrested case" were twelve monthly consecutive negative bacteriological examinations. In addition, the patient had to be clinically inactive. If a positive count appeared during the year, examinations started over again. The new policy was more flexible. Under certain conditions patients would now be eligible for a medical discharge during the "so-called communicable stage" of the disease. To qualify, four conditions applied: (1) The patient's family would pay for the cost of outpatient treatment; (2) the treating physician would issue monthly reports on the patient's progress; (3) no children and few adults would live at home with the patient; and (4) the state health department would concur in the disposition. The new policy applied to relatively few of the patients who came to Carville. Even so, *The Star* hailed the move as a "crack in the wall of tradition" when, in October 1948, a patient was discharged from the hospital as an arrested case after six consecutive negative bacteriological examinations.[62]

Veterans' groups, however, were impatient with the progress of the PHS. In May 1949, hearings were held before a Senate subcommittee on a proposed bill to improve the leprosy situation in the United States. The National Leprosy Act (S. 704) was an omnibus bill.[63] Lobbying on behalf of veterans and in the name of disability, proponents obtained the support of labor unions, who were also interested in extracting special benefits and more generous concessions from a post-war Congress.

The bill was backed by Colonel G. H. Rarey, U.S. Army (retired) and southern representative of the American Federation of the Physically Handicapped. The incidence of leprosy in the country was expected to increase as a result of the war. Rarey argued the case for overhauling leprosy policy on the grounds that, as persons who had acquired a socially stigmatized disease while in the service of their country, veterans were entitled to better treatment than that currently accorded to leprosy patients. In his testimony before the Senate, Rarey pointed out that the PHS had postponed or rejected the recommendations of "forward-looking leprologists" in favor of an "ultraconservative" policy of compulsory segregation. Federal policy, the committee was told, had failed to control the disease and had contributed to the "perpetuation of lepraphobia among our people."[64]

Almost all phases of national policy came under attack at the hearings. Veterans hospitalized at Carville did not receive the rehabilitation or educational benefits granted by the G.I. Bill of Rights. The PHS was faulted for its conservative medical discharge policy, its provision of "hazard duty" pay to leprosarium workers, its lack of medical research, and its failure to establish outpatient centers. One document presented noted that there were fewer than six scientists in the United States who were working on the disease, that no research was going on at the federal level, and that at Carville the laboratory was inadequately staffed. Only the Leonard Wood Memorial at Harvard Medical School was conducting research, but no patients were available there. The burden of exploring new chemotherapies rested exclusively with commercial pharmaceutical firms.[65]

Witnesses at the hearings charged that an "illogical discrimination" was practiced by the federal government with regard to leprosy. Dr. C. D.

Bowdoin, Georgia State Health Department, was quoted as saying that "there were 254 known typhoid carriers, all of whom were walking bundles of the deadly typhoid germs, in Georgia. . . . Being kept under surveillance by the State health department is quite different from the isolation decreed for the patient having the far less communicable disease of leprosy."[66] In 1945, the American Public Health Association had recommended that the segregation of persons with leprosy was unnecessary where the disease showed no tendency to spread. Suitable medical and nursing care in general hospitals or in the patient's home was regarded as sufficient.[67] Rarey pointed out that the APHA recommendations had been approved by the PHS and printed as a public document, but that "it would appear that this Service has not fully acquainted the Army, the Navy, the Veterans Administration, and the medical profession with this new policy."[68] The military branches of the government were especially hard to convince. An article in the St. Louis *Post-Dispatch* asserted that "An ordinary layman's misapprehensions about Hansen's disease . . . are understandable. . . . Governmental officials, however, ought to know better. That's why it is depressing to find Defense Secretary [James V.] Forrestal passing on to Congress a report which recommends special 'hazard duty' pay to uniformed personnel handling lepers."[69]

For six years (1948–1954) the American Federation of the Physically Handicapped lobbied hard to have the National Leprosy Act introduced in both houses of Congress. There was strong opposition in Washington to the many generous provisions of the bill. Harsh criticism came from the Federal Security Agency, which contended that "new knowledge of the disease seems to weaken, rather than strengthen, the case for singling it out and its victims for such special consideration as . . . [the bill] would provide."[70] Among its special considerations, the bill called on the PHS to arrange for medical care and hospitalization in centers across the country as well as in the patient's own home. Financial assistance to the families of patients and their dependents and special compensation for disability were also requested. The Federal Security Agency questioned "the advisability of singling out members of this group and their dependents to receive federal help solely on the grounds that they have leprosy." The agency totally rejected the recommendation that employable discharged leprosy patients be given job preference in filling vacancies at service hospitals, noting that such a provision was not in the best interest of medical care.[71]

The immediate postwar years had brought a great deal of national publicity to Carville. Many officials, leprologists, and news reporters came. In addition to these visitors, there were those who came as patients. Some had served or lived in leprosy endemic regions of the Pacific during the war. One such patient was Gertrude Hornbostel, the wife of Bataan death-march survivor Major Hans Hornbostel. Both the Major and his wife were interned at prisoner-of-war camps when the Japanese overran the Philippines in 1942. Both were war heroes. Reunited with her husband after the war, Mrs. Hornbostel was diagnosed in San Francisco as having leprosy. Her arrival at Carville in 1946 and the anger of her husband at being denied the right to live with his wife at the institution were extensively covered by the news media. The Hornbostels held press conferences and voiced their criticism of the PHS's policy toward leprosy. The Hornbostels' presence at Carville and their refusal to conceal her illness also had a local effect on the custom whereby patients assumed aliases on entering the leprosarium. "Since that time," Stanley Stein wrote, "there has been an increasing tendency among Carville patients to face the world on their own terms and under their own names."[72] The Hornbostels' behavior at Carville and their sharp criticism of PHS policy strengthened the argument for congressional leprosy reform.

Section 902 of the proposed reform Act contained a controversial provision. The section "would supercede and invalidate the provisions of other national Acts and instructions which are contrary to this Act as applicable to the national plan for the control and elimination of leprosy in the United States."[73] The specific issue involved was the power of the federal government in the matter of "enforced detention." The officials of the Federal Security Agency took an adamant position on this proposed change and stated that they were unwilling to relinquish their authority. They claimed that the issue played "no part in the present leprosy program of the Public Health Service (all admissions of patients to Carville being accompanied by the written consent of the patient)." The existing authority of the Public Health Service, agency officials argued, "should not be repealed or cast in doubt without careful consideration and provision for alternative methods of meeting the problem, *should need arise*."[74]

The National Leprosy Act was never passed by Congress; it died in committee. Although Congress and the PHS were disinclined to restructure leprosy policy along the broad lines recommended by the Act, life at the leprosarium continued to improve. Some changes were directly initiated by the PHS, some by other federal agencies, and some were brought about locally in Louisiana through the combined efforts of patient activists working together with friends and allies within the state. Following the earlier recommendations of the National Advisory Committee on Leprosy, a number of added paramedical and medical appointments to the institution were made. Within a few years, a branch of the U.S. Post Office was opened at the leprosarium. Patients employed at the hospital by the PHS became eligible for social security coverage. Locally, the state of Louisiana amended its constitution and granted eligible patients the right to vote, removed leprosy from the category of quarantinable diseases, and allocated a small monthly allowance to indigent patients who were residents of the state.[75] There were also indications that changes were taking place worldwide. In 1950, the newly formed World Health Organization gave recognition to leprosy as an international health problem, and new programs and approaches were being discussed.

There were conservative trends as well. The Surgeon General's National Advisory Committee on Leprosy had not convened for years. The issue of conducting basic research at Carville remained unresolved. In 1950 the

United States was again at war in the Far East, in Korea. And in 1951 Great Britain, for the first time in modern history, made leprosy a reportable disease.[76] At Carville, colony residents were worried that Clinical Director Dr. Rolla R. Wolcott, a "hard liner," would succeed Dr. F. A. Johansen as the leprosarium's medical officer in charge. It was well known among patients that Dr. Wolcott wanted to shut down *The Star*.[77] In Washington the U.S. Immigration Department was about to deport Josefina V. Guerrero, Carville patient and Filipino war hero, back to the Philippines.[78] In the early 1950s, U.S. leprosy policy was at a crossroad. Clearly, the leprosarium could not go back to being what it once was. On the other hand, no new direction was immediately apparent.

In the summer of 1953, however, the PHS revealed its own thinking on the policy matters. The opportunity came with the mandatory retirement of Johansen after twenty-nine years of service at Carville, the last six as medical officer in charge. Dr. Edward M. Gordon was appointed as his successor. The changes that were about to be made were not announced ahead of time, nor were they shared in advance with veterans' groups and patients. This time the PHS acted unilaterally. The shape of things to come only emerged gradually as they unfolded locally at the administrative level. What followed was open confrontation between an angry reform group and the PHS. PHS officials had decided not to reorganize the leprosy control program by liberalizing it, as the reformists had hoped, but instead to tighten control over the institution. The confrontation lasted three years.

What the PHS officials intended was to reshape Carville into a formal communicable disease facility. They had two objectives: (1) to dismantle the community structure that had developed within the colony at the leprosarium, and (2) to invoke a harder line on contagion.

Directives in support of reshaping Carville along more formal lines were announced within six months. The PHS proposed to discharge patients from the leprosarium in instances where medical opinion concurred that continued hospitalization was no longer justified. At the time the policy was announced, there were 365 patients at Carville; ninety-two, or 25 percent, of them were listed as "arrested cases," that is, bacteriologically negative. Arrested cases were divided by the administration into three categories: (1) physically able-bodied patients, (2) partially disabled, or borderline patients, and (3) the "permanently disabled," such as the blind and the severely handicapped.

Early in January 1954, patients in the first category were asked to leave. It was suggested to patients in the second category that they also consider leaving. Patients in the third category were assured that they would not be asked to leave but told that they could leave if friends or relatives were willing to care for them. In addition to discharging eligible patients, Gordon sought to change a series of other long-standing practices. His objective was to permanently disrupt patient community life. Able-bodied dischargeable patients, it was announced, "were no longer eligible to hold either part-time government jobs or positions with such private enterprises as patient-owned shops or the canteen operated by the Patients' Federation." While

The Star was not specifically mentioned, patients understood that the newspaper was also targeted. Patient employees who were declared to be arrested cases were given three months, with the aid of the social service department, to make arrangements to live on the outside.[79]

The patients agreed in principle with the spirit of the new discharge policy, insofar as Gordon claimed it was intended to further public understanding about leprosy. However, they sharply disagreed with the administration over the criteria used in formulating the policy. The Patients' Federation argued that "patients who came to Carville in the pre-sulfone era, prior to 1941, had been here for 12 years, and in many cases much longer, and even though some of them might fortunately fall in the first and second categories, their homes had been broken, contact with relatives lost, and they had no place to go, and without some sort of rehabilitation, they were unable to enter the competitive world."[80] With respect to the question of public understanding, patients argued that "unwarranted social stigma, discrimination and fear" were still too often associated with the disease even though an individual might be classified as an "arrested" case. Patients were angry that the administration was burdening them with the task of testing public perception without first engaging in public health education.

Patients eligible for a medical discharge who remained at the leprosarium were termed "colonizers." For years such patients had been uneasy about remaining at Carville and feared that falling into disfavor with the administration would jeopardize their continued residence at the institution. The strength of the administrative pressure in reducing the number of patients at the leprosarium was decisively demonstrated in February 1955, when a group of fourteen patients from the Virgin Islands, who had been transferred from St. Croix to Carville early in the 1950s, before Gordon's arrival, was suddenly discharged from the hospital. The patients were notified on February 26, and seven were flown back home within three days. The other seven had in the meantime absconded.[81]

The new administration leaned toward a more extreme view on contagion than patients had experienced in years. These views came to light concurrently as patient extramural activities were curtailed. In July 1956, the administration banned all golf, baseball games, and dances between the patients and outsiders. Patients were advised to inform the American Legion that "in deference to the fact that leprosy is a communicable disease . . . patients should have as few and as casual contacts with non-patients as possible. The exposure of more or less the same group of outside Legionnaires . . . is a cause of concern."[82]

Patient uneasiness had meanwhile turned to action, and the Patients' Federation announced that it had retained the services of an attorney to represent them. They hired Robert L. Kleinpeter of Baton Rouge, who was on the state executive board of the American Legion and the son of one of the pioneers of American Legion work at Carville.[83] In addition to sending Kleinpeter to Washington to discuss matters with the PHS, the Patients'

Federation also sent a letter to the Surgeon General outlining their grievances with the Gordon administration. The letter, part of which later appeared in a Baton Rouge newspaper, noted that "the doctor-patient relationship [at Carville] has deteriorated to the point where it has become intolerable. . . . The patients no longer have the respect for and confidence in the Medical Officer in Charge [MOC] which this position merits." The letter specifically charged Gordon with lacking a "human touch," with being "arbitrary and unjust" in his relations with patients, and with engendering a fear among patients "that if they express an opinion contrary to that of the MOC, they may be singled out for personal retaliation." Convinced that "the MOC is the root of the troubles" at Carville, the Patients' Federation called for Gordon's removal. At Carville, graffiti denouncing Gordon began appearing on the walls of the covered walkways at the leprosarium.[84]

In addition to poor patient morale induced by the Gordon administration, the letter registered other long-standing patient complaints. Patients protested that members of the small medical staff, usually composed of young physicians just entering the PHS, seldom remained at Carville for more than a two-year rotation, although knowledge of the disease and its treatment required years of experience. Dentures had formerly been bought from a professional laboratory, but now ill-fitting ones were ordered from a federal prison. The patients had difficulties in obtaining specially built shoes. As gum tissues and feet are physically sensitive areas in persons with leprosy, these complaints reflected on medical care. The letter also commented on the absence of vocational and rehabilitation programs at the leprosarium. This situation was perceived by patients as a major deficit in a chronic disease institution and particularly glaring in light of the new discharge policies.[85]

While still in Washington, Kleinpeter wired the Patients' Federation that his meeting with the PHS was "most successful." However, Gordon had in the meantime banned all patient activities with outsiders. The next blow came the following month with an announcement from the PHS Division of Hospitals that all private cottages occupied by patients would be demolished. In the future all patients would be housed in dormitory facilities.

Of all the changes that were proposed at Carville, the plan to demolish the private cottages and relocate its inhabitants closer to the mainstream of hospital life was the most explosive. In targeting Cottage Grove, the PHS had taken on the power structure of the community. The citizens of Cottage Grove were the "elite" among the patients. Cottage Grove was for the most part inhabited by, or was accessible to, community leaders at the leprosarium. The destruction of Cottage Grove, *The Star* warned, meant that "Carville would become an institution again, instead of a liberal hospital community."[86]

The PHS had concerned itself with Cottage Grove earlier. In 1947, the head of the Federal Security Agency noted that many of the cottages were in need of repair and promised to secure funds to build new ones. In 1953, the issue of the PHS's acquiring title was discussed, and the PHS proposed to compensate owners for their cottages. Until mid-1956 it had been assumed by patients that after acquiring title the PHS would continue to allow patients to occupy the houses. This belief was reinforced when Dr. C. K. Himmelsbach, chief of the Division of Hospitals, testified before the House Appropriations Committee in Washington in July of that year. Transfer of the cottages to the PHS with compensation to the owners was supported on the grounds that the houses "have helped to preserve family relationships" and that the PHS "should use them . . . in a therapeutic fashion." Accordingly, the hospital administration released a statement to patients reassuring occupants "that they will continue to be assigned their present houses assuming good behavior and therapeutic need."[87]

However, in August, one month after his congressional testimony, Himmelsbach visited Carville and told the patients that the plan now was to compensate owners for their cottages and then to demolish the buildings. Cottage dwellers would be housed in kitchenless apartments in the old dormitories, which would be remodeled. All patients would be required to take their meals in the cafeteria. Stein commented bitterly that this latest plan was "the last straw."[88]

Threatened by the fact that Carville was changing in ways not to its liking, the Patients' Federation contacted all their outside supporters. Within a few days, the local chapter of the American Legion adopted a resolution condemning the administration for attempting to convert Carville into a "quarantine hospital." Copies of the resolution were sent to the state and national organization for "appropriate action" and to the press, where the resolution was printed in a Baton Rouge newspaper. Similar resolutions were adopted by other veterans' groups, and delegates were urged to contact their congressmen.[89] A friend from Monroe, Louisiana, was also contacted— Congressman Otto E. Passman.

With the patients' opposition out in the open, conflict within the hospital turned acrimonious. Patients were divided from the administration, and divisiveness developed within the ranks of the hospital staff itself. The new policy was enthusiastically supported by the pro-Gordon faction. *The Star* reported that this "same group of employees (including two department heads)" had circulated "a petition among hospital personnel [asking] 'Do you want the patients to run the hospital instead of the doctors? If they win out, there is no stopping them.'"[90]

On August 22, two Louisiana officials of the American Legion, the editor of the Monroe *Morning World*, and Congressman Passman met separately with the executive board of the Patients' Federation and with Gordon. The "crisis" at Carville, as it was now called, attracted the attention of the state's newspapers. *The Star* enjoyed excellent relations with the local press, which was uniformly propatient. Passman's active interest in the patients' cause was immediately noted, as was the fact that his position was soon endorsed by other congressional representatives and senators. One month later, events at Carville would reach *Time* magazine.

As the story unfolded, many of the details of the August 22 meeting surfaced. Gordon defended his actions as being "in the interest of protecting the public health, which is our job." As far as the cottages were concerned,

Gordon explained, "I thought . . . the folks understood . . . that the ultimate decision rests with the Public Health Service headquarters and the Public Building Authority." The reasons advanced by Gordon for the decision about Cottage Grove were considered by his critics to be inadequate. He cited their "substandard" condition and said that because the hospital was converting from DC to AC current, there would be limits to "the electric appliances patients will be permitted to have." As for the policy that all patients eat in the cafeteria rather than in their homes, Gordon explained that this was necessary because "treatment of Hansen's disease requires a controlled diet."[91]

Critics of the administration soon attacked Gordon's competence both as an administrator and as a leprologist. The Monroe *Morning World* questioned Gordon's record, noting that he had held nineteen assignments in the twenty-eight years he had been with the PHS. "Apparently he has not been very satisfactory anywhere."[92] Gordon's career mobility would also be noted by *Time* magazine.[93] *The Star* called Gordon "a newcomer" to the field of leprosy whose answer is "to cite authorities who recommend the segregation of all known victims of Hansen's disease." *The Star* further charged Gordon with being "a disciple of Dr. L. F. Badger [chief of the PHS Leprosy Control Unit], an extremist in his views on contagion."[94]

"Tensions Mount" and "Smoldering Unrest" were the way Louisiana newspapers headlined events at Carville in the last week of August 1956. Passman, who was a member of the powerful House of Representatives Appropriations Committee, and other congressmen threatened a full-scale investigation of the PHS. The local press demanded Gordon's immediate resignation. The Monroe *Morning World* rhetorically characterized the leprosarium under Gordon with an editorial entitled "Soviet-Type Prison Camp at Carville?"[95] On the same day, the Baton Rouge *Morning Advocate*, on the front page, endorsed the Monroe newspaper's editorial and picked up on the theme that the Gordon administration was engaged in "a scheme to regiment the Carville patients along the lines of Soviet disciplinary barracks."[96]

The campaign against Gordon came to a head on September 13, 1956, with a statement issued by Congressman Passman in Washington to the Associated Press that Gordon would immediately be replaced at Carville and that his successor had already been chosen.[97] On the same day that Passman announced Gordon's removal, Dr. Jack Masur, assistant Surgeon General, flew to Carville to meet with the executive board of the Patients' Federation. Masur would not comment on Gordon's removal. The real reason for his visit, he said, was to "cool the situation," especially the national publicity it was receiving. "The *Time* article," Masur was quoted as telling the Patients' Federation, "is unfortunate for all of us. It smacks of yellow journalism. . . . I am asking all people concerned to lay hands off, and quiet things down."[98]

On November 16, 1956, Dr. Edgar B. Johnwick became the sixth medical officer in charge of the leprosarium. Within a few days, *The Star* reported, "the tension which hung over this hospital like a heavy fog had lifted. There was a sudden and profound change in climate." Johnwick arrived at Carville on a Friday. On Monday, he called a meeting with the medical staff, patients, and hospital personnel—"a radical departure," Stein later wrote, "not only from Dr. Gordon's nonfraternization policy, but from an old Carville custom which had always kept the three groups apart."[99] Speaking to a full house, Johnwick outlined his "mission"—medical care, research, and health education. "These three things are not done separately by different members of the staff but by a team that is made up of the staff and patients." Johnwick closed his address with two final remarks that put to rest the turbulence of the Gordon years: "No one should be discharged from this hospital against his will. No one should be kept in this hospital against his will."[100]

Among the items of unfinished business that Johnwick inherited was Cottage Grove. As with a number of other undesired changes, the issue of Cottage Grove was also resolved in favor of the patients. In June 1957, the federal government assumed title to the cottages and checks totalling $24,120 were distributed among former owners. Along with the checks, letters were distributed that assigned each patient to the cottage he occupied, as resident now rather than as owner. "Within the budgeted means of this hospital," Johnwick announced, "the cottages will be maintained by the hospital," and priority in assigning cottages in the future "will be given to married couples."[101] In 1960, new cottages were built by the PHS to replace the old ones. For other married couples at Carville, three-room apartments were constructed, each with a built-in kitchen, living-dining room, bath, and bedroom.[102] In the September 1956 magazine article that had upset the PHS by bringing the unrest at Carville to national attention, *Time* had hailed the end of the Gordon administration as a "clear-cut victory" for the patients. With this opinion, *The Star* heartily concurred: "Another good fight won," was the way it phrased it.

9

The National Hansen's Disease Center: New Managers and Old Habits

Under the Johnwick administration, Carville entered a new era. The era marked the fulfillment of many of the goals envisioned when postwar plans for broad changes in leprosy policy were being discussed. The changes that were introduced were welcomed by the patients; for years patients and their allies had argued their need. As welcome as these changes were, they nonetheless produced strains within the institution. The new goals and programs intruded on entrenched values and traditional attitudes and practices within the leprosarium and on the fabric of patient life in the colony.

Medical care at the hospital was soon expanded to include rehabilitation and plastic surgery. An opthalmologist and an epidemiologist joined the staff, and the number of visiting consultants increased. Research in the laboratory, in physical therapy, and in new surgical procedures received high priority. Programs of health education for professionals, as well as for the public, were introduced. In 1961 the hospital at Carville reached out and announced intentions of fulfilling "responsibilities of leadership" in the field of leprosy.[1] International seminars in collaboration with the American Leprosy Missions were conducted annually. By the late 1970s, Carville had so grown in terms of research and training that the hospital was officially renamed the National Hansen's Disease Center.[2] The event concurred with having the editorial and publishing offices of the *International Journal of Leprosy* housed there. On the face of it, Carville was being turned around. All the components essential for the creation of a proper treatment facility— long-term for some, short-term for others—were being assembled. The philosophy of the new administration stressed the importance of a team approach in carrying out the function of the institution, with patients and staff working together in mutual partnership.

Along with medical care, patient rehabilitation was accorded a high priority. One of the primary functions of the newly created rehabilitation branch at the hospital was "to motivate and prepare the patient for return to his own community outside of Carville as an acceptable and contributing member of society."[3] The rehabilitation branch was composed of personnel from several subspecialties. Also included were Protestant and Catholic chaplains and schoolteachers from the accredited high school for patients that was located on the hospital grounds. Patient employment was incorporated as an important subsystem of rehabilitation. Patients had been employed at the leprosarium for some time. Earlier, employment had been thought of simply as a way of getting certain necessary work done and as a means of providing patients with "something to do" as well as a way to earn extra money. Now, with more modern treatment methods and with a new perspective on rehabilitation, patient jobs were perceived as having "therapeutic" or "rehabilitative" value.[4] A physician was in charge of the rehabilitation branch.

In time Carville would achieve many of the goals set by the administration. However, the goal of motivating patients to leave Carville for a life outside the leprosarium would prove to be the most difficult task. For years the federal government had tried to get people with leprosy to come to Carville. Now the problem was to get them to leave. Starting in 1953 with the Gordon administration, a new policy had emerged. The PHS no longer viewed leprosy as a disease for which indefinite asylum was encouraged. Between 1953 and 1956 the PHS had sought to prevent patient colonization via administrative fiat. Under Johnwick, rehabilitation became the means whereby eligible patients were encouraged to leave voluntarily. Although the approach of the two administrations differed sharply, the policy itself represented a radical departure from past practices, in which the release of patients was not actively pursued. In attempting to implement the new policy via decree, Gordon had encountered strong patient resistance. Under Johnwick and subsequent administrations, the rehabilitation approach met with a different and paradoxical fate. Programs designed to motivate patients into leaving voluntarily brought into sharp focus conflicting institutional dynamics inherent in the leprosarium setting.

When the new administration strove to involve patients in hospital functions, it faced a more difficult task than simply breaking down preexisting barriers and trying to motivate patients. Events during the Gordon administration had driven home the point that the leprosarium was unlike other hospitals. Generally, hospitals are identified with their managers and with the medical and nursing staff. Although patients are acknowledged to be a part of a hospital system, their relevance to social organization is generally thought to be secondary to that of the hospital structure. In Talcott Parsons's view, the career of patients within hospitals tends to be overly regularized by hospital managers.[5] In Goffman's view, it is ruined by managers.[6] Exceptions are chronic disease situations where patients are long-term residents: "then their impact upon structure is more obvious to everyone concerned."[7] In elevating the status of patients at Carville, the new administration acknowledged the reality of leprosarium life. It further acknowledged that patients at the leprosarium possessed a considerable degree of power and autonomy and that they exercised it both within the institution and outside of it.

The new administrative philosophy called for a sharing of responsibility between patients and staff, especially in matters of patient care and disease

management. Implicit in the idea of shared responsibility within an organizational setting is the view of the organization as a "system of purposely
coordinated activities designed to produce some over-all explicit ends."[8] At
Carville the intended product was improvement in the medical condition
of patients and their release to the community. Although the concept of a
team approach had an egalitarian appeal, there nonetheless existed among
clinicians, rehabilitation personnel, and patients serious and at times incompatible differences in values and objectives. When coupled with the
medical uncertainties of leprosy and the specter of public stigma, these
differences conspired to produce considerable indeterminateness in reaching
and implementing decisions on important aspects of patient treatment and
disposition.

The professional mandate at Carville now was to provide medical treatment, to assist in patient rehabilitation, and to anticipate the departure of
patients from the leprosarium. In terms of the age of patients and the length
of time many had been at the institution, the new philosophy, although
applied to patients presently in residence, seemed designed more for a future
generation of patients. In November 1962 (when I took my first patient
census), of the 306 patients in residence, the median age was 50 years and
the median length of elapsed time this group had been at Carville from
the date of first admission until the end of 1962 was 15.4 years. For the
99 patients who had been admitted prior to the introduction of the new
chemotherapy in 1941, the median length of elapsed time since first admission
was 28.6 years. As patients had been assured that leaving the leprosarium
was now a voluntary decision, the inherent conflict between staff objectives
and patient colonization did not lead to outright protest. Instead, it led to
a complicated intramural struggle. That the new policy was incompatible
with the demographic characteristics of the present generation of Carville
patients was perhaps understood by the PHS, for when Surgeon General
Luther L. Terry visited Carville in October 1961, he spoke of the hospital's
future in terms of research. Carville was perceived as a receiving hospital
for all new cases of the disease in the United States, where patients would
be admitted "for at least a year so that evaluation . . . can be made upon
which to base future out-patient treatment." Patients would be admitted in
the early stages of the disease and would not have to remain at Carville
so long, and the plan "would give the medical staff . . . an opportunity to
study previously untreated cases."[9]

Generally, the cooperation of a patient in a treatment program is based
on a set of objectives that stresses the hospital's identification with the
interest of the patient. At Carville the staff had a difficult time convincing
patients of an identity of interest. The medical uncertainties associated with
the disease, the problematic nature of social acceptance, and the history
and structure of the leprosarium all conspired to make life difficult for a
staff wedded to ideas of treatment, rehabilitation, and discharge.

Young physicians, trained in medical school according to an acute illness
model, found Carville an unusual place. Staff had little formal control over

patients' behavior and no authority to discharge them from the institution. A senior member of the clinical staff explained in an interview that the colony aspect of patient life constrained the work of the staff:

> The patient community, the apartments and quarters that patients occupy, patient organizations, social activities and liberal passes, all these things defy comparing Carville with a hospital as I know a hospital. The hospital I know is the one in which you make daily rounds to see your patients and they are confined to their beds or rooms. . . . If a patient feels he doesn't want to leave here, even though we think he's ready to leave, he doesn't have to go. There's no way for us to move him out. All of this influences our relations with the patients.[10]

The freedom of colony life gave patients control over decisions about whether to engage in rehabilitation programs or even to take medication. Life in the colony, according to one physician, permitted residents to behave like outpatients:

> The thing about the community that I personally don't like is the freedom that the patients have which almost makes it equivalent to [their] living outside. It defeats the aim that we try to set of rehabilitating a patient. Some patients in the community may go for long periods of time without seeing a physician . . . [even] when it's just a matter of him receiving medication.

Data obtained by a research assistant who spent two days a week for a period of nearly one year observing life in the colony corroborated the picture of patient freedom described by the physician in the above interview:

> Unlike many other institutions operating for the treatment and rehabilitation of inmates, staff has very little control over the activities of patients. The daily lives of the patients are not scheduled by staff; participation in treatment and rehabilitation programs is voluntary. Indeed, about one-third of the patients at Carville do not even make appointments with the doctors for treatment of their leprosy. Some of these are arrested cases, but because of the physical arrangements of the hospital, it is quite possible for a patient at Carville to have practically no interaction with staff. For example, a patient couple living in one of the cottages and operating their own business on the grounds prepares breakfast at home, goes to work, goes back home for lunch, returns home after work, prepares dinner, and perhaps attends a meeting of a patient organization or has another patient couple over for cards during the evening. The couple may own their own car and take frequent short passes to Baton Rouge or New Orleans to shop, go to a football game, or dine out.[11]

The length and uncertainty of medical treatment in leprosy made it difficult for staff to convince patients of the need to follow a long treatment regimen. Some patients "just walk off" and leave the institution. One staff member said that others return to Carville "when they are quite ill [and] when they improve sufficiently [so] that they are able to ambulate again . . . they just say goodbye to us and leave. And there isn't anything doctors can do about it. You can't say we just won't admit him the next time he comes because . . . invariably the next time he is usually worse off than the first time." A major complaint voiced by the physicians was that patients did not heed the medical advice of the staff. In matters having to do with leprosy-related treatment, they listened to other patients and to the Patients' Federation. As one physician put it: "You can just talk and talk to these people over and over again and they just sit there and agreeably smile and they acknowledge what you say and turn around and do the opposite. . . . On the other hand, the Patients' Federation guides and advises the other patients. These members are very influential and they exert a lot of influence in the community."

As despairing as physicians were of the "freedom" that the patients at Carville possessed, another leprologist, experienced in a variety of treatment settings throughout the world, observed that Carville was not unique among leprosaria with long-term admission policies. Such centers have special management problems. Of Carville, this physician commented:

> Some patients have been here longer than any of the staff and many patients feel and actually do know more about the disease than the medical staff, and especially the doctor who has not encountered leprosy before. Some of the patients who have been treated by a succession of doctors over the years know what's good for them, I mean they really know. Therefore [there's a] kind of political feeling about the place, where the patients feel like they have a right to advise on what can be done for them, and in other ways try to run the place.

Patients who had been at Carville for many years were "old hands" at dealing with inexperienced staff, changing personnel, and the vicissitudes of medical treatment. In light of their own experience, patients, particularly the "old-timers," felt they were just as capable as the doctors at the leprosarium, or even more so, in treating their own condition and advising on the condition of others. "One of the attitudes around here," one patient, a relative newcomer, explained, "is that the patients seem to think they are better doctors than the doctor himself." To this another patient added: "The ones that have been here a long time, they think they can doctor themselves. They say, 'I am my own doctor.'" One of the young Sisters, a member of the nursing staff, reported encountering this attitude frequently. She observed:

> For oral medication, they [the patients] go to their doctor and get a prescription say for DDS, a hundred milligrams four times a week for a month. They hand that to the Sister in the pharmacy. She hands them a bottle of pills and that's that. Some of them will come right out and tell you, "Sister, if I take more than two of these a week, I get a reaction and I'm not going to take them." And they won't. And they'll tell you they won't. They don't mind telling you. Now, here's the doctor writing down on his card, "Patient doing well on 400 mg a week." He's no more taking 400 mg a week than I am. A lot of them save it up to take it home on a pass. They figure if they go

AWOL [absence without leave] or can't come back for a couple of months or so, it gives them something to take when they're out.

Old-timers were very adamant about which medicines worked for them and which did not. The Sister continued:

A lot of patients are very opinionated. They're sure they know what is best for them and God help the doctor if he tries to change it. They think their own remedies are better in the long run, and a while back a group of the old patients got up a signed petition that they absolutely wanted Promin put back on the treatment regimen. I don't know what was done about putting it back [but] they'll tell you about such and such in the old days. Well, I've been here only a short time, so usually I just keep my mouth shut and don't say anything because if you agree with them, boy, they've got you right where they want you.

Disagreement among experts about medical treatment in leprosy created confusion among patients and eroded their confidence in physicians. One patient reported: "Dr. _____ [a visiting leprologist] told me, yes, your doctor is going too fast with you. He just told me, 'Don't take too much [sulfone] because that's the trouble here, they go too fast with the treatment. You should go slow.'"[12] Because leprosy is frequently misdiagnosed by physicians in general practice, some patients' confidence in medical expertise began to erode long before they arrived at Carville. "Many doctors can't tell what you have," another patient reported. "That happened to me. They about to kill you before they find out what's wrong with you. They said it was rheumatic fever for two years. . . . But the doctor should know at least a little bit about leprosy. Or the dermatologist, they should know of leprosy."

Other patients reported receiving conflicting information about medication from the professional staff at the leprosarium: "That's what I can't understand. Sister [a nurse] told me to take it [medication] as long as I live and the doctor said to take the medication about a year. I don't know which one I'm gonna listen to."

At times, the source of patient confusion stemmed from the conflicting advice they received from fellow patient-experts. It "all builds up in a person's head," one patient explained, and "you think of what each patient tells you and you get all mixed up. Some have told me, 'You don't have to tell the doctor, just stop taking the medicine when you don't feel good.' And others say, 'Why don't you take this other drug? It's doing wonders for me.' And you start to think, is this medicine doing me good or should I ask for the other kind?" Patient-experts defended their role as decision makers in recommending medication by arguing that it was made necessary by the inexperience of the clinical staff, many of whom rotated in and out of the hospital. Patients pointed out that the assignment to Carville of junior medical officers, many only one year out of medical school, where they received no clinical experience with leprosy, perpetuated a staff unskilled in the disease. They argued that this encouraged reliance on self-diagnosis and self-medication.

The inexperience of the junior staff was not accidental. It was part of PHS policy that the "assignment of junior officers to Carville should be for limited periods of two to three years."[13] This practice, patients contended, denied physicians the opportunity to learn more about the disease, fostered a lack of physician concern for patients, and made frequent "get-acquainted" sessions necessary between new physicians and long-term patients. The short time that many physicians remained at Carville was a frequent topic of conversation among patients. At one group meeting patients discussed the matter at length. "The doctors haven't been here long," one patient said.

> They're always changing the doctors here. I have been here twenty years. I think I can tell when I'm better or worse. If the doctors would be here longer, if they wouldn't recommend changing them like they do every two years, the doctors would get to know more about the disease and do more research. . . . If I lose my doctor and go to another doctor, it seems to me I have to start all over again for him to get acquainted with my case. . . . When the doctors become familiar with the patient, he can tell more about what medicine to give him and what not to give him.

Instead of starting over again with another doctor, some patients would stop seeing a physician altogether in instances where their own doctor had left:

> I had a reaction and Dr. _____ prescribed cortisone. I was taking two tablets a day. I was supposed to see him again in a couple of days to change the amount I was taking. Then he was gone. I was supposed to see him yesterday [but] he wasn't here, so I had to see other doctors. If some patients here don't care about their own well-being, they use this as an excuse and say, "Well, I don't have to go, my doctor is not here [anymore]."

Patients who refrained from seeing a physician for extended periods complained that physicians new to Carville, and therefore unacquainted with the institution and its residents, made them feel like "guinea pigs" or else treated them as "disease entities." Others questioned whether "nerve pains" alone would legitimize making an appointment with a new staff member assumed to be unfamiliar with the disease. Consequently, some patients allowed their conditions to deteriorate. One nurse, upset at the indifference that some patients seemed to display toward their symptoms, commented:

> I hate to use the word "lax," but after a while they either get so used to living with leprosy, or because they don't know any better, they tend not to pay attention to things. And they'll let something go, like an ulcer or a sore or swollen glands [and] they'll only just mention it in passing. Well, by this time they've got a dandy infection and they end up in the infirmary.

Citing a specific case, the nurse said that one day she noticed a young patient with "one eye very red, and he kept rubbing it." He repeatedly refused to see the ophthalmologist, explaining that the irritation was due to "reading too much under a bad light." Later, the patient was found crying, his eye badly tearing. "But he wouldn't go until I practically had to twist his arm [and] sure enough he had a corneal ulcer." She explained that "nurses here have to keep an eye on things like this."

Surgeons who performed reconstructive surgery encountered many problems similar to those faced by their medical colleagues. One surgeon observed that while patients readily accepted professional advice "to correct functional problems that interfere with the use of their hands or in walking," they were very reluctant when it came to "disfigurements and deformities of the face, for example." Instead of listening to what the surgeon had to tell them, "they wait around; they seek other sources of opinion; they compare results; they see what other patients have done, what good they have derived from it, and what improvements they think they will obtain." In instances where a flare-up of the disease later attenuated earlier cosmetic benefits, patients became skeptical of surgery. The surgeon commented, "Then they look on the patient two or three years later and say, 'Well, that surgery didn't do any good. He's lucky he got back to where he started,' as if implying the uselessness of surgery altogether. . . . It's the patient's premise that is wrong," the surgeon explained. "And that's where we need to educate the patient, to let them know that even though we could obtain an immediate good result, if they don't watch themselves and don't continue to take medication, they could have a setback."

In addition to their frustration with a system that allowed patients to seek treatment on a voluntary basis, new physicians at Carville were frustrated upon discovering that leprosarium life asked them to experience a shift in professional role from being in command of medical decisions to working at modifying patient behavior. When questioned about the most satisfying aspects of their work at the leprosarium, most young physicians spoke of the technical aspects of working in leprosy. As one physician put it: "There is a tremendous intellectual kick that I get out of the disease. . . . Not many physicians know much about leprosy and the new things I find out, I enjoy. I'm not the dedicated sort that you find in the jungle [who] go out and take care of the needy."

When questioned about the least satisfying aspects of their work, most physicians mentioned the difficulties experienced in motivating patients to adhere to a treatment plan, enlisting the patients' cooperation in rehabilitation programs, handling disciplinary problems, "playing cop," and dealing with "station politics." In the mid-1960s, physicians, along with the Sisters of Charity and two chaplains, were the only members of the hospital staff to live on the grounds of the leprosarium. Physicians' duties as "officer of the day" and the close proximity of their living quarters to the rest of the hospital resulted in their being contacted for a variety of nonmedical reasons. Often they were called at night to investigate a disturbance in the colony or to attend someone drunk or disorderly, "which, after all," one doctor complained, "is not a physician's function. . . . You get disgusted most of the time, because I hate to get called out of bed and come over here for something like that. . . . It's hard the next morning to maintain an occupation when you've had to chase a patient all over the colony that night. It puts you in a weird position." The "weird position" this doctor spoke of involved the intrusion on the formal relationship with patients that physicians sought to maintain.

The system of voluntary treatment at Carville collided with the professional expectations of the medical staff. Young physicians, trained in acute illness situations where patients behaved in accordance with the dictates of the "sick role," reacted to Carville patient autonomy by limiting their own role as much as possible to purely medical responsibilities. As another doctor explained:

> I'm a bit authoritarian. I usually give a patient the choice of doing what I tell him or get out. When the time comes that I tell a patient, you can go home now, and they say, "Well, I don't want to go home," I just say that's fine and I put them on a chronic care basis and see them once a week, once every two weeks, or even every two months, just to make sure they are not getting into trouble from the disease. . . . I try to keep myself limited purely to the medical management of patients.

As there were no formal sanctions that could be applied that would not disrupt the voluntary treatment relationship, the incentives available to doctors to induce cooperation were limited. Thus, nonmedical involvement in the personal lives of patients was doubly resented.

The rehabilitation staff, on the other hand, sought a more personal relationship with patients. In emphasizing the hospital's commitment to patients, rehabilitation personnel stressed the relevance of patient participation in rehabilitation programs within the leprosarium and the importance of maintaining social ties outside the institution, especially with their families. To deal with the contingencies of public response to leprosy, the rehabilitation branch urged patients to adopt their doctrine on "information control." The doctrine stated that the patient should inform his immediate family and his employer of the disease but that telling others may not be beneficial. In order to foster patient identification with the aims of the institution, the rehabilitation staff attempted to engage patients in activities closely supervised by the staff, such as patient jobs in the hospital, rather than in colony activities. The rehabilitation staff emphasized that a "personalized" approach in working with patients was essential.

One outcome of this position was that the rehabilitation personnel tended to accept a wider range of patient behavior as legitimate than did the medical staff. Such practices as patients leaving the hospital on a pass during the hours they were scheduled to be in school, or participating irregularly in physical therapy because they were otherwise engaged in a colony recreational program, were upsetting to the rehabilitation staff. This behavior, nevertheless, was usually accepted as valid or, if not, was considered by the staff to be due to the failure of the hospital to help patients organize their activities into "meaningful therapeutic" designs. Similarly, in matters regarding a patient's "readiness" to leave the institution, rehabilitation members tended to take a broader view of the situation than physicians, especially when patients feared leaving because of societal stigma.

Unlike tuberculosis, leprosy has few benchmarks whereby physicians can reasonably predict clinical progress. Just as the work of the medical staff at Carville was hampered in enlisting the patients' cooperation in their own treatment by the absence of lasting physical signs of improvement, the work of the rehabilitation staff was hampered by the lack of precise standards to evaluate a patient's rehabilitation. In response to a survey questionnaire to determine the meaning of "rehabilitation," most members of the staff spoke in very general terms: restoring "the individual to his highest possible potential" or "helping the individual adjust to his handicaps." Few mentioned returning patients to society, and one member, in fact, saw rehabilitation as an adjustment to Carville.[14] In the absence of better standards by which to evaluate rehabilitation, personnel tended to consider the amount of a patient's participation in institutional activities as an indication of how the patient was doing. Participation in one set of activities was often used to explain poor performance in other activities. Thus, with the emphasis placed on the amount of participation, the staff members were at a loss in helping patients organize their activities therapeutically.

Although the rehabilitation staff spoke more often about invoking minor sanctions against patients—such as denying requests for a pass, removing a patient from his hospital job, or assigning less preferential living quarters— patient participation in rehabilitation was as voluntary as medical treatment. With only minimal formal sanctions at hand, the major reward system available to the rehabilitation staff in securing patient participation took an informal turn. There was less social distance between the rehabilitation staff and patients than between patients and clinicians. Specifically, rehabilitation personnel relied on giving patients social approval, exchanging "private" information about outside interests, and interacting frequently with patients on a personal basis; in short, they provided status rewards.[15]

Important differences existed between the clinical and rehabilitation members in their approach to patient management. Each group acted in accordance with its own set of objectives. The behavioral standards of both groups were established by the norms of their specialization, with one group rooted in a medical model and the other in a rehabilitation model. The two models presented conflicting viewpoints. One outcome of this divergence in approach was that it often created a dilemma for the staff when trying to reach consensus about specific patient goals.

In debating whether patients should be allowed to remain at Carville after they became eligible for a medical discharge, the two groups were often at odds. The stance of the medical branch was that patients should be encouraged to leave once the staff had determined that maximal hospital benefits had been received. The rehabilitation branch, on the other hand, argued that psychosocial considerations must also be weighed in planning for discharge. The two branches were generally split along professional lines, but the matter was further complicated by how long members of the staff themselves had been at Carville, regardless of their professional affiliation.

Among other things, the leprosarium was a socializing agency. The longer one was there, the more socialized to the world of leprosy one became. At Carville, staff as well as patients were inducted into the darker side of the disease and the public stigmas outside. New patients were indoctrinated into a bleak world of deformity and fear by the large number of old-timers at Carville, by the various treatment failures, and by those who remained behind as colonizers for social reasons. Fledgling staff members were indoctrinated by their peers. One young member of the rehabilitation staff, whose work required close physical contact with patients, recalled that when he first arrived, he was reprimanded by one of the Sisters for "fraternizing" with patients. He was cautioned to "wash" his hands often and that alcohol dispensers were distributed for staff use. This same Sister, he went on, "plays this role with new patients as well as with other Sisters" who came as young nurses. Early during my own fieldwork at Carville, I was taken aside by one member of the rehabilitation staff who, on hearing that I had been to the patient canteen, expressed the hope that I had not bought anything there to eat. "Coca-Cola or cigarettes, that's OK," she said.

Most staff personnel new to leprosy, regardless of professional affiliation, in time became converted to the perspective on public stigma pervasive at the leprosarium and to the view that patients needed protection "from the trauma of social ostracism." Conversion to this perspective represented a transition point in the socialization of new arrivals. In speaking about patient colonization, one member of the rehabilitation staff, who had been at Carville nearly five years, remarked that "three years ago I would have said, as long as they [patients] don't require hospital care, they should not stay. Now, I think I've mellowed a little because of stigma and because of the length of time many of them have been here."

For years, patients at Carville had colonized at the leprosarium in order to conceal their disease and to live unencumbered by public prejudice; and in the past this practice had received the approval of the hospital administration. Older patients and those members of the staff who had been at Carville for years, together with long-term employees at the hospital, formed a cohort in keeping alive ideas and memories about leprosy and about stigma that more properly belonged to the past. According to Johnwick:

There are employees on the station who have been here for 20 or 30 years and there are patients who have been here for the same length of time. These long-term employees have identified themselves with the patients rather than with the staff, which keeps changing. I recall an example when a patient with good eyesight and a good physique and negative tests was being prepared for a discharge and for employment outside of Carville by the Social Worker. At the same time this patient was being told by one of the nurses [Sisters of Charity] that his place was in Carville.

When the new administration made it known in 1956 that it would not force patients to leave, this was not construed to mean that "the purpose of the hospital was to provide a community for patients with leprosy and their families in order for them to withdraw from circulation." To break the cycle of tradition and to further the changes in leprosy management, Johnwick often spoke of the need for a system of rotation so that no one in immediate contact with patients would remain at Carville indefinitely.[16]

One of the livelier places at Carville to hear discussions about patient colonization was at the bimonthly rehabilitation staff meetings, where the status of patients was reviewed. Early during the Johnwick administration, the rehabilitation branch had been established; one of its functions was to integrate the work of the professional staff with individual patients. Typically present at each meeting were the chief of the branch, who was a physician, the patient's attending physician, a member of the nursing staff, and representatives from each of the rehabilitation subspecialties or programs at the hospital. As the clinical staff lacked the authority to unilaterally implement major decisions regarding patient disposition, these meetings became a forum for airing conflicting views between clinical and rehabilitation personnel and between new staff arrivals to the hospital and older personnel who had been at Carville for some time.

The length of employment for the clinical staff varied greatly. Of the four attending physicians whose patients were reviewed between January and June 1963, the average length of service was 2.3 years, with a range from one to four years. In contrast, the average length of service for the twelve regularly present rehabilitation personnel was 7.3 years, with a range from less than one year to more than sixteen years. Six members of the rehabilitation staff in regular attendance had been at Carville for more than ten years. In addition, in the mid-1960s there were twenty-three Sisters of Charity at Carville serving as nurses, pharmacist, and dietitian. The tenure of many of the Sisters was considerable. Sister Laura Stricker, for example, as *The Star* noted in 1976, had served at Carville for forty-seven years.[17]

The discussions that took place at patient reviews reflected staff ambivalence about the function of the institution. There was conflict between the belief that institutional life was drab at best and the belief that the hospital was made too comfortable for patients.If hospital life were less attractive, some argued, perhaps more patients would be tempted to leave and try to succeed on their own. The staff also struggled with the problem of how to minimize the impact that older patients had on newcomers, with their pessimistic stories of how bad things were in the old days and with their deformities as a visible reminder of the damage that the disease can cause when neglected. In light of the easy access that old-timers had to new patients, the staff at one time considered permanently separating the two populations. Other, more realistic proposals included upgrading patient health education in an effort to present a more optimistic picture of leprosy. Such a program would aim to break the cycle that perpetuated the view that the disease today was not much more manageable than in the past and that society ostracized those with leprosy just as much as in the days when the leprosarium was founded.

The patients at Carville had a relatively high median age and, generally, a low prehospitalization level of job skills and education. Late in the 1960s, nearly three-fourths of the patients came from ethnic minority groups. Staff members were well aware that the standard of living that the hospital environment offered surpassed what many patients could look forward to on the outside. This was one reason why staff believed the hospital "did too much for patients." The staff also anticipated that once a patient had been at Carville for some time, he was likely to "lose his courage" and hesitate to leave. Patients also recognized this tendency, and those who planned on leaving often openly criticized those "dependent" on the institution.

In reviewing the status of patients, the staff expressed uncertainty about where their responsibility toward patients ended and what they could realistically expect from patients who had received maximal medical benefits. Consequently, the staff was unable to devise general guidelines concerning patient management or to reach a uniform policy for discharge. The matter was further complicated by the professional investment that staff members had in developing new reconstructive surgical procedures. Reconstructive surgery and new developments in physical therapy were becoming important areas of research at the hospital, and the question of how long to delay a patient's discharge often arose. Despite the insistence of young clinicians that "healthy" patients (especially if they were young and male) not be allowed to "settle in," physician concern about the availability of follow-up treatment for leprosy outside of Carville and the development of secondary complications in patients often made it difficult for physicians to be adamant in their stance that patients not stay.

Excerpts from two case histories taken from tape-recorded sessions of rehabilitation branch meetings illustrate the complexity of issues and the divergent views that staff members faced in attempting to decide questions of patient disposition. (The abbreviations C and R refer to whether the speaker is a clinician or a rehabilitation staff member. The numbers indicate different speakers.)[18]

The Case of D. I.

D. I. is a twenty-two-year-old male who arrived at Carville a year prior to this staffing. Born in the Philippine Islands, he was diagnosed as having leprosy while a steward with the U.S. Coast Guard. He is not a U.S. citizen. According to his physician the patient is nearly ready for a medical discharge.

C1: He's got eleven negative skin scrapings. His lesions have responded well [to therapy]. His only lesion is on his left leg and he has a foot drop.

When we've done a tendon transfer for this, then he'll be ready to go. We gonna get him out in the fall.

R1: He has problems. He's deportable. He does not want to go back to the Philippines. The reason for joining the Coast Guard was an opportunity to come to the United States. So, he has much mixed feeling about being negative. And he's recently been notified that he will receive $200 a month from the Veterans Administration for his service-connected disability. He's also contemplating marriage to S. V. [another Carville patient].

R2: [Marriage] would keep him here until he can become a citizen. He won't be the first one that has stayed here that way.

C2: Immigration feels inordinately strong about his departure from this country.

R3: Well, why put the pressure on this individual, when they don't on others?

C2: I think it relates to the fact that the man was a noncitizen in the service of our country.

[At this point, the staff are unclear why his leprosy is being considered a service-connected disability, and if he will, in fact, receive disability payments for it and whether such payments will continue if he is returned to the Philippine Islands. It is also noted that if he is returned home within a year from his discharge then the Coast Guard will provide free transportation. The deadline is less than four months away.]

R4: Would she [his wife-to-be] go with him back to the Philippines?

R1: Neither one of them wants to go to the Philippines.

C2: Well, we made a lot of noise. Now, what's the recommendation? Do you want to tell the chaplain to marry them or not? (Laughter).

R5: Marry him and live happily ever after in the cottage in the back and $200 a month of our money.

[The question of his surgery is raised and the issue of his being deported before surgery is discussed.]

C1: He's already been warned. We had a meeting about him with the medical staff. We have never pushed anybody out of here, but we're going to push him out and he knows it.

C2: Irrelevant of his marital status?

C1: He's too young and he's got to go.

R4: That isn't something you can actually control here.

C2: What?

R4: Well, you can recommend that he stay for treatment longer. Would they [immigration] honor that?

C2: It seems that we agree that this boy should be out of the hospital as soon as possible, regardless of everything but his ability to benefit from his hospitalization. He stays only as long as he is accomplishing something here.

R2: In other words as far as the clinical staff is concerned he will be ready to accept his free transportation by the 8th of October?

C1: Not necessarily. But he'll go as soon as he's done.

C2: Well, this is a good fact. You might want to get everything done in time, so he can take advantage of this free trip.

C1: Well, it will probably take a while.

C2: Well, what's our recommendation?

R6: We can't stop them from getting married.

R1: At this point immigration has consistently told him that he's deportable.

R4: Unless he gets married.

R1: If he married an American citizen immigration might do something else. I don't know. I haven't asked.

R3: Dr. _____ , after his surgical procedure, are you going to force him out as soon as he's completely healed?

C1: Yes.

R3: The dropped foot. Are you going to let him stay until the [tendon] transfer has been properly tested?

C1: Well, yes.

R3: This may hinder his improvement if he knows he's going to leave as soon as he improves.

C1: We'll give him a reasonable length of time.

R3: I also want to ask, why the big rush to kick him out?

C1: He's too young to stay here. I think his disease is arrested.

R1: I don't think it is helping him to stay in the hospital.

C2: Let's avoid the use of words such as one, force; two, kick out. We can say that this man will be actively encouraged to depart.

R1: I don't think he is resisting leaving the hospital. But he doesn't want to leave the country. Of course, the thing is as long as he's in the hospital he knows he can't be deported.

Two and one-half years later, married and medically eligible for discharge, this couple left the institution voluntarily. They return periodically for check-ups.

The Case of Mr. and Mrs. R. S.

R. S. is a white male from Louisiana who was first admitted to Carville in 1934 at the age of fourteen with a diagnosis of lepromatous leprosy. He is at the time of this review forty-three years old. Mrs. R. S. is a white southern woman who was first admitted in 1962 at the age of thirty, with a diagnosis of tuberculoid leprosy. The R. S.'s were married in July 1962, six months after her arrival. Their situation is somewhat special in that it is now believed that Mrs. R. S. does not have leprosy but instead some other "rather rare disease." In addition, she is an amputee.

C1: R. S. was admitted here in 1934. He absconded a year later, was readmitted in 1937, then absconded again in 1939. He was admitted again in 1939 and has stayed on our rolls since then, having had frequent vacations. He was first treated with chaulmoogra oil and then later with the sulfones and was declared arrested bacteriologically as of June 1959, following which time his treatment has been relatively uneventful. He has no particular orthopedic deformities. Looks to be in good health. In fact, is in good health. However, the new method around here now of declaring people inactive is to take a biopsy. And so this gentleman having had numerous negative skin scrapings plus a biopsy in September was found to have quite a few acid-fast bacteria in the skin. So, he was therefore declared reactivated. But this shouldn't be taken too literally. He's probably as good or bad a candidate for or against discharge as before the skin biopsy was taken. This same problem will undoubtedly come up with other patients as our standards for active, inactive, and arrest are altered. The only problem that he has that I can think of that would require him to be followed closely here is in regard to his eyes. He's had numerous attacks of red-eye during his earlier years which has left him with glaucoma in the left eye that was detected a year ago and only in the last two months has the pressure gotten high enough to require therapy. So, he'll be under our observation from that point of view almost indefinitely.

R1: Six months ago, just before their marriage, we were thinking in terms of their leaving. After their marriage we encouraged this couple's discharge from the hospital, subsequent to the wife's surgery.

C1: The only difficulty with having a man like this out of the hospital is that he'll be lost, like so many others. There are many exceptions, people who have faithfully returned on a monthly basis, or every other month. Large hospitals are full of outpatients who came back regularly for check-ups. There is no reason why he can't do it. I don't know if he will or not.

R1: Do you think it is our duty to keep him here? How often would you have to see him?

C1: We put him on therapy before Christmas. And I was thinking of checking him a week later, but he was gone on Christmas vacation. So, I can't say right now. Perhaps about four times a year.

R1: He could commute from _____ [a town in Louisiana], if he'll do it. Anyway, he will be here until his wife's surgery is completed.

C1: Which will probably be months, which will give us ample time to decide.

R1: Do you think we should board him again in three months, six months?

C1: Three months maybe.

R1: If the surgery was started now, I would think three months would be fine, but I doubt whether they're considering it now. Let's put it down as six months.

R2: I know he's a ham operator or a radio technician. Is there much planning that needs to be done vocationally for his community adjustment?

R1: I don't know whether he has enough skill. He did operate a radio repair shop here at Carville, but he finally closed it. He was supposed to keep a profit-and-loss statement to submit to the administration twice a year. I'm not sure he's competent enough to go out into a community and find a job as a radio technician. What do you think?

R3: No, I don't think so. If he had a supervisor to lay out the work for him and tell him everything. . . . He needs a lot of extra help besides. He's quite a marked introvert type.

C1: I spoke with him about leaving last summer and he said he likes it here. He wants to be a permanent resident here. Not so much because this is the best place to be, but because he doesn't want to be outside, from a negative point of view. But he knew he was getting married at that time.

R1: But he had stated that he and his wife were planning to leave. They had bought a trailer or had planned to buy one.

R4: He has one already.

R2: He has no insurance on his automobile and therefore can't bring it out of the state. [The state of Louisiana did not require automobile liability insurance at that time.]

R1: Has he been given any vocational tests?

R5: He won't take them.

C2: He can't do fine work. He has difficulty picking up change.

R6: When he was talking about getting out, did he plan to work? I never heard it mentioned. I don't know how they thought they'd get along.

R7: I think they indicated a few months ago that they wouldn't be here long, only until she finished her program. I think that if she decided, they would leave. But I sort of think that he will make the final decision on whether to go or stay and if they go, when they go.

R4: I wonder if he's getting any social security?

R1: He can't make social security here, that I know of. And he's been in the hospital so long. There's nothing in his chart that states that.

C1: He talks about leaving but whether he will or not is another question. He was pretty discouraged when he found out he was reactivated. It seems reasonable that he would be discouraged. However, he doesn't look at it the same way we do. I told him we'd altered our standards. This biopsy makes it pretty hard. You've really got to be clean through to have a negative biopsy. It's pretty easy to be negative on the skin scrapings.

R5: If he had twelve negatives and the biopsy was positive, would the hospital frown on allowing him to go if he came and said he wanted a discharge?

C1: No. We've got a lot of people with positive skin scrapings that are out with a so-called medical discharge.

R8: My impression in talking to him is that they are not in a hurry to get out.

R7: I'd like to suggest that perhaps we talk to them about some kind of employment in his home town and try to get social service help place him in a job of some type. I don't think she wants to go. I think she won't go as long as he wants to stay.

R9: Sounds like they are saying both things. They really don't know what they want to do.

R1: Perhaps he could be interested in some vocational training.

R6: They could still go on three-month vacations and then come back and go on another three-month vacation, just like they're doing now.

C1: I don't know what we can do to force him. These patients seem to be able to do anything they want to do or not to do what they don't care to do.

Despite all the indecision and uncertainty displayed about this couple, the staff continued to lay plans for their departure. Twenty years later this couple was still in residence at Carville.

*   *   *

The leprosarium at Carville will soon have been in continuous existence for 100 years. It has been situated on the same isolated site in rural Louisiana since 1894 and is still "pretty far from everything and everybody," as one issue of *Rehabilitation Record* noted in 1968.[19] Some of the older buildings evoke antebellum memories. Contagion, "public horror," and the protection of lepers were the reasons given in 1916 for the continuation of the state leper home under federal control. The contagiousness of leprosy no longer frightens the Western world. Newer and more effective chemotherapies are available, to be sure, but more important than medical intervention is the fact that leprosy has not proliferated in advanced urban settings. In the United States, there are today at least thirteen regional Hansen's disease outpatient centers throughout the country and an indeterminate number of private sources of care. Thus, many patients live in communities, marry, work, and rub elbows with fellow commuters on buses, subways, and trains. Most of them have never been to Carville. Many conceal the disease as best they can and many pass; others make no special secret of it. Individual citizens may privately be squeamish about leprosy, but the general public is not alarmed.

At Carville, however, life has been lived at a different pace. Throughout much of its long history Carville had been a closed community and a repository of stigma, with those who worked there sharing in the ideology of a society that sent patients there. For patients, the stigma of leprosy transformed their lives and gave them a new, undesired social identity. Later, stigma became the central concept that patients organized their energies and talents to combat. Collectively, the patient body at Carville was forced into an investment in stigma. Stigma gave patients a "spoiled identity" and created the leprosarium as a place of refuge, some of whose benefits patients later found hard to give up. Some patients believe that the subsidized life their special status accords them is justified in view of society's attitude. More important, the idea that strong social stigma exists has continued to be preached in the pages of *The Star*. In a 1974 article reviewing the events that had led to the construction of new patient cottages and apartments at Carville fifteen years earlier, *The Star* reminded readers: "Yes, these living quarters meet a deep human need for privacy and a de-institutionalized manner of living, but those who occupy them would gladly trade them for any mean hovel in the world—if only they could live there in health and without the terrible stigma which society imposes upon all who suffer from Hansen's disease."[20]

The socioeconomics of leprosy are such that for a number of patients the problems of coping, and of stigma, may be at least as much a consequence of socioeconomic status and level of functioning as they are of the disease itself. Furthermore, with the social emphasis on physical comeliness in the United States, disfigurement and deformity, whatever their source, pose adaptive problems. In a sense, such persons already experience social discrimination. Leprosy only compounds the disadvantage.[21] Those who colonize, and those who may wish to colonize in the future or return to the leprosarium at any time—even to use the institution as a retirement center—need to rationalize their actions, if only to mollify the staff. That there is an incentive to resort to Carville for economic reasons seems to be borne out by the history of length of hospitalization. For the decade 1931–1941, during the Great Depression, the mean time in the hospital in total months increased 19.6 percent over the previous decade and then declined in the following decade, during more prosperous times, by 34.5 percent.[22]

In adapting to the leprosarium on a long-term or permanent basis, patients stress the pervasiveness of stigma as their rationale for colonizing. The history of public stigma and the vicissitudes of societal acceptance favor the patient's viewpoint. Patients who colonized defined their position by reference to the standards at the hospital. Those who utilized medical standards emphasized the uncertainties of the disease—including contagion. These patients maintained that to adjust to society was impossible; rather, the "solution" lay in removing the mythology that surrounds leprosy. Conversely, other patients used the protective and supportive rehabilitation standards to justify a sheltered existence within the leprosarium. These patients also emphasized stigma, but used it to legitimize the protective functions of the institution.[23]

In upholding the pervasiveness of stigma, Carville patients were not being uncompromising or merely clinging to the past, as it were. Although the leprosy situation in the United States in the second half of the twentieth century has changed considerably, there are still enough references available today reflecting stereotypic ideas about the disease, and enough patients experiencing discrimination and hardship, to keep the militant view simmering. And some things have not changed: The PHS still pays employees at Carville "hazard duty pay"—called "incentive pay" by those who receive it. The rules and regulations for governing the leprosarium established in the 1920s still remain on the books unaltered—"one more bit of unfinished business for *The Star*," Stein wrote in his autobiography four years before he died.[24] Finally, and ironically, patients will point to the existence of the leprosarium itself and to the patients' special status as evidence that the stigma continues.

Just as some patients had a vested interest in believing that strong public stigmatization of leprosy continued, some older members of the staff found it difficult to accept the idea that leprosy was no longer an issue in the United States. Some members of the staff were too close to the personal situation of individual patients at Carville, or too familiar with the frustrations of state health officials in overcoming specific barriers to a successful social outcome for patients (or too busy erecting barriers themselves), to always grasp the larger contours of change. The successful patient rarely returned to Carville where he might have acted as a role model (though *The Star* did print success stories whenever possible). Furthermore, the staff at Carville, and especially its medical officers in charge, were highly sensitive to unfavorable publicity about leprosy and to adverse patient behavior and activities, which, they hoped, would not elicit unwanted public attention. Those staff members with long experience in certain countries where the stigma of leprosy is acute, such as India, continued to hold a mental set of stigma as being universally overwhelming.

My own need for some objective data on public response to leprosy led, in the mid-1960s, to a community study of public knowledge and attitudes toward the disease. The survey was conducted by a member of the occupational therapy staff with eight years of experience at Carville, James D. Ebner, then on sabbatical leave from the PHS for graduate study. It produced the interesting finding that strong public stigma could not be demonstrated. The evidence for leprosy stigma was equivocal, at best: The disease might be stigmatized to some extent, but so were a series of other chronic conditions, notably tuberculosis, cancer, and mental illness. More important, most respondents did not consider leprosy salient.[25] One conclusion reached was that those responsible for the treatment of leprosy patients might need to consider alternatives to the presumption of public stigma, at least insofar as it emanated from the disease itself.[26]

In light of the belief held at the leprosarium that stigma was pervasive, the findings were unexpected. They received little recognition from Carville, and the rehabilitation staff at the hospital soon commissioned its own studies of stigma as part of a larger vocational rehabilitation grant. Investigations were conducted by the School of Social Welfare, Louisiana State University, in collaboration with members of the Carville staff. These hospital-commissioned studies leaned uniformly to the position that the attitude of the general public in the United States toward leprosy was not encouraging.[27] The findings reaffirmed the ethos of the hospital—and the past. Since the 1960s, however, the subject of leprosy stigma has been investigated in a number of regions of the world where the disease is prevalent and by investigators trained in epidemiology and the social sciences, and one historian has examined the literature on medieval Islamic society. None of these studies has revealed a picture of societal stigma of leprosy as intractably devastating as it has been portrayed in ingrained Western attitudes. Where fear and aversion were found, stigma was often the result of the Western practice of isolating lepers.[28]

Since the early 1960s, the United States has been seeking to curtail the operations of its large federal hospital system. Today, most of the PHS hospitals in this country have been closed. With a federal policy of deregulation now in effect to reduce the role of government and the number of federal employees, the federal government has sought to contract out to the private sector many of the functions of those hospitals that remain open. In the fall of 1982, a special congressional hearing was held at Carville to debate the merits of the proposals of the Office of Management and Budget and the Department of Health and Human Resources regarding how the policy of deregulation was to be applied to the leprosarium.[29]

The hearing drew a large audience: patients, staff, hospital employees, representatives from the American Legion, members of the neighboring community civic government, officials of the hospital employees' AFL-CIO union, Louisiana representatives to the U.S. Congress, administrative officials from the Department of Health and Human Resources, and the chairman of a House of Representatives Subcommittee on Energy and Commerce.

All those in attendance agreed that leprosy was a special disease, that a special community for leprosy patients was needed, along with special personnel to attend them, and that things ought not to change. Representative Lindy Boggs of Louisiana put into the record that "leprosy is on the rise throughout the world . . . [in] refugee camps in the Far East, in Haiti, and in various other places. . . . We have seen some of it coming to California . . . and into Texas and Florida, with some of the illegal aliens."[30] Tom Strom, former chairman of the Patients' Federation, told the committee that "public fear . . . is still very strong. . . . You can imagine how tough it must be for victims of this disease and their families when many of them are forced to live in . . . constant fear that their secret will be discovered."[31] Others, less mindful of the spread of leprosy and of the stigma of the disease, spoke of the leprosarium as a local industry and pointed to the number of jobs that would be lost in the neighboring community and the incomes that would be reduced if private contractors took over the nonmedical functions at the hospital from federal employees.

Opponents of deregulation viewed the actions of the Office of Management and Budget as an effort to curtail activities at the National Hansen's Disease Center. An intense lobbying campaign against deregulation argued the importance of maintaining the leprosarium intact. Leprosy was described as a disease that had afflicted humanity "for at least seventeen centuries," a disease whose victims society had refused to accept. The disease was noted to be the "single most frequent cause of disability in the world" today. The research facilities and treatment programs provided at the National Hansen's Disease Center were praised as the "best hope" for combatting the physical disabilities of leprosy.[32]

In the end, federal officials reluctantly gave the administration at Carville the authority to decide the issue of deregulation for itself, but not before making it clear that the federal government no longer considered leprosy to warrant special federal sponsorship and direct ongoing subsidization. Although the policy of the federal government is changing, Carville, for now, remains.

PART 5

Conclusion

10

The Secularization of Leprosy

The competition among disease conditions for public recognition, for a sense of social importance, for special funds and exemptions is intense. To achieve those ends and then to maintain them, a special case for support must be made, and once that support has been gained, it must actively be accounted for if it is to be continued.[1] In the competitive struggle for public attention, those seeking support for leprosy have been remarkably successful. For a physiologic condition to attain such eminence, it must resonate to wider public concerns. It must become lodged within a general universe wherein suppositions about the condition arouse public thoughts and feelings of involvement or obligation that presuppose some philosophical point of view.

Leprosy attracted international attention more than a century ago as a contagious, foreign disease. The alleged contagiousness of leprosy, when coupled with its identification as a disease of "inferior" populations, was considered, at the time, sufficient reason for the alarm that it created. Early in the twentieth century, however, the fear of a pandemic had abated; in fact, the contagiousness of leprosy had been considerably downgraded. Leprosy did not become a significant disease in Western nations, although it was abundant in tropical and colonial areas of the world. By all accounts, special Western attention to leprosy should have diminished; but it did not. On the contrary, the aversion toward leprosy and the attention to its taint grew. Conventional historians have attributed this continued attention to leprosy to the influence of tradition and maintain that the stigma and the symbolism of the disease were upheld by biblical description and proscription. It has been the argument of this book that such was not the case. As with other diseases and human conditions that have captured and then held the public imagination, attention to leprosy has been sustained by powerful social and political events, forces, and institutions.

In an article published in *Leprosy Review* in 1973 about stigma and the harm that biblical connotations have caused to contemporary leprosy, T. A. Stringer of the British leprosy organization LEPRA noted that a "most extraordinary" coincidence had taken place in 1874. The Mission to Lepers was formed only one year after Armauer Hansen publicly announced that leprosy was a contagious germ disease. Prior to this discovery, Christian tradition had made use of biblically defined lepers only in a very general way, which reflected the vagueness of the original usage. That the modern disease might have been represented in the assemblage of original meanings is considered by some authorities to be possible; nonetheless, the biblical meaning remains vague. The work of Hansen in the 1870s made it possible to define leprosy in scientific terms. According to Stringer, the Christian concern for "lepers" had reached a crossroads by Hansen's time, and what had once been a vague and inexact set of terms was now applied exclusively to those who suffered from this newly and specifically defined clinical entity. At the same time that "lepers" became clinically a much more restricted set of people, the Christian world advanced to take up their cause. The idea that the modern disease and the "leprosies" of biblical and medieval tradition shared a common experience was a dramatic theme. "Christian motivation," Stringer noted, incorporated "all the Biblical connotations" into the identity of modern sufferers. Evangelization aided the process. "It has, through the desire to evangelize and through misconception, been in the interest of Christians to see modern leprosy sufferers as 'Biblical lepers.'"[2]

The organized involvement of Western missionaries in leprosy work, which started in the early 1870s in India, had less to do directly with Hansen's scientific work than with the religious revival that was then taking place and with the expansion of overseas empires. In Great Britain the new imperialism was brought on by the intense industrial competition now coming from other advanced countries. The economic prosperity enjoyed by many Europeans required an increased supply of raw materials, much of which came from the colonial world. An expanded manufacturing base at home in turn demanded a growing market. A decline in world prices in the early 1870s led to the raising of tariffs to stem the inflow of cheaper goods. A new form of mercantilism was about to be born.

Earlier, colonialism had been largely commercial in nature. Western territorial ambitions did not extend much beyond protecting trading centers and way stations. With the growth of industrialism, however, European countries could no longer survive on what could be purchased by or traded with colonial markets. Now what was needed were goods of a special kind or in quantities sufficient to sustain an expanding industrial base. Consequently, Western nations began to move more thoroughly into the affairs of "backward" nations and as a result began to transform their productive and economic capacities. In order to secure their investments, European nations sought political and territorial domination. Soon, some parts of the world became outright colonies, directly governed by European administrators. Others became protectorates, where native authority was maintained with a European commissioner on hand. In other regions, spheres of influence were bargained for, with European privileges, investment, and trade opportunities the main goal.

Many pressures lay behind the new expansion. For one, Europe could no longer maintain the style of life it had created for itself except by bringing the rest of the world within its orbit. The social economic argument of the time was that, out of necessity, an industrial country must develop a dependent colonial empire—an area of "sheltered markets," as the phrase went—in which the home country would supply manufactured goods in return for needed raw materials. The idea was to create a large self-sufficient trading unit that embraced a variety of resources. It would be protected from outside competition by tariffs, if necessary; it would guarantee a market for the goods of all its members and wealth for the home country.[3]

In moving more thoroughly into the "backward" areas of the world, Western nations sought more than the restructuring of the colonial economies in order to make them fit European needs. The people of the colonial countries were also to be "civilized" and converted to Christianity. The development of the new imperialism in the 1870s and 1880s in England was accompanied by a revival of religion and patriotism. As the British Empire expanded and consolidated its colonial position, the overseas missionary movement, itself an expression of imperialism, also consolidated its own smaller empires. Imperialism, patriotism, and religion provided a strong impetus to overseas missionary activity and evangelical work, both in the Church of England and among the Nonconformists. For many Protestants, the death of David Livingstone in Africa in 1873, and the "intercession" that affected both the Society for the Propagation of the Gospel and the Church Missionary Society late in 1872, revived their congregations and their treasuries and spurred the business of empire building forward. At mid-nineteenth century, India was Great Britain's most important overseas possession. With its millions of non-Christians and with a history of Protestant missionary effort that dated back to the early nineteenth century, India became fertile soil for the "uplifting" work of mission societies. In the 1870s, Africa had not yet been "opened up," and China was less than receptive to foreigners. India acted as a magnet to missionaries from many countries. By 1910, there were more than 4,500 European missionaries (including wives) in India, representing 122 societies, and the number of natives converted to Christianity had increased accordingly.[4]

India was known, moreover, to have a large leper population. The first all-India leprosy census was conducted between the years 1867 and 1872; at that time a prevalence of 5 lepers per 10,000 population was enumerated.[5] The census had followed immediately upon the publication of the leprosy survey ordered by the British Colonial Office in 1862 in all colonies of the empire. This survey, in turn, had been a response to the public announcement of the epidemic of leprosy in Hawaii.

Concern about leprosy in India, as well as in Great Britain's other nearby Eastern possessions, led the Anglo-Indian Government, in 1873, to send Surgeon-Major Henry Vandyke Carter of Her Majesty's Bombay Army to Norway to inquire into how the disease was dealt with in that country. Dr. Carter was no stranger to leprosy. He had been observing the disease in India since 1860. At the time that Carter submitted his report to the secretary of state for the colonies in November 1873, he was of the opinion that leprosy was transmitted by heredity, although he expressed great enthusiasm for Hansen's theory of contagion.[6]

The cornerstone of the leprosy control program that Carter recommended was the isolation of lepers from society and the sexual segregation of lepers from each other. Carter proposed that India establish a nationwide system of leper asylums, especially in the hyperendemic regions of the country. The "sequestration of . . . parents of a diseased offspring [is to] directly check the propagation of an inherent malady," Carter wrote. "From the nature of the case, no other plan can be so effective; for, time and due perserverence being granted, the aim of eradicating the morbid taint must inevitably be successful."[7] In recommending isolation, Carter did not directly address the question of how segregation was to be achieved other than to suggest that "perhaps fresh laws [are] needed." In recommending that lepers be isolated in asylums, Carter was at odds with the 1867 report of the Royal College of Physicians, which had pronounced leprosy noncontagious and had come out against compulsory segregation.

Aside from disease eradication, Carter had other motives in mind for segregating lepers—motives more lofty and moral in nature:

> It is most desirable to remove from sight of, and contact with, healthy men, women, and children, the diseased and repulsive leper, who when a beggar is obtrusive, and who is almost naturally, considering his sad lot, careless of all social restrictions. But even when the affected person is harboured in the midst of a tolerant family the moral and physical evil which may ensue are not imaginary, but, on the contrary, real and grievous. Familiar contact with a loathsome malady can have but one effect upon young and old, when it is not accompanied (as here) by any regular or constant attempt to palliate or cure, such as would be sufficient to keep alive the feelings of pity or compassion which are alone the beneficial sentiments familiartity of this kind can excite.[8]

In speaking of the native Indian indifference to the lepers within their midst, Carter was addressing the larger question of the Hindu character, which perplexed and bothered the British.

> Passive tolerance of frightful disease is surely the mark of blunted sympathies, or, still worse, of reprehensible indifference—failings which in the long run cannot but react upon the whole pertaining community. . . . One might surmise that much of the indifference to the sufferings of others amongst Hindoos, which is wondered at by Europeans, is due to a persistence of the condition now hinted at. I would add that on the broad ground of social policy, even, it would be desirable to deal with this disregarded subject. It is for the better informed to set example.[9]

The cost of establishing leper asylums throughout India would be high, as Carter well knew, having explored the matter in Norway. But even in Norway, the government was not the sole source of funding. Some of the "old lazarettos in Norway," Carter had learned, "are endowed by private gifts; thus St. Jørgens Hospital has from this source a considerable income." The notion of private gifts held out hope for Carter. At the same time that he condemned the indifference of the Indian people to matters of human suffering, Carter nevertheless saw the "custom of endowing public charities by charitable bequests [a trait] peculiarly grateful to the Oriental mind" and thought the practice "would probably become common in India, if leper asylums were openly sanctioned and encouraged by the heads of the several Governments."[10]

The charity that Carter had envisioned was to come less from the "charitable bequests . . . grateful to the Oriental mind" and more from the growing missionary movement. In the early years of the 1870s, missionaries in Britain were beginning to organize themselves for overseas evangelical work.

Missionaries were field workers; they knew something not only of local conditions but also of the concerns of Western nations as these concerns applied abroad and were thought about at home. Thus, it can hardly be fortuitous that the plight of India's lepers came to missionary attention and that the issue of providing for them was relayed back to an England awash with religious enthusiasm. At the same time the Anglo-Indian government was seeking a solution to its leprosy problem and Western missionaries were beginning to enlarge their scope of activities on that subcontinent. Wellesley Cosby Bailey, who founded the Mission to Lepers in 1874, had first encountered leprosy only five years earlier. Until then, he wrote, he had "never seen or heard anything of lepers, except what one reads in the Bible."[11] He had been introduced to a small leper settlement near the American Presbyterian Mission, Ambala, in the Punjab, in December 1869, by senior missionary Reverend J. H. Morrison, whose station he had just joined. Bailey later remarked on their disfigurement and their "look of utter helplessness. I almost shuddered," he wrote, "yet I was at the time fascinated, and I felt, if ever there was a Christ-like work in this world, it was to go among these poor sufferers and bring to them the consolation of the Gospel. I was struck by the way in which their poor, dull faces would now and then light up as Dr. Morrison explained some precious, comforting truth from the Word of God."[12]

Bailey was excited by his encounter with lepers and "convinced that their first and greatest need was the Gospel." He wrote enthusiastically to his wife-to-be in England about his newly found mission in life: to bring to the lepers "the power of God unto salvation." Bailey later reflected that "thus was born the germ of what has ever since been the watchword of our beloved Mission, *viz.*: The Gospel for the lepers." Alice Grahame, who became Mrs. Bailey when she journeyed to Bombay in 1871, shared Bailey's letters with her three Dublin friends, the Misses Pim, and "found them keenly interested." In 1873, the Baileys returned to England because of Alice Bailey's health, and the connection with the Pims was re-established. Of the three sisters, Charlotte Pim was the most deeply concerned about "procuring friends for the lepers." Together with Wellesley Bailey, she began to organize small meetings in her drawing room for the purpose of describing "the terrible condition of India's lepers, physically, mentally and spiritually, and of what we were trying to do, for just a few of them, at Ambala, in the Punjab." It was Charlotte Pim's idea, at least "I think it was," noted Bailey, to try to raise money annually to send to the Baileys for their work with lepers on their return to India. About 30 pounds a year was what Charlotte Pim thought they could manage.[13]

Interest at home in missionary work in India and the fate of India's lepers proved far greater than Charlotte Pim's modest expectation of 30 pounds annually. At the end of the first year alone, between 500 and 600 pounds had been raised. When Bailey wrote a small pamphlet entitled "Lepers in India," she first asked him for 100 copies—thinking that would be enough—but ended up distributing 2,000; those copies, too, were soon exhausted and further editions were prepared. Things went even better in the second year, when 809 pounds were received. By the end of its first decade of operation, The Mission to Lepers had received nearly 9,000 pounds with which to carry on its work; this sum quadrupled in the second decade and then continued to grow exponentially in the years that followed.[14]

Bailey was overwhelmed by the liberal response for funds, which provided more than enough to assist the Ambala leper asylum and to erect another one at Chamba, in the Himalayas, where the Baileys were now stationed. He sought to deploy financial aid to other missions in India in the vicinity of whose stations small groups of lepers had gathered. In place of sending out "missionaries of our own," Bailey wrote, we "began building asylums . . . in districts where they were badly needed, always putting them in [the] charge of missionaries who we know would 'seek first the Kingdom of God,' [and] who would have the spiritual interests of the lepers at heart." In pursuing this strategy, the incipient Mission to Lepers became interdenominational almost from the very beginning.[15]

The new society on behalf of lepers was off to a splendid start. By 1924, Bailey was able proudly to announce that in the fifty years of the Mission's history, over one million pounds sterling had been raised. Not a single year had gone by in which the Mission was ever in debt. The Mission was international now as well as interdenominational, carrying on its work in cooperation with nineteen British, sixteen American, and three European Protestant societies.[16]

In 1907, a Mission committee report noted that local governments in India, Siam, and Korea were beginning to openly acknowledge the work of the Mission and to cooperate more fully with it.[17] This increase in cooperation between local authorities and the Mission to Lepers, especially in India, was related to the interest caused by the death of Father Damien in 1889 and to the work of the National Leprosy Fund created in England on his behalf. One of the main tasks undertaken by the National Leprosy Fund had been to conduct a survey of leprosy in India in order to formulate policies in the management of the disease in that country. A commission was appointed that consisted of the Executive Committee of the National Leprosy Fund, members from the Royal College of Physicians and the Royal College of Surgeons, and two delegates from India.

After reviewing leprosy data from censuses between 1867 and 1891, the commission pointed to a gradual decrease of the disease in India and maintained that the amount of contagion was so small "that it may be disregarded." The commission concluded that "neither compulsory nor voluntary segregation would . . . effectively stamp out the disease." The commission also noted that the decline of leprosy earlier in Europe had been due to improvements in hygiene and in increased material prosperity. It therefore recommended that no legislation be enacted to segregate lepers or to prohibit their marriage.[18]

The view of leprosy reported by the commission was unpopular. The Royal College of Physicians had endorsed a similar position after conducting the leprosy survey of 1862 among all the colonies of the empire; this position, too, had been attacked a number of times. With many voices now leaning toward a harder line on contagion and with mission societies actively in the field establishing leper asylums, the commission's report was challenged. The National Leprosy Fund set up a special commission to re-examine the report. This commission, headed by George N. Curzon, under secretary for India, issued a strong dissenting statement. The members of the special commission declared that they "entertain a precisely opposite opinion and would be sorry if the Government of India were encouraged by the *Report of the Commission* to refrain from taking the necessary steps in the direction of such segregation of lepers as may be found possible."[19] Within a few years, in 1897, delegates to the First International Leprosy Conference, including representatives of a number of colonial nations, declared that they agreed with the policy of segregation.

By the turn of the century leprosy was widely acknowledged to be a contagious disease to be managed by segregating lepers in colonies and asylums. The Mission to Lepers enjoyed a very favorable position. Bailey had already demonstrated its special willingness to care for lepers and had also demonstrated the organization's quite exceptional strength in raising large sums of money from private donations for this purpose. "It was during this period," Bailey wrote, "that the local governments in India increasingly acknowledged the value of the Mission's care of the destitute lepers in the different provinces." Thus, "a new relationship" between local authorities and the Mission "more definite and far reaching in effect had begun. Certain local institutions for lepers, ill-equipped and indifferently conducted, were brought under the management of the Mission. These institutions were either remodelled or re-established on other sites and placed under the supervision of experienced missionaries."[20] With the responsibility of providing care for lepers being turned over more and more to the Mission to Lepers, local governments in India responded with grants of their own out of public funds. "These grants," Bailey acknowledged, "have enabled the Mission to enlarge its institutions and to care for increased numbers of lepers." Far more important, there were no restrictions placed on the Mission. "Anything of that nature," Bailey commented, "could not, in fact, have been accepted, but none were suggested."[21]

Increasingly, the Mission to Lepers became the dominant organization devoted to leprosy work in India. Within the space of a few decades it expanded to include other countries. In commemorating the hundredth anniversary of the Mission's work, Dr. Stanley G. Browne credited that agency with having "made a greater contribution to the cause of leprosy in its hundred years of existence than any other organization."[22] Changes in the Mission's name reflected its ever-widening sphere of activities. First called the Mission to Lepers in India, it became the Mission to Lepers of India and the East in 1893 as the work of the society expanded to China and Japan. It became the Mission to Lepers in 1914 as its work encompassed the globe. Finally, in 1966, the name was changed to the Leprosy Mission, as the term "leper" was being phased out.[23] In 1924, Bailey reported that in the fifteen countries where work on behalf of lepers was being conducted, the Mission aided, owned, or managed seventy-three institutions. The number of lepers under its care was placed at 7,850, with assistance to an additional 683 healthy children of lepers, most of whom were living in separate homes.[24] In the years that followed, the work of the Mission grew, and, according to Browne, writing in 1974, the Mission was now "responsible for the treatment of about 240,000 sufferers from leprosy in 30 countries, and assists in the leprosy programmes of about 90 Protestant missionary bodies."[25]

In focusing on the destitute leper for special care and attention, and with local governments cooperating more fully, the Mission moved toward becoming part of the colonial infrastructure. "Now established as a serious organization with a reputation for cooperation with government [the Mission] offered to set up in every State in India a model institution for the care of leprosy sufferers." To this offer, the local and central administrations responded with financial grants, "a happy augury for future cooperative working."[26]

As the Mission expanded its field of operations, it also moved into the loftier arena of participating in intergovernmental scientific conferences. In 1897, Wellesley Bailey, founder and director of the Mission, was the only nonmedical delegate to the First International Leprosy Congress held in Berlin; according to Browne, he was invited to present a paper. Twelve years later, at the Second Congress, held in Bergen, Norway, Bailey was "an honoured visitor." The Mission also began to influence the leprosy policies of foreign governments, including the United States. "In Japan and Korea," Browne had noted, "the public conscience [toward leprosy] was aroused, and in the United States of America the Mission was influential in establishing Carville as a Leprosy Hospital and in fostering the passage of legislation in aid of leprosy sufferers."[27]

When Bailey described the relationship that developed between the Mission to Lepers and local governments in India with respect to the establishment of asylums for the care of lepers in his history of how the work of the Mission expanded, he recorded an event of special importance: the institutional transfer of responsibility for indigenous lepers from local state authority to Western religious private philanthropy. Such transfers are uncommon.

A similar transfer took place in Louisiana when the Daughters of Charity of St. Vincent de Paul assumed responsibility for the care of lepers at the state leprosarium at Carville. This transfer of responsibility was marked ceremonially on April 16, 1896, in a highly structured, publicly visible event aboard the steamer *Paul Tulane* when four Sisters of Charity departed from New Orleans for the leper colony upriver. The transfer of the care of lepers to a religious order was occasioned in Louisiana by the failure—many claimed the indifference—of the state to create a proper facility for persons with the disease. With the state unable to attract patients to the isolated colony or to secure personnel to attend them, the future of the home was in jeopardy, as was the goal to eradicate the disease in Louisiana. A large audience came to bid the Sisters "goodbye"; it included the archbishop of New Orleans, a delegation of twenty-six members of the Society of St. Vincent de Paul and the Society of the Holy Spirit and other prominent Catholic laymen, along with the Sisters Superior of the New Orleans Charity Hospital corps of nurses and the Louisiana Retreat (an asylum for the insane). Albert G. Phelps, a member of the state board of control, was also present to see the Sisters off. He told the audience:

> There are at least 100 lepers in Louisiana, some hiding anywhere the law cannot find them. We have thirty-one in the Indian Camp; as soon as it becomes known that the Sisters of Charity are actually there, the others roaming at large will take confidence and come into our retreat. The very name of the Sisters inspires confidence. . . . The Sisters will be in entire control in the household management, and everything except prescribing for the patients, for of course the resident physician must attend to this.[28]

But Wailes, the resident physician, tendered his resignation and departed the same month that the Sisters arrived. For the remaining years that the home received appropriations from the state legislature (1894–1921), the colony was without a resident physician. According to Charles H. Calandro, the home was almost totally under "ecclesiastical control."[29]

A PROPRIETARY RELATIONSHIP

Just as the imperialist nations sought to bring the colonies into an interdependent economic orbit with the home country, so too missionaries sought to bring colonial people into the Christian kingdom of God. The purposes of the missionaries in the colonies were multiple, to be sure, but evangelism was uppermost in their minds; in the case of lepers, it was foremost. Preaching and proselytizing were the chief tools of missionaries. In confronting the destitute leper, spiritual salvation was accorded the highest priority. In summing up the work of the Mission to Lepers from 1874 to 1910, John Jackson, who in 1908 became honorary secretary to the Mission, emphasized that the "ultimate aim" of the Mission "is essentially *Christian*, inasmuch as [it] is to lead the leper to a vital faith in Jesus Christ. It is eminently *philanthropic* as it sees that they are sheltered, clothed and fed, and only then does it seek to evangelize them."[30]

Lepers were described as particularly receptive to the Gospel. Quoting from a committee's report representing all of the missions in China, Jackson said, "No class of the population have shown themselves so ready to receive the Gospel and to receive it with their whole hearts."[31] By describing the despair of lepers and their eagerness for the sympathy of Christian help, Jackson reached a height of Victorian rhetoric in reminding his overseas readers of the large number of lepers yet to be helped:

> Let it never be forgotten that in the field of its operations these stricken people number from a quarter to half a million! Accursed, as they believe, by their gods: cast out by their own kindred: shunned by their fellows, this vast throng of the sons and daughters of death lift up their hoarse voices in a bitter cry, and stretch out their fingerless hands in a pitiful plea, for the help and sympathy of the healthy and happy people of the Christian lands in whose language the sweetest word is Love.[32]

Native religious conversions and baptisms were recorded as faithfully as funds received and expended. By 1910, at which time 10,619 lepers were reported to have been aided, 3,615 were noted to have been "returned as Christians."[33] By 1916, the number of conversions had increased to 5,104.[34] Medical work with lepers, wrote Jackson, was important, but was secondary to the "ultimate aim."[35]

Sixty-three years later, the emphasis had changed only somewhat. Writing about the Leprosy Mission in 1973, A. D. Askew, deputy international general secretary to the Mission, spoke of the role of spirituality as a crucial dimension in the Mission's service to lepers: "The Leprosy Mission is a Christian organization. It does not use its medical services as a tool for pressurized or indiscriminate evangelism, but believes that the effectiveness of modern treatment is increased when it is allied with a concern for the total personality of each patient, whose true happiness demands physical, mental, and spiritual fulfillment."[36]

From the perspective of both the Protestant and the Catholic missionary worlds, lepers were no ordinary persons.* They were a very special group of people. The question of why leprosy work was special has been answered by missionaries themselves. The matter has been explained quite candidly in a preface to a case study in Christian technical cooperation published as recently as the middle of this century:

> Some friends of the missions may ask why so much attention should be given to leprosy work, since it is after all only one small sector of the great field of medical missions, which in turn is but one subdivision of the entire vast and

---

*I am aware that there are fundamental differences between Protestant and Catholic interpretations about the place of lepers in Christian history and between their respective involvements with modern-day sufferers. For one, Protestants have been far more organized in their approach to leprosy work. Denominational differences, however, are not the issue here.

varied mission apostolate. There are at least two convincing answers to this important question.

First, in no other realm of experience is there to be found, on the one hand, so much human suffering—psychological as well as physical—and such utter abandonment, cruel neglect, and desperate need on the part of the victim of this disease, and on the other hand, such sublime selflessness and heroic charity on the part of those who give them shelter, care, and treatment. And in no other field do we find so many thrilling examples of complete spiritual regeneration and rebirth through the love of Christ—even among Moslems and Tibetan Buddhists.

Another striking feature is the fact that the incidents leading to the foundation of nearly every Christian leprosy home have been a *literal re-enactment of the parable of the Good Samaritan.*

Perhaps most significant of all is the truth that the operation of a leprosarium is in itself a well-nigh perfect fulfilment of the requirement for eternal life which Our Lord declared (St. Matthew 25:31–46) that He will apply to all men at the Last Judgment.

Thus . . . this small and apparently insignificant section of the whole mission field can in a certain sense contribute more to the extension of the Love of Christ among men than any other single aspect of mission work.[37]

The involvement of missionaries in leprosy work initiated a remarkable chapter in the history of religion that allowed missionaries to bring to life and to experience an ancient Western religious allegory. In this paradigm the parable of the Good Samaritan was re-enacted and the modern leper was retainted. In staking out leprosy in the name of doing "God's work," missionaries laid total claim to the leper. To their modern caretakers the lepers of the present day became as the lepers of old. Their caretakers, in turn, wrote the Protestant Bailey, tread "literally . . . in the footsteps of the Divine Master."[38]

The Catholic message is similar. In a written address to Catholic leprosy workers, the Reverend Tomás Aspe, bishop of Cochabamba, Bolivia, himself afflicted with Hansen's disease, spoke of the

leprosy apostolate . . . [as] a flower born of the charity which was taught by Our Lord Jesus Christ by example and by word. In no other state or condition of human affliction—with the exception of insanity—do these words of the Divine Master carry a fuller and more intimate application: "I was sick and you visited Me.—What you did to one of these, My least brethren, you did unto Me." For in no other sickness does one feel and is one considered so afflicted as in leprosy.[39]

Missionary belief and conviction thus wove a complex design wherein modern sufferers of leprosy were wedded to an ancient Christian allegory: The leper became the "ultimate sufferer," and leprosy work, in redeeming the leper, epitomized the essence of Christian charity.

From its early beginnings in the 1870s to the present day, the relationship of missionary societies to leprosy has been a very special one. The involvement of missionaries with lepers brought the disease to popular world attention in a directly personal way and in a far more systematic fashion than notice of an epidemic in Hawaii, Chinese immigration, or the prediction of pandemicity could ever do. The appeal for funds and the description of the condition of lepers intensified as missionaries expanded their network to encompass a good portion of the globe. By and large missionaries are an energetic lot, and with their own means of reaching a large audience via the pulpit and the private missionary press, their influence in bringing leprosy to world attention has been considerable. Missionary efforts to sponsor asylums on an international scale represented a "cause." During a period in Western history when "manifest destiny" was a prevalent idea, the care of lepers, although not the "white man's burden," nonetheless was the Christian's: Imperialism had relegated lepers to the missionaries.

The funds that missionaries raised to carry on their work with lepers came largely from donors in the industrialized countries, where leprosy was virtually a nonexistent disease. On the other hand, the work of erecting asylums and caring for lepers took place in far-off countries and continents. To the general Western public leprosy was, at best, a vague unstructured perception. It was not a salient Western disease. Nonetheless, within a short space of time an army of supporters had emerged willing and eager to contribute large sums of money to help the lepers of India, Asia, Africa, and elsewhere. Appeals, if they are to be successful, must reach potential donors who have thoughts and feelings supportive of the cause at hand. While Charlotte Pim was modest in her expectations of arousing public interest on behalf of the "poor lepers," Bailey seemed to have his ears better attuned to the sympathies and religious concerns of the day. The phenomenal growth of the Mission to Lepers, especially as expressed in its early financial statements, testified to a considerable receptiveness among Christians in the Western world among people who, for the most part, had never seen a leper. But like Bailey himself before he arrived in India, they knew of them in connection with "what one reads in the Bible."

The emergence of a structured, biblically oriented Western perception of leprosy came about through the organized activities of mission societies as they raised funds for leprosy work. Modern communication theory reminds us that the less that is known about a given topic, the easier it is for opinion makers to influence their audience and to supply them with images with which to structure their beliefs and ideas.[40] Once missionary agencies, ecclesiastics, and members of religious orders were firmly entrenched in leprosy work, the important opinion makers in matters relating to leprosy became the caretakers themselves. Their influence in shaping the general public's point of view was greatly enhanced by virtue of their having direct, personal contact with victims of the disease around the world, an experience that few Westerners ever shared. The importance of this group of caretakers in structuring the public view was also enhanced by the monopoly it exercised. No other organized groups holding different or competitive views were concerned with the disease.

THE HISTORICAL "CONTINUITY" OF LEPROSY

It is unfair, however, totally to fault Christian missionaries for interpretations equating modern leprosy sufferers with the "lepers" of biblical tradition. Mission societies have played an important role in articulating this view and in disseminating it to the general public, but they were not alone in formulating it. The misconceptions about modern leprosy that Stringer attributed to Christian motivation and to the missionary desire to evangelize must be examined alongside a larger body of beliefs about leprosy held by late nineteenth-century historians and leprologists generally.

The epidemic of leprosy in Hawaii, the death of Father Damien, colonialism, racism, and the movement of peoples that characterized the second half of the nineteenth century created a milieu in which the people of Western nations came to fear that the disease might spread alarmingly. But, beyond fear and some highly stereotyped ideas about leprosy, very little was known about the disease. The existence of leprosy abroad had not been totally unknown earlier in the century to European travelers, explorers, and missionaries. The presence of the disease was noted, but without remarkable comment. Scant attention was paid to the disease prior to the period of alarm, even by universities instructing students about diseases encountered in foreign lands. It was an "extinct deinotherium of the palaeontology of disease," declared Sir Morell Mackenzie in 1890.[41]

Armauer Hansen's work investigating the endemic Norwegian disease *spedalskhed* established the existence of *Mycobacterium leprae* in 1873. With leprosy now considered by many to be a germ disease, contagion was implicated. *M. leprae* soon proved to be intransigent to laboratory efforts to develop an antitoxin serum, and leprosy was classified as incurable. Much of what Norwegian scientists late in the nineteenth century were not able to learn about the behavior of *M. leprae* still eludes medical science today. Whatever Norwegian scientists knew about the disease, the rest of the world knew less.

International interest in leprosy late in the nineteenth century centered on practical matters. The chief concerns were how the disease was transmitted and how it might best be controlled. Leprologists of the day who sought answers to these questions received little help from the laboratory; they returned instead to the methodologies used earlier by medical scientists and historians before bacteriology came to prominence: They investigated leprosy by tracing its geographical distribution and by studying its history. In their search for historical antecedents, leprologists thoroughly combed Western history. Two periods in Western history were rich in leprosy lore: the period encompassed by the Old and New Testaments and the Middle Ages. Both periods were rooted in ecclesiastic tradition.

The more that leprosy was perceived as a threat late in the nineteenth century, the more historians and alarmists of the day were able to find leprosy in the pages of history. Philology was a highly respected field of knowledge, and historians and leprologists relied heavily on an earlier body of historical and comparative studies. Linguistic data and reasoning were marshalled to document that earlier terms roughly translatable into "leprosy" had been employed for millennia to describe a variety of phenomena; some of these descriptions actually reflected an affliction of the skin. The controversies and confusions contained within the accumulated historical literature—much of which constituted a continuous, unchanged narrative dating from the Renaissance on through the eighteenth century, along with considerable linguistic hyperbole—were considered less important, however, than the premise that a contagious, disfiguring, and stigmatized condition labeled "leprosy" had existed in an unbroken continuum from antiquity to the present. The more history they read, the more lazar houses they found that contained lepers, the more severe were the social restrictions imposed on lepers—the more convinced they became of the accuracy of earlier diagnoses.

Some late nineteenth-century historians of leprosy openly eschewed factual evidence in order to confirm their belief in the antiquity of the disease. For them, leprosy was so remarkable, so unique and specific in the severity of its symptoms, and so grossly disfiguring that it had "in all ages assumed exceptional prominence by the extraordinary and long-enduring misery it inflicts on its victims."[42] The fact that "the earliest references to leprosy are vague, incomplete, and even inaccurate," Dr. George Thin wrote in 1891, should not obscure our acknowledging its history. Rather, we should "feel astonished that the disease should be mentioned at all. The mere fact that, in the earliest sacred writings of the world, there are allusions to a disease which evidently, more than all others, impressed primitive peoples by its gravity and terrible nature, at once points to leprosy as the malady which was likely to stamp itself on the popular imagination."[43]

The history of leprosy from which late nineteenth-century Western leprologists sought guidance was a history that provided answers to the fears produced by the threat of leprosy from abroad. Thin, who began his book *Leprosy* with a chapter on the history of the disease, noted that "the allusions to leprosy in the Biblical record possess for us, in these times, more interest than the references in any other ancient literature. They are fuller and they are familiar to all readers in every Christian country."[44] He ended the chapter with a discussion of the Middle Ages and spoke of the "horror and fear" that leprosy had inspired throughout "the whole of Christendom" and of the "genius of Christianity . . . [in] providing 'lazar houses' for the reception of the unfortunate outcasts." Thin concluded his discussion by directly comparing leprosy in the Middle Ages with the situation in the late nineteenth century: "[In] the present day, [we] have to deal with countries in which leprosy is now as great a scourge as it was in Europe at that time. With extraordinary rapidity . . . it [leprosy] began to disappear simultaneously with the adoption of the strict measures that were put in force, the disappearance being as rapid and complete as the onset of the disease amongst the population had been swift and intense."[45]

Late nineteenth-century historians matched biblical and medieval leprosy with the disease from abroad, certain that parallels existed. The restrictions that were placed on lepers in the past were held to apply to the present contagion. These methods had been advised once before, and the earlier disappearance of leprosy from Europe was cited as testimony to their effectiveness. The lessons of the past were applied to the present, and the leprosy from abroad, along with *M. leprae*, was joined historically to the leprosy of the Bible and the Middle Ages. Europe and Christendom had fought an evil called leprosy before and had won. Now they would battle again.

Not all historians at the time were as convinced of the identification of biblical and medieval leprosy with the present-day disease. Charles C. Creighton, the social epidemiologist and eminent translator of August Hirsch, distrusted "the popular and clerical notions of leprosy" as "too superstitious and inexact, even if the diagnostic intention had been more resolute than it was, to permit any clear separation of the leprous" from patients with syphilis, lupus and cancer of the face, scrofulous sores, or neglected skin eruptions.[46] Creighton also criticized leprosy historians of the day for their failure to view the disappearance of leprosy in medieval Europe in epidemiological terms and for their failure to differentiate among different types of leprosy. Their method for tracing leprosy history was a continuous narrative, a form of historiography that Kalisch notes is still employed as the traditional genre and found inserted at the beginning of many present-day scientific articles and monographs.[47] Such a history is static and uncritical and presents the disease without reference to the particular circumstances of the times.

Creighton reserved his harshest criticism, however, for the widespread attention then being paid to leprosy. Pellagra, Creighton noted, which was still endemic in parts of Europe, shared many pathological characteristics with leprosy and showed no evidence of declining even in the richest province of Italy; yet it aroused little concern. Unlike leprosy, Creighton wrote, pellagra "is not mentioned in the Bible, therefore it has no traditional vogue; it is not well suited to knight-errantry, because it is a common evil of whole provinces; its causes are economic and social, therefore there is no ready favor to be earned by systematic attempts to deal with them; and there is absolutely no opening for heroism and self-sacrifice of the more ostentatious kind."[48]

Today there is probably as much criticism of the late nineteenth-century historians of leprosy as there once were writers of leprosy history. Commenting on the wealth of misinformation to be found in works published since 1835, Stanley G. Browne recently wrote that the

> perusal of . . . classical secondary sources with their wealth of references to such monumental tomes as Dugdale's "Monasticon Anglicanum" (1655) is a somewhat intimidating experience: it is impossible to see the wood for the trees. . . . the frequent uncritical acceptance of a lay diagnosis of leprosy, or a designation of intent in a bequest or ecclesiastical document, and the over-zealous repetitive copying from dubious sources, reduce the value of much of

this comment. The use of the word leprosy is no guarantee that the specific mycobacterial disease called leprosy is intended.[49]

A detailed examination of the description of medieval lepers bears little resemblance to modern leprosy. Saul N. Brody, a historian of medieval literature, has written:

> It is intriguing . . . to discover that the lepers in medieval tales—whether French or German or English—bear remarkably close resemblance to one another and to the medieval textbook cases, but it is unsettling to find that the clinical accounts of the time bear only the most superficial likeness to those written in this century. . . . The picture of leprosy offered by medieval medicinal tracts departs in significant ways from the contemporary representation. The medieval practitioner never spoke of leprosy as "slightly contagious"; he saw it everywhere. Nor did he find that prolonged, intimate contact with a leper was necessary for the onset of the disease. . . . He had no conception of a long incubation period. . . . From time to time he might hesitate in making a diagnosis; symptoms *could* be equivocal. Yet if a sufferer showed a particular combination of a limited number of signs, the physician believed that he was confronted with a leper; . . . the forms the disease might take were few and the symptoms fell into simple patterns. The doctor of the Middle Ages viewed one leper as not very different from another, either physically or morally. The contemporary physician does not see so simple a disease.[50]

The missionaries who entered the field of leprosy work in the latter part of the nineteenth century and who saw in modern lepers analogues to their own Christian past were heirs to a tradition already laid down by men of science and men of scholarship who had traced contemporary leprosy to roots in antiquity. The belief that the leprosy from abroad was the same entity as a "disease called leprosy" was an established part of the conventional wisdom of the day. Organized missionary involvement in the care of lepers reinforced and popularized the belief as a shared experience. Missionary elaborations of and accretions to the theme of similitude heightened its impact on public thought and feelings.

THE USES OF SENSATIONALISM

In late Victorian England during Bailey's day, a renewed Christianity stirred the social consciousness. A multitude of social organizations run by the middle class explored, exposed, and strived charitably to relieve some of the miseries of the working-class poor. In 1878, four years after Bailey founded the Mission to Lepers, William Booth founded the Salvation Army. The first large-scale effort to take Christianity into the urban back streets of London, the Salvation Army was an "army of the saved at war with the Devil." The salvationism of the day systematically combined the saving of souls with attending to the physical demands of the poor and the unwanted. Contributing to the enormous success of these social missions, noted the

British historian L.C.B. Seaman, "may have been the insatiable Victorian desire for facts and particularly sensational ones."[51]

In pamphlets, tracts, books, and speeches about leprosy, sensationalism is what mission societies exported to listeners, readers, and overseas donors. A dramatic appeal for funds based on an extreme picture of the disease has been the pattern employed by missionary agencies since the 1870s. For some agencies, the pattern has remained relatively unchanged to the present day. The materials reek with lurid accounts of disfigurement, familial and societal rejection, despair, and poverty. The same material also spells out the sublime joy and happiness of lepers at the salvation offered by Christian love and charity. The format of pity, rejection, and deformity—especially of the hands, feet, and face—appeared in 1874 in the first tract that Bailey wrote, when fundraising for leprosy work began to be organized:

> In India the lepers are often turned adrift by their friends, and cast out of house and home, to wander about the country in the most pitiable condition imaginable. Their hands and feet drop off bit by bit, joint by joint, until they have nothing but the bare stumps left. As they are unable to work for themselves, they have to eke out their living by begging from door to door, and take whatever is thrown to them—and *thrown* to them it often is, as if they were dogs. When too ill to totter along on their poor stumps, they sometimes lie down and die from exhaustion. The disease attacks them generally in the hands and feet, and often in the nose and face. The bridge of the nose falls in, and gives them a most forbidding appearance.[52]

The emphasis that mission societies placed on aggravated cases of leprosy furthered the public stereotype that such descriptions characterized all of leprosy. Leprosy is a polymorphous disease, however. Gross facial disfigurement and the deformity of extremities can occur, to be sure, in advanced stages where the disease has been neglected. But these deformities are not inevitable sequelae of leprosy; in fact, they are comparatively rare. The distinctive leonine features of advanced lepromatous leprosy were described by some writers in antiquity. However, the difficulties involved in differentiating less conspicuous forms of the disease from a wide variety of other skin and neurological conditions made the advanced lepromatous leprosy the prototype of the disease. Sometimes it was called *Leo*, also *Heraclean*, more often *elephantiasis*. Stanley G. Browne nevertheless has cautioned that even with so distinctive a physiognomy, diagnostic errors still occurred.[53]

Nerve damage and deformities due to bone absorption and decalcification were described far less frequently by ancient writers than leonine features and were almost totally absent from descriptions of the disease in the medieval literature. Trophic changes in the shafts of the phalanges of the hands and feet are the result of decalcification and of the contraction of soft tissues, which then produce a shortening of digits.[54] Appendages do not "fall off," and the process is gradual, not sudden. As noticeable as such deformities are, they do not appear in the descriptions of leprosy provided by medieval writers. In his detailed examination of the medieval literature,

Brody cites only one reference to nerve damage. This instance, involving a claw hand malformation, was recorded by Prudentius, a poet writing in the fourth or fifth century A.D.[55] The failure of medieval commentators, who were strong on images, to record evidence of the deterioration of the flesh as part of their description of leprosy may be testimony to their greater attention to spiritual deformity than to physical details in matters relating to the disease.

The myth that appendages literally "drop off" is widespread in leprosy. Such a misconception is part of the general public's perception of the disease. The image that such occurrences are part of the disease process has been exploited by numerous popular authors since late in the nineteenth century and continues to be exploited by some of them today. James A. Michener, for example, used this stereotype extensively in his novel *Hawaii*. He described lepers "whose lips and nose had fallen away" and whose "feet had fallen away," leaving the impression that lepers actually experienced a "loss" of body parts. He wrote, "Her shattered husband had already begun to lose his toes and fingers."[56] The stereotype about digits formed part of the fantasies held about the disease by newly diagnosed patients whom I interviewed at Carville in the 1960s[57] and, at one time, was a popular in-joke among the more knowledgeable patients at the leprosarium.[58] Leprosy patients have earned the right to parody their own situation, but "jests" about "fingers falling into the soup" or Paolo Zappa's literary reference to fingers snapping off "like a dry twig,"[59] convey a grossly misleading visual image about leprosy. Examples of such "humor" can still be found in "joke" books published today.[60]

Physicians working with leprosy patients in countries where the disease is uncommon have noted that psychological difficulties found in their patients can be traced to the skewed pictures and misinformation about the disease that are disseminated by mission societies. Abel and van Soest, both attached to the German Institute for Medical Missions, Tübingen, West Germany, have commented that "medical malinformation can be cured relatively easily," if only the "leprosy relief organizations [would] give up fund-raising by means of 'horror-pictures'. . . . It must be possible to promote the much more important prevention of the disease to the main theme for fund-raising. Surely this would . . . influence . . . the image of leprosy in the eyes of the public."[61]

Verbal and pictorial descriptions of leprosy as horribly deforming and physically repulsive have probably contributed more to the modern stigmatization of leprosy than its alleged contagiousness. Earlier in this century, when the contagiousness of leprosy was being downgraded, leprologists began to cite deformity as the principal reason for public concern. In fact, in 1925, Rogers and Muir claimed that contagion was never the reason for the age-old practice of isolating lepers; rather, that the "terrible deformities of the face and extremities brought about by" leprosy exaggerated public opinion about how contagious the disease really was: "The disease is probably but little, if at all, more infective than tuberculosis, though the serious facial disfigurement in the nodular form, and the crippling loss of fingers and toes in the little-infective nerve variety, ultimately make the sufferers so repulsive, that in all historical ages, and in many parts of the world, compulsion has been used to destroy or isolate them. . . . ''[62]

As they exported an extreme picture of the disease to donors, mission societies catered to the increasing interest in the spiritual and temporal welfare of lepers awakened among Christians at home and to the late-Victorian desire for sensational facts. In doing so, they laid the foundation for a structured public perception of leprosy as an especially loathsome disease. This observation is not new. Jonathan Hutchinson, who had a long familiarity with leprosy in India, made this point in 1906 when he wrote:

> It is upon these, the later stages, that all our popular notions of the disease are based. . . . Pictorial illustrations of leprosy are plentiful. The conditions displayed in aggravated cases are conspicuous and lend themselves readily to the camera of the photographer and to the artist's pencil. For the most part, however, only aggravated cases are selected and it is the so-called tuberous form which is almost invariably depicted.
>
> Thus the leonine physiognomy, with its repulsive hypertrophies, has assumed a very false position in the imagination of those not personally conversant with the disease. It is thought to be the ordinary characteristic of the malady, whereas it is a comparatively rare one. . . . [63]

Although mission societies engaged in high rhetoric in describing the condition of lepers in foreign countries as especially appalling, they were not being altogether deceptive. They mostly described what they saw. The diseased persons who attracted the missionaries' eyes, the lepers who gathered at the doorsteps of missions, and the ones most eager to exchange care for Bible classes were among the most destitute and disabled. As Hutchinson noted, "it is of subjects in this stage that the inmates of leper-houses chiefly consist."[64] Furthermore, the missionary and colonial practice of locating large numbers of destitute and disabled lepers in settlements and in leprosaria visually magnified the deficits produced by the disease and by the poverty associated with it. Recently, Iman Bijleveld, in reporting on leprosy in Kenya, commented on the visual impact of concentrating many patients in single camps:

> It strikes me as inevitable that concentration of leprosy patients in camps, despite the social benefits to them of their confinement, had negative consequences for stigmatization. Scattered patients in huts along scattered rivers do not appall the imagination, not the way hundreds of deformed, ulcerating patients in a limited space are likely to do. The sheer numbers of camp populations, the density of suffering, are sure to have contributed heavily to popular horror at the mention of the disease.[65]

Bijleveld, who studied leprosy practices in Kenya and in Nigeria, further observed that leprosy workers tend to lose their objectivity about leprosy after working with the disease over an extended period of time:

> There is a risk that people who concern themselves with leprosy for any protracted length of time, whether doctors or social scientists, become so immersed in the visible horror of the disease and the stigmatization for patients which derives from this horror that they will no longer be able to see leprosy for what it is, only one of a range of dire sicknesses, and will elevate it to a unique malady which demands extremely special forms of health care.[66]

The social environment of the countries in which leprosy has been prevalent and where missionaries conducted the bulk of their activities must also be weighed in assessing the attitude toward the disease found within missionary circles. The countries of Great Britain's eastern empire, especially India, were far more complex, highly stratified social entities than England in the late nineteenth century. India's hierarchical caste structure was held in place by an ideology of impurity and notions of sin along with rigid caste beliefs and practices relating to avoidance and the concept of the "untouchable." This system equated disease with defilement and ritual pollution, and was equipped to sustain a "leper" category.[67] Nineteenth-century Hindu social rules for dealing with untouchables and other culturally defined outcaste groups fit in well with the Christian caretakers' own picture of biblical stigma. For many missionaries, Hindu social structure provided them with their first cross-cultural experience of the societal treatment of devalued persons, and the experience strengthened their own beliefs in the lessons of the biblical and medieval proscription of lepers. The strength of leprosy stigma in India has been such that it is still a major obstacle today in providing effective treatment.

As long ago as the 1930s, enlightened leprologists recognized that the popular belief that equated the modern disease with biblical leprosy also contributed to the public stigmatization of leprosy and that the stigma was a barrier to treatment. Early efforts to destigmatize leprosy were directed at changing the name of the illness and at discontinuing the use of opprobrious terms, like "leper" and even "leprosy," in order to diffuse the taint that surrounded the modern condition. Today, leprologist scholars are highly skeptical about, and often openly disavow, a clinical connection between the entity mentioned in the Bible and medieval tracts and the disease that is observed today. On the other hand, they believe that the general Western public is ill-informed about leprosy and clings to the traditional view. The task of raising private funds for leprosy work is far more difficult today than in the past. Whatever competition for funds that Bailey and the Mission to Lepers faced in the golden years of that organization, it was slight when compared with the situation today. Stringer has noted that in the early 1970s in Great Britain alone, the proponents of some 77,000 different charities were vying for a share of the public goodwill.[68] In the United States, according to a Gallup poll commissioned by the American Leprosy Missions in 1982, no more than one percent of the population surveyed was aware of the name of a church or mission-related agency that helped people with the disease.[69]

The question becomes one of how to keep the public interest in leprosy alive in the face of increasing competition from other charitable organizations seeking donations for a host of other worthy purposes. Mission society fundraisers today find themselves in the paradoxical position of having to rely on public misunderstanding about leprosy in order to keep the disease salient to their Christian donors. Stringer has outlined the strategy involved:

> The process is one of relying on the existence of misunderstanding, and making the correction reveal the case for concern and generosity. It is a process of associating the traditional "disease called leprosy" with the actual currently defined disease to provide for the dissociation of fiction from fact. To attempt to do this without a total reliance on the abundant misuse of the word "leprosy" would be a complex and vain exercise and would, moreover, lose the interest and imagination of the public. . . . Because of all the factors which frustrate the efforts of field workers, the word "leprosy" invites curiosity and attention, and provides for a strategy in gaining support. This seems a legitimate and harmless process.[70]

There was one stratagem that Stringer was prepared to do without: "Pictorial representation of leprosy sufferers provides immediate information about the nature of the disease, but, stressing the unaesthetic aspects of it, seems calculated to reinforce its stigma."[71]

Mission societies working with leprosy have generally been loathe to abandon "last year's words," even though, as T. S. Eliot reminds us, they "belong to last year's language." Their dilemma, in part, lies with the next line of the poem: "And next year's words await another voice."[72] The question of how to present leprosy to the general public became a relevant issue in the 1940s, when modern chemotherapy first became available. Along with it came the possibility of being able to do more for patients. Rehabilitation could now be emphasized, and greater attention could be paid to the prevention of deformities. In the case of the American Leprosy Missions, a decision was made in the 1950s to make a film with a "happy" message about leprosy instead of emphasizing the unaesthetic aspects of the disease. Robert M. Wulff, in his book *Village of the Outcasts*, recalled the controversy this decision evoked when he described his visit to the Reverend Raymond B. Buker at the McKean leper colony in Thailand in 1953. Wulff, who first went to the Orient in 1946–47 when the U.S. Army stationed him in China, returned to the Far East in 1951 after graduating from St. Olaf College in Wisconsin. There he "found his life's calling," establishing leper colonies in Thailand. Wulff arrived at McKean in time to witness the arrival of an American movie crew that had come to make a color film about leprosy work. The movie had been commissioned by the American Leprosy Missions. Writing about this event, Wulff recalled:

> I remember that I was really excited about the filming. . . . Dr. Buker was more interested in the content of the film than in its technique and I remember his saying, "I am sure you are making a technically good film, Alan [Alan Shilen, owner and director of the company], but it won't say anything. I

have watched you at work and you haven't photographed one single bad case of leprosy. When people at home see your film they won't know what leprosy can do to a person. If you want to film the truth, film the toeless feet, the clawed hands, the sunken noses, the ulcers and the sores. Film the misery of many of the patients. Try to show their bitterness and despair."

But Alan explained that the American Leprosy Missions had insisted that the film should be "horror-free." He had been instructed to make a happy film about happy lepers in a happy leprosy colony. Apparently the American Leprosy Missions felt that it would be easier to raise money with a happy film than with a tragic one.[73]

Buker and Wulff both, though in different ways, stand as representatives of "last year's words that belong to last year's language," a frame of mind that has contributed to the public's view of leprosy as an extreme and unusual phenomenon. For Buker, the teaching of Christ was paramount. He noted that since the Mission to Lepers began its work, "thousands of patients . . . have been dismissed as 'symptom-free'" and added: "Praiseworthy as these results are, it is even more creditable that an estimated more than ten thousand men and women and children have accepted Jesus Christ as their Lord and Savior."[74] For Wulff, "leprosy is one of the most terrible diseases to afflict human beings." Angry over the American Leprosy Missions' decision that the film be "horror-free," Wulff replied: "I believe that the world must be shocked into a realization that leprosy is a terrible problem, and the techniques used to solicit help should show it as it really is."[75]

"Happy films about happy lepers in a happy leprosy colony," or Buker's recipe, "toeless feet, clawed hands, sunken noses, ulcers, sores, misery, bitterness and despair," both rest their case with a heavy dose of emotionalism and stereotyped messages. In time, however, another language began to emerge. Early in 1970, the American Leprosy Missions placed an advertisement in the intellectual magazine *Saturday Review*. In the ad, Dr. Oliver W. Hasselblad, then president of ALM, reflected on his return to the United States a few years before, after spending twenty years as a surgeon in India. He had been appalled at the enthusiasm shown by the U.S. public in "the fight against polio, cancer and multiple sclerosis, while leprosy was thought of in terms of the cry that greeted Ben Hur's mother and sister, 'unclean, unclean.'" This contrast in public reception caused him to have second thoughts about how leprosy was presented to the public. "Perhaps part of the blame," he wrote, "lies with leprosy organizations. Emotional appeals have been the major means used to loosen purse strings. Little wonder Americans have never been able to view leprosy as a disease, rather than a curse."[76] Accompanying the text of this new perspective on leprosy there was a line drawing of a laboratory scientist at work.

Most large leprosy relief organizations today eschew sensationalism and now build their public relations and fundraising campaigns around the provision of medical and surgical services, rehabilitation, health education, and vocational training; the construction and maintenance of facilities; the recruitment and training of leprosy workers; and scholarships and research grants. The problem they face is how to interest the public in supporting their work without resorting to dramatic appeals or to heavy emphasis on Christian motivation. These societies, however, still wish it to be known that no other disease has been so stigmatized; often they will go into some detail explaining past misconceptions about leprosy. This, perhaps, is the Stringer strategy of "relying on the existence of misunderstanding, and making the correction reveal the case for concern and generosity."

Some smaller organizations, however, still speak in the language of yesterday. The Salesian Missions, for example, mail out a brochure showing photographs of forlorn Indian children. The photographs are accompanied by the following text:

> A fingerless hand clutches two loaves of bread . . . the other presses a coin into the folds of tattered garments . . . then the leper hobbles off back to the city streets, which are his home; or, if he is more fortunate, to a flimsy shack in the wastelands. Exposed to the scorching sun and the driving monsoon rains, to rats that gnaw at their open wounds in the night—these outcasts of humanity have nowhere to turn but to the one man [Father Maschio] who has spent his life helping the miserable.[77]

In this brief tract of about 1,000 words, the word "leper" is used eleven times.

RESTRUCTURING THE CARE OF LEPROSY PATIENTS

The historical role played by mission societies—now generally known as "voluntary agencies"—in caring for lepers worldwide, in raising funds for their support, and in influencing governmental policies about the disease has been truly enormous. One consequence of missionary involvement has been that the care of lepers has evolved into a distinct and separate social and medical service, with its own outlook and tradition, its own staff structure and funds, and its own vested interest. From early in the 1870s until the middle of the present century, the care and, later, the medical treatment of lepers—first through enforced segregation, later in voluntary agricultural communities, leprosy hospitals, and outpatient dispensaries—existed in near-total isolation from other world health problems and health delivery systems. Leprosy workers themselves were isolated. "We have become a select society, a clique, almost a secret sect," wrote one recent critic of leprosy separatism.[78] The separatist tradition has had an undesired effect on treatment programs and a profound effect on fundraising, Stanley G. Browne has noted: "Far from being the neglected and utterly unprivileged outcast of society, the ex-leprosy patient in some communities is becoming an over-privileged and expensive non-productive citizen, making inordinate demands on the budget. And it is the crippled and mutilated, rather than the patients with early active disease, who succeed in capturing the sympathy and the money of many charitable organizations."[79]

Following World War II, major changes in leprosy policies and practices took place, and with these changes public attitudes toward the disease have been changing accordingly. Three series of events, all war-related, contributed to ending the tradition of leprosy separatism and thus to bringing the disease closer to the mainstream of clinical medicine: the development of modern leprosy chemotherapy; the dissolution of colonial empires; and the formation of the World Health Organization (WHO). With these developments leprosy has lost much of its former public fascination and its status as a special disease.

The coming of World War II quickened the search for new drugs to combat disease and to deal with war-related injuries. Sulfones, the basis of modern leprosy treatment, emerged from investigations carried on in the 1930s on the sulfonamides, chemical substances that proved effective in the development of agents capable of dealing with a wide variety of bacterial infections. An effective leprosy chemotherapy that could be administered orally greatly increased the scope for leprosy control programs in endemic countries with large rural populations; another factor was the development of expanded case-finding methods. Leprosy suspects could now be examined, treated, and maintained on an outpatient basis. The use of outpatient dispensaries had been advocated early in the century and had been tried with some success on a small scale in Calcutta and, later, in the Philippines, Nigeria, and other parts of British Africa.[80] Treatment using chaulmoogra oil was usually available only in clinics that were connected to hospitals or to other centers with laboratory facilities; thus it was of limited value in reaching populations far removed from such centers.

Formal dissolution of colonial empires in Asia and in Africa occurred during the period between the end of World War II and the 1960s. The war and its aftermath had restructured the world map. With independence, former colonies became responsible for their own problems and for their own citizens, including their own lepers. Under colonialism the voluntary agencies had assumed much of this latter responsibility. Now the voluntary agencies became expatriate organizations, "guests," so to speak, in countries they once considered home.

WHO came into being as a specialized agency under the charter of the United Nations and was established at the end of World War II "to act as the directing and co-ordinating authority on international health work." For the first time, a single worldwide intergovernmental agency had emerged to consider all aspects of human health. Unlike previous international health organizations, whose main concerns rested with preventing the spread of communicable diseases across national boundaries, WHO had as its objective "the attainment by all peoples of the highest possible level of health." In 1952 WHO began to tackle the problem of leprosy.

Prior to the formation of WHO, the care of lepers—or the lack of it— was a matter left to individual governments or nations. For years a loose arrangement existed between governments, international scientific associations, leprosy conferences, a few private foundations, and a vast network of voluntary agencies, all of which conferred occasionally to discuss policies. Within this informal structure, there was a less than satisfactory agreement about leprosy and little coordinated effort among leprologists and health planners, as many of them had encountered leprosy in different regions of the world and under widely differing sets of conditions.

The emergence of WHO and its acceptance by the world community in matters of international health had a unifying effect on leprosy work. When the World Health Assembly passed a resolution in 1951 urging WHO to assist developing countries in national health planning, the opportunity to reassess leprosy policies and practices had arrived. WHO, noting the many disagreements and changes in disease classification that had marked the efforts of international leprosy congresses since 1931, observed that "the pattern of leprosy . . . changes considerably from one country to another. There are few leprologists with a wide knowledge of all the regional variations of the disease. . . . The majority of leprologists have in mind one static and immutable disease."[81] WHO argued that from the point of view of public health, and especially if mass campaigns against leprosy were to be inaugurated, "it is more important to classify the population in which the disease appears, than it is to classify the disease itself into categories meeting the approval of all leprologists."[82]

As a first step in coordinating leprosy work, the WHO Expert Committee on Leprosy, in its initial report, undertook the important task of removing the disease from its nineteenth-century position as a special and unique malady. "Leprosy," committee members asserted, "is not a disease apart; it is a general public-health problem in the countries where it is endemic."[83] The long tradition of thinking of leprosy as a separate disease and of maintaining distinct and separate services isolated from other medical and health concerns was about to end. For the first time since Norway had tackled the problem, leprosy policies and practices would be planned within a framework of public health.

Leprosy has always been most prevalent in the developing nations. Many of those countries today are former colonies and are among the poorest countries in the world. The socioeconomic, fiscal, and administrative policies of the colonial governments left these countries with serious deficits in many areas, and independence brought them face to face with their own enormous problems of poverty and disease. Moreover, the past efforts of colonial governments to deal with leprosy by establishing leper asylums had failed to reveal the magnitude of the problem. If leprosy were now to be dealt with on a mass scale, new models of controls were needed.

In communicable disease theory, isolation of all infectious cases ideally should break the chain of infection. The practice works best in the acute infectious diseases, where the period of infection is relatively short. In a chronic disease like leprosy, with its lengthy incubation and lengthy treatment, isolation, though long advocated in the past, has been ineffective and, by the early 1950s, was considered obsolete by many leprologists and health planners. The new chemotherapies were considered to be capable of rendering many cases noninfectious. The disadvantages of isolation outweighed any possible benefits; rather than reduce disease incidence, it increased the number of cases that were concealed. It did little to encourage case-finding and early treatment and provided little opportunity to engage in health education to prevent deformity. Isolation also impeded drug trials, as persons with advanced leprosy were the ones usually confined. In addition, the idea of promoting a policy of compulsory segregation within newly independent nations was politically unthinkable and logistically impossible.

In its attempt to deal with the problem of leprosy in hyperendemic areas, WHO recommended that programs of intensive outpatient sulfone treatment of all known cases of the disease be undertaken and that systematic surveys be made in order to detect the unknown cases. The idea behind this approach was that in countries with high endemicity it was more important to reduce the infectiousness of many than to concentrate on only a few. Such an approach was economical, when compared to isolation, in terms of both treatment costs and the patient's ability to maintain himself and his family. Recommendations were also made to combine the treatment and control of leprosy with campaigns against other diseases, such as tuberculosis. The need to improve the physical resistance of whole populations through better nutrition and through mass treatment of other common infectious and parasitic diseases was deemed essential.

The isolation of leprosy patients was downgraded; it was placed on a voluntary basis and reserved for selected cases. Patients were to be discharged from isolation promptly on becoming noninfectious. Home and special village confinement were considered adequate in many instances. The idea that leprosy was so infectious that isolation must be in areas far removed from the centers of population was deprecated. This principle applied as well to the construction of new facilities. Questions of medical discrimination and coercive legislation against leprosy patients were also addressed by WHO. The importance of health education in leprosy, laboratory and field research, and continued efforts in physiotherapy, surgery, ophthalmology, orthopedics, and other clinical specialties have consistently been urged by WHO. Health education was considered to be especially important in combating public ignorance and prejudice and in preventing disease progression and deformity. Medical administrators, doctors, and nurses all needed to know more about the disease in order to diagnose leprosy accurately and earlier.[84]

The WHO model for directing antileprosy campaigns developed along lines already employed in other communicable diseases: (1) an attack phase aimed at case-finding and early treatment, (2) a consolidation phase of case-holding, and ultimately, (3) the integration of leprosy programs into the general health service system of a nation. In the developing countries especially, the problem of disease control more often than not relates to the fact that general health services are lacking or are below minimal levels of effectiveness. To maintain a separate leprosy service would be expensive, and the developing countries have more than their share of other major health problems to be tackled. The integration of leprosy into the general health system—as such systems evolved—was therefore not only a logical and economical move, it was also one that promised an end to the long tradition of leprosy separatism.[85]

The new leprosy policies represented a radical departure from past practices. They collided with the work of the voluntary agencies, where fundraising and caretaking activities had long been vested in leprosaria, disease deformity, and salvation. The exclusive focus on one disease in countries plagued by multiple problems of health and nutrition, many of which were far more serious than leprosy, called the activities and intent of the voluntary agencies into serious question. Pressure on the voluntary agencies to adopt newer methods and to broaden their base of activities became intense. For despite their expatriate status, the voluntary agencies have retained a considerable presence in many of the developing countries, where they provide facilities and expertise and contribute money for treatment and hospitalization. The voluntary agencies are caught between the past and the present; they do not want to see 100 years of effort on behalf of leprosy sufferers slip away from them. They are aware that integration of health services, along with the urgency of assisting in other health areas, threatens to lessen the dramatic cause for leprosy. The voluntary agencies are being pulled in two directions. For some, the integration of leprosy is desirable and necessary; for others, it is a catch-phrase, a possible long-term solution, but one that has not yet proved itself.

The primary responsibility of WHO is to the national governments that request its help and to international health. Most Third World countries have limited resources and embryonic health care systems. The presence in these countries of the voluntary agencies is therefore a potential asset. Many leprologists affiliated with the voluntary agencies now serve on WHO expert committees, in special study groups, and as field consultants. An ongoing task of WHO has been to co-opt the participation of the voluntary agencies into supporting plans in Third World nations that further the long-term development of basic health services. "It would be appropriate," according to a WHO report in 1977, "for the voluntary agencies to seek to pattern their own services on those of the government."[86] As the voluntary agencies struggle to retain their own identity and their own special sense of service, the nature of their work is being changed for them.

As a transmissible disease, leprosy is still far from being under control. *M. leprae* remains a baffling bacillus; the number of scientific investigators actively working in leprosy are few; and the search for a vaccine continues. The worldwide magnitude of leprosy has not decreased since the period of alarm in the late nineteenth century. If anything, owing to modern surveys and improved case-finding methods, the known number of cases is greater. Moreover, of the estimated 10 million cases of leprosy in the world today, from one-third to one-half of them have not been detected. Of the more than 3.5 million registered cases, only 41 percent in Africa and 47 percent in Asia are thought to be receiving regular treatment.[87] Yet, although the magnitude of leprosy remains high, the amount of public attention that the disease now receives has declined appreciably.

It is tempting to attribute this lessening of public interest in leprosy to advances in chemotherapy, to the belief that modern medicine has the disease under control. But such is not the case. Few compounds are available. The major drug companies are not interested in leprosy, as there is little profit in tropical disease.[88] To deliver to millions throughout the world those drugs that are available requires stability of government, comprehensive health care facilities, and adequate staffing levels, which more often than not are lacking. Furthermore, most treatment procedures for leprosy are lengthy affairs, and for success to be ensured, treatment must be regular and cases must be carefully monitored. Prejudice against leprosy is still encountered in many quarters. Leprosy is primarily a disease of rural impoverishment, and WHO has recently predicted that satisfactory results in leprosy control may be delayed until there is a significant rise in the standard of living and in education in many parts of the world.[89]

In approaching the question of why public interest in leprosy has declined, it is important to look at how the public interest was once deeply aroused because of entrenched social values and attitudes and to examine how these values and attitudes have changed. The formation of newly independent nations out of old colonial empires that followed World War II, and the formation of WHO, permanently altered the nature of the work that mission societies had formerly engaged in and, in so doing, changed the character of the overseas missions themselves. Pressured by national governments and by WHO into assisting with health-related problems other than leprosy— and with sensationalizing the disease now out of the question—the lessening role of missionary societies in leprosy has lessened the drama of leprosy. With missionary societies no longer a part of the colonial infrastructure and with the developed nations now less involved with their former colonies than before, there has been a lessening of public attention to leprosy as a dramatic disease and with it a decline in religious fundraising for leprosy work.

The institutional structures of the past that enveloped leprosy in racism and stigma and cloistered it behind religious symbols and metaphors have shifted and today are giving way to secular arrangements. This shift in institutional base may be the most significant change that has taken place in leprosy history in the past 100 years, new scientific knowledge and chemotherapies notwithstanding. The negative stereotypes that once elevated and then held leprosy prominent as an international social problem are diminishing. Now the disease remains.

◇——— *Notes*

Chapter 1

1. Sontag, Susan. *Illness as Metaphor* (New York: Farrar, Straus and Giroux, 1978).
2. Brody, Saul N. *The Disease of the Soul: Leprosy in Medieval Literature* (Ithaca: Cornell University Press, 1974): 11.
3. Ibid., 197.
4. Kellersberger, Eugene R. "The Social Stigma of Leprosy." *Annals of the New York Academy of Medicine* 54, art. 1 (1951): 132.
5. Terris, Milton, ed. *Goldberger on Pellagra* (Baton Rouge: Louisiana State University Press, 1964).
6. Blumer, Herbert. "Social Problems as Collective Behavior." *Social Problems* 18, no. 3 (1971).
7. Strickland, Stephen P. *Politics, Science, and Dread Disease: A Short History of United States Medical Research Policy* (Cambridge: Harvard University Press, 1972).
8. Kunitz, Stephen J. "Some Notes on Physiologic Conditions as Social Problems." *Social Science & Medicine* 8, no. 4 (1974).
9. Stinchcombe, Arthur L. *Constructing Social Theories* (New York: Harcourt, Brace and World, 1968): 101–103.
10. "International Work in Leprosy 1948–1959." *World Health Organization Chronicle* 14, no. 1 (1960): 8.
11. Cochrane, Robert G., and Davey, T. Frank. *Leprosy in Theory and Practice* (Baltimore: Williams and Wilkins Co., 1964); Trautman, John R., and Enna, Carl D. "Leprosy," in *Tice's Practice of Medicine*, vol. 3 (Hagerstown, Md.: Harper and Row, 1970); Arnold, Harry L., and Fasal, Paul. *Leprosy: Diagnosis and Management* (Springfield, Ill.: Charles C. Thomas, 1973); Bryceson, Anthony, and Pfaltzgraff, Roy E. *Leprosy for Students of Medicine* (Edinburgh: Churchill Livingston, 1973); *World Health Organization Chronicle* 31, no. 12 (1977); Shepard, Charles C. "Leprosy Today." *New England Journal of Medicine* 307, no. 26 (1982); Young, Donald B., and Buchanan, Thomas M. "A Serological Test for Leprosy with a Glycolipid Specific for *Mycobacterium leprae*." *Science* 221 (September 9, 1983).
12. Some examples of strategies and even prototheories may be found in Goffman, Erving, *Stigma: Notes on the Management of Spoiled Identity* (Englewood Cliffs, N.J.: Prentice-Hall, 1963).
13. Skinsnes, Olaf K. "Leprosy in Society, I." *Leprosy Review* 35, no. 1 (1964): 13–15.
14. Ibid., 15.
15. Skinsnes, Olaf K. "Leprosy in Society, I." *Leprosy Review* 35, no. 1 (1964); ———, II, 35, no. 3 (1964); ———, III, 35, no. 4 (1964); Skinsnes, Olaf K., and Elvove, Robert M. "Leprosy in Society, V." *International Journal of Leprosy* 38, no. 3

(1970); Skinsnes, Olaf K. "Notes from the History of Leprosy." *International Journal of Leprosy* 41, no. 2 (1973).

16. Skinsnes and Elvove, 304.

17. Ibid., 294, 305.

18. Ibid., 305.

19. Sontag, 58.

20. Kalisch, Philip A. "Lepers, Anachronisms, and the Progressives: A Study of Stigma, 1889–1920." *Louisiana Studies: An Interdisciplinary Journal of the South* 12, no. 3 (1973).

21. Ibid., 525.

22. Ibid., 489.

23. Ibid., 530, 531.

24. Ibid., 529.

25. Brody, 107.

26. Ibid., 108.

27. Ibid., 190.

28. Ibid., 197.

29. Skinsnes, 1973: 245.

30. *The Star*, back cover of every issue until recently.

31. McCoy, George W., and Goodhue, William J. "Studies upon Leprosy. XX. The Danger of Association with Lepers at the Molokai Settlement." *Public Health Bulletin* 61 (1913); Gray, Herman H., and Dreisbach, John A. "Leprosy Among Foreign Missionaries in Northern Nigeria." *International Journal of Leprosy* 29, no. 3 (1961).

32. Gussow, Zachary, and Tracy, George S. "Status, Ideology, and Adaptation to Stigmatized Illness: A Study of Leprosy." *Human Organization* 27, no. 4 (1968).

33. Brody, chapter 1.

34. I deal with this issue in more detail throughout the book. See also: Rogers, Sir Leonard, and Muir, Ernest. *Leprosy* (Bristol: John Wright and Sons, 1925): 53; Shiloh, Ailon. "A Case Study of Disease and Culture in Action: Leprosy Among the Hausa of Northern Nigeria." *Human Organization* 24, no. 2 (1965); Marshall, Carter L., Maeshiro, Mieko, and Korper, Samuel P. "Attitudes Toward Leprosy in the Ryukyu Islands." *Public Health Reports* 82, no. 9 (1967); Bijleveld, Iman. "An Appraisal of Diverse Actual and Potential Public Health Activities in Kaduna State, Northern Nigeria: A Report on Fieldwork May–July 1977." (Department of Social Research, Royal Tropical Institute, Amsterdam, n.d.); Dols, Michael W. "Leprosy in Medieval Arabic Medicine." *Journal of the History of Medicine and Allied Sciences* 34, no. 3 (1979); Waxler, Nancy. "Learning to Be a Leper: A Case Study in the Social Construction of Illness," in *Social Contexts of Health, Illness, and Patient Care*, Elliot G. Mishler, ed. (New York: Cambridge University Press, 1981).

35. Sagarin, Edward, ed. *The Other Minorities: Nonethnic Collectivities Conceptualized as Minority Groups* (Waltham, Mass.: Ginn and Company, 1971): 164.

36. Osgood, Charles E. *The Measurement of Meaning* (Urbana, Ill.: University of Illinois Press, 1957); Shearer, Lois A., and Hoodwin, Jean. "Hansen's Disease: A Modern Approach." *International Journal of Leprosy* 27, no. 4 (1959); Barker, Donald G. "Concepts of Disability." *Personnel and Guidance Journal* 43, no. 4 (1964).

37. Ebner, James D. "Community Knowledge and Attitudes About Leprosy: A Social-Psychological Study of the Degree of Stigmatization of a Chronic Disease." Master's thesis, Department of Sociology, Louisiana State University, Baton Rouge, 1968; Gussow, Zachary, and Tracy, George S. "The Phenomenon of Leprosy Stigma in the Continental United States." *Leprosy Review* 43, no. 2 (1972).

38. Foucault, Michel. *Madness and Civilization: A History of Insanity in the Age of Reason* (New York: Random House, 1965).

39. Dubos, Rene and Jean. *The White Plague: Tuberculosis, Man and Society* (Boston: Little, Brown and Company, 1952); Ackerknecht, Erwin H. *History and Geography of the Most Important Diseases* (New York: Hafner Publishing Company, 1965).

40. Browne, Stanley G. "Leprosy: The Christian Attitude." *International Journal of Leprosy* 31, no. 2 (1963): 230.

41. Brinckerhoff, Walter R. "Studies upon Leprosy. VI. Leprosy in the United States of America in 1909." Treasury Department, Public Health and Marine-Hospital Service of the United States (Washington, D.C.: Government Printing Office, 1909): 14; Trautman and Enna, 3.

42. *A Guide to Leprosy Control* (Geneva: World Health Organization, 1980): 9–11.

Chapter 2

1. Duffy, John. *Epidemics in Colonial America* (Baton Rouge: Louisiana State University Press, 1953).

2. East, Dennis, II. "Health and Wealth: Goals of the New Orleans Public Health Movement, 1879–1884." *Louisiana History* 9, no. 3 (1968); Ellis, John H. "Business and Public Health in the Urban South During the Nineteenth Century: New Orleans, Memphis, and Atlanta." *Bulletin of the History of Medicine* 44, nos. 3 and 4 (1970).

3. Duffy, John. *Sword of Pestilence: The New Orleans Yellow Fever Epidemic of 1853* (Baton Rouge: Louisiana State University Press, 1966): 169–170.

4. Baughman, James P. "Gateway to the Americas," in *The Past as Prelude: New Orleans, 1718–1968*, H. Carter, ed. (New Orleans: Pelican Publishing House, 1968): 381.

5. Smillie, Wilson G. "The Period of the Great Epidemics in the United States (1800–1875)," in *The History of American Epidemiology*, Franklin H. Topp, ed. (St. Louis: The C. V. Mosby Company, 1952): 57–58.

6. Caplan, Harry B. "History of Smallpox in Louisiana." Louisiana State University Medical Center Rare Book Collection, typescript, 1944; Duffy, John, ed. *The Rudolph Matas History of Medicine in Louisiana*, vol. 2 (Baton Rouge: Louisiana State University Press, 1962): 433.

7. Ibid., 437.

8. Duffy, John. "Pestilence in New Orleans," in *The Past as Prelude: New Orleans, 1718–1968*, H. Carter, ed., 100.

9. Barton, Edward B. *The Cause and Prevention of Yellow Fever at New Orleans and Other Cities in America*, 3rd ed. (New York: H. Bailliere, 1857): Comparative Table: Estimate of the Salubrity of New Orleans, As affected by Her Epidemics, 1st—of Yellow Fever, n.p.

10. Ibid.; Augustin, George. *History of Yellow Fever* (New Orleans: Searcy and Pfaff, 1909): 868ff.

11. *Mortality Statistics of the Seventh Census of the United States, 1850* (House of Representatives, 33d Cong., 2d sess., Executive Document no. 98, Washington, D.C., 1855).

12. Ibid., table 24.

13. *Report of the Sanitary Commission of New Orleans on the Epidemic Yellow Fever of 1853* (New Orleans: Picayune Office, 1854): chart A.

14. Ibid.

15. *Mortality Statistics of the Seventh Census*, 5.

16. *Report of the Sanitary Commission*, iii.

17. Ibid., 257; Reinders, Robert C. *End of an Era: New Orleans, 1850–1860* (New Orleans: Pelican Publishing Company, 1964): 98; Duffy, *Sword of Pestilence*, 171.

18. Reinders, 98.

19. Duffy, *The Rudolph Matas History of Medicine*, 131.

20. Moe, Christine. "Yellow Fever in New Orleans." *Publications of the Louisiana Historical Society* 1, series 2 (1973): 15.

21. Duffy, "Pestilence in New Orleans," 112.

22. Fenner, E. D. *History of the Epidemic Yellow Fever at New Orleans, La., in 1853* (New York: Hall, Clayton and Company, 1854): 69; Moe, 13.

23. *Report of the Sanitary Commission*, chart A; Chaille, Stanford E. "Life and Death Rates: New Orleans and Other Cities Compared." *New Orleans Medical and Surgical Journal*, n.s., 16 (August 1888): table 4.

24. *Report of the Sanitary Commission*, iii.

25. Simonds, J. C. "The Sanitary Commission of New Orleans as Illustrated by the Mortuary Statistics." *Charleston Medical Journal and Review* 6, no. 5 (1851): 677–678.

26. *Report of the Sanitary Commission*, iii.

27. Barton, Edward H. "Sanitary Report of New Orleans, La." *Transactions of the American Medical Association* 2 (1849).

28. *Mortality Statistics of the Seventh Census*, 8, 15.

29. *Report of the Sanitary Commission*, 220–223 (italics in original).

30. Ibid., 247–248 (italics in original).

31. Ibid., table H.

32. Sartwell, Philip E. *Preventive Medicine and Public Health*, 9th ed. (New York: Appleton-Century-Crofts, 1965): 310.

33. *Report of the Sanitary Commission*, 249.

34. *Mortality Statistics of the Seventh Census*, table 7.

35. *Report of the Sanitary Commission*, 460–461.

36. Ibid., 244.

37. Simonds, 709.

38. Ibid.; Sigerist, Henry E. "The Cost of Illness to the City of New Orleans in 1850." *Bulletin of the History of Medicine* 15, no. 5 (1944).

39. Simonds, 709.

40. Sigerist, 507. In reviewing Simonds's work and noting that he "deserves more attention and credit for his courageous and far-sighted report than he has been given in the past," medical historian Henry Sigerist added the comment that, had Simonds reasoned as Pettenkofer did in 1873, the annual cost of preventable sickness to the city of New Orleans, capitalized at 5 percent, would have represented an amount of $70 million.

41. Dowler, Bennet. *Tableau of the Yellow Fever of 1853 with Topographical, Chronological, and Historical Sketches of the Epidemics of New Orleans Since Their Origin in 1796, Illustrative of the Quarantine Question* (New Orleans: Office of the Picayune, 1854): 29.

42. *Report of the Sanitary Commission*, 254.

43. Duffy, *Sword of Pestilence*, 167.

44. Ibid., 134.

45. Jackson, Joy J. *New Orleans in the Gilded Age: Politics and Urban Progress, 1880–1896* (Baton Rouge: Louisiana State University Press, 1969): 171.

46. Duffy, *Sword of Pestilence*, 172.

47. Barton, Edward H. "Report upon the Meterology, Vital Statistics and Hygiene of the State of Louisiana." *Southern Medical Reports* 2 (1851). Of New Orleans's

"insalubrities" Barton had the following to say: "The greatest sources of *impurity of air* arise from privies, the offal from kitchens, stables, stores, markets, streets, manufactories, etc. It is estimated that a population of 130,000 produces annually 5633 tons of night soil, and 43,000 tons of urine: these may be doubled from domestic animals, and from other sources are at least as much more; making the frightful aggregate of about 150,000 tons, (including more than 3000 dead bodies buried in the Cemetaries in the *city limits*), of organic matter submitted to the putrefactive fermentation every year, under our very noses, on an area of 7¼ square miles! It is in vain to say that the night soil is removed to the river, urine sunk into the soil, and the offal carried a mile or two in the rear, and bodies buried in vaults: all are long enough exposed to contaminate the atmosphere, and those buried are constantly impairing the purity of the air we breathe, and poisoning the water we daily drink. Bad water is probably more injurious to health than bad air, as it acts far more rapidly. . . . Hence it is, that our cisterns, and particularly when near the privies, (*as they usually are!*) are sure to be contaminated thereby, and, indeed, every source of filth in the neighborhood. . . . This presses on us, with all its force, the necessity of ventilation, and it becomes doubly important when with the *damp, still air* of our backyards, the accumulation of the concentrated filth of a family, including the privy and kitchen offal, in the direct neighborhood of that which is of the last [sic] importance to keep pure, viz., the water we drink and use for all domestic wants. . . . It is impossible to overlook the effects of intemperance, especially in a warm climate; probably no cause is so effective in undermining the constitution, impairing the *vis-vitae*, and increasing the liability to disease. . . . The most cursory examination of our cemetary reports of the causes of death will satisfy any professional man, at least, how vast have been the additions to it from an undue indulgence in this vicious habit. . . . *Bad Milk.*—The mortality in the city of New Orleans of all under five years of age is upwards of 30 per cent, notwithstanding the proverbial kindliness of the climate to our young population, and the mildness of most of the diseases to which they are everywhere subject, such as cholera-infantum, whooping-cough, croup, etc., which, in the northern cities, takes off more than 50 per cent, and in New York, 55 per cent of all under that age! This immense mortality has been ascribed, nay, almost demonstrated, to arise, with every reasonable probability, to BAD MILK. That the same cause exists here, to some extent, there is no doubt," 135–138 (italics in original).

48. Augustin, 868ff.

49. Ellis, no. 4, 349.

50. Ibid., 346.

51. Orto, John D. "Yellow Fever." *New Orleans Medical and Surgical Journal,* n.s., 6 (February 1879): 642–643.

52. *Official Report of the Deaths from Yellow Fever as Reported by the New Orleans Board of Health—Epidemic of 1878* (New Orleans: W. L. Murray's Publishing House, n.d.).

53. Jackson, chapter 2.

54. Ibid., 171.

55. Freedman, Ben. "The Louisiana State Board of Health, Established 1855." *American Journal of Public Health* 41, no. 10 (1951); Jackson, chapter 7.

56. Jackson, 175–178.

57. Ellis, no. 4, 352–356.

58. Layton, Thomas. "An Address. . . ." *New Orleans Medical and Surgical Journal,* n.s., 6 (January 1879): 513.

59. *Daily Picayune*, March 14, 1880.

60. Jackson, 145–146, 179–181.

61. Twain, Mark. *Life on the Mississippi* (New York: Harper and Brothers, 1927): 339–343.

62. Ellis, no. 4, 370.

63. Jackson, chapter 7.

Chapter 3

1. Romans, Bernard. *A Concise Natural History of East and West Florida*, a facsimile reproduction of the 1775 edition, with an introduction by Rembert W. Patrick (Gainesville: University of Florida Press, 1962): 255–257.

2. Jones, Joseph. "Leprosy in Louisiana," in *Annual Report of the Board of Health for the State of Louisiana for the Year 1880* (New Orleans, 1881): 194–195.

3. Gayarré, Charles E. A. *History of Louisiana*, vol. 3 (New York: Redfield, 1854): 167.

4. Duffy, John, ed. *The Rudolph Matas History of Medicine in Louisiana*, vol. 1 (Baton Rouge: Louisiana State University Press, 1958): 259.

5. Gayarré, 167.

6. Records and Deliberations of the Cabildo, 1769–1803, book 3, vol. 1: 49–50. Louisiana Division, New Orleans Public Library.

7. Duffy, 262.

8. Alliot, Paul. *Louisiana Under the Rule of Spain, France, and the United States, 1785–1807*, vol. 1. James Alexander Robertson, ed. (Freeport, N.Y.: Books for Libraries Press, 1969): 97–99.

9. City Council. Proceedings of Council Meetings, 1803–1829. Vol. 1: 25. Louisiana Division, New Orleans Public Library.

10. Quoted in Dyer, Isadore. "Endemic Leprosy in Louisiana, with a Logical Argument for the Contagiousness of this Disease." *Philadelphia Medical Journal* 2, no. 12 (1898): 568.

11. Duffy, 265.

12. Jones, 208.

13. Duffy, John, ed. *The Rudolph Matas History of Medicine in Louisiana*, vol. 2 (Baton Rouge: Louisiana State University Press, 1962): 390–391.

14. Jones, Joseph. "Observations on the African Yaws . . . and on Leprosy . . . in Insular and Continental America." *New Orleans Medical and Surgical Journal*, n.s., 5 (March 1878).

15. Ibid., 690.

16. Ross, John W. "Leprosy. . . ." *New Orleans Medical and Surgical Journal*, n.s., 3 (September 1875).

17. Gayarré, 167–168.

18. Layton, Thomas. "An Address. . . ." *New Orleans Medical and Surgical Journal*, n.s., 6 (January 1879): 520–521.

19. Salomon, L. F. "Report to the Louisiana State Medical Association of the Existence of Leprosy in the State." *New Orleans Medical and Surgical Journal*, n.s., 6 (June 1879): 1030.

20. Duffy, 1962: 450.

21. Salomon, 1031–1032.

22. Ibid., 1030–1031.

23. Ibid., 1035.

24. Jones, 1881.

25. Page, J. D. "Leprosy in Canada." *Canadian Medical Association Journal* 16, no. 9 (1924): 824; Kato, Laszlo, and Marchand, Jocelyne. "Leprosy: 'Loathsome Disease in Tracadie, New Brunswick'—A Glimpse into the Past Century." *Canadian Medical Association Journal* 114 (March 6, 1976).

26. Jones, 1881: 205–206, 219. In October 1881 there was correspondence about leprosy between Canadian officials and the State of Louisiana. See Jones, *Medical and Surgical Memoirs . . . 1855–1886*, vol. 2 (New Orleans, 1887): 1214–1215.

27. Jones, 1881: 193.

28. Ibid., 218.

29. Ibid.

30. Ibid.

31. Ibid.

32. Ibid., 220.

33. Ibid., 210–217.

34. Duffy, 1962: 450.

35. Simonds, J. C. "Report on the New Orleans Charity Hospital." *Southern Medical Reports* 2 (1850): 286.

36. *Mortality Statistics of the Seventh Census of the United States, 1850* (House of Representatives, 33d Cong., 2d sess., Executive Document no. 98, Washington, D.C., 1855): 101–107.

37. Dyer, 567.

38. Matas, Rudolph. "The Surgical Aspects of Leprosy." *New Orleans Medical and Surgical Journal* 67 (June 1915): 1020.

39. Bulkley, Duncan L. "Leprosy." *Medical Records* 76, no. 2, 1909: 46.

40. Blanc, Henry W. "Leprosy in New Orleans." *New Orleans Medical and Surgical Journal*, n.s., 16 (September, October, November 1888).

41. "Leprosy Question in Louisiana." *New Orleans Medical and Surgical Journal*, n.s., 22 (July 1894): 31.

42. Jones, 1881: 219.

43. Ibid., 221.

44. Ibid., 222.

45. Ibid.

46. Ibid., 213.

47. Ibid., 214–215.

48. Ibid., 223.

49. Jones, 1887.

50. Ibid., 1246.

51. Ibid., 1245.

52. Ibid., 1252.

53. Ibid., 1245.

54. Ibid., 1275.

55. Ibid., 1246–1247.

56. *Daily Picayune*, May 2, 1893. The U.S. census of 1910 lists 507 Chinese in Louisiana, 344 of whom resided in New Orleans; from the 13th Census of the United States, taken in the year 1910 (Department of Commerce and Labor, Washington, D.C., 1913): 583.

57. "Our Leprosy Iniquity and the State Medical Society." *New Orleans Medical and Surgical Journal*, n.s., 20 (April 1893): 748–749; "Leprosy Question in Louisiana." *New Orleans Medical and Surgical Journal*, n.s., 22 (July 1894): 31–32.

58. "Leprosy and Boards of Health." *New Orleans Medical and Surgical Journal*, n.s., 16 (August 1888): 140–141; "Leprosy in Louisiana—Necessity of Providing for

Lepers." *New Orleans Medical and Surgical Journal*, n.s., 18 (November 1890): 396; "The Leprosy Question." *New Orleans Medical and Surgical Journal*, n.s., 18 (December 1890): 478–479; "Our Leprosy Iniquity and the State Medical Society." *New Orleans Medical and Surgical Journal*, n.s., 20 (April 1893): 748; *Times Democrat*, November 12, 1890; *New Orleans Daily States*, November 18, 1890.

59. "Leprosy Question in Louisiana." *New Orleans Medical and Surgical Journal*, n.s., 22 (July 1894): 33.

60. *Times Democrat*, July 12, 1892.

61. "Care of Lepers in the United States and Elsewhere." *New Orleans Medical and Surgical Journal*, n.s., 18 (January 1891): 550.

62. *Times Democrat*, May 16, 1894.

63. *Bi-Annual Report of the Board of Control for the Leper Home of the State of Louisiana to the Governor and General Assembly*, 1902: 8.

64. "Leprosy and Boards of Health." *New Orleans Medical and Surgical Journal*, n.s., 16 (August 1888): 140.

65. Ibid.

66. Ibid., 141.

67. Ibid., 139.

68. "Leprosy in Louisiana—Necessity of Providing for Lepers." *New Orleans Medical and Surgical Journal*, n.s., 18 (November 1890): 394.

69. Ibid., 394, 397; "Care of Lepers in the United States and Elsewhere." *New Orleans Medical and Surgical Journal*, n.s., 18 (January 1891): 551; "Our Leprosy Iniquity and the State Medical Society." *New Orleans Medical and Surgical Journal*, n.s., 20 (April 1893): 748–749; "The Care of our Lepers." *New Orleans Medical and Surgical Journal*, n.s., 21 (July 1893): 53–54.

70. "The Control of Leprosy." *New Orleans Medical and Surgical Journal*, n.s., 22 (July 1894): 39–40.

71. Ibid.

72. *Bi-Annual Report of the Board of Control for the Leper Home of the State of Louisiana to the Governor and General Assembly*, 1904: 33.

73. *Bi-Annual Report of the Board of Control*, 1902: 6, 8.

74. Duffy, 1962: 518–519.

75. *Daily Picayune*, February 18, 1893.

76. *Daily Picayune*, February 18, 1893; *Daily Picayune*, March 2, 1893; Dyer, Isadore. "The History of the Louisiana Leper Home." *New Orleans Medical and Surgical Journal* 54 (May 1902): 714, (?) in original.

77. Dyer, 1902: 714, 716.

78. *First Annual Report of the Louisiana State Board of Control of the Leper Home to the Governor and the General Assembly of the State of Louisiana*, 1896: 3.

79. *Daily States*, December 2, 1894.

80. *Daily States*, November 10, 1894.

81. *First Annual Report of the Board of Control*, 1896: 7.

82. Dyer, 1902: 3.

83. *Bi-Annual Report of the Board of Control*, 1902: 4.

84. Ibid., 4–5.

85. Ibid., 7.

86. Ibid., 8.

87. Ibid., 11.

88. Ibid., 11–12.

89. *First Annual Report of the Board of Control*, 1896: 4; Dyer, 1902: 719.

90. *First Annual Report of the Board of Control*, 1896: 4.

91. Ibid., 14–15.

92. Dyer, 1902: 722.

93. Morrow, Prince A. "The Prophylaxis and Control of Leprosy in This Country." *Transactions of the American Dermatological Association* 24 (May 1900): 88.

94. *First Annual Report of the Board of Control*, 1896: 10–11.

95. *Biennial Report of the Board of Control for the Leper Home of the State of Louisiana to the Governor and General Assembly*, 1906: 29.

96. Dyer, Isadore. "Leprosy in the United States." *New Orleans Medical and Surgical Journal* 73 (August 1920): 60.

97. Calandro, Charles H. "From Disgrace to Dignity: The Louisiana Leper Home, 1894–1921." Master's thesis, Department of History, Louisiana State University, Baton Rouge, 1980: 119.

98. Ibid.

99. *Tenth Biennial Report of the Board of Control for the Leper Home of the State of Louisiana to the Governor and General Assembly*, 1914: 3–4.

100. Stein, Stanley. *Alone No Longer* (New York: Funk and Wagnalls Company, 1963): 92.

101. Ross, Sister Hilary. "The Louisiana Leper Home, 1894–1921: U.S. Public Health Service (National Leprosarium 1921–1958)." Bound letters, papers, photographs, n.d.

102. Cited in Calandro, 114.

Chapter 4

1. Steen, Sverre. "The Democratic Spirit in Norway," in *Scandinavian Democracy*, J. A. Lauwerys, ed. (Copenhagen: Danish Institute, 1958): 144.

2. Derry, Thomas K. *A Short History of Norway* (London: George Allen and Unwin, 1960): 130.

3. Ibid., 140.

4. Ibid., 141.

5. Carter, Henry Vandyke. *Report on Leprosy and Leper-Asylums in Norway: With Reference to India* (London: G. E. Eyre and W. Spottiswoode, 1874): appendix A.

6. Derry, 142.

7. Ibid., 148.

8. Allwood, Martin S. *Eilert Sundt: A Pioneer in Sociology and Social Anthropology* (Oslo: Olaf Norlis Forlag, 1957).

9. Irgens, Lorentz M. "Leprosy in Norway: An Interplay of Research and Public Health Work." *International Journal of Leprosy* 41, no. 2 (1973): 189–190.

10. Ibid.

11. Ibid., 190; Irgens, Lorentz M., and Bjerkedal, Tor. "Epidemiology of Leprosy in Norway: The History of the National Leprosy Registry of Norway from 1856 Until Today." *International Journal of Epidemiology* 2, no. 1 (1973): 82.

12. Ibid., 84.

13. Ibid., 82.

14. Irgens and Bjerkedal, 81.

15. Skinsnes, Olaf K. "Notes from the History of Leprosy." *International Journal of Leprosy* 41, no. 2 (1973): 224.

16. Carter, 13.

17. Yoshie, Yoshio. "Advances in the Microbiology of *M. leprae* in the Past Century." *International Journal of Leprosy* 41, no. 3 (1973): 361.

18. Irgens, 192.

19. Ibid.

20. Richards, Peter. "Leprosy in Scandinavia: A Discussion of Its Origins, its Survival, and its Effects on Scandinavian Life over the Course of Nine Centuries." *Centaurus* 7, no. 1 (1960): 117–118.

21. Carter, 12–13.

22. Ibid., 29.

23. Ibid., 14.

24. Ibid., 13.

25. Ibid., 28.

26. Rosen, George, trans. "Jacob Henle: On Miasmata and Contagia." *Bulletin of the History of Medicine* 6, no. 8 (1938).

27. Ibid., 908.

28. Carter, 26.

29. Hansen, G. A., trans. *The Memories and Reflections of Dr. Gerhard Armauer Hansen* (Würzburg: German Leprosy Relief Association, 1976); Larsen, Øivind. "Gerhard Hendrik Armauer Hansen Seen Through His Own Eyes: A Review of His Memoirs." *International Journal of Leprosy* 41, no. 2 (1973).

30. Singer, Charles, and Underwood, Ashworth E. *A Short History of Medicine*, 2nd ed. (New York: Oxford University Press, 1962): 329.

31. Irgens, 193.

32. Hansen, 70.

33. Hansen, Gerhard A. "Foreløbige Bidrag til Spedalskhedens karakteristik." *Nordisk Medicin Arkiv* 1, no. 13 (1869).

34. Hansen (1976): 72.

35. Ibid., 83–84.

36. "Causes of Leprosy," translated by Pierre Pallamary. *International Journal of Leprosy* 23, no. 1, 1955. (Reprinted from Hansen, Gerhard A. "Spedalskhedens Arsager." *Nordsk Magazin for Laegevidenskaben* 4, 1874). According to the editor of the *International Journal of Leprosy*, "this material was not in the form of a separate article . . . but was a part of Hansen's annual report for 1873, thus establishing that year as the time he made the observations recorded."

37. Ibid., 308.

38. Roose, Robson. *Leprosy and Its Prevention as Illustrated by Norwegian Experience* (London: H. K. Lewis, 1890): 89.

39. Irgens, 195.

40. Ibid., 195–196.

41. Roose, 14.

42. Lie, H. P. "Why Is Leprosy Decreasing in Norway?" *International Journal of Leprosy* 1, no. 2 (1933): 216 (italics in original). Reprinted from *Transactions of the Royal Society of Tropical Medicine and Hygiene* 22 (1929).

43. Collins, W. J. "Notes on the Leprosy Revival." *Lancet* 1 (May 17, 1890): 1064.

44. Irgens, Lorentz M. "Epidemiology of Leprosy in Norway: The Control of a Public Health Problem." Paper presented at the Tenth International Leprosy Congress, Bergen, Norway, 1973.

45. Lie, 211.

46. Irgens, *International Journal of Leprosy* (1973): 195.

47. Lie, 212.

48. Irgens and Bjerkedal, 85.

49. Hansen, 1976: 100.

50. Irgens, Lorentz M., Head, Institute of Hygiene and Social Medicine, University of Bergen. Letter to author, October 5, 1976.

51. Goffman, Erving. *Stigma: Notes on the Management of Spoiled Identity* (Englewood Cliffs, N.J.: Prentice-Hall, 1963).

52. Irgens and Bjerkedal, 82.

53. Blom, Knut. "Armauer Hansen and Human Leprosy Transmission: Medical Ethics and Legal Rights." *International Journal of Leprosy* 41, no. 2 (1973); Vogelsang, Th. M. "A Serious Sentence Passed Against the Discoverer of the Leprosy Bacillus (Gerhard Armauer Hansen), in 1880." *Medical History* 7 (April 1963).

54. Blom, 200; Hansen (1976): 20.

55. Blom, 203.

56. Ibid., 206, footnote 2.

57. Lie, H. P. "Norwegian Lepers in the United States: The Investigations of Holmboe, Boeck and Hansen." *International Journal of Leprosy* 6, no. 3 (1938).

58. Cited in Washburn, Walter L. "Leprosy Among Scandinavian Settlers in the Upper Mississippi Valley, 1864–1932." *Bulletin of the History of Medicine* 24, no. 2 (1950): 129.

59. *New York Times*, December 27, 1852.

60. Blegen, Theodore C. *Norwegian Migration to America, 1825–1860* (Northfield, Minn.: Norwegian-American Historical Association, 1931): 347.

61. _____ . *Norwegian Migration to America: The American Transition* (Northfield, Minn.: Norwegian-American Historical Association, 1940): chapter 15.

62. Carter, 5.

63. *Report on Leprosy by the Royal College of Physicians Prepared for Her Majesty's Secretary of State for the Colonies* (London: George Edward Eyre and William Spottiswoode, 1867).

64. Drognat-Landré, C. L. *De la Contagion, seule Cause de la Propogation de la Lepre* (Paris: Germer-Baillière, 1869).

65. Irgens, 193.

66. Thompson, Richard A. "The Yellow Peril, 1890–1924." Ph.D. diss., University of Wisconsin, 1957: 1–2.

67. Currie, D. "The Second International Conference on Leprosy, held in Bergen, Norway, August 16–19, 1909." Treasury Department, Public Health and Marine-Hospital Service. *United States Public Health Report* 24, pt. 2, no. 38 (1909): 1361.

68. Brinckerhoff, Walter R., and Reinecke, A. C. "Studies upon Leprosy. VII. A Statistical Study of an Endemic Focus of Leprosy." Treasury Department, Public Health and Marine-Hospital Service. *United States Public Health Bulletin* 33 (1910): table 1.

69. Currie, 1361.

70. Ibid.

Chapter 5

1. Mouritz, A.A.St.M. *The Path of the Destroyer: A History of Leprosy in the Hawaiian Islands and Thirty Years Research into the Means by Which It Has Spread* (Honolulu: Honolulu Star-Bulletin Press, 1916): 32. This 424-page volume contains a history written by Mouritz, former physician to the leper settlement on Molokai, and a compilation of early official reports and personal reminiscences of various residents in Hawaii.

2. The work of the following historians has been useful in summarizing the history of Hawaii: Bradley, Harold W. *The American Frontier in Hawaii: The Pioneers, 1789–1843* (Palo Alto, Calif.: Stanford University Press, 1944); Tate, Merze. *The United States and the Hawaiian Kingdom: A Political History* (New Haven, Conn.: Yale University

Press, 1965); _____ . *Hawaii: Reciprocity or Annexation* (East Lansing, Mich.: Michigan State University Press, 1968); Kuykendall, Ralph S. *The Hawaiian Kingdom, 1854–1874: Twenty Critical Years* (Honolulu: University of Hawaii Press, 1953); _____ . *The Hawaiian Kingdom, 1874–1893: The Kalakaua Dynasty* (Honolulu: University of Hawaii Press, 1967).

3. Cordy, Ross H. "The Effects of European Contact on Hawaiian Agricultural Systems—1778–1819." *Ethnohistory* 19, no. 4 (1972): 409.

4. Nordyke, Eleanor C. *The Peopling of Hawaii* (Honolulu: The University Press of Hawaii, 1977): 14.

5. Bradley, 2.

6. Nordyke, 17.

7. Strode, J. E. "The Progress of Medicine in Hawaii." *Transactions of the Hawaii Territorial Medical Association* (April 1932): 15; Nordyke, 18.

8. Nordyke, 8.

9. Kamakau, Samuel M. *Ruling Chiefs of Hawaii* (Honolulu: Kamehameha School Press, 1961): 404.

10. Schmitt, Robert C. *Demographic Statistics of Hawaii, 1778–1965* (Honolulu: University of Hawaii Press, 1968): 39.

11. Quoted in Bradley, 124.

12. Tate (1968): 25.

13. Ibid., 40.

14. Tate, Merze. "Decadence of the Hawaiian Nation and Proposals to Import a Negro Labor Force." *Journal of Negro History* 47, no. 4 (1962).

15. Thompson, J. Ashburton. "Leprosy in Hawaii: A Critical Enquiry." *Mittheilungen und Verhandlungen der internationalen wissenschaftlichen Lepra-Conferenz zu Berlin im Oktober, 1897*, pt. 2 (Berlin: A. Hirchwald, 1898): 273.

16. Ibid.

17. Tate (1962): 250.

18. Ibid., 250–251.

19. Kuykendall, 1953: 183.

20. Cited in Kuykendall, 1953: 180–181.

21. Kuykendall, 1953: 181.

22. Kuykendall, 1967: 148.

23. Mouritz, 199.

24. Ibid., 358.

25. Thompson, 279.

26. Ibid.

27. Mouritz, 32.

28. *Report on Leprosy by the Royal College of Physicians Prepared for Her Majesty's Secretary of State for the Colonies* (London: George Edward Eyre and William Spottiswoode, 1867): iii.

29. Ibid., vii.

30. Ibid., vi.

31. Ibid.

32. Mouritz, 33–34.

33. Ibid., 65.

34. Brinckerhoff, Walter R. "The Present Status of the Leprosy Problem in Hawaii." Treasury Department, Public Health and Marine-Hospital Service of the United States. (Washington, D.C.: Government Printing Office, 1908): 5.

35. "Detention Hospital for Lepers at Honolulu." *Journal of the American Medical Association* 27 (October 24, 1896): 923.

36. Kuykendall, 1953: 257.

37. Arnold, Harry L., and Fasal, Paul. *Leprosy: Diagnosis and Management*, 2nd ed. (Springfield, Ill.: C. C. Thomas, 1973): 50.

38. Ibid., 53.

39. Thompson, 280.

40. Mouritz, 54; See also *Leprosy and Libel: The Suit of George L. Fitch Against the Saturday Press* (Honolulu: Saturday Press Print, 1883).

41. Thompson, 274, 289.

42. Worth, Robert M. "The Disappearance of Leprosy in a Semi-Isolated Population (Niihau, Hawaii)." *International Journal of Leprosy* 31, no. 1 (1963): 34.

43. Brinckerhoff, 5.

44. Ibid., 9.

45. Ibid.

46. Thompson, 289.

47. Mouritz, 59.

48. Woods, George W. "On Some Peculiar Diseases Encountered in Naval Cruising and Recent Observations on Hawaiian Leprosy," in *Transactions, Pan-American Medical Congress* (September 1893). Washington, D.C. (1895): 2044.

49. Mouritz, 58–59.

50. "Report of R. W. Meyer," in Mouritz, 273.

51. Thompson, 283.

52. Mouritz, 403.

53. Thompson, 283.

54. Mouritz, 71–82.

55. Thompson, 282.

56. Mouritz, 166–167.

57. Brinckerhoff, plate 1; Mouritz, 166; Kuykendall, 1953: 257–258.

58. Bradley, Harold W. Letter to author, November 30, 1976.

59. Kuykendall, 1953: 258–259.

60. Bradley. Letter to author, November 30, 1976.

61. *Leprosy and Libel*, 2.

62. Ibid., 23.

63. Ibid., 22.

64. Ibid., 23.

65. [A Hawaiian Government School Teacher]. "Shall We Annex Leprosy?" *Cosmopolitan* (March 1898).

66. For documentation, see Tate, 1962: 248–263.

67. Yzendoorn, Father Reginald. *History of the Catholic Missions in the Hawaiian Islands* (Honolulu: Honolulu Star-Bulletin, 1927): 197.

68. Farrow, John. *Damien the Leper* (Garden City, N.Y.: Doubleday and Company, Image Books, 1966): 80.

69. Yzendoorn, 198.

70. *Encyclopaedia Brittanica*, 11 ed., 1910, s.v. "Hawaii: charities"; Mouritz, 204–207, 211–228, 265–282, 295–312, 313, 319, 357, 380.

71. Reverend Joseph Damien. "A Personal Experience," in Mouritz, 218.

72. Ibid., 211.

73. Ibid., 227.

74. "Report of R. W. Meyer," in Mouritz, 274.

75. Reverend Joseph Damien, in Mouritz, 227–228.

76. Kuykendall, 1967: 69.

77. Ibid., 72.

78. Mouritz, 170.

79. Ibid., 93.

80. "Report of Dr. Edward Arning," in Mouritz, 329.

81. Mouritz, 151 (capitals in original).

82. Ibid., 152.

83. "Report of Dr. Edward Arning," in Mouritz, 327.

84. Mouritz, 154.

85. Ibid., 174 (italics in original).

86. Farrow, 159–160.

87. Letter from Father Damien to Joseph Dutton, March 10, 1889. Quoted in Yzendoorn, 208.

88. Mouritz, 244.

89. Hutchinson, Jonathan. *On Leprosy and Fish-Eating* (London: Archibald Constable and Company, 1906): 76.

90. *Report of the Leprosy Commission to India, 1890–1891.* Published for the Executive Committee of the National Leprosy Fund (London: William Clowes and Sons, 1893): vii–viii.

91. Ibid., 265.

92. Ibid., 389–390.

93. Ibid., 3ff.

94. Currie, D. "The Second International Conference on Leprosy, held in Bergen, Norway, August 16–19, 1909." Treasury Department, Public Health and Marine-Hospital Service. *United States Public Health Report* 24, pt. 2, no. 38 (1909): 1361.

95. Smyser, A. A. "Hawaii's HD Policy: Accent on Outpatient Treatment." *The Star* 34, no. 3 (1975): 7.

Chapter 6

1. Mackenzie, Sir Morrell. "The Dreadful Revival of Leprosy," in *Wood's Medical and Surgical Monographs,* vol. 1 (New York: William Wood and Company, 1890): 614.

2. Ackerknecht, Erwin H. *History and Geography of the Most Important Diseases* (New York: Hafner Publishing Company, 1965): 4.

3. Ibid., 5.

4. Hirsch, August. *Handbuch der historisch-geographischen Pathologie,* 2 vols. (Erlangen: F. Enke, 1860–1864).

5. Ackerknecht, 4–5.

6. Ibid., 3.

7. Creighton, Charles. *A History of Epidemics in Britain,* vol. 1, 2nd ed. (London: Frank Case and Company, 1965): 107–108.

8. Hirsch, August. *Handbook of Geographical and Historical Pathology,* vol. 1, translated from 2nd German edition by Charles Creighton (London: The New Sydenham Society, 1883): 7.

9. Hutchinson, Jonathan. *On Leprosy and Fish-Eating* (London: Archibald Constable and Company, 1906): 30.

10. Macnamara, C. N. *Leprosy a Communicable Disease,* 2nd ed. (London: J. and A. Churchill, 1889): 3.

11. Ibid., 58, 64–65.

12. Ibid., 45.

13. Yzendoorn, Father Reginald. *History of the Catholic Missions in the Hawaiian Islands* (Honolulu: Honolulu Star Bulletin, 1927): 212ff.

14. Mackenzie, 614.

15. Mulhane, Reverend L. W. *Leprosy and the Charity of the Church* (Chicago and New York: D. H. McBride and Company, 1896).

16. Ibid., 48.

17. U.S. Congress. Senate. *Report of the Commission of Medical Officers of the Marine Hospital Service . . . to Investigate the Origin and Prevalence of Leprosy in the United States, in Compliance with an Act of Congress Approved March 2, 1899.* 57th Cong., 1st sess. S. Doc. 269, Serial 4239: 87.

18. Cantlie, James. "Report on the Conditions Under Which Leprosy Occurs in China, Indo-China, Malaya, the Archipelago, and Oceania. Compiled Chiefly During 1894," in *Prize Essays on Leprosy,* vol. 162 (London: The New Sydenham Society, 1897): 363.

19. Wright, Henry P. *Leprosy an Imperial Danger* (London: J. and A. Churchill, 1889).

20. Mackenzie, 610.

21. Ibid., 621–622.

22. Coolidge, Mary R. *Chinese Immigration* (New York: Henry Holt and Company, 1909).

23. Barth, Gunther. *Bitter Strength: A History of the Chinese in the United States, 1850–1870* (Cambridge: Harvard University Press, 1964).

24. Miller, Stuart C. *The Unwelcome Immigrant: The American Image of the Chinese, 1785–1882* (Berkeley: University of California Press, 1969; reprint, 1974).

25. Ibid., chapter 2.

26. Ibid., 38–39.

27. Ibid., 56.

28. Ibid.

29. Ibid., 79.

30. Ibid., 76.

31. Palmer, R. R., and Colton, Joel. *A History of the Modern World,* 3rd ed. (New York: Alfred A. Knopf, 1965): 652.

32. Bode, Carl. *The Anatomy of American Popular Culture, 1840–61* (Berkeley: University of California Press, 1959): x.

33. Coolidge, 498.

34. Miller, 140.

35. Ibid.

36. Thompson, Richard A. "The Yellow Peril, 1890–1924." Ph.D. diss., University of Wisconsin, 1957: iv.

37. Haller, John S., Jr. *Outcasts from Evolution: Scientific Attitudes of Racial Inferiority, 1859–1900* (Urbana: University of Illinois Press, 1971; reprint, McGraw-Hill, 1975): vii.

38. Ibid., 210.

39. Brinton, Daniel G. *Races and People: Lectures on the Science of Ethnography* (Philadelphia: David McKay, 1890): 48.

40. Morgan, Lewis Henry. *League of the Ho-dé-no-sau-nee or Iroquois* (Rochester: Sage and Brothers, 1851): 143.

41. Haller, 147.

42. Ibid., 141.

43. Ibid., 148.

44. Morris, Charles. *Man and His Ancestor: A Study in Evolution* (New York: Macmillan Company, 1902): 194.

45. Cited in Haller, 150.

46. Ibid., 128.

47. Miller, 147.

48. Haller, 68.

49. Nott, J. C. "Thoughts on Acclimation and Adaptation of Races to Climates." *American Journal of Medical Sciences*, n.s., 64 (October 1856).

50. Miller, 161.

51. Stout, Arthur B. *Chinese Immigration and the Physiological Causes of the Decay of a Nation* (San Francisco: Agnew and Deffebach, 1862): 20ff.

52. *Congressional Record*, 47th Cong., 1st sess., March 6, 1882: 1636.

53. *Congressional Globe*, 41st Cong., 2nd sess., January 25, 1870: 752–756; *Congressional Record*, 44th Cong., 1st sess., July 6, 1876: 4418–4420; *Congressional Record*, 47th Cong., 1st sess., March 6, 1882: 1634–1636.

54. *Congressional Record*, 44th Cong., 1st sess., July 6, 1876: 4418.

55. Cited in *Congressional Globe*, 41st Cong., 2nd sess., January 25, 1870: 752.

56. *Congressional Record*, 47th Cong., 1st sess., March 6, 1882: 1636.

57. Sims, J. Marion. "Address of the President." *Transactions of the American Medical Association* 27 (1876): 106–107.

58. Ibid., 107–108.

59. *Congressional Globe*, 41st Cong., 2nd sess., January 25, 1870: 752–756; see also Miller, 147–148, 182–186, 199.

60. *Congressional Record*, 44th Cong., 1st sess., July 6, 1876: 4419.

61. *New York Times*, February 20 and March 1, 1877.

62. *Congressional Globe*, 41st Cong., 2nd sess., January 25, 1870: 756.

63. Miller, 161.

64. Ibid., 140.

65. Cantlie, 361, 363 (italics in original).

66. Mulhane, 43–44.

67. Morrow, Prince A. "The Prophylaxis and Control of Leprosy in this Country." *Transactions of the American Dermatological Association*, 24th Annual Meeting (May 1900): 75.

68. Ibid.

69. Miller, 231, n114.

70. Morrow, 76.

71. McCoy, George W. "Leprosy in California—Danger of Infection." *Public Health Reports* 63, no. 22 (1948).

72. *New York Times*, September 28, 1878.

73. Cited in Miller, 164.

74. *New York Times*, September 28, 1878; Miller, 164.

75. *New York Times*, March 6, 1880.

76. Ibid., December 22, 1880.

77. "Leprosy in California." *New York Times*, July 20, 1881.

78. Montgomery, Douglass W. "Leprosy in San Francisco." *Journal of the American Medical Association* 23 (July 28, 1894): 137.

79. Handlin, Oscar. *The Americans: A New History of the People of the United States* (Boston: Little, Brown and Company, 1963): 296.

Chapter 7

1. *Descriptive Catalogue of the Government Publications of the United States, September 5, 1774–March 4, 1881.* (Washington, D.C.: U.S. Government Printing Office, 1885).

2. U.S. Congress. House. *Comprehensive Index to the Publications of the U.S. Government, 1881–1893.* 58th Cong., 2nd sess., H. Doc. 754, 1905. Vol. 1.

3. "Memorial of A. Berger, M.D., of Tampa, Florida, in Relation to the Treatment and Suppression of Leprosy in the United States." 50th Cong., 2nd sess., Senate Miscellaneous Doc. 31, January 5, 1889.

4. Unpublished memorandum regarding leprosy dated December 23, 1889, in Records of the U.S. Public Health Service (RG 90), National Archives, Washington, D.C. Manuscripts from this collection are hereafter cited as RG 90, NA.

5. Bennett, Marion T. *American Immigration Policies: A History* (Washington, D.C.: Public Affairs Press, 1963): 23.

6. Kalisch, Philip A. "Lepers, Anachronisms, and the Progressives: A Study in Stigma, 1889–1920." *Louisiana Studies: An Interdisciplinary Journal of the South* 12, no. 3 (1973): 517.

7. *Annual Report of the Surgeon General of the Public Health Service of the United States, 1919* (Washington, D.C., 1919): 81.

8. Kalisch, 505–506.

9. The systematic segregation of lepers began in earnest in the Philippines soon after U.S. occupation of the islands. The "selection of a proper place for isolating all the lepers," Lara noted, "began in 1901. . . . The actual work of preparing Culion was however delayed for at least a year due to epidemics of cholera and plague in the country; but in the meanwhile, since 1901, a general census of all the known lepers was attempted. In December, 1904, the leper hospital at Nva. Caceres was closed and the patients transferred to the San Lazaro Hospital, Manila. On May 22, 1906, the Cebu leper hospital was also closed, the patients being sent out as the first contingent of lepers for Culion" (Lara, Casimiro B. "Leprosy Research in the Philippines: A Historical-Critical Review." Bulletin no. 10, National Research Council, Philippine Islands, 1936: 2).

10. *Annual Report of the Supervising Surgeon-General of the Marine-Hospital Service, 1894* (Washington, D.C., 1895): 349.

11. Washburn, Walter L. "Leprosy Among Scandinavian Settlers in the Upper Mississippi Valley." *Bulletin of the History of Medicine* 24, no. 2 (1950): 125ff.

12. Hewitt, Charles N. "Leprosy." *Public Health in Minnesota* 5, no. 5 (July 1889): 42.

13. Grönvold, Chr. "Leprosy in Minnesota and the Northwest." *Public Health in Minnesota* 6, no. 1 (March 1890): 5.

14. Ashmead, Albert S. "Did Norway Send as an Official Representative a Leper to America?" *St. Louis Medical Gazette* ii (1899).

15. Hansen, G. Armauer. "An Explanation of the Causes Which Have Led to the Decrease of Leprosy in Norway." *St. Paul Medical Journal* 1, no. 4 (1899).

16. Hirsch, August. *Handbook of Geographical and Historical Pathology*, vol. 2, translated from 2nd German edition by Charles Creighton (London: The New Sydenham Society, 1885): 27.

17. Scott, Harold H. *A History of Tropical Medicine*, vol. 1 (Baltimore: Williams and Wilkins Company, 1939): 597–598.

18. *Annual Report of the Supervising Surgeon-General, 1894*, 348.

19. Ibid.

20. Lee, Benjamin. "Does the Presence of Leprosy in the United States, Canada, and Mexico Call for the Supervision of Their Several Federal Governments?" *Transactions of the 1st Pan-American Medical Congress, September 1893*, pt. 2 (Washington, D.C., 1895): 2048.

21. "Lepers in Siberia." *New York Times*, June 13, 1892; see also Marsden, Kate, *On Sledge and Horseback to Outcast Siberian Lepers* (London: The Record Press, 1892).

22. Rake, Beaven. "The Communicability of Leprosy." *Transactions of the 1st Pan-American Medical Congress, September 1893,* pt. 2 (Washington, D.C., 1895): 2052–2053.

23. Hutchinson, Jonathan. "The Proposed Leprosy Congress." *Journal of the American Medical Association* 27, no. 18 (October 31, 1896): 967.

24. Kalisch, 527.

25. Quoted in Bulkley, L. Duncan. "Leprosy." *Medical Record* 76, no. 2 (July 1909): 45.

26. Osler, William. "Leprosy in the United States, with the Report of a Case." *Bulletin of the Johns Hopkins Hospital* 9, no. 84 (March 1898): 48–49.

27. "Leprosy Scare Unfounded." *New York Times,* February 18, 1905.

28. "Transactions of the Eighth Annual Conference of State and Territorial Health Officers with the United States Public Health and Marine-Hospital Service." Treasury Department. *Public Health Bulletin* no. 40 (1910): 13.

29. Dyer, Isadore. "The Duty of the Government in Leprosy Care and Control." *Journal of the American Medical Association* 63 (July 25, 1914): 299.

30. *Annual Report of the Supervising Surgeon-General, 1895,* 350.

31. Ibid., 348–349.

32. Ibid., 350.

33. Dyer, Isadore. "Leprosy in the United States." *New Orleans Medical and Surgical Journal* 73, no. 2 (1920): 58; _____ . "Leprosy From a Sanitary Standpoint." *Journal of the American Medical Association* 41 (November 7, 1903): 1130.

34. U.S. Congress. Senate. *Report of the Commission of Medical Officers of the Marine-Hospital Service . . . to Investigate the Origin and Prevalence of Leprosy in the United States, in Compliance with an Act of Congress Approved March 2, 1899.* 57th Cong., 1st sess., S. Doc. 269, Serial 4239: 8.

35. Brinckerhoff, Walter R. "Studies upon Leprosy. VI. Leprosy in the United States of America in 1909." Treasury Department. Public Health and Marine-Hospital Service of the United States. (Washington, D.C.: Government Printing Office, 1909): 14.

36. *Annual Report of the Surgeon-General of the Public Health and Marine-Hospital Service of the United States, 1905* (Washington, D.C., 1906); 208.

37. Ibid., 209.

38. *Congressional Record,* 58th Cong., 3rd sess., March 2, 1905: 3911.

39. Kalisch, 505–506.

40. Stein, Stanley. *Alone No Longer* (New York: Funk and Wagnalls Company, 1963): 205–206.

41. *Annual Report of the Surgeon-General, 1905,* 206.

42. Cited in Stein, 205–206.

43. *Congressional Record,* 58th Cong., 3rd sess., March 2, 1905: 3909.

44. Ibid., 3908.

45. Ibid., 3911.

46. Ibid., 3909.

47. Ibid., 3910.

48. Ibid.

49. Ibid., 3911.

50. A questionable bill to establish a leper colony in Alaska for Creoles, Indians, and Eskimos was introduced in 1910, but died in committee, as did another bill introduced in 1913 (*Congressional Record,* 61st Cong., 2nd sess., June 17, 1910: 8448). In June 1914, the subject of leprosy was debated in the House of Representatives, and Representative Albert Johnson of Washington suggested using one of the Aleutian

islands as a place to confine lepers. But the delegate from Alaska protested and Johnson simply introduced a bill providing for a national leprosarium (*Congressional Record*, 63rd Cong., 2nd sess., June 3, 1914: 9772–9773). Another bill was introduced that same day, followed by one in September 1914, but none were reported out of committee (*Congressional Record*, 63rd Cong., 2nd sess., September 15, 1914: 15190). On December 15, 1914, hearings were held on the necessity for a national leprosarium and a bill passed the House on February 24, 1915, but the Senate failed to act on the matter before the 63rd Congress adjourned (*Congressional Record*, 63rd Cong., 3rd sess., December 16, 1914: 291; *Congressional Record*, 63rd Cong., 3rd sess., February 15, 1915: 3814–3815; *Congressional Record*, 63rd Cong., 3rd sess., February 24, 1915: 4545–4547.

51. *Congressional Record*, 64th Cong., 2nd sess., January 25, 1917: 1965–1966.

52. Hasseltine, Hermon E. "Leprosy in Men Who Served in United States Military Service." *International Journal of Leprosy* 8, no. 4 (1940); Aycock, W. Lloyd, and Gordon, John E. "Leprosy in Veterans of American Wars." *The American Journal of the Medical Sciences* 214, no. 3 (1947); Brubaker, Merlin L., Binford, Chapman H., and Trautman, John R. "Occurrence of Leprosy in U.S. Veterans After Service in Endemic Areas Abroad." *Public Health Reports* 84, no. 12 (1969); *American Medical News*, October 30, 1967.

53. U.S. Congress. Senate. Committee on Public Health and National Quarantine. *Hearings on S. 4086. A Bill to Provide for the Care and Treatment of Persons Afflicted with Leprosy*, 64th Cong., 1st sess., February 15–16, 1916 (Washington, D.C., 1916): 39. Hereafter referred to as S. 4086.

54. Handlin, Oscar. *The Americans: A New History of the People of the United States* (Boston: Little, Brown and Company, 1963): 314.

55. Ibid., 316.

56. Ibid., 322.

57. Ibid., 336.

58. Ibid., 352.

59. Ibid., 232–233.

60. Quoted in Sinclair, Andrew. *Era of Excess: A Social History of the Prohibition Movement* (New York: Harper and Row, 1964): 29.

61. Crafts, Dr. and Mrs. Wilbur F., and Leitch, Mary and Margaret W. *Protection of Native Races Against Intoxicants & Opium: Based on Testimony of One Hundred Missionaries and Travelers* (Chicago: Fleming H. Revell Company, 1900): 14.

62. Macht, David I. "The History of Opium and Some of Its Preparations and Alkaloids." *Journal of the American Medical Association* 64, no. 6 (1915): 477.

63. Szasz, Thomas. *Ceremonial Chemistry: The Ritual Persecution of Drugs, Addicts, and Pushers* (Garden City, N.Y.: Anchor Press, 1974).

64. Quoted in Musto, David F. *The American Disease: Origins of Narcotic Control* (New Haven, Conn.: Yale University Press, 1973): 191.

65. Bennett, 26.

66. "Unreasonable Fear of Leprosy." *American Journal of Public Health* 30, no. 5 (1940): 550.

67. S. 4086: 3.

68. Ibid., 39.

69. Ibid., 162, 190.

70. Ibid., 153.

71. Hasseltine, 501–508.

72. Aycock and Gordon, 329–339.

73. Kalisch, Philip A. "The Strange Case of John Early: A Study of the Stigma of Leprosy." *International Journal of Leprosy* 40, no. 3 (1972): 292.

74. Stein, 181.

75. Early, John. *John Early, World Famous Leper: Twenty-eight Years at the Quarantine "Bat"* (Carville, Louisiana: privately printed, 1935).

76. Cited in Kalisch, 1972: 291–305.

77. S. 4086: 146.

78. Ibid., 159.

79. Ibid., 121.

80. The hospital at Lexington, Kentucky, and another one opened at Fort Worth, Texas, in 1938, were for the treatment of narcotic addicts. Initially they were designed for federal prisoners, but a policy permitted probationers from courts as well as ordinary citizens who voluntarily committed themselves for treatment. First called "narcotic farms," these institutions were later renamed USPHS hospitals; the name change, however, in no way altered the fact they were intended as prisons, built with security in mind, with all windows barred and automobile entrances fitted "for ever-watchful guards." See Williams, Ralph C. *The United States Public Health Service, 1798–1950.* (Washington, D.C.: United States Public Health Service, 1951: 52; Furman, Bess. *A Profile of the United States Public Health Service, 1798–1948.* (Washington, D.C.: United States Department of Health, Education, and Welfare, DHEW Publication no. 73-369 [NIH], 1973): 388.

81. In 1848 Dorothea Dix had petitioned Congress to declare the indigent insane "wards of the nation." The bill passed both houses of Congress in 1854, but was vetoed by President Franklin Pierce on the grounds that "if Congress have powers to make provision for the indigent insane without the limits of this district [District of Columbia], it has the same power to provide for the indigent who are not insane, and thus to transfer to the federal government the charge of all the poor in all the States." (Cited in Deutsch, Albert. *The Mentally Ill in America: A History of Their Care and Treatment From Colonial Times,* 2nd ed. [New York: Columbia University Press, 1952]: 178).

82. Stein, 100–101.

83. Section 6, entitled "Detention and Discipline of Patients Afflicted With Leprosy," contained these provisions:

a. No patient shall, under any circumstance, proceed beyond the limits of the reservation set aside for the detention of patients suffering from leprosy.

b. Any patient who shall proceed without the bounds of the reservation, or shall induce or connive at any person proceeding beyond such limits, shall be guilty of an offense.

c. Any person who, seeing a patient outside or having reason to suppose, that a patient is intending to proceed outside the said limit and fails to report the circumstance immediately to an officer, attendant, or guard, of the hospital, shall be guilty of an offense.

d. Patients shall, on no account, visit the quarters allotted to, or hold communication with, patients of the opposite sex unless authorized to do so by special permission of the Medical Officer in Charge. Visiting between patients of the opposite sex shall be permitted in the appointed visiting place only and at such hours as may be set aside for that purpose.

e. No patient shall willingly permit himself to come in physical contact with any person who is not a patient under treatment for leprosy, except when such a person is a member of the hospital staff and it is necessary for such person to come into physical contact with a patient for the purpose of medical treatment or other necessary attendance.

f. No animals or birds, of any kind, shall be kept by the patient without permission of the Medical Officer in Charge.

g. Any patient who shall willfully destroy, damage, deface, or make away with any building, fixture, implement, article of equipment, clothing, or any other article, the property of the Government, and any patient who shall receive at the public expense issues of clothing, equipment, or foodstuffs, for personal use and shall willfully destroy, damage, deface, or make away with such articles by gift, sale, barter, or otherwise, shall be guilty of an offense and shall, in addition, be liable to pay for or make good the damage or loss incurred by the Government in consequence of such action.

h. Any patient, who feels aggrieved by any act, or omission, on the part of any officer, or attendant, of the hospital, shall lay his complaint before the Medical Officer in Charge. Any person who considers that proper redress has not been given by the Medical Officer in Charge, may bring the matter before the Surgeon General of the United States Public Health Service.

Section 7, entitled "Provisions for the Enforcement of Discipline," contained these regulations:

a. There shall be provided the necessary accommodations within that part of the reservation set aside for persons afflicted with active leprosy, for the isolation and confinement of patients awarded imprisonment with, or without labor, or restriction of liberty as a minor punishment.

b. The Medical Officer in Charge shall not award imprisonment with hard labor as a punishment to a patient if the performance of labor is likely to accentuate the physical suffering caused by the disease of leprosy or will act detrimentally on the patient's bodily health.

c. The award of imprisonment, with or without labor, shall be reserved for the only serious offenses and shall not be made when a minor punishment would ordinarily act as a sufficient punishment to the offender and exercise a deterrent effect on other patients.

d. The Medical Officer in Charge is impowered to award to any patient for every act of misconduct or minor breach of order such degree of restriction on his liberty within the reservation, or such deprivation of privileges, or such special tasks or duties as may in his discretion suffice as an adequate punishment and exercise a deterrent effect on other patients.

e. The Medical Officer in Charge shall keep a separate register recording all punishments awarded by him to patients, each record of punishment shall state distinctly the nature and duration of the punishment and the offense for which it has been awarded, and such further particulars as may be pertinent (RG 90, NA).

84. Ibid.
85. Ibid.
86. *Public Health Reports* 37, no. 51 (1922): 3151–3154.
87. Stein, 101.

Chapter 8

1. Public Law No. 299, "An Act to Provide for the Care and Treatment of Persons Afflicted with Leprosy and to Prevent the Spread of the Disease in the United States." *Congressional Record*, 64th Cong., 2nd sess., January 25, 1917: 1965–1966.

2. In 1916, Mouritz wrote that leprosy is "limitedly contagious . . . its specific contagion, compared to that of Tuberculosis, is less than one-tenth of one per cent." (Mouritz, A. A. St. M. *The Path of the Destroyer: A History of Leprosy in the Hawaiian Islands and Thirty Years Research into the Means by Which It Has Spread* (Honolulu: Honolulu Star-Bulletin Press, 1916: 9); Rogers, Sir Leonard, and Muir, Ernest. *Leprosy* (Bristol: John Wright and Sons, 1925): 72ff; Gelpi, Paul. "Sanitary Control of Leprosy." *New Orleans Medical and Surgical Journal* 67, no. 12 (1915): 1008. Also see testimony of expert witnesses at Senate hearing on bill S. 4086, U.S. Senate. Committee on Public Health and National Quarantine. *Hearings on S. 4086*, 64th Cong., 1st sess., February 15–16, 1916 (Washington, D.C., 1916): 13–200 (hereafter referred to as S. 4086).

3. Rogers and Muir, 102.

4. Rogers, Sir Leonard, and Muir, Ernest. *Leprosy*, 2nd ed. (Baltimore: The Williams and Wilkins Company, 1940): 134–136.

5. S. 4086, 95–96, 126, 127.

6. Ibid., 96.

7. Ibid., 120.

8. Kalisch, Philip A. "Lepers, Anachronisms, and the Progressives: A Study in Stigma, 1889–1920." *Louisiana Studies: An Interdisciplinary Journal of the South* 12, no. 3 (1973): 529–531.

9. "Regulations Governing the Care of Lepers." *Public Health Reports* 37, no. 51 (1922): 3154.

10. Glucosulfone sodium (Promin) was originally developed for use in tuberculosis, but it proved disappointing.

11. Michael, Jerrold M. "The Public Health Service Leprosy Investigation Station on Molokai, Hawaii, 1909–13—an Opportunity Lost." *Public Health Reports* 95, no. 3 (1980).

12. Long, Esmond R. *Forty Years of Leprosy Research: History of the Leonard Wood Memorial (American Leprosy Foundation), 1928–1967* (Washington, D.C.: Leonard Wood Memorial, 1967).

13. Goffman, Erving. *Asylums* (Garden City: Anchor Books, 1961): xiii.

14. Ibid., 6.

15. Stein, Stanley. *Alone No Longer* (New York: Funk & Wagnalls, 1963): 92.

16. Ross, Sister Hilary. "The Louisiana Leper Home, 1894–1921: U.S. Public Health Service (National Leprosarium 1921–1958)." Bound letters, papers, photographs, n.d.; Calandro, Charles H. "From Disgrace to Dignity: The Louisiana Leper Home, 1894–1921." Master's thesis, Department of History, Louisiana State University, Baton Rouge, 1980.

17. *The Star* 12, no. 6 (1953): 6–7.

18. Memorandum, April 7, 1958. Edgar B. Johnwick, MOC, USPHS Hospital, Carville, Louisiana, to staff (copy sent to author).

19. *The Star* 33, no. 3 (1974): 8.

20. *The Star* 18, no. 6 (1959): 4.

21. Ibid.

22. Stein, 117–122.

23. Quoted in Stein, 119.

24. Lisio, Donald J. *The President and Protest: Hoover, Conspiracy, and the Bonus Riot* (Columbia, Mo.: University of Missouri Press, 1974): 8.

25. Rainer, Robert R. "A History of The Star: Bimonthly Publication of Patients at the United States Public Health Service Hospital, Carville, Louisiana, 1931–1963." Master's thesis, School of Journalism, Louisiana State University, Baton Rouge, 1963: 35. Rainer was assistant editor of *The Star* for eight months while Stanley Stein was writing his autobiography.

26. Feeney, Patrick. *The Fight Against Leprosy* (London: Elek Books, 1964): 166.

27. Rainer, 98–100; *The Star* 8, no. 8 (1949): 6.

28. Faget, Guy H., Pogge, R. C., Johansen, F. A., Dunn, J. F., Prejean, B. M., and Eccles, C. G. "The Promin Treatment of Leprosy: A Progress Report." *Public Health Reports* 58, no. 48 (1943).

29. Stein, 219–223.

30. Quoted in Rainer, 48.

31. *The Star* 1, no. 7 (1942): 3–4; *The Star* 1, no. 8 (1942): 3–4; *The Star* 1, no. 9 (1942): 2–3.

32. Rainer, 68.

33. *The Star* 1, no. 7 (1942): 3–4; *The Star* 1, no. 8 (1942): 4.

34. Stein, 163.

35. "The Words 'Leper' and 'Leprosy.'" *International Journal of Leprosy* 16, no. 2 (1948): 243–244.

36. *The Star* 8, no. 2 (1948): 6; *The Star* 9, no. 3 (1949): 13.

37. Stein, 332.

38. Ibid., 331.

39. *The Star* 17, no. 3 (1958): 2.

40. Ibid.

41. U.S. Congress, Senate. National Leprosy Act. Senate hearings on bill S. 704. Subcommittee on Health, Committee on Labor and Public Welfare. 81st Cong., 1st sess., May 9, 1949 (hereafter referred to as S. 704).

42. Aycock, Lloyd W., and Gordon, John E. "Leprosy in Veterans of American Wars." *The American Journal of the Medical Sciences* 214, no. 3 (1947): 338.

43. *Newsweek*, January 3, 1944.

44. *New York Herald-Tribune*, May 22, 1945.

45. "Leprosy." *Journal of the American Medical Association* 124, no. 4 (January 22, 1944): 256.

46. *The Star* 3, no. 5 (1944): 7.

47. Faget, Guy H. "Leprosy in Military Service." *International Journal of Leprosy* 12, (December 1944): 65–66.

48. *The Star* 2, no. 8 (1943): 2.

49. Stein, 136.

50. *The Star* 2, no. 9 (1943): 5.

51. *The Star* 5, no. 8 (1946): 8–9; Stein, 278–280.

52. *The Star* 2, no. 11 (1943): 6.

53. *The Star* 6, no. 4 (1946): 9.

54. *The Star* 6, no. 5 (1947): 9–10, 12–13.

55. Browne, Stanley G. "Memorandum on Leprosy Control." Reprinted in *Hanseniasis: Abstracts and News* 3, no. 1 (1972). Instituto de Saúde, Publicacão no. 14, 1972, Serie B, São Paulo, Brasil; Arnold, Harry J., and Fasal, Paul. *Leprosy: Diagnosis and Management*, 2nd ed. (Springfield, Ill.: C. C. Thomas, 1973): 16–18.

56. "Social Aspects of Tuberculoid Leprosy." *Journal of the American Medical Association* 135, no. 3 (September 20, 1947): 178; Rotberg, A. "The Brazilian Phase III of Prevention of Hanseniasis." *International Journal of Dermatology* 18, no. 8 (1979).

57. *The Star* 7, no. 2 (1947): 8; *St. Louis Post-Dispatch* (September 24, 1947), quoted in *The Star* 7, no. 2 (1947): 8; Arnold and Fasal, 17.

58. Letter. From Colonel Rarey to Major General Kirk, Surgeon General, United States Army. Quoted in *The Star* 6, no. 11 (1947): 5–6.

59. *The Star* 6, no. 12 (1947): 4–5, 15.

60. *New Orleans States*, May 9, 1947.

61. *New Orleans Times-Picayune*, May 13, 1947.

62. *The Star* 8, no. 2 (1948): 8–10.

63. S. 704.

64. Ibid., 17–34, 94–109.

65. Ibid., 54.

66. Ibid., 24.

67. Reprinted in *The Star* 5, no. 5 (1946): 1–2.

68. S. 704, 26–27.

69. Ibid., 92; *The Star* 8, no. 6 (1949): 10.

70. S. 704, 10.

71. Ibid., 12–13.

72. Stein, 37. For a brief account of the Hornbostels at Carville, see Stein, 247–254.

73. S. 704, 9.

74. Ibid., 11 (italics added).

75. *The Star* 7, no. 1 (1947): 6; *The Star* 7, no. 5 (1948): 1; *The Star* 9, no. 10 (1950): 1; *The Star* 12, no. 10 (1953): 8.

76. "Leprosy Notifiable in England." *International Journal of Leprosy* 20, no. 1 (1952): 132–133.

77. Stein, 303.

78. *The Star* 11, no. 4 (1951): 8; *The Star* 11, no. 10 (1952): 10; *The Star* 12, no. 9 (1953): 8; Stein, 254–258.

79. *The Star* 14, no. 4 (1955): 4–5; Stein, 303–305.

80. *The Star* 14, no. 4 (1955): 4.

81. *The Star* 14, no. 6 (1955): 4.

82. *The Star* 16, no. 1 (1956): 12; Baton Rouge *State Times*, August 23, 1956.

83. *The Star* 15, no. 11 (1956): 6.

84. Baton Rouge *State Times*, August 24, 1956.

85. Baton Rouge *State Times*, August 25, 1956.

86. *The Star* 15, no. 11 (1956): 16.

87. *The Star* 6, no. 12 (1947): 15; *The Star* 15, no. 11 (1956): 11; *The Star* 16, no. 1 (1956): 8.

88. *The Star* 15, no. 11 (1956): 16; Stein, 308.

89. *The Star* 16, no. 1 (1956): 8–10; Baton Rouge *State Times*, August 25, 1956.

90. *The Star* 16, no. 1 (1956): 10; Stein, 308.

91. Baton Rouge *State Times*, August 22, 25, 1956; Baton Rouge *Morning Advocate*, August 24, 25, 1956; Monroe *Morning World*, August 24, 25, 1956.

92. Monroe *Morning World*, August 24, 1956.

93. *Time*, September 17, 1956.

94. *The Star* 16, no. 1 (1956): 12.

95. Monroe *Morning World*, August 26, 1956.

96. Baton Rouge *Morning Advocate*, August 26, 1956.

97. Baton Rouge *Morning Advocate*, September 13, 1956; Monroe *Morning World*, September 13, 1956; *The Star* 16, no. 1 (1956): 10.

98. *The Star* 16, no. 1 (1956): 10.

99. Stein, 309–310.
100. *The Star* 16, no. 2 (1956): 7.
101. *The Star* 16, no. 6 (1957): 4.
102. *The Star* 21, no. 1 (1961): 22.

Chapter 9

1. *Annual Report* (USPHS Hospital, Carville, Louisiana, 1961): 1.
2. According to *The Star* 40, no. 1 (1980), frontispiece, the "marker" announcing the name change was "erected by the Louisiana Department of Culture, Recreation and Tourism," a form of publicity that has caused more than one raised eyebrow.
3. *Annual Report* (1961): 1.
4. Nichols, Dorothy S. "The Function of Patient Employment in the Rehabilitation of the Leprosy Patient." Master's thesis, Department of Sociology, Louisiana State University, Baton Rouge, 1966.
5. Parsons, Talcott, and Fox, Renee. "Illness, Therapy, and the Modern Urban American Family." *Journal of Social Issues* 7, no. 4 (1952).
6. Goffman, Erving. "The Moral Career of the Mental Patient." *Psychiatry* 22, no. 2 (1959).
7. Strauss, Anselm; Schatzman, Leonard; Ehrlich, Danuta; Bucher, Rue; and Sabshin, Melvin. "The Hospital and Its Negotiated Order," in *The Hospital in Modern Society*, Eliot Freidson, ed. (New York: The Free Press of Glencoe, 1963): 160–161.
8. Goffman, Erving. *Asylums* (Garden City, N.Y.: Anchor Books, 1961): 175.
9. *The Star* 21, no. 2 (1961): 3.
10. All staff interviews were conducted in 1963.
11. Nichols, 17–18.
12. The patient data presented in this chapter were collected as part of a monthly patient group meeting conducted by Marvin F. Miller, M.D., in 1963 and 1964; also see Rutledge, Carolyn M., "Treatment Models and Patient Adaptation: A Study of Life in a Leprosarium." Master's thesis, Department of Sociology, Louisiana State University, Baton Rouge, 1970.
13. *The Star* 15, no. 11 (1956): 13.
14. Nichols, 71–73.
15. Spray, S. Lee. "The Organizational Management of Uncertainty in a Chronic Illness Community: The Leprosarium." Paper presented at the Pacific Sociological Association, 1965.
16. Johnwick, Edgar B., Medical Officer in Charge, USPHS Hospital, Carville, Louisiana (personal communication).
17. *The Star* 35, no. 3 (1976): 14.
18. Ten consecutive sessions of the rehabilitation branch meetings were tape-recorded between January and June 1963, using the expensive conference equipment generously provided by the hospital.
19. "What Carville Looks Like." *Rehabilitation Record* 9, no. 4 (1968): 31.
20. *The Star* 33, no. 3 (1974): 14.
21. Gussow, Zachary, and Tracy, George S. "Disability, Disfigurement, and Stigma: A Brief Overview," in *Combating Stigma Resulting From Deformity and Disease*. Proceedings of the Leonard Wood Memorial Conference, New York, November 1969.
22. Rolston, Richard H., and Chesteen, Hilliard E. "The Identification of Psychosocial Factors Related to the Rehabilitation of Leprosy Patients." (Washington, D.C.: Division of Research and Demonstration Grants, Social and Rehabilitative Service, Department of Health, Education, and Welfare, 1970): 25–26.

23. Spray, 1965.

24. Stein, Stanley. *Alone No Longer* (New York: Funk & Wagnalls, 1963): 333–334.

25. Ebner, James D. "Community Knowledge and Attitudes About Leprosy: A Social-Psychological Study of the Degree of Stigmatization of a Chronic Disease." Master's thesis, Department of Sociology, Louisiana State University, Baton Rouge, 1968.

26. Gussow, Zachary, and Tracy, George S. "The Phenomenon of Leprosy Stigma in the Continental United States." *Leprosy Review* 43, no. 2 (1972).

27. Rolston and Chesteen; Moskal, E. T., and Nolen, R. H. "Social Stratification as a Factor in Attitudes Towards Persons with Hansen's Disease." Master's thesis, School of Social Welfare, Louisiana State University, Baton Rouge, 1968; Brown, N. A. "A Survey of Attitudes of Certain Medical and Paramedical Professionals toward Hansen's Disease." Master's thesis, School of Social Welfare, Louisiana State University, Baton Rouge, 1969.

28. Shiloh, Ailon. "A Case Study of Disease and Culture in Action: Leprosy Among the Hausa of Northern Nigeria." *Human Organization* 24, no. 2, 1965; Marshall, Carter L., Maeshiro, Mieko, and Korper, Samuel P. "Attitudes Toward Leprosy in the Ryuku Islands." *Public Health Reports* 82, no. 9, 1967; Bijleveld, Iman. "Leprosy in the Three Wangas, Kenya: Stigma and Stigma Management." Koninklijk Instituut Voor De Tropen, Royal Tropical Institute, Amsterdam, 1978; _____ . "An Appraisal of Diverse Actual and Potential Public Health Activities in Kaduna State, Northern Nigeria: A Report on Fieldwork, May–July, 1977." Department of Social Research, Royal Tropical Institute, Amsterdam, n.d.; Dols, Michael W. "Leprosy in Medieval Arabic Medicine." *Journal of the History of Medicine and Allied Sciences* 34, no. 3, 1979; _____ . "The Leper in Medieval Muslim Society," in *Medicine, Society and History*, Basim Musallam, ed. (in press); Frist, Thomas F. "Employer Acceptance of the Hansen's Disease Patient and Other Handicapped Persons." *International Journal of Leprosy* 48, no. 3, 1980; _____ . "Community Factors Influencing the Leprosy Patient and His Treatment." Paper presented at the 11th International Leprosy Congress, Mexico City, 1978.

29. U.S. Congress. House of Representatives. Subcommittee on Health and the Environment, Committee on Energy and Commerce. *Hearing on the National Hansen's Disease Center.* 97th Cong., 2nd sess., September 3, 1982.

30. Ibid., 5.

31. Ibid., 9–10.

32. Ibid., 1.

Chapter 10

1. See Freidson, Eliot. "Disability as Social Deviance," in *Sociology and Rehabilitation*, Marvin B. Sussman, ed. (American Sociological Association, 1965): 82–86.

2. Stringer, T. A. "Leprosy and 'A Disease Called Leprosy.'" *Leprosy Review* 44, no. 2 (1973).

3. Palmer, R. R., and Colton, Joel. *A History of the Modern World*, 3rd ed. (New York: Alfred A. Knopf, 1965): 615–618.

4. *Encyclopaedia Brittanica*, 11th ed., 1911, s.v. "Missions."

5. *Report of the Leprosy Commission in India, 1890–91.* Published for the Executive Committee of the National Leprosy Fund (London: Willilam Clowes & Sons, 1893): 49.

6. Carter, Henry Vandyke. *Report on Leprosy and Leper-Asylums in Norway: With Reference to India* (London: G. E. Eyre & W. Spottiswoode, 1874): 27.

7. Ibid., 24.

8. Ibid., 23.

9. Ibid.

10. Ibid., 14.

11. Bailey, Wellesley C. *Fifty Years' Work for Lepers, 1874–1924* (London: The Mission to Lepers, 1924): 7.

12. Quoted in Jackson, John. *Lepers, Thirty-six Years' Work Among Them: Being the History of the Mission to Lepers in India and the East, 1874–1910* (London: The Mission to Lepers, 1910): 12.

13. Bailey, 8–11.

14. Ibid., 83.

15. Ibid., 13–14.

16. Ibid., 16, 82.

17. Ibid., 20–22.

18. *Report of the Leprosy Commission in India*, 265, 389–390.

19. Ibid., 3–7.

20. Bailey, 21.

21. Ibid., 21–22.

22. Quoted in Browne, Stanley G. "The Leprosy Mission: A Century of Service." *Leprosy Review* 45, no. 2 (1974): 166.

23. Ibid., 167.

24. Bailey, 41.

25. Browne, 169.

26. Ibid., 167.

27. Ibid.; see also Bailey, 31.

28. *New Orleans Daily Picayune*, April 17, 1896.

29. Calandro, Charles H. "From Disgrace to Dignity: The Louisiana Leper Home, 1894–1921." Master's thesis, Department of History, Louisiana State University, 1980: 80.

30. Jackson, 39 (italics in original).

31. Quoted in Jackson, 192.

32. Ibid., 196.

33. Ibid., 197.

34. Bailey, 25.

35. Jackson, 39.

36. Askew, A. D. "The Leprosy Mission—A Crucial Dimension of Service." *Leprosy Review* 44, no. 4 (1973).

37. Brown, Raphael. *World Survey of Catholic Leprosy Work: A Case Study in Christian Technical Cooperation* (Techny, Ill.: The Mission Press, 1953): 14–15 (italics added).

38. Bailey, 25.

39. Cited in Brown, 10.

40. Berelson, Bernard. "Communication and Public Opinion," in *Reader in Public Opinion and Communication*, Bernard Berelson and Morris Janovitz, eds. (Glencoe, Ill.: Free Press, 1953).

41. Mackenzie, Sir Morell. "The Dreadful Revival of Leprosy," in *Wood's Medical and Surgical Monographs* (New York: William Wood and Company, 1890): 608; also Thin, George. *Leprosy* (London: Percival and Company, 1891): 197–198.

42. Thin, 1.

43. Ibid.

44. Ibid., 3.

45. Ibid., 42.

46. Creighton, Charles. *A History of Epidemics in Britain, Vol. 1: From A.D. 664 to the Great Plague,* 2nd ed. (London: Frank Cass and Company, 1965): 69.

47. Kalisch, Philip A. "An Overview of Research on the History of Leprosy." *International Journal of Leprosy* 41, no. 2 (1975): 132.

48. Creighton, 110.

49. Browne, Stanley G. "Some Aspects of the History of Leprosy: The Leprosie of Yesterday." *Proceedings of the Royal Society of Medicine* 68, no. 8 (1975).

50. Brody, Saul N. *The Disease of the Soul: Leprosy in Medieval Literature* (Ithaca: Cornell University Press, 1974): 21, 24–25.

51. Seaman, L. C. B. *Victorian England: Aspects of English and Imperial History, 1857–1901* (London: Methuen and Company, 1973): 304.

52. Quoted in Jackson, 15.

53. Browne, 1975: 486.

54. Arnold, Harry L. Jr., and Fasal, Paul. *Leprosy: Diagnosis and Treatment,* 2nd ed. (Springfield, Ill.: C. C. Thomas, 1973): 36.

55. Brody, 131.

56. Michener, James A. *Hawaii* (New York: Random House, 1959): 487–496.

57. Gussow, Zachary, and Tracy, George S. "Status, Ideology, and Adaptation to Stigmatized Illness: A Study of Leprosy." *Human Organization* 27, no. 4 (1968).

58. Stein, Stanley. *Alone No Longer* (New York: Funk & Wagnalls, 1963): 43.

59. Zappa, Paola. *Unclean! Unclean!,* translated by Edward Storer (London: Dickson, 1933): 93, 97–98, 118–129, 136.

60. Knott, Blanche. *Truly Tasteless Jokes* (New York: Ballantine Books, 1983). Pt. 1: 97–98; pt. 2: 74–77.

61. Abel, G., and van Soest, A. H. "Psychologic Difficulties in the Treatment of Leprosy Patients in a Nonendemic Country." *International Journal of Leprosy* 39, no. 2 (1971).

62. Rogers, Sir Leonard, and Muir, Ernest. *Leprosy* (Bristol, Engl.: John Wright and Sons, 1925): 56, 101.

63. Hutchinson, Jonathan. *On Leprosy and Fish-Eating* (London: Archibald Constable, 1906): 21–22.

64. Ibid., 1.

65. Bijleveld, Iman. "Leprosy in the Three Wangas, Kenya: Stigma and Stigma Management." Koninklijk Instituut Voor De Tropen, Royal Tropical Institute, Amsterdam, 1978: 15.

66. _____ . "Leprosy and Other Diseases in the Three Wangas: Community Thought Patterns about Health Care and their Consequences for Emergent Patients." Department of Social Research, Royal Tropical Institute, Amsterdam, 1976: 1.

67. See Waxler, Nancy. "Learning to be a Leper: A Case Study in the Social Construction of Illness," in *Social Contexts of Health, Illness, and Patient Care,* Elliot G. Mishler, *et al.,* eds. (New York: Cambridge University Press, 1981).

68. Stringer, 70.

69. "A Study of Public Perceptions and Awareness Concerning Leprosy." Poll conducted for the American Leprosy Missions, Inc., by The Gallup Organization, Princeton, New Jersey, July, 1982: 8–9.

70. Stringer, 71.

71. Ibid.

72. Eliot, T. S. *Four Quartets* (New York: Harcourt, Brace & World, 1943): 35.

73. Wulff, Robert M. *Village of the Outcasts* (New York: Doubleday and Company, 1967): 57–58.

74. Buker, Raymond B. "The Contribution of Christianity in Leprosy Colonies," in *A Study of Leprosy Colony Practices*, Thomas, Howard Elsworth, ed. (American Mission to Lepers, Inc., 1947): 98.

75. Wulff, 57, 59.

76. *Saturday Review*, February 14, 1970: 83.

77. Salesians Missions, brochure, 1982 (Ellipses in original).

78. Browne, Stanley G. "The Integration of Leprosy into the General Health Services." *Leprosy Review* 43, no. 1 (1972).

79. Ibid.

80. Rogers, Sir Leonard, and Muir, Ernest. *Leprosy*, 2nd ed. (Baltimore: The Williams and Wilkins Company, 1940): 134–136.

81. "International Work in Leprosy, 1948–1959." (Geneva: World Health Organization, 1960): 8.

82. Ibid.

83. WHO, Technical Report Series, No. 71. Expert Committee on Leprosy, First Report. (Geneva: World Health Organization, 1953): 6.

84. Ibid., 6–18.

85. WHO, Technical Report Series, No. 189. Expert Committee on Leprosy, Second Report. (Geneva: World Health Organization, 1960): 13–14.

86. WHO, Technical Report Series, No. 607. Expert Committee on Leprosy, Fifth Report. (Geneva: World Health Organization, 1977): 33.

87. "A Guide to Leprosy Control." (Geneva: World Health Organization, 1980): 11.

88. Morrison, Norman. *Johns Hopkins Magazine* 32, no. 1, (1981): 34–35.

89. "A Guide to Leprosy Control," 37.

Index